—For more reviews, please see next page

1942: The Year That Doomed The Axis

By Henry H. Adams, Capt., USNR

WARNER
PAPERBACK
LIBRARY

A Warner Communications Company

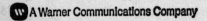

CONTENTS

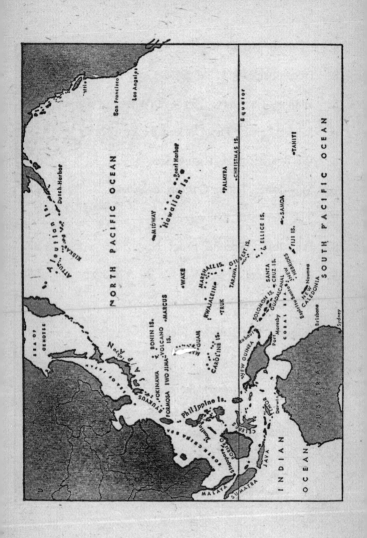

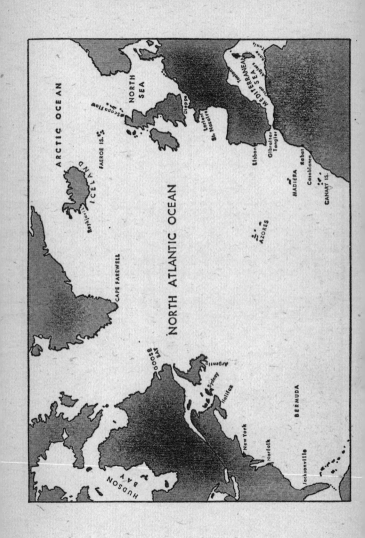

Preface

This book is the story of how America went to war and began to win. It is a story of heroism and brutality, of brilliance and stupidity, of tragedy and comedy, of baseball and football, of songs and sorrows, of theater and movies, of books and typewriters, of ships and automobiles, of tanks and guns, of oil and gasoline, of rubber and riveters, of shortages and abundance, of what men needed and what men wanted.

I have attempted to tie together the feeling of a year, the life of a year. Everyone old enough to remember can never forget the surprise attack on Pearl Harbor and the dramatic events that followed. Yet memory plays tricks, and what we remember didn't always happen that way. We were not privy to the command decisions of the time, so we could not understand what was going on. Now these matters can be explained, and wartime secrets can be told.

A work like this necessarily rests on the work of the giants in the field of the history of World War II. Their books will be found listed in the bibliography. But four names stand out so much that they must be mentioned here: Captain S. W Roskill, RN, author of the official history of the Royal Navy in World War II, *The War at Sea*, in four volumes; Rear Admiral Samuel Eliot Morison, USNR, author of the fifteen-volume *History of United States Naval Operations in World War II;* Kent Roberts Greenfield, editor of the multi-volume official Army history; and, most important, because he made the history before he wrote it, the late Sir Winston S. Churchill, Prime Minister of Great Britain and author of the thoroughly biased, thoroughly delightful, completely indispensable *History of the Second World War.*

As I write these words twenty-five years after the Japanese surprise attack on Pearl Harbor, I remember most the men I knew and those I never knew who made the victory possible.

9

The great leaders played their parts, and that story is told here. But so did the men who manned the guns, flew the planes, sailed the ships, pushed the paper, served the meals, and trained the boots and rookies. So did the men and women at home who built the ships and planes and tanks and guns, who grumbled but accepted rationing, who kept the wheels of the family car turning occasionally (at not over thirty-five miles per hour), who kept the wheels of production turning with no speed limit. Everyone who lived during the war had a part in writing this book, because he was a part of the time it represents.

To my family, friends, and colleagues, my thanks for their help. Some have given aid without knowing it by their encouragement, questions, idle conversations, and reminiscences. I owe most to my wife, Catherine, for criticism, for backing my efforts, and for shoving me to the typewriter when there were so many things I would rather have done. My friend James B. King was a participant in the defense of Malaya and Java and has helped me in details of those operations. More than that he has endured my questions and has been a tower of strength throughout the writing and revisions.

My colleagues on the faculty of the United States Naval Academy have assisted by providing an atmosphere of criticism. I would like to mention especially Professor E. B. Potter, Professor William H. Russell, Professor Robert W. Daly, Professor Vernon D. Tate, Professor William W. Jeffries, and Professor Allen B. Cook.

Lieutenant Commander David W. Waters, RNR, FRHS, of the Greenwich National Observatory, the late Commander F. Barley, RN, Captain T. Armour, RN, Commander G. Titterton, RN, and Lieutenant Commander Peter Kemp, RN, of the Historical Section, British Navy Department (formerly Admiralty), have made me welcome, as has M. Harvé Cras (Jacques Mordal), head of the Section Historique du Ministère de la Marine.

To all these and more I owe thanks, but they can bear no responsibility for any deficiencies in this book.

HENRY H. ADAMS

Annapolis, Maryland
December 7, 1966

CHAPTER ONE

"This Is No Drill"

> *Long is the way*
> *And hard, that out of hell leads up to light.*
> Milton, Paradise Lost

Nothing would ever be the same again. The end of an era had come. Somewhere—somehow—the postwar years had become the prewar years.

Sunday, December 7, 1941, dawned fair over much of the country. In the unseasonably warm weather, most Americans planned a long, lazy day. Some rose early to attend church. Others piled clubs in the back of the car and headed for the golf course, heedless of the gasoline they were using. Some merely slept on; some padded out in bathrobes and slippers to get the Sunday papers.

There was much in the news that morning. Uppermost in the people's minds was Japan. Not that one man in ten believed the Nipponese would dare to take on the mighty battle line of the United States Navy. The eight battleships of the Pacific Fleet stood guard. Formidable monsters they were, whose pictures decorated the walls of many a boy's room. Recite their names, ye haughty, and tell the numbers thereof, and take heed: *Pennsylvania, California, Oklahoma, Tennessee, West Virginia, Arizona, Maryland, Nevada.*

Since late November a special Japanese Ambassador Extraordinary, Saburu Kurusu, had been in Washington to talk peace in the Far East. Mr. Kurusu had an American wife. He had served in the United States and loved baseball. He was a walking embodiment of Japan's peaceful intentions toward America. The only danger lay in the Far East.

Americans' thoughts and way of life were far from war on that last morning of peace. The new-model cars, little changed from those of the previous year, were selling for as low as $659 F.O.B. Detroit for a two-door Chevrolet coupe. Automobile traffic was considerably up from normal, since train service was going from bad to impossible, the result of increasing demands of the military. The only bright spot in rail travel was

11

the New York Central's new crack Empire State Express running on a daily schedule between New York and Detroit in thirteen hours.

For those who wanted to get away for Christmas, there were special excursion trips to Miami starting at $89.50, all expenses paid, for fourteen days. The war in Europe and the rampaging Nazi U-boats had suspended the lucrative transatlantic passenger trade for shipping lines, but rather than let their vessels lie in idleness, neutral owners assigned them to West Indian cruises. "Why not get away from the cold and disagreeable weather? Think of dancing on deck beneath a gorgeous moon. Meet gay, congenial people." The *Kungsholm* promised such delights for sixteen days beginning December 19, all for a fare of $195 up.

The football season was drawing to a close, but a few important games had been played the day before. Rice had beaten Southern Methodist 6 to 0, while U.C.L.A. had had to be content with a 7 to 7 tie in its game with Southern California. Texas A. & M. had downed Washington State 7 to 0, but had been greatly overshadowed by Texas, which had humiliated Oregon 71 to 7.

The Stock Exchange, recently in a slump over the crisis in the Far East, had staged an unexpected rally at week's end. American Tel. and Tel., one of the leaders, closed at 146, up 1¾ for the week. Other blue chips were: General Electric, 27, up an eighth; General Motors, 36¾, up a quarter; Parke Davis 26 1/8, off an eighth; Socony Vacuum, 10, up an eighth; U.S. Steel, 52¼, up a quarter.

Movie houses were playing to bumper crowds. Especially popular was the *Andy Hardy* series, starring Mickey Rooney and Lewis Stone. In New York, Cary Grant and Joan Fontaine in *Suspicion* crammed Radio City Music Hall, which also featured the famous Rockettes in a revue called "Nice Going." Walter Pidgeon headed the cast of *How Green Was My Valley* at the Rivoli. *Rise and Shine* was playing at the Roxy, while Walt Disney's flying elephant, *Dumbo*, packed them in at the Broadway.

A new young soprano, Dorothy Kirsten, had sung the role of Musetta in *La Bohème* at the Civic Opera House under the sponsorship of her friend and guide, Grace Moore, who had appeared as Mimi. At the Metropolitan, Astrid Varney made an unexpected debut in *Die Walküre,* singing the role of

Sieglinde opposite Lauritz Melchior when Lotte Lehmann was indisposed. Also making her debut in the same opera was Helen Traubel in the role of Brünnhilde.

Broadway was enjoying a rich season. The oldest feature was the *New Hellzapoppin*, then in its fourth year, with a $2.20 top. *Life With Father*, co-starring Howard Lindsay and Dorothy Stickney, had been filling the Empire Theatre ever since its opening twenty-five months earlier. Ethel Barrymore starred in *The Corn Is Green* at the Royale. Other top attractions were: *Angel Street* with Vincent Price; *Arsenic and Old Lace* with Boris Karloff; Clifton Webb and Peggy Wood in Noel Coward's *Blithe Spirit; Claudia; Junior Miss;* Gertrude Lawrence in *Lady in the Dark;* Maurice Evans and Judith Anderson in what the *New York Herald Tribune* called "the finest *Macbeth* of our time." The Plymouth Theatre featured an extra performance that night of Edmund Gwenn in *The Wookey* for the benefit of the Actors' Fund.

The war had so far had little effect on Broadway. Only Lillian Hellman's *Watch on the Rhine* with Paul Lukas allowed such somber thoughts to disturb playgoers. Most plays commanded a price range of $1.10 to $3.30 for a ticket, although prices would be increased a dollar or so on New Year's Eve.

Popular books of the time included, symbolically enough, Margaret Leech's *Reveille in Washington* and *The Sun Is My Undoing* by Marguerite Steen. Other items in the bestseller list were William L. Shirer's *Berlin Diary, The Keys of the Kingdom* by A. J. Cronin, *Saratoga Trunk* by Edna Ferber, and *Windswept* by Mary Ellen Chase. On the nonfiction side was Carl Van Doren's *Secret History of the American Revolution, Reading I've Liked* by Clifton Fadiman, star of the popular radio program "Information, Please," and the latest offering by that perennial insider, John Gunther, *Inside Latin America.*

Over this scene of life as usual were daubed the harsh realities of war in Europe, where Britain still struggled to contain the German fury at home, in North Africa, and most dangerous of all in the North Atlantic, where convoys fought their way through ever growing numbers of U-boats. Although the Russians were not only resisting but even counterattacking near Rostov, the Germans had opened a new drive between Moscow and the Donetz basin.

But most on the minds of Americans who cared—or dared—to think about it was the danger of their own involvement in war in the Far East. Japan's drive into Southeast Asia was rapidly bringing on a showdown with the United States and Great Britain. In a desperate effort to avert calamity, President Roosevelt only the day before had sent a personal message to Emperor Hirohito.

The situation was fast approaching a breaking point. According to the newspapers, 135,000 Japanese troops were in French Indochina, or in transports ready to move. "Two large and heavily escorted convoys," reported the B.B.C., as quoted in the papers, "were seen steaming toward the Gulf of Siam this morning."

Nothing, it seemed, could keep the Japanese out of Thailand. Japan's hunger was for the resources of Southeast Asia: rice for her people; rubber and oil for her industry, for the war machine, for the unsettled "China Incident"—the unadmitted war that had ravaged China for nearly ten years.

Japan was on the march. Would she have the good sense to avoid trouble? Where was Thailand, anyhow? Oh, it was Siam. Why can't these Orientals make up their minds what to call themselves? Who cares what happens way out there?

But the itch of worry remained. Suppose the Japanese did not have the good sense to keep hands off British and American possessions in the Far East. Suppose an American ship got in the way and was sunk. What then?

Nonsense! The Japanese wouldn't dare. The American Navy is superior to any. Secretary of the Navy Frank Knox had said so only the day before in a statement accompanying the Navy's Annual Report.

"I am proud to report," stated Knox, "that the American people may feel fully confident in their Navy. In my opinion, the loyalty, morale and technical ability of the personnel are without superior. On any comparable basis, the United States Navy is second to none."

Japan would never dare provoke Uncle Sam. That way lay madness. Besides, Special Ambassador Kurusu had an American wife, and he loved baseball.

Over the country the last few hours of peace were spent as though they were unending. In the churches, the congregations heard sermons on every conceivable topic, but few were on the state of the world. A notable exception was Harry Emerson

14

Fosdick, preaching from the pulpit of New York's Riverside Church, high on an embankment overlooking the Hudson. "The world splits up," said Dr. Fosdick, "dictatorships naturally emphasizing loyalty but not liberty, democracy naturally emphasizing liberty but not loyalty. Somehow we must get these two indispensable qualities together."

Official Washington, too, had accepted the glorious weather as a respite from tension. For weeks, months, as the crisis had mounted, lights burned late in the Navy, War, State, Justice, and Treasury buildings and in the White House. Only last night, United States intelligence officers had intercepted the first thirteen parts of a long, fourteen-part message from Tokyo to the Japanese Embassy. It was Japan's final answer to the American proposal for a settlement in the Far East. Broken from its code by the aid of American "Magic," the message passed by hand to various responsible officers. By 9:30 P.M. it had reached President Roosevelt. According to the courier who brought it, Lieutenant Lester R. Schultz, Assistant Naval Aide in the White House, the President read the wordy rehash of previous diplomatic correspondence and the implied rejection of the American proposals. Then he handed the papers to his close friend and assistant, Harry Hopkins. When Hopkins had read them, the President spoke.

"This means war."

No one, even Mr. Roosevelt, could have deduced from the turgid prose of the Japanese note that it implied an attack on Pearl Harbor. Probably the President had in mind the threatening Japanese movements into the Malay area. He planned to address the Congress on Monday or Tuesday to state that Japanese movements into that area would have to be met with military action. Lieutenant Schultz later testified that Hopkins and the President had discussed the implications of the note, recognizing that Japan was determined to embark on war in Southeast Asia. The only geographic name mentioned was Indochina. Harry Hopkins remarked wistfully that since war was undoubtedly going to come at the convenience of the Japanese, it was too bad that we could not strike the first blow and avoid being surprised ourselves.

"No, we can't do that," replied the President. "We are a democracy and a peaceful people. But we have a good record."

Then followed some discussion of sending a further warning

to the military commands, and Mr. Roosevelt picked up the phone to call Admiral Harold R. Stark, then Commander in Chief, U. S. Fleet. On learning that Admiral Stark was attending a play at the National Theatre, the President decided not to have him paged, for fear that it would cause public alarm.

Lieutenant Schultz was then dismissed, and no record remains of the subsequent conversation between the President and Mr. Hopkins. Shortly afterwards, Hopkins took his departure and Mr. Roosevelt retired after calling Admiral Stark when the latter had returned home. No one knows the substance of that conversation, but it kept neither the Admiral nor the President from his bed.

Sometime before ten o'clock the next morning, the President and his chief advisers received the final (fourteenth) section of the Japanese message. Although this was the decisive part, it added nothing to the implications contained in the sections already intercepted.

Obviously [read part fourteen] it is the intention of the American Government to conspire with Great Britain and other countries to obstruct Japan's efforts toward the establishment of peace through the creation of a new order in East Asia, and especially to preserve Anglo-American rights and interests in keeping Japan and China at war. This intention has been revealed clearly during the course of the present negotiations. Thus, the earnest hope of the Japanese Government to adjust Japanese-American relations and to preserve and promote the peace of the Pacific through cooperation with the American Government has finally been lost:

The Japanese Government regrets to have to notify hereby the American Goverment that in view of the attitude of the American Government it cannot but consider that it is impossible to reach agreement through further negotiations.

Mr. Roosevelt, upon reading these words, took no action. He had already discussed the essence of the message with Hopkins and with Stark, and he saw no need to take further steps at the moment. Instead, he intended to devote the day to rest, to working on his famous stamp collection.

Mrs. Roosevelt, too, carried on the normal White House

routine. Thirty people were expected for lunch, but the President did not join them. It was a mixed group of friends and minor Government officials—by no means the kind to draw the President from his day of relaxation. He had his luncheon served on a tray in his study.

The principal cabinet officers who had seen the "Magic" message continued to work on the President's address to Congress.

In the Navy Department building, Captain Alwin D. Kramer delivered the fourteen-part note to Admiral Stark at about nine o'clock that morning. Stark read it and is reported to have exclaimed: "My God! This means war. I must get word to Kimmel at once!"

Instead, he reached for the telephone and called the home of General George C. Marshall, Chief of Staff of the Army.

General Marshall and Admiral Stark had consulted each other at every stage of the growing crisis. On November 27, they had agreed that a formal warning should be issued to all commands, advising them that hostilities with Japan might begin at any moment. Each leader sent a message to his command with instructions to inform the other service. Admiral Stark's message to Admiral Hart in Manila and Admiral Kimmel at Pearl Harbor was:

THIS DISPATCH IS TO BE CONSIDERED A WAR WARNING X NEGOTIATIONS WITH JAPAN LOOKING TOWARD STABILIZATION OF CONDITIONS IN THE PACIFIC HAVE CEASED AND AN AGGRESSIVE MOVE BY JAPAN IS EXPECTED WITHIN THE NEXT FEW DAYS X THE NUMBER AND EQUIPMENT OF JAPANESE TROOPS AND THE ORGANIZATION OF NAVAL TASK FORCES INDICATES AN AMPHIBIOUS EXPEDITION AGAINST EITHER THE PHILIPPINES THAI OR KRA PENINSULA OR POSSIBLY BORNEO X INFORM DISTRICT AND ARMY AUTHORITIES X A SIMILAR WARNING IS BEING SENT BY WAR DEPARTMENT X

General Marshall had risen that Sunday morning and after breakfast, according to his custom, had taken a horseback ride. Accordingly, Admiral Stark's phone call was useless. The Admiral, however, kept on trying for the next two and a half

17

hours. Finally he reached the Marshall, who agreed to come to see Stark at once. After the General had read the fourteen-part message, they agreed they had better send another warning to the commanders in Hawaii, particularly in view of the instructions contained in the "pilot message" from Tokyo that the fourteen-part message was to be presented at 1 P.M., Washington time. This was 7:30 A.M., Honolulu time, but no one seems to have fully appreciated the significance of that point.

When finally drafted by General Marshall for transmission to General Short, the message read:

JAPANESE ARE PRESENTING AT ONE PM EASTERN STANDARD TIME TODAY WHAT AMOUNTS TO AN ULTIMATUM X ALSO THEY ARE UNDER ORDERS TO DESTROY THEIR CODE MACHINE IMMEDIATELY X JUST WHAT SIGNIFICANCE THE HOUR SET MAY HAVE WE DO NOT KNOW BUT BE ON ALERT ACCORDINGLY X INFORM NAVAL AUTHORITIES OF THIS COMMUNICATION X

Marshall said he would take care of its transmission and left the room. He hesitated to use the scrambler telephone on his desk for fear of interception. The Army Signal Corps station was dubious about reaching Hawaii with its equipment, so Marshall sent the message by commercial radio after it had been enciphered. For some unknown reason, he ignored both the Navy and the FBI communications systems, which maintained constant contact with the islands.

The message reached Honolulu some minutes before the attack began. A messenger boy was riding along the streets of the city to deliver it when the bombs began to drop. Quite naturally, he lost all interest in his errand and took shelter until after the attack. He delivered it then, where it joined a pile of messages waiting for decryption. Because it was not marked for priority, it had to wait its turn and did not reach General Short until after three o'clock that afternoon, Honolulu time, some nine and a half hours after it had been sent. By this time it had become a mere curiosity.

Secretary Hull reached his office in the State Department building about 10:45 that morning to confer with his Far

Eastern experts and then with Secretaries Stimson and Knox. "The faces of my visitors were grim," wrote Hull. "From all our reports it appeared that zero hour was a matter of hours, perhaps minutes."

The three Secretaries devoted their time to a reading and discussion of the fourteen-part note. They speculated upon the meaning of the instruction that it be delivered at one o'clock that afternoon.

About noon the phone rang. It was Japanese Ambassador Nomura requesting an appointment for himself and Special Ambassador Kurusu at 1 P.M. Keeping a straight face, Hull agreed. His visitors left.

A few minutes after one o'clock, the phone rang again. The Japanese requested that the appointment be postponed until 1:45. Without comment, Hull consented.

In Radio Central in the Navy Department building, Radioman First Class E. E. Harris glanced at the clock. It read 1848 Greenwich Civil Time. That was 1:48 P.M., Washington time. His earphones began to chatter. His fingers moved automatically over the keys to his typewriter: NSS NSS V NPM NPM O O O. A pause. NSS NSS V NPM NPM O O O. An urgent message was coming in from Pearl Harbor.

His right hand moved to his sending key. NPM NPM V NSS NSS K K K. Go ahead, Pearl Harbor.

* * * * *

It was 7:49 A.M. in Hawaii. In a Mitsubishi attack bomber, Type 97, Commander Mitsuo Fuchida gazed down on the splendid beauty of Oahu bathed in the soft light of the rising sun. Under his right wing he could see Barbers Point. Far in the distance loomed the unforgettable silhouette of Diamond Head. At a lesser distance he could see the city of Honolulu, Wheeler Field, Hickam Field, Ford Island, and—Pearl Harbor.

He flew on toward the naval base. Behind him, under his command, were 182 aircraft, bombing types, torpedo planes, and fighters. He looked for signs of resistance.

There were none. All was peaceful.

Casting his eyes on Pearl Harbor, he counted the battleships. One by one he spotted them until he came to the total of eight. But there were no carriers.

19

Sadly disappointed, Commander Fuchida ordered his radioman to send the signal to begin the attack. The code signal went out: "TO . . . TO . . . TO . . . [Tiger . . . Tiger . . . Tiger]"

The dive bombers and torpedo planes began their downward runs, bomb bays open, eager eyes waiting for the targets to come into their sights.

At last.

Fingers closed on the releases. Hawaii slumbered in the bright morning sun, enjoying the last few seconds of peace.

* * * * *

At dawn that morning U.S.S. *Enterprise,* known affectionately throughout the fleet as the "Big E," under the command of Captain George D. Murray, was about two hundred miles from Pearl Harbor. On her flag bridge Vice Admiral William F. Halsey watched a dawn launch of planes he was sending in to Ford Island. The ship had just returned from delivering twelve Wildcat (F4F) fighters to Wake Island. All the way, the ship and its escorts had operated under war conditions. Halsey had given instructions that any ships encountered were to be sunk and any planes shot down.

"Goddammit, Admiral," protested Commander William H. Buraker, "you can't start a private war of your own!"

Halsey did not have to start his private war. The mission went off without incident. The fighters arrived at Wake safely, and the *Enterprise* turned back for Pearl. Head winds had delayed her, or she would have entered harbor on the evening of December 6, where she would have been a prime target for Japanese bombs.

Once the planes were off, Admiral Halsey went to flag quarters to shave, shower, and eat breakfast.

"We were on our second cups of coffee when the phone rang," wrote Halsey. "Doug [Lieutenant H. Douglas Moulton, Flag Secretary] answered it. I heard him say, 'Moulton. . . . *What?* . . . Roger!' He turned to me: 'Admiral, the staff duty officer says he has a message that there's an air raid on Pearl!'

"I leaped up. 'My God, they're shooting at my own boys! Tell Kimmel!'"

* * * * *

In Radio Central, Navy Department, Washington, the hands of the clock moved to 1850 Greenwich Civil Time (1:59 P.M., Eastern Standard Time). Radioman Harris gave the receipt and then stared at the message he had just copied.

NPM 1516

Z ØF2 1830 ØF3 ØF4 Ø2FØ O

AIR RAID ON PEARL HARBOR X THIS IS NO DRILL K

The message was passed from Harris to his superior, Chief Radioman Frank A. Ackerson, and from him to the communications watch officer, Lieutenant William L. Tagg, USN. Tagg passed it on to Rear Admiral Richmond Kelly Turner, Chief of the War Plans Division. Turner informed Admiral Stark, and they took it to Secretary Knox. Knox picked up the telephone to call the White House.

"I lunched with the President today at his desk in the Oval Room," wrote Harry Hopkins in his diary. "We were talking about things far removed from war when at about 1:40 [*sic*] Secretary Knox called and said that they had picked up a radio from Honolulu from the Commander in Chief of our forces there advising all our stations that an air raid attack was on and that it was 'no drill.'

"I expressed the belief that there must be some mistake and that surely Japan would not attack in Honolulu.

"The President discussed at some length his efforts to keep the country out of war and his earnest desire to complete his administration without war, but that if this action of Japan's were true, it would take the matter entirely out of his hands, because the Japanese had made the decision for him.

"The President thought the report was probably true and thought it was just the kind of unexpected thing the Japanese would do, and that at the very time they were discussing peace in the Pacific they were plotting to overthrow it.

"At five minutes after two he called Hull and told Hull of the report and advised Hull to receive Nomura and Kurusu, who had an appointment with him, and not to e..t on that he, Hull, had the news but to receive their reply formally and coolly and bow them out."

It was physically impossible for the peppery-tempered Mr.

Hull to follow the President's instructions literally, for he could not be cool when he was outraged. He waited fuming in his office until the tardy Japanese representatives arrived: Mr. Hull kept them cooling their heels in an anteroom for fifteen minutes before sending for them. He did not ask them to be seated.

Nomura handed him the fourteen-part note, stating that they had been instructed to deliver it at one o'clock that afternoon, but that difficulties in decoding had delayed them.

Hull solemnly read the document through, letting no expression or action reveal that he was already thoroughly familiar with its content. Only when he had finished did he look at the two Japanese diplomats. Taking a deep breath, he let them have it with all the force of his righteous Tennessee indignation.

"I must say," he said, "that in all my conversations with you during the last nine months I have never uttered one word of untruth. This is borne out absolutely by the record. In all my fifty years of public service I have never seen a document that was more crowded with infamous falsehoods and distortions—infamous falsehoods and distortions on a scale so huge that I never imagined until today that any Government on this planet was capable of uttering them."

Hull permitted his visitors no reply. He made a motion toward the door, and the Japanese left, their heads down.

At 2:30, the President called in Steve Early, his press secretary and dictated an immediate release for the press. By the time Mr. Nomura and Mr. Kurusu left the State Department building, the news was on the streets.

Guards appeared at the White House and at military establishments throughout the country. Summoned by the newscast, officers and men of the Army, Navy, Air Corps, Marines, and Coast Guard reported to their stations for duty. Cabinet officials and Government workers went to their offices. A crowd gathered outside the Japanese Embassy, watching in menacing silence as Mr. Nomura and Mr. Kurusu scuttled inside. Soon the gray smoke of burning papers arose from the chimneys of the Embassy.

Some super-patriot chopped down one of the Japanese cherry trees ringing Washington's Potomac Basin.

War had come. The morning was dead. The afternoon of war was upon us.

22

* * * * *

The war that had come to America had been long a-borning. It began in 1853 when Commodore Perry forced Japan to abandon its policy of isolation from the world. It came nearer when the Versailles Treaty at the end of World War I left unsettled the conditions that had brought four years of agony to the world. It came closer still when the United States rejected the League of Nations. It became inevitable when Mussolini and Hitler came to power and Japan found her interests closer to those of Germany and Italy than to those of her former allies, the United States, Britain, and France. These three great powers might have stopped the dictators in their tracks, but they did not.

Then the war came to Europe.

Americans passionately desired to avoid involvement. But it was not to be.

To avoid offending Japan, the American Congress refused to vote adequate military strength for the Pacific. The bitter fruits of this policy were the costs America and Britain had to pay in the months ahead. The first installment was paid at Pearl Harbor.

Long before war came to America, President Roosevelt and Prime Minister Churchill had established cordial relations in the hope of speeding the victory against tyranny. They had exchanged letters, cables, advisers, and military confidences. There is no example in history of such complete cooperation and trust as was displayed by these two great leaders of these two great nations.

One of their most important decisions was to provide plans for concerted operations if and when America should enter the war. Their representatives, military and civil, met in Washington in March 1941 in the ABC-1 Staff Conference to determine Allied strategy. There was unanimous agreement that the defeat of Germany would be the chief task of the combined efforts of the two nations, even if Japan became a major belligerent. Germany clearly offered the greater menace. The Pacific must, if necessary, be sacrificed to the needs of the war in Europe. But, and this was a large *but,* certain positions in the Pacific could not be yielded: Dutch Harbor in the Aleutian Islands, which commands the Great Circle Route between

Japan and North America; the Hawaiian Islands, which shelter the American base at Pearl Harbor; Australia and New Zealand, whence a major portion of the drive against Japan would be staged; and those island positions necessary to afford protection to ships plying between the United States and Australia. All else would be considered expendable, temporarily.

Through the lazy spring, summer, and fall of 1941 the United States slumbered away the last months of peace: President Roosevelt, on January 20, 1941, inaugurated as the first third-term President in history, had in a "Fireside Chat" on December 29, 1940, proclaimed America the Arsenal of Democracy. "Suppose," he said at a press conference a few days earlier, "my neighbor's home catches fire, and I have a length of garden hose . . . If he can take my garden hose and connect it up with his hydrant, I may help him put out his fire." From these statements was born the Lend-Lease Act, which eliminated the necessity for Britain to pay spot cash for the arms she needed in her struggle against Hitler.

By no means all the nation was ready to follow Mr. Roosevelt in his determination to defeat tyranny even at the risk of war. When the Lend-Lease Bill was introduced to the Congress—was it by accident or by design that its designation was H.R. 1776?—isolationists assailed it on the floor of Congress, in the press, and on the platform. "Never before," roared Senator Burton K. Wheeler of Montana, "has this Nation resorted to duplicity in the conduct of its foreign affairs. . . . The lend-lease program . . . will plow under every fourth American boy." America's "Lone Eagle," Charles A. Lindbergh, argued that "a complete victory on either side would result in prostration such as we have never seen." These efforts were defeated by the political astuteness of the Administration and by the realization on the part of the Congress that failure to pass H.R. 1776 would go a long way to assure Axis victory. Its passage was aided by Hitler's frenetic denunciations of the bill and perhaps in some small measure by Mr. Churchill's urgent plea: "Give us the tools, and we will finish the job." On the afternoon of March 11, 1941, President Roosevelt signed the measure into law, shortly after the House had agreed to the Senate version.

As winter waned and spring moved toward summer, the Axis opened its spring offensives. In North Africa the successful British drive in the Western Desert ground to a halt as the

24

Afrika Korps intervened under the dramatic leadership of General Erwin Rommel; Germany invaded Greece, thrusting the British relief force into the sea and back to Crete. A few weeks later Crete fell before the onrushing tide of German victories; Rommel bypassed Tobruk and so established his front on the Egyptian border.

These disasters in the Mediterranean faded from the world's attention when the great battleship *Bismarck* broke out into the Atlantic. Brought to action by the new British battleship *Prince of Wales* and the venerable battle cruiser *Hood,* the *Bismarck,* on May 24, 1941, obliterated the *Hood* with a lucky salvo and drove off the *Prince of Wales.* Then the *Bismarck* disapppeared. Discovered again on May 26, she was brought to bay by other British units and finally sunk by H.M.S. *Rodney* and *King George V.*

The same day President Roosevelt broadcast to the American people. "The war," he declared, "is approaching the brink of the Western Hemisphere itself. It's coming very close to home." He concluded by proclaiming a state of unlimited national emergency, "which requires the strengthening of our defense to the extreme limit of our national power and authority."

Despite the President's proclamation, the country lagged behind in its appreciation of danger, and members of the Congress lagged behind the country. A reluctant majority on Capitol Hill on September 14, 1940, had passed the Burke-Wadsworth Selective Training and Service Act, the first peacetime draft in the nation's history; the President signed it into law two days later. On October 16, 1940, every man between the ages of twenty-one and thirty-five years had gone to the school, the firehouse, the armory, the courthouse, to register for Selective Service and receive a draft number. Weeks later Secretary of War Henry L. Stimson had been blindfolded and reached into a large glass bowl containing thousands of capsules. Under the blinding floodlights of the newsreel photographers, he drew out one of the capsules and handed it to President Roosevelt. Breathless people over the length and breadth of the land listened intently for the familiar voice to announce the result.

"The first number which has been handed me," stated the President, "is serial number one five eight." Six thousand men held that number.

"The second number is serial number one nine two."
"The third number is serial number eight two three nine."

The first "draftees," as the newspapers called them, were bewildered, confused, resentful. It was only for a year, but a year of the *Peacetime* Army? Most young men lived in a climate of opinion that it was all a plot on the part of "That Man in the White House." Some dedicated liberals denounced the draft, the war, the Army, the Navy, and the role of the United States in the world. Their lapels bore buttons reading "OVER HERE" or "THE YANKS AREN'T COMING," or, oddly enough, "V.F.W." These letters did not stand for the honorable veterans' organization, Veterans of Foreign Wars, but rather for "Veterans of Future Wars." These young men demanded the bonus now, while they were still alive to enjoy it.

In most Army camps, living conditions were vile. The Army simply had not been ready to receive the selectees—another name for the drafted men. The bewildered, harassed, unhappy victims called themselves poor bastards.

Herded off the trains, tired, dirty, unkempt men found themselves greeted by a gravel-voiced, leather-lunged sergeant, who herded them into buses for the trip to camp. All the while he cast reflections on their mental capacity, their physical appearance, and their ability ever to achieve the high eminence of Private in the United States Army.

The buses pulled up in front of a monstrously ugly building that would be their home for the next few months—their first Army barracks. It was a gray clapboard building, whose exterior belonged to no architectural period and might have been designated "Army Uninspired." Inside they found canvas cots on an unpainted pine board floor, a few mud-covered windows letting in meager rays of dispirited sunshine. Outside, the temperature was in the 80s. Inside, it was in the hundreds. It was the only building in existence that could leak simultaneously through the roof, all four walls, and the floor.

Directed to put their bags in the barracks, the men next fell in outside the building. Their unloving sergeant proceeded to tell them in greater detail of their complete unfitness for the honor that had been done them. To his commands of right face and forward march, the column of men shuffled off,

26

looking much like an uncertain centipede.

The rest of the day remained something of a haze. A few moments stood out. The uniform issue room. Here there were only two sizes: too big and too small. They put on massive high shoes and stood on a platform, holding a bucket of sand in each hand. This established shoe size. Back to the barracks to put on fatigues, stow gear, pack civilian clothes for shipping home. Back to the supply center for blankets, mattresses, pillows. Back to the barracks to make bunks. Men called on summer-camp memories to try to achieve the necessary neatness and rigidity of blankets. Then the sergeant, overturning bunks, stripping off blankets: "Do it over, dammit! Do it right!" Back to supply. Draw buckets, mops, blitz cloths, soap. Back to the barracks. "Get this place clean—I mean clean! I'll be back in an hour."

A frantic hour of work. The sergeant again. "Do it over! It's lousy!" Bunks overturned. Packs ripped open. "Do it over! Do it over!"

More frantic work. "Fall in outside." The column of men, now brown-clad instead of parti-colored, headed off for the messhall. "Get ya tray! Ya tray! Ya gotta eat!" Grinning messmen doled out the food. A slab of nondescript meat. A scoop of grayish mashed potatoes. Beans. A salad. A bowl of unidentifiable soup. A dab of ice cream on top of the mashed potatoes. A dill pickle on the ice cream. The long tables to which they made their uncertain ways bore pitchers of milk and coffee, both the same temperature.

Lunch over, then to the dispensary. "Strip!" The men shed their sweaty fatigue uniforms. A bored enlisted corpsman with a bowl of Mercurochrome in one hand and a small brush in the other painted a number on the chest of each victim as he passed. Down the assembly line of health. Eyes, ears, nose, throat. Blood pressure, temperature, chest, heart, lungs, abdomen, feet, hands. "Bend over and spread!" Shots. The biggest man in line crumples under the needle and is drawn off to one side. More shots. Blood test. "Okay, get dressed. Next man."

Back to the barracks. Clean up. Fall in outside. Close order drill. "In the position of Attention, the body is held erect but not tense, hands curled naturally at the side, thumbs next to the trouser seams. . . ." Right face! Left face! About face! For-wa-a-a-rd Harch! By your left, your *left,* your LEFT! Detail

Halt! Goddammit, don't you know your left from your right? Forwa-a-a-a-rd Harch. By your left . . . *left* . . . LEFT. HUP, HOO, HREEP, PO! HUP, HOO, HREEP, PO!

Drill. Cleanup. Inspection. Lectures. Drill. Cleanup. Inspection. Chow. Taps. Reveille. Inspection. Cleanup. Inspection. Chow. Drill. Drill.

Shortages were everywhere. There were not enough rifles to go around. Some men carried brooms. Others had nothing.

"Jones!"

"Sir?"

"Describe your rifle!"

"Sir, it is a breech-loaded, magazine fed, bolt-operated shoulder weapon, United States Rifle, Caliber .30, model 1903. It holds five rounds in a clip and the weight is 8.69 pounds without bayonet, sir."

"Is that all, Jones?"

"Yes, sir."

"You forgot the serial number."

"Yes, sir. Serial number 1487621725, sir."

"Take one hour extra duty marching around the company area at port arms."

"Yes, sir."

"And sing out the proper description of your rifle while you're doing it."

"Yes, sir."

A new uniform was on the way, but not enough had arrived, so the draftees wore khaki breeches left over from World War I. This meant that they had to wear puttees. There is a trick to wrapping puttees about the calves of the legs. If they are too tight, they cut off the circulation. If they are too loose, they fall in a tangle on the feet. Most men walked on numb feet and legs rather than face the sergeant's wrath for tripping over brown spaghetti.

Thank God it was only for a year. *Only* for a year. Men crossed out the days in pocket diaries, much as a prisoner will. The day of release was circled with appropriate symbols of freedom.

For serving their country in peacetime by drill, drill, drill, draftees were paid $21 a month, out of which they had to buy their cigarettes, shaving equipment, soap, toothpaste, stationery, stamps, and beer or Cokes at the canteen. There was little left to send home for a savings account.

Life continued to be monotonous and frustrating at basic training camps. Most were located miles from the nearest town, and that place had no recreational facilities for so many men. During these years of peace, soldiers were generally regarded as ill-mannered, rough, uncouth, and best let alone. Not yet had come the citizen Army and the effective U.S.O. organization with its dedicated workers who would take the American G.I. to their hearts.

As world conditions worsened during the rest of 1940 and into 1941, it became increasingly clear to the Administration that the draftees could not be released. National safety demanded otherwise. Yet the draft would expire in September. As Commander in Chief, Mr. Roosevelt would permit the disintegration of the Army.

The President's request to extend the terms of service of the draftees was accompanied by his demand for authority to permit employment of the drafted men overseas if necessary. Congressmen hotly protested that the required legislation would break faith with the men and would pave the way for a new American Expeditionary Force, all without a declaration of war. After bitter debate, the proposal passed the Senate, but came close to defeat in the House. On August 12, the roll-call vote was taken. Representatives and guests in the visitors' gallery sat nearly breathless as the voice of the clerk called the roll. First one side and then the other would be in the lead. It was so close that no one dared believe his private tally sheet. At length the Speaker announced the results. For the extension of selective service: 203; opposed: 202. The bill that saved the Army from complete disintegration less than four months before Pearl Harbor had passed by a single vote.

Meanwhile, Hitler had astounded the world by repeating the error of Napoleon; he attacked Russia while leaving an undefeated Britain in his rear. On June 22, 1941, the Nazi armies smashed into Russia. American reaction was mixed. Some exclaimed, "Let's hope neither side runs out of bullets!" Prime Minister Churchill and President Roosevelt saw a God-given opportunity that would lead to the eventual downfall of the Nazi Government. Mr. Roosevelt promptly extended the provisions of Lend-Lease to Russia.

At sea, American ships had encounters with the Germans; on May 21, the American freighter *Robin Moor* had been torpedoed and sunk by a U-boat. When the news reached America, the President responded by freezing all German and Italian assets in the United States. A few days later, German and Italian consulates in the United States were closed by Executive Order. On September 4, the American destroyer *Greer* had a brush with the German submarine *U-652*. As a result, Mr. Roosevelt proclaimed the "shoot on sight" policy. Four days later, Secretary of the Navy Knox announced that the United States Navy would convoy ships as far as Iceland, where American troops had been stationed.

As America's neutrality passed to "non-belligerency" in the Atlantic, it was inevitable that clashes would occur. On October 17, the destroyer *Kearney* was torpedoed by a U-boat while she was escorting a British convoy. Although heavily damaged, she managed to reach port. Two weeks later, the ill-starred destroyer *Reuben James* took a German torpedo and sank with the loss of some hundred men. Partly as a result of this tragic event, Congress amended the Neutrality Act to permit arming to U.S. merchant ships. President Roosevelt signed the amendment on November 17, 1941, and from that date the United States waged undeclared war on Germany and Italy in the Atlantic.

It was in the Pacific, however, that hostilities exploded. The long friendship between the United States and Japan, inaugurated by Perry's visit in 1853, began to decline after the First World War. By the Thirties, mutual suspicion shaded most relationships between the two nations. In 1931, Japan invaded Manchuria and the following year extended operations to China itself, all without a declaration of war. She marked the attack by wanton bombing of Shanghai, followed by a landing of Japanese troops. Then, honor satisfied, Japan withdrew her forces from Shanghai near the end of May.

In the year before the outbreak of war, Japan was unique among nations in that she had embraced modern industrialism without ever abandoning feudalism. Along with complex economic ideas her rulers gloried in their Samurai tradition and its Bushido code, which glorified war and the warrior. Face and honor were more important than life itself. The highest hope of the soldier was to die for the Emperor and join the spirits who eternally guarded the islands. The Japanese warrior, assured of the divine descent of the Emperor from Jimmu Tenno, "Son of the Sun," regarded all other beings as inferior, fit subjects for servitude. Those who were unaware of their inferiority and those who opposed Japan's rightful aspirations must be exterminated.

Such was the attitude of the military clique in Japan. More moderate, wiser counsels prevailed during the 1920s, in spite of the indignities Japan saw in her receiving the small end of the stick in the Washington Naval Conference. An American reservoir of friendship and good will as a result of American aid to Japan after the disastrous earthquake at Tokyo in 1923 was speedily emptied by the United States Immigration Act of 1924, which completely forbade Japanese immigration into the United States. These two insults to Japan spurred the militarists to greater efforts, and a wave of assassinations followed, as Army extremists strove to intimidate or liquidate the liberal statesmen. From their plotting grew the Manchurian Incident of 1931 and the overthrow of the enlightened governments.

The Army enjoyed extraordinary strength in the Japan of the 1930s. Not only could they appeal to the code Bushido for popular support; their political strength was no less real. They held a veto power over the appointment of the Prime Minister, in practice if not in theory, for the Japanese constitution provided that the Minister of War must be an Army officer. Thus by refusing to permit one of their officers to accept the War portfolio, they could prevent the formation of any government.

In the mid-Thirties, the Japanese Army exercised its prerogative, forced out the moderate cabinet then in office, and installed one of its own selection. By 1936, Japan had renounced the Washington Naval Treaty and had embarked on a rapid armament program, including heavy munitions and large warships.

The following year, Japan turned its attentions once again to China. The "China Incident" began on July 7, 1937. "Japan," declared Prime Minister Prince Konoye, "never looks upon the Chinese people as an enemy." His statement did little to reassure the Chinese as Japanese troops advanced, leaving behind them thousands of raped, mutilated, tortured women and bayonetted, headless corpses of men, women, and children. Japanese aircraft rained bombs on helpless cities, so many bombs falling on American property that a Chinese cynic remarked that the most dangerous place to be in an air raid was in an American mission. Americans in Chinese cities were humiliated and mistreated by Japanese troops, while the Japanese Government blandly denied the incidents or disavowed responsibility.

On December 12, 1937, Japanese aircraft deliberately bombed and sank the American naval gunboat U.S.S. *Panay*, assigned to the Yangtze River Patrol. Three passengers were killed and eleven others wounded when the planes strafed the survivors.

This time the Japanese realized that they had overstepped themselves and offered apologies and reparations. Anxious to avoid war, the United States accepted the apologies, and the American people breathed a collective sigh of relief. American acquiescence had purchased four years of peace.

Far from restraining their activities as a result of the *Panay* incident, the Japanese, if anything, intensified them. The Rape of Nanking followed; indignities to American citizens went uncurbed, but no major events affecting the United States transpired.

Meanwhile America sold oil and scrap iron to Japan.

In 1939 Shanghai fell to the Japanese, and then the strategic island of Hainan. In the midst of these events, the Japanese Ambassador to the United States, Hiroshi Saito, died. As a gesture of good will, the American Government sent his ashes to Japan in an American cruiser, U.S.S. *Astoria*, under the command of Captain Richmond Kelly Turner, USN. Both the ship and her captain had a rendezvous with the Japanese at Guadalcanal.

A few months later, Japanese bombs fell near the American Embassy in Shanghai and also near the American gunboat U.S.S. *Tutuila*. In reprisal, the Congress denounced the Commercial Treaty of 1911 as a first step in imposing economic sanctions on Japan.

Meanwhile America sold oil and scrap iron to Japan.

Expanding into China, the Japanese proclaimed that they planned to unite all of eastern Asia in a giant economic community, the Greater East Asia Co-Prosperity Sphere. Other Asiatic countries recognized this move as an attempt to establish economic hegemony by Japan. The United States and the United Kingdom recognized it as a threat to their interests in the Far East. In response, the United States changed the

32

base of the U.S. Fleet from California to Pearl Harbor in the Hawaiian Islands.

Meanwhile America sold oil and scrap iron to Japan.

During the summer of 1940, Japanese pressure forced the British to close the Burma Road for three months. Since Japan controlled the coast of China, this tortuous, storm-swept path was the only way supplies could reach the Chinese. Six weeks later, the Vichy Government of France succumbed to Japanese and German pressure and agreed to permit Japanese troops to "maintain order" in northern Indochina. The United States, Great Britain, and the Netherlands countered with a partial oil embargo. The growing alignment of Japan and the Axis marked by this move was formalized by the efforts of the Germanophilic Foreign Minister of Japan, Yosuke Matsuoka. Militarists in Japan were overjoyed to learn that Matsuoka had taken Japan formally into the Axis by signing on September 27, 1940, the Tripartite Pact by which the Germans (and Italians) on one hand and the Japanese on the other divided the world among themselves. Each power promised to come to the aid of the other if "attacked by a power at present not involved in the European war or in the Sino-Japanese conflict." By this treaty Japan had no responsibility to declare war on Russia, an undertaking that would have seriously hampered her drive into Southeast Asia. It was perfectly clear to everyone that the unnamed power referred to was the United States. America could not move in either ocean without facing war in both. Each of the Axis powers hoped to terrify the United States into paralysis on both Europe and Asia by this diplomatic blackmail.

Three days later, the United States gave its response. Steel and scrap iron were completely embargoed to Japan, and severe limitations were placed on petroleum products. The challenge had been offered, and the response was given. The way led to war. How soon it would come, no one could foretell.

By the end of January 1941, matters had grown so tense that the American Ambassador to Japan, Mr. Joseph Grew, noted in his diary: "There is a lot of talk around town to the effect that the Japanese, in case of a break with the United States, are planning to go all out in a surprise mass attack at Pearl Harbor. Of course, I informed our government." The Navy

33

Department "places no credence in these rumors," stated the Chief of Naval Operations, Admiral Harold R. Stark, in passing the warning on to Admiral Kimmel at Pearl Harbor. It was just at this time that Japanese Admiral Isoroku Yamamoto, Commander in Chief, Combined Fleet, set his staff to work planning the attack on Pearl Harbor.

During the spring and summer of 1941, Japanese-American relations continued to deteriorate. On July 25, the Japanese announced Vichy's agreement to Japanese protectorate of all of Indochina. The next day (also July 25, because of the time difference) President Roosevelt froze all Japanese assets in the United States. Japan retaliated with a similar freeze on American assets in Japan. America's economic boycott of Japan was complete. From that date on, there was no turning back.

In a desperate effort to maintain the peace, the Premier of Japan, Prince Konoye, proposed a meeting with President Roosevelt. The President was willing, but Secretary of State Cordell Hull believed such a meeting would be inadvisable until subordinates had defined the areas of discussion. Mr. Roosevelt, just back from the Argentia meeting with Prime Minister Churchill, did not press the point, and the opportunity was lost. Two months later Prince Konoye, the last of the "moderate" premiers, resigned and was replaced the next day, October 17, 1941, by the militarist General Hideki Tojo.

The complex story of the negotiations between the United States and Japan has been told elsewhere. Each side seems to have been genuinely anxious to reach a settlement, but neither would yield anything the other considered significant. At the request of the War and Navy departments, Mr. Hull attempted to keep the talks going, while the Japanese pressed their Ambassador, Admiral Kichisaburo Nomura, to reach an early settlement. To assist him they dispatched a veteran diplomat, Saburo Kurusu, with the hope of reaching agreement by November 25. Mr. Kurusu left Japan on November 5. The same day, Japan took the decision for war if negotiation failed. They would smash into the Philippines, Guam, Malaya, Hong Kong, and Borneo, covering their flank by a surprise attack on Pearl Harbor. Japanese military leaders wished to jump off by December 1, so they could complete operations in the south before the monsoon season set in.

Mr. Hull received Mr. Kurusu on November 15, but discussions were unpromising. A week later, Tojo extended the November 25 deadline by four days. After the new date, cabled Tojo, "things are automatically going to happen." By the "Magic" of cryptanalysis, Mr. Hull and Mr. Roosevelt were well aware of the approaching deadline. They were often reading the Japanese diplomatic messages before the Japanese diplomats themselves, so efficient were the American decoding experts. Unfortunately for thousands of Americans in Hawaii, the Japanese allowed no hint of the forthcoming attack on Pearl Harbor to enter their dispatches to their Embassy in Washington. By December 6, 1941, Mr. Hull and Mr. Roosevelt had agreed that an impasse had been reached. As a last effort to preserve the peace, the President sent his personal appeal to the Emperor of Japan.

It was too late. Events were fast moving to disaster. On November 26, 1941 (East Longitude Date), a Japanese task force built around six aircraft carriers left Tankan Bay in the Kurile Islands. Shortly before sailing, the bullhorns on the thirty-one Japanese ships announced their destination—Pearl Harbor. On December 1, the Japanese Privy Council in the Emperor's presence approved the decision for war. Nothing now remained except to stall the negotiations until the striking force could get into launching position. At 0600 on December 7, 1941, the first aircraft flew off the flight deck of the *Shokaku, Zuikaku, Akagi, Kaga, Hiryu* and *Soryu*. At 0755 the first bombs fell on Pearl Harbor.

CHAPTER TWO

December 1941: America Goes to War

> *"Praise the Lord and pass the ammunition!"*
> Remark attributed to a
> chaplain at Pearl Harbor

The U.S.S. *Ward*, a four-piper relic of the 1918 construction boom, steamed peacefully off the entrance to Pearl Harbor. It was her first patrol under her new skipper, Lieutenant William W. Outerbridge, USN. As he dozed in a wire bunk slung for him in the charthouse, he felt some apprehension—the kind shared by all captains in their first commands. He had no way of knowing that in a few hours he would fire the first shots of the war between the United States and Japan. It happened at 0645 on the morning of December 7, 1941. He promptly reported the incident to the authorities at Pearl Harbor.

No one believed him.

Early in the morning watch* on that day, the *Ward* received a message from the minesweeper *Condor* that she had spotted a suspicious vessel, probably a submarine, in the prohibited area south of the harbor entrance. Outerbridge sent his ship to General Quarters [battle stations] and searched. There were no results, so after an hour, the *Ward* went back to her patrol and Outerbridge to his bunk.

He did not have long to sleep. At 0637 the Officer of the Deck called him to the bridge. Ahead they could see the U.S.S. *Antares,* and astern of her the periscope and conning tower of a midget submarine, apparently attempting to sneak into the harbor in the wake of the old stores ship. One look was enough. Outerbridge sent his ship to General Quarters again, and eight minutes after he had been summoned, opened fire. The first round missed by inches, but the second was a direct hit. To make certain, Outerbridge dropped four depth charges on the stricken submarine.

The first attack of the war was a complete success. The midget disappeared forever.

Lieutenant Outerbridge immediately sent a message to Pearl Harbor: WE HAVE ATTACKED FIRED UPON AND DROPPED DEPTH CHARGES UPON SUBMARINE OPERATING IN DEFENSIVE AREA.

The message reached shore with the speed of light. Its progress thereafter was considerably slower. First it was delayed in decoding. Eventually it made its way up the chain of command, only to be dismissed as "another sub sighting." A request for verification went out to the *Ward*, but just to be on

* Aboard U.S. and Royal Navy ships, watches retain the old, traditional names from the days of sail.

Time	Watch
0000–0400	midwatch (or middle watch)
0400–0800	morning watch
0800–1200	forenoon watch
1200–1600	afternoon watch
1600–1800	first dogwatch
1800–2000	second dogwatch
2000–2400	first watch (or evening watch)

the safe side, the duty officer called Admiral Husband E. Kimmel, Commander in Chief, Pacific Fleet. Kimmel asked whether any verification had been received. When told no, he decided to take no action.

Near Kahuku Point on the north side of Oahu, two privates manned the Army's Opana Radar Station. They were there only for training; the station was not yet operational. According to the plan, they were to shut down at 0700, when a truck would come to pick them up. Their transportation was late that morning, and Private George Elliott kept the set running for practice. Over his shoulder, Private Joseph Lockard gazed at the screen, giving his buddy a few tips from time to time.

Then at 0702 the biggest target either of them had ever seen appeared at a range of 137 miles, three degrees east of north. Lockard began plotting the mysterious aircraft, and four minutes later telephoned the Fort Shafter Information Center. As the aircraft came closer minute by minute, Lockard reported their progress to an unimpressed Lieutenant Kermit Tyler. Tyler listened and then shrugged. Some carrier planes were due in. Also, there was a large flight of B-17 Flying Fortresses coming from Stateside.

"Don't worry about it," he concluded.

Elliott continued tracking until the breakfast truck came. By that time the Japanese planes were only twenty-two miles away.

But no one knew they were Japanese.

Just before 0755 on every one of the ninety-four ships in Pearl Harbor, signalmen were standing ready to hoist the Blue Peter or "Prep" flag, which warned of five minutes until morning colors. Condition Three was set on all ships, and some antiaircraft batteries were manned, although the ammunition was in locked boxes. At the Naval Air Stations on Ford Island and Kaneohe, and at the Army's Hickam Field, planes were drawn up in neat, orderly rows to make it easy to guard against sabotage. Church bells sounded the call to eight o'clock Mass. Some irate householders peered up and down the street for the paper boy with the Honolulu *Advertiser*. No papers would be delivered that morning; the presses had broken down.

It was a normal, peaceful Sunday morning.

At that precise moment, startled eyes noticed strange planes

37

high in the sky. They began to slant down. Tiny objects separated from the aircraft, followed by—chaos.

As a stone thrown in a pool of water will shatter the reflections mirrored in its surface, so those first bombs shattered the peace of that morning.

When the attack was over at 0945, every one of the eight battleships in Pearl Harbor was either sunk or damaged. The *Oklahoma* and *Arizona* would never fight again. The others eventually rejoined the fleet. The old battleship *Utah*, ending her days ignominiously as a target ship, and the minelayer *Oglala* were on the bottom. The destroyers *Cassin, Downes,* and *Shaw* were damaged; so were the seaplane tender *Curtis* and the repair ship *Vestal.* The Army had lost 144 aircraft and the Navy 89, but grimmest of all were the losses of men and women. In all, 2,403 persons died in the raid, 68 of them civilians.

There were a few bright spots.

All three of the aircraft carriers assigned to the Pacific Fleet were safe. The *Saratoga* was undergoing repairs on the West Coast; her sister ship *Lexington* was delivering aircraft to Midway; the *Enterprise*, near Pearl Harbor at the time of the attack, spent the next few days in a gallant but futile search for the Japanese Striking Force.

Equally important, the Japanese had overlooked the shore facilities at Pearl Harbor. Intact were most of the installions of the navy yard, oil storage for 9,500,000 barrels of fuel oil,* and the submarine base. For each of these omissions the Japanese were to pay dearly in the months to come.

News of Pearl Harbor sped westward over the waste of waters of the Pacific—to Midway, Wake, Guam, the Phillipines, Singapore, Australia. Garrisons braced for the shocks they knew must come—if not now, then later, but they would come.

Both Wake Island in Mid-Pacific and Guam, the American base in the southern Marianas, felt the weight of Japanese fury. Guam was overwhelmed by five thousand Japanese on December 10. Wake, after repulsing the first Japanese attempt, fell two days before Christmas.

---

* A barrel of oil contains forty-two gallons. Thus the Pacific Fleet had 189 million gallons available after the attack, not counting the oil already in the fuel tanks of the ships.

The Sons of Heaven, as they called themselves, smashed through Thailand with ease, and on December 8 and 9 landed in force at Kota Bharu on the eastern coast of the Malay Peninsula and began an ominous advance toward Singapore.

* * * * *

Most Americans learned of the attack about 3 P.M. The weekly broadcast of the New York Philharmonic Orchestra was interrupted to promise "more news about Pearl Harbor." Soon the news was on all stations, although details were pitifully few or nonexistent.

Men began to appear at their places of duty. Vice President Henry A. Wallace phoned from New York to say he would arrive on the next plane. Loudspeakers summoned men from the Redskin football game; telephones brought others from their homes. The White House quickly became a headquarters for war. Amid widespread confusion the Commander in Chief presided, wearing a turtleneck sweater, quietly issuing the necessary orders.

Every American old enough to remember that day knows precisely what he was doing when he heard the news of the Japanese attack. Some sought out friends to find companionship. Some went back to church to pray. Others sought courage in a bottle. Not a few headed for recruiting stations, to stand quietly waiting the long night hours through.

New York's mercurial Mayor Fiorello H. La Guardia, who was also U.S. Director of Civil Defense, careered across the city in a police car, siren shrieking, to reach WNYC studios, his own "personal radio station. Into its microphones he read the "funnies" to the kids during newspaper strikes. Now he had a grimmer message:

"Calm! Calm!" he commanded. "We are not out of the danger zone, by any means!"

New York's radio station WQXR canceled a scheduled broadcast of Gilbert and Sullivan's *The Mikado* and instead presented *H.M.S. Pinafore* "in honor of the Royal Navy."

* * * * *

In Manila, General Douglas MacArthur, until recently Field Marshal of the Philippine Army, but now on active duty as a

General of the U. S. Army, slept in his penthouse in the Manila Hotel. A few floors below, Admiral Thomas C. Hart, USN, Commander in Chief, U.S. Asiatic Fleet, was roused from slumber at about 0300* by the duty officer. "Admiral, put some cold water on your face," he telephoned. "I'm coming over with a message." It was, of course, the news of the attack. General MacArthur learned of it about an hour later.

The alert quickly went to all ships and stations. On all airstrips, every aircraft that could fly was drawn up ready for takeoff as soon as word should come of the inevitable Japanese attack. There they waited. No planes appeared. What was wrong?

The weather at Clark Field and at Nichols Field near Manila was good. Not so over Formosa, where the Japanese awaited their chance to knock out the American air strength before it could flee to the south. At last, by about 1015, weather improved enough for 192 planes of the Japanese Eleventh Air Fleet to take off.

Meanwhile, a false alarm at 0830 had sent the American planes from Clark Field clawing their way into the air. By 1000 most had returned from this fruitless mission to be refueled. There the Japanese found them, sitting ducks on their hardstands. No one had signaled the Japanese approach. Suddenly the Japanese aircraft were overhead and as suddenly dropping bombs and spitting tracer bullets from their guns. At the end of the attack, a third of the American fighter strength was gone, and half of the bombers. This single strike finished whatever tiny chance there might have been of holding the Philippines. It made inevitable the tragedies of Bataan and Singapore.

* * * * *

The time in Hawaii was 0945. The last Japanese planes had

---

* This was within minutes of the attack itself. Because of the International Date Line, which runs generally along the 180th meridian, the date in the Far East is one day ahead of that in the United States and Europe. For example, 1 P.M. in Washington, December 7, 1941, was 6 P.M. Greenwich Mean Time, 7 P.M. in London, which was observing Summer Time [*Sic.* In summer, they observed "Double Summer Time."], 7:30 A.M. in Honolulu, December 7, and in Tokyo, 2 A.M., December 8.

departed, and there was time to look around at the rubble. But who could know that the attack was over? Rumors were everywhere. The Japanese were reported landing at Barbers Point. Covered by carriers, the forces at sea spent their time searching for the Japanese—in the wrong directions. A radio direction finder picked up a Japanese transmission from the north and reported it was from the south. The *Lexington* force, under Rear Admiral J. H. Newton, and the *Enterprise* force under Halsey spent two frustrating days before they gave it up and entered port.

Not all of the pilots from those carriers came in with them. Some were lost at sea. Others had been ordered to land at Ford Island with messages and to take on fuel before returning to their carriers. A few, tragically, were shot down after dark by nervous gunners—this, in spite of ample warning and the use of lights on the aircraft. A few made it safely down in spite of the gunfire. One pilot counted eighteen holes in his F4F Wildcat fighter.

Two pilots of Scouting Squadron Six from the *Enterprise*, deciding that Ford Island was too hot, headed across the mountains to Kaneohe. Uable to raise the tower, they came in anyway. As Ensign Bucky Walters set his SBD Dauntless dive bomber down, he noticed an obstruction ahead. He swerved to dodge. Another. He swerved again. Soon he was whipping down the runway like a slalom skier. He brought his maltreated dive bomber to a stop only inches from a mobile crane. His wingmate repeated his experience, ending up eyeball-to-eyeball with a concrete mixer.

The commanding officer of the Kaneohe Naval Air Station was furious. He had given strict orders to make the field absolutely unusable.

* * * * *

On the other side of the world, Winston S. Churchill was entertaining U.S. Ambassador John C. Winant and Lend-Lease Expediter W. Averell Harriman at Chequers, the Prime Minister's official country estate. The three men had just finished dinner when Churchill turned on a small portable radio for the nine o'clock news. The Prime Minister was apparently only half listening, for he did not catch the statement made in the cultivated tones of the B.B.C. announcer of "an attack by the Japanese on American shipping at Hawaii." When Harriman called it to his attention, Churchill promptly put in a call to President Roosevelt. In a few moments the familiar voice came over the wire.

"Mr. President, what's this about Japan?" asked Churchill. "It's quite true," replied Mr. Roosevelt. "We are all in the same boat now."

Immediately Churchill made up his mind that he must go to Washington. He secretly feared that the Japanese attack would turn all American attention to the Pacific. This would violate the ABC-1 agreement providing that the defeat of Germany would be the first objective in the event of American entry into the war. America, he felt, must be guided along the path of victory.

> No American will think it wrong of me [he wrote in 1951] if I proclaim that to have the United States at our side was to me the greatest joy. . . . So we had won after all! . . . England would live, Britain would live. . . . Once again in our long Island history we should emerge, however mauled or mutilated, safe and victorious. . . . Hitler's fate was sealed. Mussolini's fate was sealed. As for the Japanese, they would be ground to powder. . . . The British Empire, the Soviet Union, and now the United States, bound together with every scrap of their life and strength were, according to my lights, twice or even thrice the force of their antagonists. . . . United we could subdue everybody else in the world. Many disasters, immeasurable cost and tribulation lay ahead, but there was no doubt about the end. . . . I went to bed and slept the sleep of the saved.

* * * * *

When Americans woke the next morning, shock had been replaced with rage and by an urgent, overwhelming desire to get on with the job. Throughout the country, recruiting stations were swamped. Block-long lines of men waited patiently in the cold, crisp morning air. In New York, stations opened an hour early at 7 A.M. to accommodate the volunteers, or at least to permit those who had been waiting all night to come in and get warm. All day and into the evening, recruiters labored on. Groups of men were sworn in whenever an officer could be found to spare a minute from his pressing duties. Soon orders came that in the major cities recruiting stations were to remain open twenty-four hours a day. The young and the old, the halt and the hale, the college boy and professor, the butcher, the baker, the candlestick maker—all doubts gone, all questions set aside—they came in thousands to pay back in kind the bloody attack on their country.

World-famous names appeared on enlistment rosters. Cleveland pitcher Bob Feller was sworn into the Naval Reserve as a Chief Boatswain's Mate in Lieutenant Commander Gene Tunney's physical fitness program.

Toward midday those who could do so began to turn on their radios, for the President of the United States was to address a joint session of Congress soon after noon. Just at twelve, six limousines drew up in front of the White House. The big glass doors opened, and Mr. Roosevelt came out, leaning on the arm of his son James, who was wearing the uniform of a Major in the Marine Corps. Without a word the President descended the steps and entered his car, which moved off immediately. Mrs. Roosevelt and members of the President's offical family followed in the other cars.

The chamber of the House of Representatives was jammed with people. Klieg lights for newsreel cameramen blazed down on the assembled Representatives and their eighty-two Senatorial guests. In spite of greatly increased security measures, the galleries were jammed with the diplomatic corps, official guests, Government officials, and the few soldiers and sailors and members of the public who had managed to get passes.

At 12:23 the Sergeant at Arms announced, "Mr. Speaker, the President of the United States."

After a brief prayer by the chaplain, Mr. Roosevelt advanced to the lectern. The radio networks carried his words to all the country and to all the world, while movie cameras preserved the scene for history.

Yesterday, December 7, 1941, [the familiar voice took tones of scorn]—a date which will live in infamy—the United States of America was suddenly and deliberately attacked by naval and air forces of the Empire of Japan. . . .

The attack yesterday on the Hawaiian Islands has caused severe damage to American naval and military forces. Very many lives have been lost. . . .

Hostilities exist. There is no blinking at the fact that our people, our territory, and our interests are in grave danger.

With confidence in our armed forces—with the unbounded determination of our people—we will gain the inevitable triumph—so help us God.

I ask that the Congress declare that since the unprovoked and dastardly attack by Japan on Sunday, December seventh, a state of war has existed between the United States and the Japanese Empire.

Completing his speech, Mr. Roosevelt looked up to acknowledge the cheers. His familiar smile had a touch of grimness as he waved.

Within minutes, the Senators had reassembled in their own chamber and had passed a declaration of war against Japan by a vote of 82 to 0. The House followed shortly with a vote of 388 to 1. The lone holdout was Representative Jeannette Rankin of Montana, who had also voted against the American declaration of war on Germany in 1917.* This near-unanimity reflected the feelings of the American people. Isolationism was dead. In the words of its principal spokesman, Senator Burton K. Wheeler, "The only thing to do now is to lick the hell out of them."

It would be a long time before America could "lick the hell out of them." In the months ahead lay tragedy, defeat, despair. The Germans held all of Europe from North Cape to the Pyrenees, from Brest to Central Russia. Only Sweden, Switzerland, Spain, and Portugal stood aloof.

* * * * *

On June 22, 1941, turning his back on the west where an impudent Britain continued to thwart his dreams of complete victory, Hitler smashed into Russia. Operation Barbarossa, postponed a month because Hitler had had to rescue his improvident junior partner, Mussolini, from his ill-considered assault on Greece, had been planned for months. In spite of intelligence gathered at extreme cost in lives, in spite of warn-

* She abstained three days later when the declarations of war against Germany and Italy passed both Houses unanimously.

ings from Churchill, who had his own means of knowing, the German attack caught the Russians badly unprepared. Hitler's aim was to subdue European Russia, to seize control of everything west of a line running from Archangel to Astrakhan. This was the Heartland of which Mackinder, the British geographer, had written—the Heartland his disciple, the Nazi Haushofer, had memorialized in the pithy proposition: He who controls the Heartland controls the World Island; he who controls the World Island controls the World.*

For three and a half months the Germans had a nearly unbroken series of successes. In the first two weeks the Russians lost most of their Air Force, thousands of tanks, and upwards of a million men. By the middle of July, many German generals believed they had won the war.

Three massive Army Groups attacked along a 950-mile front from the Baltic to the Black Sea. At the southern end of this front, Army Group South under the command of Field Marshal von Rundstedt pushed toward Kiev and the Ukraine. In spite of the fifty-seven divisions that composed this Army Group, progress was disappointingly slow, held up by stubborn, if abandoned, small bands of Russian patriots.

Army Group Center, under Field Marshal von Bock, made rapid advances in the direction of Smolensk and Moscow. Led by panzer divisions, the Second and Third German Armies sent long spearheads eastward and joined up east of Minsk, trapping thousands of disorganized Soviet soldiers. It spite of desperate efforts to break out, the Russian forces were soon mopped up, 290,000 prisoners being taken. By mid-July, the Smolensk area was caught in a similar pincers movement; 100,000 more men were captured, and the way to Moscow lay open.

In the north, Field Marshal Ritter von Leeb led Army Group North toward Leningrad. As his troops moved northeast past Riga, Ostrov, and Pskov, Finnish troops were supposed to invest Russia and Leningrad from the north.

By July 16, when the first phase of the German drive had ended, Hitler's forces were fifteen miles from Kiev, a hundred and seventy miles from Moscow, and seventy miles from Len-

* The World Island is the combined land mass of Europe, Asia, and Africa. North and South America, Australia, etc., were, in this theory, called Oceana.

ingrad. They would come closer. Much closer.

* * * * *

When the news of the German attack on Russia reached Churchill, he immediately promised the Soviets all aid Britain could give. "No one," he said in a broadcast that very night, "has been a more consistent opponent of Communism than I. . . . I will unsay no word that I have spoken about it. . . . This blood-thirsty guttersnipe must launch his mechanized armies upon new fields of slaughter. . . . I see the Russian soldiers standing on the threshold of their native land. . . . I see the ten thousand villages of Russia where there are still primordial joys, where maidens laugh and children play. I see advancing on all this in hideous onslaught the Nazi war machine. . . . I see the dull, drilled, docile, brutish masses of the Hun soldiery plodding on like a stream of crawling locusts. I see the German bombers and fighters in the sky, still smarting from many a British whipping, delighted to find what they believe is an easier and safer prey. . . . We are resolved to destroy Hitler and every vestige of the Nazi regime. From this nothing will turn us—nothing. We will never parley, we will never negotiate with Hitler or any of his gang. . . . Any man or state who fights on against Nazidom will have our aid. Any man or state who marches with Hitler is our foe."

While Russian men and women in their agony might have derived some comfort from Churchill's ringing broadcast, they had a long wait for a rallying cry from their own leaders. In all of vast Russia there was no one they could look to as a figure of trust and leadership. Comrade Stalin was more feared than admired. Remember the purges of 1937 and 1938. Remember the ruthless war on the Kulaks. Remember the "testament of Lenin": "Stalin is too rough." Remember the exile and murder of Trotsky.

The Russians had rather to look to "Mother Russia" and their intense patriotism for inspiration.

On July 3, twelve long days after the German invasion, all that changed. Stalin addressed the nation in a speech that has been compared to Churchill's "blood, toil, tears and sweat" appeal in 1940.

"Comrades, citizens," he began; "brothers and sisters, fighters of our Army and Navy. I am speaking to you, my friends." Could this be the mysterious, aloof, dangerous Stalin speaking? "My friends!" He called on all to unite in wiping out Russia's "most wicked and perfidious enemy, German fascism." He pronounced a scorched-earth policy. "Millions will rise," he concluded. "All the strength of the people must be used to smash the enemy. Onward, to victory!"

President Roosevelt did not immediately make a public statement about the new German aggression. Instead he sent his friend Harry Hopkins to England to see how the United States could help in the aid to Russia. To many this seemed a futile gesture. Many Americans were impartially antagonistic to both Germany and Russia. "I hope they both keep going and neither side runs out of bullets" was an observation frequently heard in offices and in cocktail lounges, in factories and in poolrooms. Military analysts were divided. Some thought Russia could hold out six weeks; others thought two weeks more likely. Few in authority doubted that the blitzkrieg of the Wehrmacht would crush Russia as it had crushed France.

After a lengthy stop in England to consult with Churchill, Hopkins decided to go on to Moscow to learn the real situation. Suffering an uncomfortable flight north about Norway and a stop at Archangel, Hopkins finally reached Moscow on July 30.

Moscow was a city of gloom, although the immediate threat to the capital had eased. Leningrad was near encirclement. In the south the drive threatened Kiev, Odessa, and the Caucasus. Hitler had weakened the drive on Moscow to concentrate on Leningrad, the Crimea, and the Caucasus. The change in emphasis may have cost Hitler the war. To move whole divisions several hundred miles in the face of the enemy is something that cannot be improvised. After a month of order-counterorder-confusion, Hitler issued a "Führer Directive" on August 21.

The most important objective to be achieved before the onset of winter is not the capture of Moscow but the seizure of the Crimea and of the industrial and coal-mining region on the Donets, and the cutting off of Russian oil supplies from the Caucasus area; in the north it is the isolation of Leningrad and the link-up with the Finns.

Meanwhile in Moscow, aware that Russia was struggling for her survival, Harry Hopkins held two conferences with Stalin and concluded to his satisfaction that Russia would hold out. Stalin asked not only for arms and ammunition for the immediate military crisis, but also for aluminum with which to build aircraft for operations in the more distant future. "Give us antiaircraft guns and the aluminum," Stalin suddenly broke in, "and we can fight for three or four years."

The German drive continued relentlessly. On September 19, Kiev fell, and by the 26th, 665,000 more Russians had been taken prisoner. On pressed the Germans. The Crimea, except for Sevastopol, was occupied by the middle of November, and the Germans pressed ineluctably closer to Moscow. Muscovites evacuated the city in large numbers, but the leadership stood firm. An ally was at hand. When the Germans were only twenty-five miles away from the capital, the terrible Russian winter closed in. German soldiers, unprovided with winter clothing, suffered agonies from frost, ice, and snow. Many froze to death. Gangrene induced by frostbite cost many an arm or leg. The common German soldiers paid in terrible measure for their Führer's shortcomings. Machines were no better off. Without winter lubricants, tanks and vehicles became inoperable. Across the whitened plains, Moscow stood stubborn as a symbol of resistance.

The siege of Leningrad has no equal in history for suffering and endurance. By the beginning of September, the city was completely cut off from the rest of Russia on the south, with Finnish troops closing the gap to the north. At this time the city had a population of just under 3,000,000 persons. When the siege was lifted in January 1943, the inhabitants numbered only 650,000. Many had been evacuated or had joined in the fighting against the invaders. But a million had died.

A million died of illness, accident, or starvation. By November rations, reduced and reduced, had reached a point where they would no longer sustain life. The daily ration scale on the facing page was announced.

Yet even these amounts of food, completely insufficient by any standards, existed on paper only. Such quantities could not be provided, for the food did not exist. On these poor scraps, men, women, and children toiled to strengthen the defenses of Leningrad. They dug, among other defenses, 340 *miles* of antitank ditches and 15,875 miles of open trenches. They worked

48

	Workers	Office Workers	Dependents	Children
Bread	260 grams	130 grams	130 grams	130 grams
Fats	20 grams	10 grams	7 grams	18 grams
Meat	50 grams	30 grams	15 grams	15 grams
Cereals	50 grams	35 grams	25 grams	40 grams
Sugar/	50 grams	35 grams	30 grams	40 grams
Candy				
Totals	430 grams	240 grams	207 grams	243 grams
Calories	1087	581	466	684

on, the dead falling in their tracks, the dying working a bit
longer.

On December 5, the Russians mounted a great counteroffensive all along the front from Kursk north. Aided by the winter and the lack of German preparedness for the elements, the
Soviet troops managed to push the Nazis back to the positions
they had held in November. Unfortunately for the citizens of
Leningrad, the drive did not go in their direction. They were
left to their own meager resources. Hitler's order to contest
every inch of ground merely threw German troops away, for
they died uselessly where they were instead of withdrawing to
positions they could hold until spring should give them the opportunity for lashing back against their Russian tormentors.

* * * * *

The Russo-German war was but vaguely understood by the
average American. It was too huge, too complex, and there
were no obvious heroes or villains. Suspicion of Communism,
distaste for Nazism, and the impersonality of the struggle as
reported in the press kept Americans' feelings from significant
involvement.

It was a vastly different story in the African desert. Here, in
an arena stretching 1400 miles from Tripoli to Alexandria, the
British battled Axis forces in a war of dash, glamour, and
élan—although to those who fought there it was a war of heat,
flies, thirst, sand.

After the fall of France, Mussolini longed to realize his
dream of "Mare Nostrum"—to make the Mediterranean an
Italian lake as it had been a Roman one in Caesar's time.

Frustrated by the sorry performance of his troops against mortally wounded France, Mussolini turned to North Africa. Peremptorily he ordered Marshal Rodolfo Graziani to drive eastward from Libya and seize the Anglo-Egyptian naval base at Alexandria. On September 13, 1940, Graziani crossed the Egyptian border. In four days he had taken the border town of Sollum (or Salum) and advanced some forty-five miles to Sidi Barrani. There, heedless of Mussolini's exhortations, Graziani discontinued his advance and constructed fortifications and waited, aghast at his own temerity. The British would be certain to punish him for his presumption.

They did not disappoint him. In December, General Wavell counterattacked and sent the Italians reeling back to the west. By early February, some 168,000 Italians had been captured, and the British had advanced nearly five hundred miles to El Agheila on the shores of the Gulf of Sirte.

Wavell wanted to keep his momentum going and push on to the vital port of Tripoli. But orders from London changed his plans. The Italian offensive into Greece in October 1940 had stalled, and a Greek counteroffensive had by March 1 the following year driven the Italians back into Albania. Then Hitler came to the rescue, attacking through Yugoslavia and on into Greece.

To parry this move, to prove to peoples struggling for freedom that they were not alone, Churchill ordered Wavell to strip his positions in the Western Desert to mere holding forces in order to send as many men as possible to help the Greeks.

The political and humane reasons may have been sound. Militarily the decision was a disaster. The Anglo-Greek force was no match for the Germans. It was driven back and back. By April 30, the Greeks had surrendered, and the remnants of Wavell's desert veterans had been evacuated at enormous cost, both in lives and in ships of the Royal Navy. The naval losses were even greater than those of Dunkirk.

Crete was the next holding point, but the story was the same, and by the end of May, British troops had been forced out and back to North Africa—those who did not leave their bodies to rot there, and those who were not fated to spend the next four years in a prison-of-war camp.

When the survivors reached North Africa, the situation was vastly different from the one they had left. A new face had appeared on the Axis scene, one whose image was better known

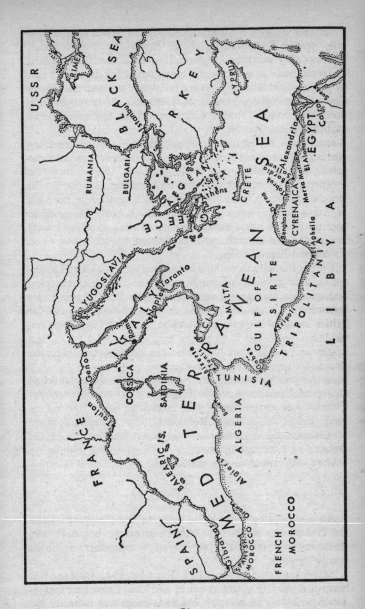

USSR

ARMEN?

BLACK SEA

RUMANIA

BULGARIA

T U R K E Y

stanbul

CYPRUS

A E G E A N

SEA

Athens

G R E E C E

CRETE

Alexandria

EGYPT

Cairo

Sollum

Bardia

Tobruk

Merso Matr

El Alamei

Derna

Benghazi

CYRENAICA

Agheila

M E D I T E R R A N E A N   S E A

YUGOSLAVIA

I T A L Y

Rome

Naples

Taranto

Genoa

Toulon

FRANCE

CORSICA

SARDINIA

BALEARIC IS.

Algiers

ALGERIA

SPAIN

Gibraltar

SPANISH
MOROCCO

FRENCH
MOROCCO

TUNISIA

Bone

MALTA

SICILY

Trapani

GULF OF
SIRTE

S. I. R. T. E

Tripoli

T R I P O L I T A N I A

L I B Y A

in Germany, Italy, Britain, and the United States than that of any other military man—General Erwin Rommel. Rommel was that rare exception, a general's general, widely respected by friend and foe alike for his competence, his dash, his complete professionalism. His arrival with the Afrika Korps changed everything. Instead of ill-trained, reluctant Italians, the British had to contend with crack troops brilliantly led by an inspired commander.

On March 24, German probes against El Agheila revealed the British weaknesses, and Rommel ordered a rapid drive eastward, to the dismay of his Italian allies, still nominally in command, and confounding his own superiors in Berlin. In less than three weeks he had driven the British completely out of Libya except for a pocket around Tobruk. Stopping at Sollum, Rommel beat off two counterattacks by Wavell, with the result that Churchill lost confidence in his commander and transferred him to India.

During the long, hot summer months, neither side made any appreciable advances. Rommel spent the time in regrouping and building up his stock of supplies. The British, now under General Sir Claude Auchinleck, also amassed supplies. All the British materials—guns, ammunition, tanks, trucks, gasoline, food, clothing—had to come the long way around Africa and up through the Red Sea. On both sides, men worked feverishly to prepare for renewed fighting.

At length Auchinleck, on November 18, 1941, launched Operation Crusader to relieve Tobruk and drive the Axis out of Cyrenaica or eastern Libya. Two months of heavy fighting ensued, and at the end of it Rommel's forces were back where they had started in El Agheila. The Desert Rats had driven the Desert Fox back into his hole.

How long would he stay there?

* * * * *

After the drama of the radio bulletins and the speeches and the declarations of war, the American people began to take stock and face up to the problem of winning the war. What was to be done, and how?

America was far better off in December 1941 than she had been in April 1917. As a result of the Lend-Lease program— the Arsenal of Democracy concept—machinery already existed in Washington to convert the productive capacity of the nation to war goods. Many factories were already humming with war orders for the British. New ships for the "two-ocean" Navy were on the builders' ways. Tanks, guns, trucks, planes, ships came out in ever increasing numbers.

The planning for harnessing America's building capacity to war needs came under the Office of Production Management (OPM), created in 1940 under the joint chairmanship of Sidney Hillman and William S. Knudsen, representing respectively labor and management. All, however, was not as simple as it seems. Mr. Roosevelt, dramatic and dynamic leader that he was, had a perfect genius for creating administrative confusion in the boards, committees, offices, commissions, and bureaus he established. The OPM existed as a part of the Office for Emergency Management (OEM) of the Executive Office of the President. But it had an associated board, partly over it and partly under it. This was the Supply, Priorities, and Allocations Board (SPAB), headed by Donald M. Nelson, which was supposed to execute the orders of OPM, but at the same time see to it that OPM issued the right orders. To cap it off, the Army and Navy Munitions Board (ANMB), answerable to the Secretaries of War and the Navy and not to OEM, was perfectly capable of issuing orders affecting the economic and productive capacity of the country without consulting either OPM or SPAB. Another office with a finger in the pie was OPACS (Office of Price Administration and Civilian Supply), headed by Leon Henderson. Its role was to see to it that the civilian economy got its share. This mission brought it into inevitable conflict with OPM. SPAB, OEM, and ANMB, since the civilian needs often competed for the same goods and materials as war production. On the other hand, OPACS was too often zealous of war needs, while OPM had to look after the consumer interests, since no one else would.

In July 1941, OPACS announced a fifty-percent cut in automobile production to be effective August 1. Execution of this order would have meant idle factories, since the automobile manufacturers were not yet ready to make the weapons of war. OPM, meanwhile, had been working to ensure that the shift would be as smooth as possible, with the minimum of production loss. This incident caused a pitched battle between OPACS and OPM. At length, a decision was reached. OPACS was bifurcated and so ceased to exist. Part of its functions, those dealing with supply, were transferred to a new office, the Division of Civilian Supply (DCS) under *both* SPAB and OPM, and the rest to the Office of Price Administration (OPA.)

Such stirring of the alphabet soup in Washington caused endless confusion among business leaders and administrators in the nation's capital. Everyone agreed that something had to be done. Whatever the sacrifices necessary for winning the war, they would be made. The question remained: which sacrifices? It was not simply a question of guns or butter. It was sewing machines or machine guns? farm tractors or tanks? railroad cars or battleships? oil pipelines or tankers?

After the attack on Pearl Harbor, when everyone knew that America's productive capacity must be exerted as never before, OPM submitted to the President an estimate that during 1942 United States production might possibly reach thirty-three billion dollars. Meanwhile OPM's own Division of Research and Statistics had shown not only that these figures were far too modest; they were based on a *decreased* rate of production from that already enjoyed by the nation. Mr. Roosevelt looked at the figures and said nothing to either Knudsen or Hillman. He simply ignored their predictions.

When a major office in Washington is ignored, it is not long for this world.

For the man below these lofty councils, changes were inevitable. Perhaps his first warning came when air raid sirens began to sound in New York on December 9. Many people went about their business, for the sirens could not be heard all over the city. Interceptor aircraft took off to look for enemy aircraft. At the Army's Mitchel Field, dependents were evacuated, and ground personnel stood to arms. Air raid wardens and spotters went to their posts, schoolchildren were sent home, and people were ordered to clear the streets. Few obeyed, lest they miss the excitement. Shipyards halted work, and the men, with nothing to do, turned their gaze to the skies. When the All Clear blew a little later, everybody was a bit sheepish about the whole affair. Still, it *might* have happened.

As a result of this event, Washington ordered that the dome over the Capitol be blacked out for the duration. Also all Federal offices were to arrange for blackouts or evacuation in the event of attack. The order was couched in these words:

Such preparations shall be made as will completely obscure all Federal buildings occupied by the Federal Government during an air raid for any period of time from visibility by reason of internal or external illumination. Such obscuration may be obtained either by blackout construction or by termination of the illumination. This will, of course, require that in building areas in which production must continue during the blackout, construction must be provided that internal illumination may continue.

On seeing this, Mr. Roosevelt said to write it this way:

Tell them that in buildings where they have to keep the work going to put something across the windows. In buildings where they can afford to let the work stop for a while turn out the lights.

Air raids or no, official Washington kept busy. Within a week, the House passed a supplemental defense appropriations bill of $8,234,839,031. This "huge sum," as the press called it, would look like peanuts before the war was over. The bill provided a billion dollars for the Navy for new ships. Over five billion went to the Army, for new equipment and for payroll for the newly authorized two million men it would soon have in uniform. They would use 100,000 multiwheel-drive trucks and 20,000 jeeps. Sixteen thousand aircraft were planned for the Army Air Forces and for the Navy. It was to be up to American industry.

Labor held a chief position in determining how much industry might turn out. Workers in key industries were quickly and indefinitely deferred from the draft, but some few labor leaders wanted to cash in on the huge appropriations. Before Pearl Harbor, several strikes had held up production. The most notable, that of the "captive coal miners," occasioned the most headlines. Bushy-browed John L. Lewis demanded the union shop in those steel-company-owned mines. The week after Pearl Harbor, an arbitration board awarded him all that he demanded. Without judging the merits of the case, it is sufficient to say that the decision outraged the country. Lewis was depicted as holding a gun to the nation's head when it was fighting for its life. The House of Representatives in its wrath passed a bill freezing present conditions in factories and practically outlawing strikes. The bill died, however, when responsible labor leaders pledged no strikes for the duration. The forty-hour week became national practice, with time-and-a-half for overtime. This provision cut to nothing workers' demands for a shorter work week. In fact, the availability of overtime became a selling point for employers seeking workers from a constantly diminishing supply. Before long, arms and ship-building industries were working 168 hours a week, fifty-six hours a week being far from unusual for individual workmen.

* * * * *

Fifty-six hours a week, or even double that, would have seemed heaven to the men and women who had to face the Japanese in the Pacific. As the Rising Sun flag moved farther south and east, there was no time for holidays—little enough for eating and sleeping.

The great naval base at Singapore stared out over the Strait of Malacca. The big guns pointed seaward; they could not be trained the other way. Only 141 aircraft were available, most of them obsolete. Britain's vaunted Far Eastern fortress seemed impregnable, but there was no lock on the back door. For years the British Cabinet had planned to send the Main Fleet to Singapore if there should be war with Japan. Now that war had come, they could not do it. Losses in the Mediterranean and threats of German breakouts in the Atlantic meant that most of Britain's naval strength was needed in Europe. Little could be sent to Singapore.

On December 2, 1941, their White Ensigns bravely flying, six British warships steamed down the Malacca Strait and entered Singapore harbor. They were the new battleship *Prince of Wales*, flying the flag of Admiral Sir Tom Phillips, the venerable battle cruiser *Repulse*, and four destroyers. Cheering crowds watched them stand in and make for their anchorages. The long arm of Britain's naval might had at last extended to the Far East.

Admiral Sir Tom Phillips was not so confident. He was keenly aware of the inadequacy of his force, particularly against air attack. His little fleet would be completely dependent on land-based air cover any time he took it to sea. He knew of the woeful lack of air strength in the peninsula.

He regretted the absence of the aircraft carrier *Indomitable,* which was supposed to have joined him. As a new ship, the *Indomitable* had been sent to the West Indies for essential training before going on to the Orient. On the way into harbor at Jamaica, she had run aground; repairs had not been completed in time to get her out to the Pacific with the others. Her aircraft might have made all the difference.

On December 8, with the news of Japanese landings in the Malay Peninsula at Singora (or Songkhla) and Kota Bharu, Admiral Phillips decided to take his meager fleet to sea and attempt to knock out the beachheads. He duly requested air cover from the Royal Air Force.

That evening, as the ships passed the Changi Signal Station at the harbor entrance, a message came to the flagship from Air Vice Marshal C. W. Pulford: "Regret fighter protection impossible."

"Well," said the Admiral with a shrug of his shoulders, "we must get on without it."

Lacking fighter cover, everything depended on surprise. For this reason, Phillips took his ships well to the east and then north until he reached the latitude of Singora. At this point he turned west to head straight for his target. Just before sunset, lookouts spotted three Japanese aircraft. Surprise was lost. Assuming the alerted Japanese would be warned and withdraw their transports, Admiral Phillips decided to return to Singapore. There was no use in risking ships to no purpose.

As the night masked the men-of-war, radio bulletins told of losses on the ground and in the air. Could nothing be done?

Word arrived that the Japanese were making yet another landing, this time at Kuantan, a hundred and ninety air miles north of Singapore. Here was an opportunity. The Japanese would be looking for the British ships two hundred and fifty miles farther north. Phillips decided to head for Kuantan.

The next morning, December 10, as Admiral Phillips peered ahead for signs of the transports and saw only open sea and dim coastline, he regretfully came to the conclusion that the report had been false. He turned once again for Singapore. He had lost only a few hours, but those hours meant everything.

About 1020, a Japanese aircraft spotted the formation, and a few minutes after eleven a group of nine planes dived on the *Repulse.* Dirty puffs of antiaircraft burst in the air around the planes. Bombs dropped on all sides. One was a direct hit, but caused only minor damage.

Twenty minutes later, torpedo planes attacked both big ships. One or perhaps two torpedoes hit the *Prince of Wales*. She heeled over and lost steering control. The *Repulse,* now some distance away, successfully dodged another bombing attack. But it was not for long. Flights of aircraft came in from all different directions. Hit after hit was made. The tormented ships slowed and stopped. The merciless pounding went on. There could be but one outcome. Both ships heeled over, capsized, and sank. Admiral Sir Tom Phillips accompanied his flagship to her grave.

The loss of these two capital ships meant the doom of Singapore, just as the decimation of the aircraft at Clark Field ensured the defeat of American and Filipino hopes of saving the Philippines.

* * * * *

Jittery after the smashing air raids of December 8 and 9, the defenders of Manila looked over their shoulders and anxiously at the sea and sky. The Japanese might be coming at any moment.

Deciding that Manila harbor was completely useless as an operating base, on December 10, Admiral Thomas C. Hart, Commander in Chief, U.S. Asiatic Fleet, ordered all ships that could steam to head south for the southern Philippines or Java. This left only a few aged submarines to carry on the fight in the central Philippines. Hampered by faulty torpedoes, these boats were fated to have little success against the oncoming Japanese.

For the Japanese were coming. Their assault on Manila was not as swift as most defenders expected. But coming they were. In two weeks they would make nine amphibious landings in the islands.

On December 8 they took the little island of Batan in Bashi Channel, north of Luzon. Two days later they arrived at the neighboring island of Camiguin and at Aparri on the north coast of Luzon. The next day they came ashore at Vigan on the west coast, seventy-some miles north of Lingayen Gulf. Simultaneously they landed at Legaspi in the tail of Luzon in order to seize control of San Bernardino Strait.

All these landings were clearly preliminary, and General MacArthur refused to commit his forces against them. He had to await the major assaults everyone knew were coming.

He was hard pressed by correspondents and by civilian officials to move into the Lingayen Gulf area on the morning of the eleventh. Reports flashed down that the main Japanese attack had come there, but that the Philippine Army had driven it off in a bloody repulse. The waters of the gulf were said to be choked with Japanese bodies and the beaches littered with their dead.

The "glorious victory of Lingayen Gulf" blazed in the headlines of U.S. papers all across the country on Sunday morning, December 14. The story had been released by MacArthur's press officers, and the correspondents had filed their stories without checking.

Carl Mydans, photographer for *Life* magazine, was not quite so credulous. Going to the area himself, he found all peaceful—no sign of a battle. On inquiring, he discovered that several Japanese motorboats had come into the gulf, presumably on a reconnaissance mission. Trigger-happy gunners had opened up on them, but had been unable to obtain a single hit.

The invasion would not take place for another eleven days.

On December 21, heavy Japanese forces steamed into Lingayen Gulf and were reported to MacArthur's headquarters at Manila. It was no false alarm this time. Admiral Hart ordered five submarines to try to break up the landing. They were too late. By the time the submarines could reach the area, the Japanese transports were already in shoal water where the undersea craft could not venture. Nevertheless, *S-38* managed to sink the 8500-ton minelayer *Hayo Maru* on December 22, and the next day the *Seal* put an end to the small freighter *Hayataka Maru*. Shore batteries made two hits on the seaplane tender *Sanuki Maru*. These three ships were the only casualties the Japanese naval forces sustained at Lingayen Gulf.

Actually the Japanese had seventy-six transports at the scene of action and a powerful fleet to cover them. By nightfall of December 22, two divisions of troops had landed, in spite of the filthy weather, which bothered the Japanese far more than the opposition of the Philippine Army.

In the next few days the Japanese built their strength up to six divisions, which made up their Fourteenth Army under Lieutenant General Masaharu Homma. MacArthur ordered General Jonathan Wainwright with his North Luzon force to the support of the Philippine Army. His remaining troops he held in reserve.

MacArthur's prudence was rewarded two days later when the Japanese made another large landing on the east coast of Luzon at Lamon Bay. This move made plain the Japanese strategy, to trap the American and Philippine defenders in the central plains east of Manila. MacArthur, therefore, sent his reserves into the central area to fight a delaying action and fall back on the Bataan Peninsula across the bay from Manila. Meanwhile, his flank thus covered, Wainwright was to fall back with all his forces, also to Bataan.

The plan worked well, and just ahead of the Japanese, MacArthur's troops established a defensive line across the neck of Bataan, their flanks protected by the ocean and bay, and presenting a comparatively narrow front to the enemy.

All Government and military officials, both Filipino and American, were evacuated from Manila, either into Bataan or completely away from the islands, employing both sea and air transport to get them out. On Deceber 26, MacArthur proclaimed Manila an open city; two days later, he ordered all units in the central and southern islands and those unable to reach Bataan to conduct unremitting guerrilla warfare against the Japanese.

Isolated groups of men carried out this order all through the three years of Japanese occupation, to the constant irritation of the Japanese. These men knew their activities would take place under the constant threat of capture. Thousands of them were captured, and many of them suffered torture and death, martyrs in their cause of freedom.

* * * * *

His Majesty's battleship *Duke of York* pitched and rolled her way westward through the gray, stormy seas of the North Atlantic. Sister ship to the ill-starred *Prince of Wales*, she carried, as her sister had done the previous August, Britain's Prime Minister Winston Churchill. With him came Lord Beaverbrook, responsible for marshaling Britain's war production, and the members of the Chiefs of Staff, Admiral Sir

Dudley Pound, First Sea Lord, representing the Royal Navy, Air Marshal Sir Charles Portal of the RAF, and Field Marshal Sir John Dill of the Army.* Ahead of them lay Washington and a personal meeting with President Roosevelt.

As the battleship plowed westward through the angry waters, Churchill and his staff prepared a series of papers to present to the Americans as a proposed strategy for the war. These papers opposed extended operations in Africa in 1942, a scheme for winning command of the Pacific by May 1942, and fixing the year 1943 for a massive landing in Europe to deliver what Churchill called the "supreme stroke" against Germany.

Preparation of these studies whiled away the hours and days of the crossing, and on December 22, the *Duke of York* reached Norfolk, Virginia. Flying from there to Washington, Churchill was soon greeting President Roosevelt. "I clasped his strong hand," he wrote, "with comfort and pleasure."

The conference which then began has been given the code name Arcadia. Like all wartime conferences between Churchill and Roosevelt, its formal meetings were supplemented by highly informal, unofficial meetings between Churchill and Roosevelt.

The story was told by Harry Hopkins of one occasion when Roosevelt, struck by a new idea, wheeled himself into Churchill's guest bedroom in the White House, only to be confronted by a pink, cherubic Churchill emerging stark naked from the bathroom. In confusion, Roosevelt apologized and began to withdraw.

"It is quite all right," protested Churchill. "The Prime Minister of Great Britain has nothing to conceal from the President of the United States."**

During his stay in Washington, Churchill took part in the

---

* Dill was no longer a member of the Chiefs of Staff, having been relieved as Chief of the Imperial General Staff (C.I.G.S.) only a few days earlier by General Sir Alan Brooke. Brooke was left behind in London with Churchill's personal Chief of Staff, General Sir Hastings Ismay, to become acquainted with his new vast responsibilities.

** Churchill later protested that the story was not quite true and that he never received Roosevelt without at least a towel around his waist.

Christmas festivities of the White House, joining in the ceremony on Christmas Eve of lighting the national Christmas tree on the White House lawn.

The day after Christmas, Churchill was driven to Capitol Hill to take advantage of an invitation to address a joint session of Congress. A twinkle came into his eyes as he gripped the speaker's rostrum and gazed out over the assembled Senators and Representatives who were looking back at him with some suspicion.

"I cannot help reflecting," he began quietly, "that if my father had been American and my mother British, instead of the other way around, I might have got here on my own."

This broke the ice. From then on, Churchill was one of the boys, as far as Congress was concerned.

The Arcadia Conference had two principal concerns: the drafting of a statement of principles for the Allies, and the formulation of a strategy for the war.

The statement of principles required much work and many revisions, particularly in view of Russian sensibilities. In its final form it included a pledge by each Government then at war with the Axis to sign no separate peace, to wage war against the Axis powers with all its resources, and to cooperate fully with all its allies. The matter was somewhat complicated by the fact that Russia was not at war with Japan. It was during these discussions of the roles of the Allies that President Roosevelt crossed out the words "Associated Powers" and substituted "United Nations." Twenty-six nations, counting British India, were signatories in this, the first declaration of the United Nations, on January 2, 1942.

* * * * *

On Christmas Day a spare, silver-haired naval officer wearing civilian clothes arrived at Pearl Harbor. A quiet, soft-spoken Texan, he had come to assume command of the Pacific Fleet from Vice Admiral W. S. Pye, who had been minding the store since the relief of Admiral Kimmel.

The new commander, Admiral Chester W. Nimitz, USN, had been graduated seventh in the class of 1905 from the U.S. Naval Academy. *The Lucky Bag*, the yearbook of the Academy, had described him as a man "of cheerful yesterdays and confident tomorrows." He assumed command on board a submarine because there was no larger ship in fit state for such a ceremony. Quickly he set about restoring confidence to the disheartened Pacific Fleet.

Rather than sweep out Kimmel's old staff, he brought only a flag secretary with him, retaining intact as a team the officers who had advised Kimmel. This was no time for recriminations. It was a time to get on with the job. No better man could have been chosen to lead the way.

* * * * *

In church that Christmas morning the President of the United States and the Prime Minister of Great Britain prayed together. Then they sang with the congregation the old familiar Christmas carols. One, previously unknown to Churchill, "O, Little Town of Bethlehem," made a deep impression on the Prime Minister. He felt these lines pointed the way ahead.

Yet in thy dark streets shineth
The everlasting light;
The hopes and fears of all the years
Are met in thee tonight.

CHAPTER THREE

January-February: Heroism Was Not Enough

Once more, dear friends, into the breach!
Shakespeare, Henry V

On Christmas Day, as Roosevelt and Churchill worshipped together at the Foundary Methodist Church in Washington, and as millions of Americans gathered around the tree to open their presents, a convoy steamed into San Francisco. On board the troopships were women, children, and wounded soldiers and sailors evacuated from Pearl Harbor. It had been a somber crossing—the women and children leaving husbands and fathers, not knowing when, if ever, they would see them again.

Ignoring the gray skies of the voyage, the women worked to ease the suffering of the wounded. On Christmas Eve they had gathered up everything they could find—cigarettes, candies, razor blades, toothpaste, sox, neckties, writing paper—and had spent hours wrapping them in fancy papers. When they took their gifts to the men, they were grieved to learn that one, the worst burned of all, had died twenty minutes earlier.

Yet the party went on. One young sailor, whose right leg had been amputated below the knee, grinned across at a despairing friend whose left leg was gone.

"Shall we dance?" he asked.

The other managed a smile. Then he began to examine his Christmas gifts.

However welcome the celebration of Christmas, there was work to be done, and it was up to the Allied leaders to do it. The members of the Arcadia Conference rolled up their sleeves and went to work planning for victory.

The great British fear was that the United Sates would turn all her attention to the Pacific theater to punish the Japanese. Churchill and his staff soon learned that these fears were groundless. One of the first papers presented was by Army Chief of Staff General George C. Marshall and the Chief of Naval Operations, Admiral Harold R. Stark.

1. At the A-B [American-British] Staff Conversations in February, 1941, it was agreed that Germany was the predominant member of the Axis Powers, and consequently the Atlantic and European area was considered to be to decisive theater.

2. Much has happened since February last, but notwithstanding the entry of Japan into the war, our view remains that Germany is still the prime enemy and her defeat is the key to victory. Once Germany is defeated, the collapse of Italy and the defeat of Japan must follow.

This view represented the professional judgment of the United States Chiefs of Staff, soon to be designated the Joint Chiefs of Staff. Initially these men were General Marshall for the Army, General Henry H. Arnold for the Army Air Corps, or as it came to be known in mid-1941, the Army Air Forces, Admiral Stark as Chief of Naval Operations, and Admiral

Ernest J. King in the newly created post of Commander in Chief, U.S. Fleet.*

Marshall proposed initially that the principle of unified command be exercised. Since no one man could possibly direct all Allied forces, at length the conferees agreed that the British and American chiefs of staff would manage the affairs of their own forces, subject to the direction of the President and Prime Minister as the respective commanders in chief.** Meanwhile, by frequent conferences, Roosevelt and Churchill would plan the broad direction of coalition warfare, advised by the Combined Chiefs of Staff, which consisted of the American Joint Chiefs and the British Chiefs of Staff, operating together.

This arrangement may sound cumbersome, but it was perfectly clear to the participants. And it worked. It was, in spite of considerable acrimony, an efficient arrangement, and it planned and won the victory of the Allied powers.

For the Combined Chiefs to function, some machinery had to be arranged for the day-to-day routine. Obviously the British chiefs could not remain permanently in Washington, nor could the Americans move to London. These officers had to run their own navies, armies, and air forces as well as function as a strategic planning board. Therefore, the official headquarters of the Combined Chiefs of Staff was established in Washington, Field Marshal Sir John Dill, just retired from the post of Chief of the Imperial General Staff, remaining in America as British representative.

Who would be in charge in areas where British and Americans were operating together? Some suggested that the forces work separately, with their respective commanders exercising liaison. Marshall would have nothing to do with this. Kimmel and Short had been ordered to maintain liaison with each other at Pearl Harbor, and look what had happened.

Instead, argued Marshall, let us use the principle of a supreme commander. We had done this with the appointment of

* Originally this title in Navy abbreviation was CINCUS. Spoken, this sounded like "sink us," and Admiral King directed that it be changed to COMINCH.
** Strictly speaking, the Prime Minister is not commander in chief, a role which belongs to the monarch. But in this case, King George had delegated the responsibility for strategic planning and conduct of the war to Churchill in his additional function of Minister of Defence.

Foch as Supreme Allied Commander in the First World War, but national rivalries had prevented its happening before 1918. By that time we had nearly lost the war.

After much discussion, the idea was accepted. Generalissimo Chiang Kai-shek was appointed to the top post in China, and British General Wavell, who had moved to India after his relief in North Africa, was named to the position of Supreme Commander of the ABDA area.*

Although these particular appointments were without much significance, the concept was of vast importance. Appointment of Chiang Kai-shek was but acknowledging an accomplished fact, and Wavell's command would collapse before he could exercise it. But future area commands of this nature would be vital.

In view of the basic decisions made, the conferees agreed that the Americans would run the war in the Pacific in regions outside Wavell's command. The British would take charge in Europe until such time as Americans entered the battle in significant numbers. Then new decisions would be made.

In the Pacific, they agreed, certain positions could not be given up. These were the Hawaiian Islands, the Aleutians, Australia, and the islands necessary for the defense of ships operating between them. These included the Fijis, Samoa, and New Caledonia; if they were lost, Australia-bound ships would have to go south of New Zealand, adding many days to the length of the voyage.

This decision meant that the Philippines, the Dutch East Indies, and the British Solomon and Gilbert Islands were all doomed. Singapore would be held, if possible, and so would Burma. Otherwise all that could be done was to delay, fight for time, fight to overcome deficiencies. Die where you are so those who come after you may live and conquer.

Plans were more optimistic for Europe. From the first, Churchill pleaded for a landing in North Africa. First named Gymnast, later grown to Super-Gymnast, the plan was to culminate in November as Operation Torch, when British and American troops went ashore at Casablanca, Oran, and Algiers. But at this moment, Churchill was thinking in terms of carrying it out in May at the latest.

* American, British, Dutch, Australian. This included all Southeast Asia, including island groups, from India to Australia.

If successful, Gymnast would take the pressure off the British Eighth Army in Egypt and would catch Rommel's Afrika Korps in a vast pincers. The plan was attractive, but not to the Americans. Much diffuculty lay ahead before it could be carried out.

A final decision of the Arcadia Conference was that an American Expeditionary Force would be sent to Northern Ireland, largely as a morale builder for both Britons and Americans, but incidentally to relieve a British division stationed there. Prime Minister Eamon De Valera of Eire indignantly protested this action. It was, he averred, a violation of Irish neutrality. Neither the British nor the Americans paid any attention to his protests.

The American people first learned of some of the Arcadia decisions through President Roosevelt's annual State of the Union Message delivered to the Congress on January 6, 1942. The speech, devoted entirely to defense matters, called up on all citizens to be prepared for heavy sacrifices and to perform such prodigies of production as the world had never seen. He demanded that 80,000 aircraft be produced in 1942 and 125,000 in 1943. Tank production was to be 45,000 in 1942 and 75,000 the following year. So the list ran, for planes, tanks, antiaircraft guns, antitank guns, rifles, field guns, merchant ships. The fact that these production figures were actually met is a tribute to the spirit of American workers, for the numbers came largely from Roosevelt's imagination. Taking the estimates arrived at after months of consultation and study, he arbitrarily revised them upward.

"Oh," he said, "the production people can do it if they really try."

War costs money [said the President to Congress]. So far we have hardly even begun to pay for it. We devoted only 15 per cent of our national income to national defense. As will appear in my budget message tomorrow, our war program for the coming fiscal year will cost $56,000,000,000,* or in other words more than half of the estimated annual national

* Strictly defense spending (including Lend-Lease) came to a little less than Mr. Roosevelt's figures. It still amounted to 89% of Federal spending.

income. That means taxes and bonds, and bonds and taxes. It means cutting luxuries and other nonessentials. In a word, it means an all-out war by individual effort and family effort in a united country.

Organization	Budget	Percentage of Federal Budget
Navy Department	$ 6,849,359,000	11.7
War Department	18,618,615,000	31.5
Defense Aid Lend-Lease)	7,500,000,000	12.7
Other	2,818,212,000	4.7
Supplemental items	17,000,000,000	28.8
Totals	$52,786,186,000	89.4

The people were already beginning to learn of the sacrifices they would be called on to make. Even before the year's end, motorists had learned that they would have to make do for the duration with the tires already on their cars. Except for vehicles "used exclusively in protection of public health and safety or for essential freight and bus transportation or industrial and commercial operations," all new tire sales were frozen as of the first of the year. With a normal monthly tire consumption of 4,000,000, national quotas for civilian use were set at 356,974 for January. Sixty-eight percent of this poor quota was set for buses and heavy trucks, leaving car, light truck, and motorcycle owners to scramble for the 114,191 tires that would be produced that month.

At first there seemed to be a way out. You could get new tires if you bought a new car. But on January 2, 1942, new car production was ordered frozen as of January 31. Except for about 200,000 cars to be built from parts already on hand, automobile production ceased at the beginning of the year. Even the 200,000 did no good to John Q. Citizen, for the retail sale of new cars was completely banned. Bicycle sales soared, but they were also in short supply. Most people had to learn to get on with what they had when the war started.

To prevent profiteering in these scarce necessities, price ceilings were imposed on tires, cars, and cigarettes. OPM ordered clothing manufacturers to cut the use of wool for civilian consumption by twenty percent.

This was but the beginning.

To many people, inability to buy tires and automobiles

seemed less a war sacrifice than a result of poor planning—by someone. New Dealers blamed anti-New Dealers, and vice versa; businessmen blamed the Army and Navy; labor blamed business; the public blamed the Administration; Republicans blamed "That Man in the White House." Everyone united in blaming the OPM and genial William S. Knudsen, its head.

The trouble was that while civilian production was cut back, nothing much seemed to be coming out for the services. Part of this was the services' own fault, for they had little idea of what and how much of this and that they wanted. The Army, in particular, had been dilatory in drawing up its "shopping list," and with recruits in ever increasing numbers pouring into training camps, the Army was hard put to feed and house, let alone equip, the men.

Public outrage was redoubled when stories came back of the defenders of Wake and Guam running out of ammunition, of four decrepit aircraft fighting hopelessly for Wake.

The problem was simply that there was no overall plan for the conversion of industry for war. When Leon Henderson, as head of OPA, froze production of automobiles, no one told the car manufacturers what use they were to make of their idled plants. The trouble was that in the maze of alphabetical bureaus no one had final authority. At the theoretical top, Knudsen, as head of OPM, was over Nelson, who, as head of SPAB, was in some respects over Knudsen.

SPAB had no authority to let contracts; that was a function of the Army and Navy Munitions Board and its purchasing agents. Nor could SPAB finance projects; that privilege was the property of Jesse Jones's Reconstruction Finance Corporation. SPAB could not touch production—a responsibility of OPM. Early in January, perhaps to complete the full circle, Roosevelt appointed Jesse Jones to SPAB.

It had become so complex that a high official had to look around to see which office he was in. Only in that way could he know whether he was boss or underling.

Businessmen, traveling to Washington in search of defense contracts, spent hours and hours, days and days, in waiting rooms, seeking appointments with officials who often were not sure whether or not they could award contracts. Often, rather than make a decision, it was easier to send the businessman on his way to another office, preferably in another agency. These men who spent so much time sitting on hard benches in waiting rooms came to be known as "Waffle Bottoms."

As always, humorists were available to ease the tension. *The Air Force News Letter* published a glossary of Washingtonese. Here are some excerpts.

Under consideration: Never heard of it.

Under active consideration: Will have a shot at finding it in the files.

Have you any remarks?: Give me some idea of what it's all about.

The project is in the air: Am completely ignorant of the subject.

You will remember: You have forgotten, or never knew, because I don't.

Transmitted to you: You hold the bag a while—I'm tired of it.

Concur generally: Haven't read the document and don't want to be bound by anything I say.

Kindly expedite reply: For God's sake, try and find the papers.

Passed to higher authority: Pigeonholed in a more sumptuous office.

Appropriate action: Do you know what to do with it? We don't.

Giving him the picture: A long, confusing, and inaccurate statement to a newcomer.

On January 13, Roosevelt took a major step toward settling the problem. He appointed Donald M. Nelson head of a new agency, the War Production Board (WPB), with broad powers to make "final decisions."

At 5:30 on that day Roosevelt welcomed Nelson in his office at the White House. Instead of opening the discussion with a wisecrack or a joke as was his wont, Roosevelt immediately got down to brass tacks. Production was in a mess, and what could be done about it? For an hour he continued in this vein, showing intimate knowledge of the problems and of the virtues and deficiencies of Knudsen, who could have been production "czar" if he had been as well acquainted wtih the ways of Washington as he was with those of big business.

Knudsen, as president of General Motors, had shown enormous capacity for getting things done. But this had been in an industrial setting. In Washington, with divided authority, and the unwillingness of too many people to take responsibility, he had been lost. When he could deal with industry, things happened. He had got all the leaders of the automotive industry together in Washington as early as October 1940 and had persuaded all except the Ford Motor Company to begin the production of aircraft parts and engines. The Ford Company, rather than deal in parts, had been inspired to go ahead and build an airplane factory. The result, the huge Willow Run plant near Ypsilanti, Michigan, was a wonder of the world. Completed in eleven months, a mile long and a quarter of a mile wide, the plant turned out thousands of B-24 four-engine heavy bombers during the war.

Yet Roosevelt knew that not enough had been done. He described the problems of conversion that lay ahead. Mass production is the least flexible of all methods of manufacturing. Dies, jigs, machine tools are geared to produce one item over and over again. The interchangeable parts of a machine mean ease of repair and speed of manufacture, but they also mean rigidity of design. A Ford factory, without expensive conversion, cannot turn out an airplane or a tank; it cannot even turn out a Chevrolet.

Nelson was, of course, perfectly aware of all these problems. He knew something had to be done. Some person or some agency had to have the requisite authority to make these decisions. He was delighted when the President told him that he had it in mind to create a super-board, with a man at its head who could make all the discordant elements work in harmony.

"I am glad you approve the name," said Roosevelt after Nelson suggested that the new agency be called the War Production Board, "because you are the chairman of the War Production Board."

Mr. Roosevelt then told Vice President Henry A. Wallace, who was attending the meeting in his role as head of SPAB, that he wanted him to resign that position, since SPAB would be absorbed by the new agency, and the chairman must have the authority as well as the responsibility. Wallace agreed immediately, although he remained as head of the Economic Defense Board, to be renamed Board of Economic Welfare.

Protesting that the job was too big for him or for any man, Nelson promised to do his best. On his arrival back at his office, Nelson was shocked to learn that the news of his appointment had already been released to the press and radio.

Knudsen had not been informed of his sudden dismissal by any official word; his first inkling of it was in a public announcement.

Hastening to see his former boss, Nelson found him sitting at his desk, the hurt and dismay stark upon his face. Apologizing for what had been done to him, Nelson begged Knudsen to stay on and give his valuable services to the Government. Knudsen thanked him, but made no promises.

In his concern, Nelson telephoned Jesse Jones and asked him to try to dissuade Knudsen from going home. Harry Hopkins, sensing how Knudsen would react, also telephoned Jones, suggesting that the former OPM head be commissioned in the Army to help Under Secretary of War Patterson with supply problems. Hopkins had already cleared the proposal with both Patterson and General Marshall, and the idea appealed to Jones. After much discussion he managed to persuade Knudsen to accept a commission as lieutenant general in the Army Services of Supply.

When Nelson rose the next morning to find the news of his appointment as head of WPB the top story of the day, he must have felt the presence of an unseen figure taking him to the mountaintop and offering him all the kingdoms of the world. For he clearly realized that the decisions he was to make in this new job would determine not only the winning of the war, but also what kind of country would come out of it.

Roosevelt had said he would back him to the hilt. Nelson had to choose: would he permit free enterprise to survive, or by taking all production under the control of WPB, would he create a socialist state?

It would be far more efficient, advisers told him, to set up the new board as a vast fountainhead of production—make the decisions on how much was needed by the Army, the Navy, the rest of the government, the public, by Joe Doakes, Susie Soakes, and all the folks. Then the board would tell Corporation A to make this, Corporation B to make that, and Corporation X the other thing. Then the board would see to it that each corporation got the materials it needed at such and such a price; the board would determine a fair profit, renegotiate contracts or use taxes to confiscate the rest, and soon the war would be won.

The difficulties with this plan were, as Nelson saw them, twofold. WPB did not have the requisite knowledge of what was needed, by what date, in what quantities. That information would have to come from the consumers—the needs of war and the needs of the civilian establishment. But far more important, the path of "efficiency" was *de facto* socialism. On the whole, it seemed to Nelson, letting the Army and Navy get economic control of the country was a sure way to totalitarianism. The scheme reminded him of the economic policy of Mussolini's Fascism.

The decisions that Nelson would have to be making in the days ahead were those that would determine the future of the country—in war and peace. Yet, they must get on with winning the war. The military forces must have what they need, but so must the people at home. A balance must be struck.

For the Army and Navy to deal simply and directly with the manufacturers would be far more convenient than going through Nelson's office. But what would be left over for the home front? For example, the Army had tried to compel Douglas and Lockheed aircraft companies to cancel contracts with civilian airlines for thirty or forty commercial planes on the excuse that their completion would interfere with Army contracts. The fact that there were not enough Army contracts to keep the plants busy and the fact that these plants were urgently needed for defense transportation made no difference. Nor did the fact that the aircraft could, in an emergency, be easily converted to troop transports. The Army preferred to have the entire capacity of those factories at their disposal. The public be damned, and devil take the hindermost. This was war!

Nelson's office was concerned with such problems. They were not simple. Suppose ABC Corporation wished to expand its facilities for making copper wire. How much copper wire was needed? Where was the raw copper coming from? How much steel from the national stockpile was needed to make the new facilities? Who, then, would not get the additional steel he needed to expand his plant to make more shoes? Round and round they go. Who has the magic answers?

Nelson, to the dismay of many of his supporters, decided to be a constitutional monarch rather than a czar. He would continue the system of letting the Army and Navy award contracts while the WPB exercised control through allocation, policy-setting, and coordination. To do otherwise, he argued, would have meant setting up a whole new section to deal with specifics; while these men were learning their jobs, production time would be lost and factories would be standing idle. The time to get on with the job was now.

A second major decision of some dismay to many in government was to retain the services of "dollar-a-year" men. These important industrial leaders, who remained on the payrolls of their own companies while working for the Government, brought to Washington an intimate knowledge of big business. No one else could know so quickly which companies could produce which commodity and thus who should be invited to submit bids. With misgivings, Nelson decided to retain this system, even though it would have removed all doubt if the dollar-a-year men had been forced to sever connections with their companies and go on the Government payroll. But this would have involved huge financial sacrifice for many of them, and, with the proviso that no dollar-a-year man was to have any part in contracts with his own company, Nelson let things ride.

> On this [Nelson said] we must get the maximun results from American industry. To do that we must have down here men who understand and can deal with industry's intricate structure and operation. In other words, we must have men with expert business and technical knowledge. For the most part we have to get them from industry itself. But no matter where we get them or how we get them, we simply must have them in the places where they are needed, when they are needed.

These were the basic decisions, and Nelson stuck to them. Senator Harry S. Truman, chairman of a committee to investigate the problem of war production, wrote: "The committee . . . will support you even on matters where it disagrees with you, and believes that all other agencies of the government should afford you a similar unquestioning support until you have had a full opportunity to achieve the success which we all hope that you will achieve."

Perhaps Nelson was lucky; perhaps there was no other way that the war production program could have been administered. But the important thing was that it worked. There were many rough places ahead. Nelson, himself, came within an ace of being fired a year later, but someone, probably Hopkins, persuaded Roosevelt to leave him where he was. Nelson remained; American war production became a wonder of the world; and the free enterprise system survived.

* * * * *

In mid-January, the control tower officer at La Guardia Airport was not sure whether it was a joke or not. In his earphones he heard: "Pacific Clipper, inbound from Auckland, New Zealand, Captain Ford reporting, due to arrive Pan American Marine Terminal in seven minutes."

No Clipper—Pan Am's huge flying boat—was scheduled in, and if one had been, it should have been the *Atlantic* Clipper. Nevertheless the controller cleared the plane to land and learned an amazing story. The Pacific Clipper had been between Noumea, New Caledonia, and Auckland on December 8, when the word of attack on Pearl Harbor crackled into Captain Ford's earphones. Arriving in Auckland, he found that no one knew what to do with him. On his own initiative, he took off from Auckland to proceed home via Australia, the Indian Ocean, Cape Town, and up the coast of South America. Scrounging fuel, avoiding aircraft of each side, Captain Ford brought the plane triumphantly home.

* * * * *

Life had to continue on the home front. As Congress pondered new taxes, men began to double up in cars—the phrase "car pool" entered the language then—and those thrown out of work by closing of automobile production began to seek new jobs. There were plenty to be had in defense industries, in shipyards, at good wages. With more money to spend than ever before, people found less and less to spend it on.

The movie industry was permitted to keep its output going as a morale builder. They responded by grinding out patriotic quickies, some of which are still shown on televison's late-late shows: *A Yank on the Burma Road, A Yank in the R.A.F., Nazi Agent, Joan of Paris, Across the Pacific.* More distinguished were *Yankee Doodle Dandy,* starring James Cagney as the beloved George M. Cohan, and the tender and moving *Mrs. Miniver,* with Greer Garson and Walter Pidgeon. A new hit song "As Time Goes By," came from *Casablanca,* starring

Humphrey Bogart and Ingrid Bergman.

On January 9, Joe Louis met Buddy Baer in a heavyweight boxing title match at Madison Square Garden. The match lasted only two minutes and fifty-six seconds, with Buddy stretched out on the canvas. Right after the bout, Louis enlisted in the Army.

"What are you going to do in the Army, Joe?" inquired a callow reporter.

"What they tell me to," answered Joe, in the perfect reply.

The public was saddened toward the middle of the summer when charming movie actress Carol Lombard, returning to Hollywood from a highly successful war bond selling tour was killed in the crash of a TWA airliner. Her husband, Clark Gable, flying to the scene, went into seclusion after viewing the wreckage. The life of violinist Joseph Szigeti was spared when he gave up his seat on the same flight to a serviceman.

To give more time for work, for leisure, to save electricity, Congress approved a bill for national Daylight Saving Time. It became effective February 9, to the usual grumbling from rural areas about tampering with "God's time." The new law meant that during the summer months, many communities would be on double Daylight Saving Time. It was enough to make the chickens wonder what the world was coming to.

On the same day that Daylight Saving Time became effective, the Navy suffered a grievous loss. The French luxury liner *Normandie* had been tied up at Pier 88, North River, in New York since the beginning of the war in Europe. Stripped of her magnificent furniture and fittings, she remained there near her rival for the Atlantic Blue Ribbon, *Queen Mary*, which was at the next pier. Then one day, after a secret, unheralded voyage across the Atlantic, the *Queen Elizabeth* had come in and taken the slip next to her sister, *Queen Mary*. There the three huge liners remained quietly. Then, just as quietly, the two *Queens* disappeared. They were set to work as troop transports, each capable of moving a whole division of fifteen thousand men in a single crossing.

Abandoned, the *Normandie* lay at her pier until after Pearl Harbor. Then she was requisitioned by the United States and turned over to the Navy as a transport. Contracts were let and the work of conversion began.

Far down in her hull a welder began to work against a bulkhead. No one checked the next compartment. It was filled with life jackets. The heat from the welding rod burned throught the metal bulkhead and reached the life jackets. A wisp of smoke arose. The workman finished his task and left. The heat grew in the life jackets.

By the time it was discovered, the fire was a raging mass of flames. It was difficult to get to, for smoke clogged the passageways. Fire engines and fire boats pumped water into the *Normandie* for over five hours. At length the flames were under control.

But the vessel had begun to list. The tons of water thrown on her were all above the center of gravity. Slowly, slowly, the great ship listed to port, then faster and faster. With a lurch, she rolled over on her port side and lay with her funnels half submerged. The Navy estimated that it would cost $5,000,000 to right her and recondition her. The work was not done. She never sailed again. After the war she was scrapped.

The Navy had much more to worry about than the fate of the *Normandie*. Things were going badly in the Pacific, and all at once German U-boats struck with a blitz off the American Atlantic coast.

This phase of the war is curiously little known today. Yet the German attack in American waters for the first six months of 1942 was more costly to the war effort than Pearl Harbor and all the naval losses in the Southwest Pacific during the same period of time. And it was done with a minimal effort on the part of the Germans. There were never more than a dozen U-boats at any one time engaged in the fantastic slaughter within sight of American ocean resorts.

Churchill once suggested that German submarines should be called U-boats at all times, as opposed to Allied "submarines," to show that "U-boats are those dastardly villains who sink our ships, while 'submarines' are those gallant and noble craft which sink theirs."

There seemed to be little of gallantry and a great deal of dastardly villainy as far as Americans were concerned in the operations of U-boats in the Second World War. Yet theirs was a hard, grueling service that was pursued with a deadly efficiency for most of the war. On the opening day of hostilities in the west, September 3, 1939, Kapitänleutnant Lemp in *U-30* torpedoed and sank the passenger liner *Athenia* outbound for New York in the North Atlantic. From then on, the Battle of the Atlantic was unremitting, although, as Nicholas Montserrat points out in his powerful novel *The Cruel Sea*, it was a war of amateurs at first. But soon a deadly professionalism ensued and as more U-boats became available, the curve of sinkings rose and rose.

When France fell, the German U-boat arm, under the command of Admiral Karl Dönitz, had bases in western Brittany, whence they could reach farther and farther out into the Atlantic. The British reeled under the attack, and hundreds of ships and thousands of men found their graves under the gray waters of the North Atlantic.

When the German battleship *Bismarck* was finally hunted down and sunk by the Royal Navy in May 1941, President Roosevelt, angered that she had come so close to American waters during her foray, proclaimed a state of unlimited national emergency, proceeded to draw a line down the middle of the Atlantic, and declared that if German ships entered those waters, they did so at "their own risk."

As has been told, the American policy of aiding Britain in the Battle of the Atlantic in the summer and fall of 1941 was bound to lead to incidents between German U-boats and American ships. Yet nothing that happened prepared the American people for the fury that would be unleashed off the East Coast in January. When Germany declared war on the United States in December, Hitler summoned Dönitz and demanded an immediate attack in American waters. It could not be done at once; on Hitler's own orders, substantial forces had been sent to the Mediterranean and to the Norwegian coast, where Hitler feared a British landing. It was a month before Dönitz was able to mount his attack, and then it was with a mere five U-boats.

Operation Paukenschlag (kettledrum roll) was scheduled to begin off New York on January 13, 1942. Two days earlier, Kapitänleutnant Reinhard Hardigen in *U-123* came upon the British freighter *Cyclops*. She was a large ship, and the temptation proved too great. Hardigen maneuvered his boat into attack position and fired. The *Cyclops*, hit in the engine room, went down with a loss of eighty-seven lives. A few days later, Hardigen bagged the Norwegian freighter *Norness*, the British tanker *Coimbra*, and the American tanker *Allen Jackson*. Then the *Norvana*, the *City of Atlanta*, and the *Malay*.

His score was typical of the Paukenschlag boats. In ten days the five U-boats sank twenty-five ships of approximately 200,000 gross register tons, and not a single U-boat was even sighted, much less attacked by any of the defending forces.

The defending forces! They were virtually nonexistent. In spite of the British experiences; in spite of ample warning of what might happen, both from the British and from the historical example of World War I, when U-boats did cross the ocean to American waters; in spite of intelligence intercepts warning of the movements of the Paukenschlag boats, the United States Navy was caught completely unprepared. U-boat skippers could hardly believe it. Ships were fully lighted. They chattered on their radios. Lighthouses and buoys gave out their navigational information after dark just as usual. It was, as the Germans called it themselves, U-boat paradise.

To protect ships in the area of his responsibility from the St. Lawrence River down to Cape Hatteras, some 280,000 square miles of ocean, Vice Admiral Adolphus Andrews had a total of twelve surface vessels—four small yard patrol craft, four subchasers, one Coast Guard cutter, and three *Eagle* boats dating back to World War I. None of these was equipped with radar. There was, he wrote, "not a vessel available that an enemy submarine could not outdistance while operating on the surface . . . in most cases the guns of these vessels would be outranged by those of the submarines."

Andrews had 103 aircraft, but only five were ready for combat. In reply to his urgent plea for reinforcements, the Navy Department informed him, "any additional allocations depend on future production." In other words, the Navy was stretched thin. But not that thin. The eyes of most naval officers were on the Pacific where, as will be told, a desperate battle of holding on was being waged. All ships that could be spared and many that could not were being sent to the west.

But the attack in the Atlantic was really an attack on American shores. It was an attack on every American in the East who depended on his car for transportation, because gasoline rationing in New England and the Central Atlantic States first came about as a result of the U-boat blitz. Yet the authorities in Washington remained singularly complacent for an unbelievable period of time.

Perhaps they were deceived by their own propaganda, for they lied to the public. There is no other word for it. The first U-boat to be sunk in American waters was *U-85* on April 14,

1942. By the end of a full six months of this blitz, only six U-boats had been sunk.

Contrast this with the figures officially released by the Navy Department:

U-Boat Losses in American Waters—1942

Months	Claims by the Navy	Actual sinkings
January–February	3–4	0
March	24	0
April–July	(no figures released)	6

With this meager expenditure, Dönitz had enjoyed unbroken success with his U-boat arm in American waters, as the following table indicates.

Sinkings of Merchant Ships in American Waters—1942

Month	Number of ships *	Gross tons	Percentage of total U-boat sinkings in all waters
January	35	202,144	76.0
February	45	250,188	62.5
March	66	384,789	75.0
April	52	313,554	80.0
May	105	516,015	87.5
June	96	516,279	83.5
Totals	399	2,182,969	84.6 (average)

Lest these figures seem cold-blooded and abstract, let us see what they really mean. It would require two freight trains of a hundred and fifty cars each to carry the cargo that can be loaded in the average 5000-ton freighter. Or, to put it another way, a naval training manual published during the war stated:

If a submarine sinks two 6000-ton ships and one 3000-

* These figures include only the American areas of responsibility in the Western Atlantic and not the American part of the trans-atlantic convoys to Britain and Russia. Total losses for the first six months of the war in all areas of American responsibility were 472 ships aggregating 2,482,508 tons.

ton tanker, here is a typical account of what we have totally lost: 42 tanks, eight 6-inch howitzers, eighty-eight 25-pound guns, forty 2-pound guns, 24 armored cars, 50 Bren carriers, 5210 tons of ammunition, 600 rifles, 428 tons of tank supplies, 2000 tons of stores and 1000 tanks of gasoline. In order to knock out the same amount of equipment by air bombing the enemy would have to make three thousand successful bombing sorties.

These dramatic figures tell the score for only the ships, and fairly small ones at that. Most tankers ran in the 5,000- to 10,000-ton range. Tankers were the particular victims of U-boats during the East Coast blitz, and to the average citizen the most telling. The loss of a single average tanker meant the loss of enough gasoline to keep 35,000 A-card holders (three gallons a week) supplied for a year.

The slaughter continued. It was a result of many things, most of them resulting from the "it can't happen here" attitude. Despite Pearl Harbor, despite the Japanese rampage in the Pacific, the public, the Navy, and the shippers all had a complacent blindness toward Germany. What the Nazis might do might be terrible, but it was on the other side of the Atlantic. When ships were sunk, people thought of them as ships bound for Britain and not as those engaged in the coastal trade of the United States.

The heavy shipping trade from Panama, the Gulf of Mexico, and the Caribbean converges near Miami and runs near the shore parallel to the coast toward the cities farther north. Northbound ships generally stand well out to sea to benefit from the Gulf Stream, while southbound ones hug the coast to avoid it.

The most precious cargoes bound from the south to the North Atlantic States were oil, sugar, and coffee. Soon all three would be rationed as a result of the U-boats' depredations. Coffee and sugar had to come by sea. Oil from the Gulf States might have come by pipeline, or by train, but no such pipelines existed at that time, and the entire oil-carrying capacity of the nation's railroads was not enough to supply the needs of the industrial Northeast. Thus the ships had to keep coming.

They kept coming and ran into trouble. The hastily improvised measures of the U.S. Navy had little effect. Neither in equipment nor doctrine was the Navy ready for the job so suddenly thrust upon it.

Budget limitations of peacetime years had caused the Navy to put every dollar available into the building of its battle fleet. It was easier to convince Congress of the need for a battleship than for small patrol vessels. Besides, battleships took three to four years to build; small antisubmarine ships could be improvised in a hurry, the Navy Department said. President Roosevelt, once Assistant Secretary of the Navy, had remarked that it was difficult to interest the Bureau of Ships in anything smaller than a ship of a thousand tons. Destroyers, in many ways ideal antisubmarine vessels, were for the most part tied up with the combatant vessels of the Atlantic, Pacific, and Asiatic Feets. Few there were to spare for antisubmarine work.

Patriotic owners turned their luxury yachts over to the Navy. Otherwise condemned to idleness because of wartime shortages, these yachts performed yeoman service during the emergency. One of them, the *Orion*, renamed *Vixen* by the Navy, was to serve as flagship of the Tenth Fleet in 1943.

It is told of one of these luxury floating palaces that as the skipper retired in what had been the owner's cabin one night, he noticed above the bunk a button he had not seen before. In idle curiosity he pressed it. There was a gently whir of machinery; the bulkhead next to him slid to one side, and he found himself staring at the astonished face of his executive officer in the next cabin, formerly the main guest stateroom.

These patrol vessels did little direct good in the battle against the U-boats. Most of them had no sonar and no radar, and few if any guns were mounted on them—sometimes a single 3-incher. Built for leisurely cruising and comfort, most of them had far too little speed to keep up with a surfaced U-boat; they could only hope to keep it in sight and send out a warning.

But the real trouble was not so much shortages of ships and equipment as it was weakness of doctrine. The Royal Navy had offered several corvettes and trawlers equipped with asdic, the British equivalent of sonar. In addition, they offered to send over some of their experienced antisubmarine officers and men to act as advisers. The U.S. Navy accepted the ships, but not the advisers. Perhaps it was professional jealousy; perhaps it was complacency. Whatever the cause, the offer was rejected and the United States continued to lose priceless ships in ever increasing numbers.

Had the advice of the British been heeded, coastal convoys would have been quickly established. In World War I, the influence of American Admiral Sims on Prime Minister Lloyd George of Britain had forced the reluctant Admiralty to institute convoy operations. At once the sinking rate of merchant ships dropped dramatically. At the same time, kills of U-boats rose in proportion. The convoy system had beaten the U-boats in the First World War and in British operations was holding losses in the Second so that they averaged well below the grim four months of February to June in 1917.

Nonetheless the U.S. Navy clung to the theory that aggressive patrolling was better than convoy—especially weakly escorted convoys. Admiral Adolphus Andrews, Commander Eastern Sea Frontier, sent his meager forces out on fruitless patrol. These were later joined by volunteer yachtsmen taking their thirty- to seventy-foot pleasure cruisers out on the high seas to look for U-boats. These members of the "Hooligan Navy," as they called themselves, did all in their power, but it was not enough. Volunteer airmen of the Civil Air Patrol, among them pianist-conductor José Iturbi, spent thousands of hours cruising over coastal waters seeking the German marauders. These efforts were in addition to the antisubmarine patrols flown by the Navy and the Army Air Force.

Meanwhile the sinkings went on. The U-boats grew bolder, and swimmers and sunbathers at the beaches of Florida often thrilled to the sight of a burning tanker near shore, oblivious of the unseen men struggling in the water, swimming for their lives through the viscous oil to avoid the onrushing flames on the water.

At night the U-boats had especially easy pickings, for the ships, blacked out at last were sharply silhouetted against the blaze of lights from cities and resort areas. Miami, especially, was urged to employ a dim-out to reduce the deadly glow, but its Chamber of Commerce refused, saying it would ruin the tourist season. They were not being unpatriotic or callous of men's lives. They simply could not understand the problem. Finally on April 18, three months after it should have happened, a dim-out of waterfront lights was ordered, extended several miles inland a month later.

By April 1, Admiral King's dictum that convoy was the only measure that offered any measure of success was partially implemented. Under Eastern Sea Frontier orders, ships would run escorted by day and hole up in sheltered bays by night. From Portland to Boston, Boston to New York, New York to Delaware Bay, Delaware Bay to Chesapeake Bay, Chesapeake Bay to Wilmington, Wilmington to Charleston, Charleston to Savannah, Savannah to Jacksonville, Jacksonville to Cape Canaveral, Cape Canaveral to Miami, and Miami to Key West: these were the leaps of the "bucket brigades." Eventually they grew into an Interlocking Convoy System extending from Halifax through the Caribbean.*

When convoys were established on the East Coast, Dönitz shifted his U-boats to the Gulf of Mexico. It was the same story all over again. Ships were sunk at the mouth of the Mississippi and in the approaches to other ports. Finally the convoy system was tried in the Gulf, and once again Dönitz shifted, this time to the Caribbean, where he found easy victims, until convoy was extended to that area in July. Then Dönitz moved his U-boats out to mid-Atlantic.

It had been a bitterly costly six months. The losses in matériel could be replaced, even though, at the time, they threatened impending operations against the Axis. The losses in lives were another matter. Had the Navy been properly prepared, they need not have happened. The dead men were victims of the peacetime habit of thought, of big-ship-mindedness of the naval authorities, and the business-as-usual philosophy that still held the public.

* * * * *

General Sir Archibald Wavell in his headquarters in India thoughtfully read a telegram. It was from the Prime Minister, and its contents were not much to his liking. But there could be no question of his compliance.

The President and his military and naval advisors [read the telegram] have impressed upon me the urgent need for unified command in Southwest Pacific, and it is unanimously desired, pressed particularly by President and General Marshall, that you should become Supreme Com-

* Halifax was the principal terminus for fast transatlantic convoys to Great Britain.

84

mander of Allied forces by land, air, and sea assigned to that theatre. . . . You are the only man who has the experience of handling so many different theatres at once, and you know we will back you up and see you have fair play. Everyone knows how dark and difficult the situation is. President will announce that your appointment has been made by his desire.

As Wavell read these words, it seemed dubious whether he would have a command to go to. The Japanese advance continued, and there was little to hold them back.

He could only try.

On January 7, 1942, Wavell arrived in Singapore and lost no time in setting out on an inspection trip of the front. Exhausted British and Malay troops, hard pressed by the Japanese, were disorganized, their morale in tatters. Wavell quickly ordered them to disengage and fall back to a line just over fifty air miles north of Singapore itself. This retreat would, he hoped, give time for regrouping and rest.

On his return to Singapore he was appalled by his examination of the island's defenses on the northern side. They scarcely existed. The city of Singapore is on the southern side of an island at the tip of the Malay Peninsula. Famed in history and legend for spies, smugglers, and sin, it, like Hong Kong, had been a British oasis in the Orient. In the cool of the lounge of the Raffles Hotel, rubber planters, civil servants, officials, and officers from the Army and Navy shared their experiences and tales of home over their pink gins or whiskeys and soda. Huge naval guns commanding the Strait of Malacca insured the invulnerability of the colony to attack from the sea.

But the attack was not coming from the sea. In normal times, nothing was to be feared from the north. The Malay and Tamil coolies were too contented with their lot. And even if they were not and tried any foolishness, the causeway to the mainland could be barricaded easily, and a few troops then could easily keep any disorganized mob in hand.

Now it was no disorganized mob. Now it was a force of crack Japanese troops, well equipped, well led, and driven by fanaticism. Nothing could stop them except modern weapons, air power, heavy artillery, and enough fresh troops. All of these were wanting.

Lieutenant General A. E. Percival, troop commander in

Malaya, was nearly at the end of his rope. Japanese planes were having their own way in the air. British experts had refused to send any tanks out to Malaya. They could not, they opined, be successfully used in the jungle. Lacking this expert advice, the Japanese had committed large numbers of tanks, and they went through the British defenders with amazingly few difficulties from the jungle terrain. Percival had none to throw against them.

As Wavell moved on to Java, his command headquarters, Percival took over coordination of defenses in Malaya, and Australian Major General Gordon Bennett assumed command at the front. More aggressive-minded than Percival, Bennett believed that the way to stop General Tomoyuki Yamashita, the "Tiger of Malaya," was by strong counterattacks. He was encouraged by the arrival at Singapore on January 13 of an American convoy having on board the 53rd British Infantry Brigade, the British 35th Light Anti-Aircraft Regiment, the 85th British Anti-Tank Regiment, and fifty-one Hurricane fighters.

At first Bennett's ideas paid off. In an ambush a hundred and twenty miles north of Singapore, the retreating troops caught and wiped out a sizeable Japanese unit. But soon the continued Japanese pressure made Bennett's plan impracticable. His counterattacks seemed to have no more effect on the Japanese than a series of light taps. On January 23, Percival decided to evacuate all of the Malay Peninsula and make a final stand on the island of Singapore itself. By the first day of February the retreat was complete, and the rear guard of the Argyll Battalion—ninety men in all—marched across the causeway to the skirl of bagpipes. The next morning the seventy-foot-wide link to the mainland was blown up. As the waters rushed in, they formed a moat serving to cut the island off from all threats.

Unfortunately for the defenders, at low tide the moat was only four feet deep in some places.

The island of Singapore is about twenty-six miles long east to west and about fourteen miles north to south, the city taking up a small area in the central southern coast. Most of the island is devoted to rubber plantations and jungle, except for reservoirs in the center and the Naval Base on the northern side on the Strait of Jonore. The strait is some eleven hundred yards wide at the causeway, but to the west it narrows to six hundred yards.

For several days there was a comparative lull in operations. Shelling and bombing were sporadic, not enough to inflict many casualties or further depress the morale of the two million people on the island.

Meanwhile General Percival had to make the fundamental decision of how to station his eighty-five thousand men for defense. Unfortunately, over fifteen thousand of these troops were noncombatant, and many of the others were poorly trained, fresh recruits who had never seen action. Since three of the four airstrips on the island were in range of Japanese shells, most of the Hurricane fighters he had so recently received were evacuated to Sumatra. Percival's problem was whether to try to repel any Japanese attempt to cross the strait at the beaches or to keep only a scouting force on the water's edge and retain strong mobile reserves to be rushed to the scene of trouble. In the end, he decided to man the beaches, largely because he felt that the reserve would not be able to respond quickly enough to do any good.

The difficulty with defending at the water's edge was that he had to spread his forces too thin. General Bennett was sent to guard the most likely point of Japanese crossing, a twenty-mile sector, with only twenty-five hundred troops.

On February 8, shelling picked up to such an extent that it was clear an assault was imminent. That night, under heavy fire from mortars and hand weapons, fifteen thousand Japanese headed for Bennett's twenty-five hundred. The first wave landed at 2230 and were given a warm reception by the Australians. All during the night the unequal battle continued. Early the next morning the Japanese landed tanks, and the position of the defenders became untenable.

With no reserve force to stop the Japanese, there remained only a perimeter defense outside the city. Soon the Japanese had seized the reservoirs; the water supply to the city was cut off. It could be only a matter of time. Refugees swarmed to the waterfront, taking their most precious possessions with them, seeking passage on any unlikely vessel that might carry them the few miles to Sumatra, or, they hoped, the greater distance to Ceylon, Java, or Australia.

Both Churchill and Wavell demanded a last-ditch fight, but

there was no chance of it. On February 15, the end came. His troops disorganized, the entire city within range of Japanese guns, with little ammunition, less food, and no water, General Percival surrendered at 1600.

Britain's symbolic Far Eastern bastion was gone.

* * * * *

In his headquarters at Bandung in central Java, General Wavell ruefully contemplated the wreck of his mission to defend the Malay Barrier. The Malay Peninsula and Singapore had fallen. Sumatra would soon follow to paratroop and amphibious attack; there was nothing he could do to save that rich island. Borneo, Celbes, the Philippines, except for a piece on Bataan, were lost. Wavell had reason to believe that even then a Japanese convoy was headed for Java, the last major Allied position, except for New Guinea, in the Southwest Pacific.

If there was any hope of saving Java, it rested on the nondescript ABDA naval forces under the command of U.S. Admiral Thomas C. Hart, a tired, sixty-four-year-old man who, Wavell believed, had insufficient aggressiveness for the job at hand. Hart, however, had repeatedly urged more offensive operations, only to be stymied by the caution of Dutch Rear Admiral K.W.F.M. Doorman. The real problem seemed to lie in Dutch reluctance to have an American commander on their soil and in command when most of the few naval forces were Dutch. Even the Dutch Ambassador in Washington urged Roosevelt to place a Dutch admiral in command.

Believing that Java was as good as lost, Roosevelt and the Joint Chiefs of Staff decided that if the Dutch wanted to be in command for the final debacle, they should have their way. On February 12, Hart was ordered to turn over operational command of Allied naval forces to Admiral C. E. L. Helfrich of the Royal Netherlands Navy. Hart nominally retained the ABDA naval post, but on February 16 he left the area on the grounds of ill health. This excuse surprised those on the scene, for in a recent inspection the Admiral had climbed all over ships "like a midshipman."

Admiral Hart was not alone in his departure. Nine days later, on February 25, Wavell dissolved the ABDA command and flew to Ceylon, following by a day U.S. General L. H.

Brereton, who had taken the Air Force command with him. This left the Dutch in sole control of the defense of Java.

Two large Japanese convoys were even at that moment headed for Java, one to land on the eastern end and the other on the western. To oppose them was a small multi-national group of ships, Dutch, American, and British. The Western Attack Group of Rear Admiral Takeo Kurita consisted of four heavy cruisers, three light cruisers, a small aircraft carrier, a seaplane tender, some twenty-five destroyers, and fifty-six transports and supply ships. Headed for the other end of the island was Rear Admiral Shoji Nishimura's Eastern Attack Group of forty-one transports, two heavy and two light cruisers, eighteen destroyers, and other smaller craft.

To meet this formidable armada, Admiral Helfrich had divided his slender resources into two groups. The Western Force of three British cruisers and two destroyers fruitlessly searched for the enemy and then fell back on Tjilatjap, thence to Ceylon. This left only Admiral Doorman's Combined Striking Force to oppose the Japanese. The name of this collection of Allied ships sounds more impressive than the fact, for Admiral Doorman had only sixteen ships—five cruisers and eleven destroyers. And not all of them would be available to him in the forthcoming Battle of the Java Sea.

After searching for the Japanese ships without making contact, Admiral Doorman led his vessels to Surabaya on the northern coast of Java to refuel. He did not even have a chance to enter the harbor, for just as he was passing the sea buoy on the afternoon of February 27, he received a message from Admiral Helfrich to attack the enemy near Bawean Island.

His ships had never operated together before; they had no common signal book. But by a combination of voice radio and signal flags he got the order out: FOLLOW ME THE ENEMY IS NINETY MILES AWAY.

Turning his force around quickly, Admiral Doorman headed for the reported contact. Three British destroyers, *Jupiter*, *Electra*, and *Encounter*, screened ahead. Then followed in column Doorman's five "heavy" ships, *De Ruyter*, a Dutch light cruiser and flagship leading, followed by H.M.S. *Exeter* and U.S.S. *Houston*, both heavy cruisers, and two more light cruisers, Australian *Perth* and Dutch *Java*, bringing up the rear. To port of the cruiser column were the Dutch destroyers. In the rear of the formation steamed the four old four-pipers of Destroyer Division 58, U.S.S. *John D. Edwards, Alden, John D. Ford,* and *Paul Jones.*

Having landed his float planes the day before in expectation of night action, Doorman was handicapped for scouting, the more especially since none of his ships had radar. He requested air support from Java, but this was denied him when the air commander at Surabaya decided to use his planes in an attack on a convoy. Like Admiral Sir Tom Phillips in the *Prince of Wales,* Admiral Doorman sailed to meet his fate without benefit of air cover.

The Japanese covering force of seventeen ships, under Rear Admiral Sokichi Takagi, was not blinded by lack of air spotting. Almost as soon as Doorman began his advance, Japanese float planes sighted him and reported his course, speed, and number of ships.

At first glance the forces do not seem badly unbalanced. Takagi had the same number of heavy cruisers as Doorman, two, the *Haguro* (flagship) and *Nachi,* two light cruisers, *Jintsu* and *Naka,* to Doorman's three, and thirteen destroyers to the Allied nine. As matters worked out, however, the Japanese edge was more than enough.

At 1612 the *Electra* sighted Takagi's force in three columns. They were headed westward in a manner threatening to cross Doorman's "T," so he swung to a northwesterly course to close the range and bring his big guns to bear. At 1616 the *Houston* and *Exeter* opened fire just at the same moment as the *Haguro* and *Nachi* did. At the extreme range of 28,000 yards, neither side made any hits, although the Japanese shells soon straddled* the Allied ships. Doorman failed to close the range fast enough and so was unable to take advantage of his superiority in light cruisers. At 1621 the *De Ruyter* was hit by a dud 8-inch shell, and Doorman turned toward the enemy. Takagi countered this move with a torpedo attack, without effect.

High-speed maneuvering continued until 1708, when an 8-inch armor-piercing shell from the *Haguro* exploded deep in the *Exeter's* machine spaces and cut her speed in half. As she

---

* A straddle is the term applied when some shells of a salvo fall short and others pass over the target. The range is the established. It is only a matter of time and luck until the shells begin hitting.

turned out of column, the ships astern mistakenly turned, too. Dorman's formation lost coherence. During the confusion the *Kortenaer* caught a torpedo, broke in two, and sank.

Seeing the Allied force in disorder, Takagi closed in for the kill. But he launched his torpedoes at too great a range. The British destroyers in a gallant counterattack, ably supported by the Dutch destroyer *Witte de With,* lost the *Electra,* but gave Doorman time to re-form his column. He ordered the *Exeter* back to Surabaya under the escort of the *Witte de With.*

About 1800, Doorman ordered the American destroyers to make a torpedo attack, then changed his mind and told them to cover his retirement. Commander T. H. Binford, the Division Commander, believed his best means of obeying was to continue the attack. Charging through a smoke screen they had just laid, the four American four-pipers closed the Japanese cruisers. As they built up speed, their wakes creaming astern in the fading light, one of the bluejackets remarked, "I always knew these old four-pipers would have to go in and save the day."

There was no chance to save the day. At a range of 10,000 yards Binford launched his torpedoes, but all missed. Firing their 4-inch guns with possibly some effect, for something hit the destroyer *Asagumo,* Binford executed the well-known maneuver known as "getting the hell out of there." When he got close enough, he received a signal from Admiral Doorman: FOLLOW ME.

Admiral Doorman by this time was attempting to work his way around the covering force to get at the transports. On a northwesterly course, Doorman was headed directly for the troop convoy, but he had no way of knowing he was so close to his goal. When Takagi's cruisers loomed up, instead of pressing on, he turned to face them. The Japanese illuminated with aircraft flares and, perforce, Doorman turned away, heading south for the coast of Java. Here he stumbled into a defensive Dutch minefield and lost the *Jupiter* before turning westward along the coast. He detached the four American destroyers, which were nearly out of fuel, and sent them into Surabaya, and, with the *De Ruyter, Perth, Houston, Java,* and the destroyer *Encounter,* turned north once more to make a final attempt to get at the enemy transports.

On the way they spotted survivors from the sunken *Kortenaer,* and the *Encounter* was told to pick them up. Without

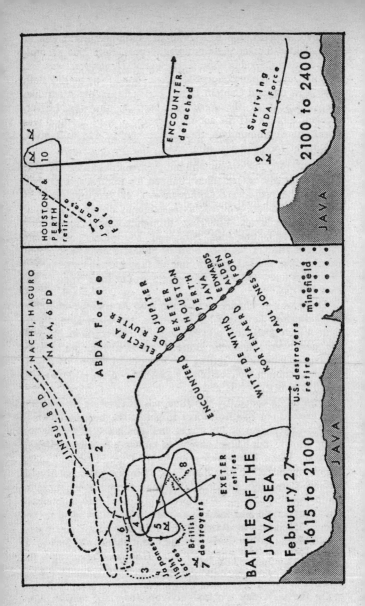

BATTLE OF THE JAVA SEA
February 27, 1615 to 2100

2100 to 2400

ABDA Force ●

NACHI, HAGURO
JINTSU, 8 DD
NAKA, 6 DD

ELECTRA
DE RUYTER
JUPITER
EXETER
HOUSTON
PERTH
JAVA
EDWARDS
ALDEN
FORD

ENCOUNTER
WITTE DE WITH
KORTENAER
PAUL JONES

minefield
U.S. destroyers retire

EXETER retires

British 7 destroyers

Japanese light forces

JAVA

ENCOUNTER detached

Surviving ABDA Force

HOUSTON & PERTH retire

Japan Force

JAVA

destroyer support, the four cruisers continued north and at 2300 sighted the Japanese cruisers to port. Both side promptly opened fire. Almost immediately the *De Ruyter* was hit, then the *Java*. Japanese torpedoes had found their marks. Both ships blew up, and Captain H. M. L. Waller of the Australian Navy, skipper of the *Perth*, the senior surviving officer, decided to break off the action. With the *Houston*, which was almost out of ammunition, the *Perth* made her way to Batavia, arriving at 1400 the next afternoon.

The battle was over, but the losses were not. The Combined Striking Force of Admiral Doorman had ceased to exist. The only thing to do was to attempt to extricate the survivors so that they might fight another day.

The *Perth* and *Houston* were ordered out of Batavia that same afternoon to pass through Sunda Strait at the western end of Java to make the best of their way to Tjilatjap on the south coast. They sailed at 2100 and an hour and a half later were approaching the strait. Unfortunately they ran into the Japanese Western Attack Force, built around four heavy cruisers and an aircraft carrier. Sighting a destroyer at 2315, the two Allied cruisers turned into Bintan Bay in Java, only to discover a Japanese amphibious landing in full swing. Shelling the transports as they raced by, they managed to sink four of them.

Their luck ran out as they tried to leave the bay. The four infuriated Japanese cruisers were waiting for them. The Allied ships did their best. They responded with everything they had,

---

KEY FOR MAP OF BATTLE OF THE JAVA SEA

1.	1616	British open fire at 28,000 yards.
2.	1633	Japanese torpedo attack.
3.	1700	Japanese torpedo attack.
4.	1708	*Exeter* hit.
5.	1715	*Kortenaer* sinks.
6.	1755	Japanese torpedo attack.
7.	1800	*Electra* sinks.
8.	1820	U.S. destroyers attack.
9.	2125	*Jupiter* sinks.
10.	2250	*Java* and *De Ruyter* sink.

firing until there was not a shell left in their magazines. In a few minutes both ships went down, their colors still flying.

The four American destroyer survivors of the Battle of the Java Sea managed to make their way to Fremantle. The American destroyer *Pope*, which had missed the battle, was not so fortunate. She, with the *Encounter*, was assigned the task of escorting the crippled *Exeter* into the Indian Ocean. They, too, were ordered through Sunda Strait. On March 1, at 0730, enemy ships loomed up ahead. Action was joined at 0940, the two destroyers shielding the cruiser as best they could until they were blown out of the water. At 1120 the *Exeter* was hit for the first time that day; then the hits mounted. Twenty minutes later she sank.

Her passing marked the end of any Allied force in the East Indies. This gallant ship was known the world over for her part three years earlier in defeating the German pocket battleship *Graf Spee* off Montevideo, Uruguay.* Now, in a different ocean, against a different enemy, she met her fate. She will always be an honored ship in the Royal Navy's annals.

With nothing to oppose them, the Japanese landed on both ends of Java and by the end of a week had received the surrender of the Allied land forces.

The end had come.

The Japanese now had complete control of their Resources Area.

How long would they be able to hold it?

CHAPTER FOUR

March-April: The Darkest Hour

> *This torture should be roar'd in dismal Hell.*
> Shakespeare, Romeo and Juliet

Little there was of cheer in the newspapers as March blew its gusty way into spring. U-boats continued their depredations along the East Coast. The Malay Barrier was gone. And Americans were just learning of shortages and hardships ahead

* See Dudley Pope, *The Battle of the River Plate*, William Kimber, London, 1956.

of them. Colleges and universities prepared for dwindling enrollments on the one hand as, on the other, they prepared for year-round operation.

Draft boards generally were sympathetic toward letting college students finish the current terms, but except for medical students, some engineers, and divinity students, the chances were slim than any healthy male would be able to complete work for his degree.

As a rule, students took matters calmly. Most men expected to go into the service. Few indeed were the wild revels based the philosophy of "eat, drink, and be merry, for tomorrow we die." Most stuck to their work, ready to go when called, but meanwhile getting as much done as possible.

Even before Pearl Harbor, college enrollments had dropped about ten percent as a result of the draft. In the spring of 1942, no one knew what might happen to colleges. Acceleration became the key word. Let the students take as much as they could as fast as they could. The colleges would remain open throughout the year, and many offerings would be added to contribute to the war effort. There was less emphasis on Greek, Latin, the humanities, and archaeology, and more on modern foreign languages—Russian, Japanese, military German, military Italian, Chinese. Courses in geopolitics, "Political and Military Geography," "Modern War Strategy and National Policy" were featured.

College population was constantly changing. Each day would see vacant chairs in the classroom as students volunteered for one of the programs that would lead to a commission in one of the services—the Navy's V-7 and V-12 plans and the Army's ASTP (Army Specialized Training Program). Nor was it only the men who went. Women had their opportunities for service in the WAVES, WAAC, SPARS, and Women Marines. Sometimes a college class would find a new instructor before it; the former one had gone into the service or had taken a job at a defense plant, where he was making far more money than he ever had in college teaching. Some students worked in defense industry, too, not only for the wages, but because defense workers were exempt from the draft. This system produced the best-educated riveters and welders in the nation's history.

In spite of fear of air raids and the popularity of the term "fifth column," the hysteria of 1917—1918 was largely lacking. Then, anyone with a German accent was regarded with suspicion; sauerkraut was renamed "liberty cabbage," frankfurters became "hot dogs," and the music of Bach, Brahms, Mozart, Beethoven, and other German composers disappeared from the concert stage. This time, in fact, the music of Beethoven was enlisted in the war. The opening four notes of his Fifth Symphony form the letter V in Morse code —the V for Victory sign, which became a symbol for fighting patriots everywhere, especially those in occupied countries.

The comic strips went to war. Skeezix in *Gasoline Alley* married his Nina and enlisted in the Army. So did Joe Palooka. Terry of *Terry and the Pirates* became a pilot in the Air Corps and found a buddy, Hotshot Charlie, with whom he was to share many exciting adventures against the Japanese. Dick Tracy fought against saboteurs at home, while Dagwood and Blondie grappled with rationing and all the other frustrations of life at home.

Immediately after the Pearl Harbor attack, the FBI moved to take into custody enemy aliens in the United States who were known to be anti-American or who were likely to be dangerous. Preparations were made to arrest 3,846 persons in the first seventy-two hours, and the roundup was carried off smoothly. These people had an opportunity for a hearing by a civilian board and the right to be represented by counsel. As a result of these precautions and the constant vigilance of the FBI and other law enforcement agencies, not a single case of enemy-directed sabotage occurred in the United States during the war.

There were, however, constant rumors and stories of espionage. Mysterious arrows plowed in fields were reported from one end of the country to the other. Most of them turned out to be natural soil markings, discernible only to the most imaginative eye. One or two were stunts by local pranksters. One lady apprehended by the police had a strange code on a slip of paper in her handbag: K1, P2, CO8, K5, etc. After experts had puzzled over it, she explained that it meant knit one, purl two, cast on eight, knit five.

The most inexcusable violation of civil liberties occurred in March on the West Coast with the forced evacuation of all Japanese-Americans from Oregon, California, Washington, Arizona, Idaho, Montana, and Utah. These people were not enemy aliens. Most of them were American citizens of the second or third generation, born in the United States and American in attitudes and loyalties. The move was carried out by the civil authorities at the demand of the military, but it was clearly a result of hysteria, politics, and in some cases local jealousy. Many Japanese-Americans were forced to sell businesses, houses, or personal property for a few cents on the dollar. Settled in relocation camps, they suffered hardships until the end of the war.

How unnecessary this wholesale relocation was can be shown by the fact that the Japanese population of Hawaii, far larger in proportion than that of the West Coast, was not made to leave the islands, yet there were no acts of disloyalty. The special Nisei Division, made up of Japanese-American soldiers, performed in an exemplary manner in Europe.

A few other acts of excessive zeal appeared. Ezio Pinza, the great opera basso, was held for several months as an enemy alien. A conscientious objector was refused admission to the Illinois bar as "morally unfit."

The whole problem of conscientious objectors was far better handled in this war than in the last. Most served in defense industry or in noncombatant military roles. The movie actor Lew Ayres, famed for his *Dr. Kildare* roles, served as a medical orderly in several military hospitals. Members of a few stricter sects chose imprisonment rather than any form of national service, even though the Government established camps somewhat on the model of the Civilian Conservation Corps for work in the forests and farm areas of the country.

Freedom of speech and of the press remained almost intact throughout the war. With the exception of military information obviously of aid to the enemy, the press was remarkably free of the restraints of censorship. There were many attempts to control the news by officials in Washington, particularly in connection with the rubber mess, but enterprising reporters generally managed to dig out distasteful facts. Under the leadership of former commentator Elmer Davis, the Office of War Information did about as good a job as could have been done. Davis had no sympathy with the bureaucrat who stamps SECRET on something merely to conceal bungling in his own office. The task of O.W.I. was aided enormously by the voluntary restraint on the part of reporters and war correspondents with respect to war news. In return the O.W.I. saw to it that credentials of war correspondents were honored and that reporters were able to get to the scenes of the actions. Few indeed were breaches of faith on either side. The result was that World War II was the best covered from a news viewpoint of any conflict up to its time. Much distinguished reporting came out of the war—Quentin Reynolds, Edward R. Murrow, A. B. Austin of the *London Herald*, John Hersey, Mark S. Watson, are a few of the names that leap to mind. But the most famous of all was Ernie Pyle. No other writer was so able to catch the spirit of the American servicemen or to make his life and death so understandable to the people back home.

The people at home needed some measure of encouragement. With the papers full of new restrictions in their daily lives and almost unbroken disaster in the war theaters, a note of success was needed. A few bright spots stood out: the defiant Marines on Wake, with their reported request to "Send more Japs." But Wake fell, and Major Devereaux and the surviving defenders entered Japanese prison camps for four years of torment and sadism. The most famous early war hero of those days was Air Force Captain Colin P. Kelly, Jr., who was reported to have crashed his crippled plane into a Japanese battleship, sinking it off the Philippines. Later the battleship was identified as the *Haruna,* and Kelly was posthumously awarded the Distinguished Service Cross. President Roosevelt left a letter for the President of the United States in the 1960s requesting that Captain Kelly's son be appointed to West Point.

Unfortunately for a great tradition, Kelly sank no battleship. There was not one within hundreds of miles, for the Japanese used none in their invasion of the Philippines. His B-17 badly hit and afire, Kelly remained with his plane to allow the crew time to bail out. Then it was too late. The plane crashed before Captain Kelly could escape. He had sacrificed his life to save the crew.*

With the loss of the Navy's battle line at Pearl Harbor, the only offensive weapons left were the submarines and the carriers. The submarine crews fought gallantly in the Southwest

---

* His son declined the Presidential appointment and made it to West Point the hard way—by competitive examination.

Pacific area, but because of faulty torpedoes, they had less success than their courage and skill deserved. It was to the carriers that the distinction fell of making the first offensive strikes against the Japanese.

The senior carrier task force commander in Hawaiian waters was Vice Admiral William F. Halsey, USN. A tenacious bulldog of a man with indomitable fighting spirit, Halsey was ready, and the new CINCPAC lost no time in employing his talents. Nimitz later remarked that among all the senior officers at Pearl Harbor, Halsey was the one he could best rely on to carry out difficult and dangerous attacks.

After several escort operations, Halsey was ordered south to cover a troop convoy for Samoa to protect that island against further Japanese advances from the newly gained Japanese positions in the Gilbert Islands. Halsey's force would then hit the Gilberts and Marshalls on the way back.

"All sorts of good luck to you, Bill,"* said Nimitz as Halsey boarded his barge to go out to his flagship, *Enterprise*.

Nimitz's wishes notwithstanding, the operation was plagued with vile luck, including lost aircraft, a collision between two destroyers in heavy rain, a man lost overboard from another destroyer. To cap it off, the *Saratoga*, not a part of Halsey's force, was torpedoed by a Japanese submarine and had to go to Bremerton for several months, keeping her out of action in the crucial battles of the Coral Sea and Midway that lay ahead.

Halsey's force consisted of two carrier groups. One, under Rear Admiral Frank Jack Fletcher in the *Yorktown*, hit the northern Gilbert and southern Marshalls. The other, built around the *Enterprise*, hit the northeastern Marshalls and, after a change in plans, added Kwajalein to the list.

No one knew what the Japanese would have in the Marshalls. Ever since World War I, when those former German possessions had been mandated to Japan, they had been closed to outsiders. Some Westerners had ventured in; some were never heard of again; others died of mysterious illnesses, and their ashes were returned by the Japanese to their relatives with appropriate expressions of sympathy. A persistent story is

---

* Halsey was known throughout the Navy as "Bill." The nickname "Bull" Halsey was only a newspaperman's idea. No one who knew Halsey ever called him "Bull."

still told that on her last flight the aviatrix Amelia Earhart strayed over the Marshalls and was shot down by the Japanese.

The charts of the area were known to be old and inaccurate, but they had to do. Early in the small hours of February 2, as the *Enterprise* was racing through the darkness at 25 knots to the launch point off Kwajalein, the staff duty officer rushed into flag plot to report that sand had just blown into his face.

At sea, sand in the air can only mean that land is near-by—very nearby, and at 25 knots it does not take long to reach it. There were tense moments in flag plot until the officer returned with a grin on his face. The "sand" was sweet. Directly below the flag bridge, a sailor was unconcernedly stirring sugar in a cup of coffee.

After a successful strike, the force returned to Pearl, only to set out again a few days later for a raid on Wake Island. When Halsey received his orders for this strike, he was appalled. His force had been designated Task Force 13, and it was to sail on Friday, February 13!

"What goes on here?" demanded Halsey, storming into CINCPAC headquarters. "Have you got it in for us, or what?"

Since no sailor would dare defy such a combination of jinxes, the force designation was changed to Task Force 16, and the sortie was postponed until Valentine's Day.

When the raid on Wake was successful, Nimitz radioed the returning Halsey requesting him to hit Marcus if he thought it practicable. With many misgivings, since Marcus is only 999 miles from Tokyo, Halsey took on the job. He little realized that in two months he would approach the Japanese capital much more closely. The raid accomplished little except for burning a few buildings, but Japanese alarm was so great that an air raid alert was sounded in Tokyo.

Meanwhile the *Lexington* force, assigned to the Southwest Pacific area, was escorting troop convoys. While the force was engaged in routine missions, the Japanese seized the Papuan peninsula on the eastern end of New Guinea, New Ireland, and New Britain. This gave them the important base of Rabaul on the northern end of New Britain.

In Simpson Harbour at Rabaul, the Japanese gained one of the finest natural anchorages in the world. Over a thousand miles closer to New Guinea and Australia than the fabled Japanese base at Truk in the Carolines, Rabaul became the principal Japanese forward outpost for over two years.

Rear Admiral Wilson Brown suggested that his *Lexington* force raid Rabaul. He planned to hit the target at dawn on February 21, but the Japanese 25th Air Flotilla scout planes spotted the *Lexington* on the morning of the previous day and attacked. For nearly two hours, heavy raids pressed against the ships, but were beaten off by the combat air patrol. Since the Japanese were thoroughly alerted, Brown called off the attack.

He had another chance a month later when the *Yorktown* joined his force. This time the targets were Lae and Salamaua in Papua, New Guinea. Rather than venture into the Bismarck Sea and risk attack from Rabaul-based aircraft, Brown, on March 10, took position in the Coral Sea and sent strikes from both carriers to fly over the fifteen-thousand-foot-high Owen Stanley Mountains and attack the targets from the landward side. The attack group of over a hundred planes found a pass seventy-five hundred feet high, and through this the heavily laden torpedo planes were able to fly, carrying their grim burdens. The raid was a complete success, catching the Japanese by surprise and resulting in heavy damage to the installations and shipping. Only one American plane was lost.

These raids, admittedly pinpricks in the face of the Japanese advances, raised morale at home and gave at least a partial answer to the oft-heard query: "Where is the Navy?"

* * * * *

The Navy was of little aid to the trapped defenders of Bataan. In spite of MacArthur's urgings, the Joint Chiefs of Staff decided that any attempt to reinforce the Philippines was too risky and would only endanger the chances of holding Samoa, New Caledonia, and Australia.

This was grim news to the Filipino-American troops. Drawn up on the Mauban-Abucay line as the New Year started were fifteen thousand American and sixty-five thousand Filipino troops. Of the latter, only ten thousand were fully trained; the others were little better than raw recruits.

The principal job was feeding and supplying the men on Bataan. With only a handful of small craft and PT boats, the Navy could do little to ease the situation, particularly in view of complete Japanese control of the air.

Flanking attacks forced Major General Jonathan Wainwright and Major General George M. Parker, commanding the western and eastern sectors respectively, to fall back ten miles or so to the Bagac-Orion line by January 26. Here the front was somewhat shorter, and the natural defenses made the going difficult for the Japanese. General Homma, unable to crack the defenders' line, tried amphibious landings on the west side of the peninsula, but these were mere footholds and did not accomplish the desired purpose. By February 8 Homma was forced to ask Tokyo for more troops. Underfed, unsupported, the Filipino-American defenders were holding their own.

The men of Bataan took a special kind of fierce pride in their predicament. Bitterly resentful of the failures of Washington and the naval forces to give reinforcement or adequate aid, these soldiers asked no quarter from the enemy and gave none. Their battle cry: "We're the battling bastards of Bataan—no papa, no mama, no Uncle Sam!"

Until the beginning of April, the situation remained a stalemate. Homma's men were reinforced as he prepared to make another trial at the defense line. Meanwhile, the defenders were suffering increasing hardships. On January 6, rations had been cut in half to thirty ounces per man per day. On April 1, they were cut again in half to fifteen ounces. The Navy attempted to relieve the shortages by running in submarines, since no surface vessels were able to get through. On February 3, U.S.S. *Trout* brought in ammunition and stores and removed two tons of gold and eighteen of silver, the Philippine national treasury, plus five tons of mail and securities. On her way out, she managed to sink two Japanese ships.

The *Swordfish* on February 20 evacuated President Manuel Quezon and his family and five other officials. Then she returned and picked up U.S. High Commissioner Francis B. Sayre, his staff and family, and took them to Fremantle, Australia.

On March 11, on direct orders from President Roosevelt, General MacArthur reluctantly turned his command over to General Wainwright and sorrowfully left Bataan. Rather than wait for a submarine, MacArthur elected to travel by PT boat. As he boarded *PT-41*, commanded by Lieutenant John D. Bulkeley, he saw to it that his family was comfortable and then looked back.

On the dock [he wrote] I could see the men staring at

me. I had lost 25 pounds living on the same diet as the soldiers and I must have looked gaunt and ghastly standing there in my old war-stained clothes—no bemedaled commander of inspiring presence. . . . Ugly dark scars marked smouldering paths where the fire had raged from one end of the island to the other. Great gaps and forbidding crevices belched their tongues of flame. . . . Darkness had fallen, and the waters were beginning to ripple from the faint night breeze. The enemy firing had ceased and a muttering silence had fallen. . . . I raised my cap in farewell salute, and I could feel my face go white, feel a sudden, convulsive twitch in the muscles of my face. I heard someone ask, "What's his chances, Sarge, of getting through?" and the gruff reply, "Dunno. He's lucky. Maybe one in five."

Through the night, as the weather deteriorated, Bulkeley and the skippers of the three PT boats with him dodged the Japanese patrol forces. The bad weather helped in evading the enemy, but it was, as MacArthur described it, like taking a ride in a concrete mixer. Eventually three of the four boats made it safely into Cagayan on the northern coast of Mindanao. There MacArthur and his party transferred to two decrepit B-17s and flew to Darwin, Australia, where the General set up his headquarters. As he stepped down from his plane, reporters besieged him. He casually spoke a magic phrase that became a symbol of hope for the Filipinos and an obligation for the United States: "I shall return."

Back in Bataan, the situation daily grew more desperate. Two submarines landed thirty-five tons of food, but this amounted to only half a day's rations.

On April 3, Homma struck savagely on the left flank of the eastern defense line, forcing a breach that could not be plugged. The advance continued relentlessly, and five days later Wainwright saw that the end had come. Evacuating naval personnel and the Philippine Scouts to Corregidor, a small island in Manila Bay two miles southeast of Bataan, Wainwright followed with his headquarters personnel and ordered the "battling bastards" to surrender.* Some of his subordinate

* Wainwright did not surrender with his troops because he was commander of all forces in the Philippines and so responsible for them as well. He surrendered when Corregidor fell in May.

commanders had already capitulated without waiting for orders, and there was nothing he could do.

Never before in U.S. history had so large a force—seventy-six thousand men, including twelve thousand Americans—surrendered to a foreign enemy. Laying down their arms, they wondered what lay in store for them.

If they had known, most of them would have chosen to fight to the last bullet, with no thought but of taking as many Japanese with them as possible.

Ahead lay the infamous Bataan Death March.

"The Imperial Japanese Army will take good care of you," shouted a Japanese officer to a group of prisoners at Mariveles, at the southern end of Bataan. "You will get good food and treatment. . . . We will abide by the Geneva Pact."

On foot, starved to the point of collapse, sick and halt, seventy-six thousand men began the long trip—a total of fifty-five miles—to San Fernando, where trains would carry them to prison camp. It was a march of despair, a journey of the damned.

In partial extenuation of what lay ahead, it must be stated that the Japanese facilities for handling prisoners were swamped. Preparations were made for at most thirty-five thousand. More than double that number set out on the hellish road. Then there is the Japanese attitude toward prisoners. Trained in the harshest of disciplinary codes, the Japanese soldier considered himself eternally disgraced if he was captured. In addition, his entire family shared his shame. Never again could they hold up their head. A Japanese soldier was trained to save the last bullet for himself or to charge out in a suicide assault on the enemy.

These facts can help to explain, but they cannot excuse, the treatment of the Filipino and American prisoners of war captured at Bataan.

At first the treatment was comparatively good, but as the march continued, more and more brutalities occurred. Prisoners were systematically stripped of rings, watches, money, even treasured photographs of loved ones.

The Japanese had assumed that the prisoners could subsist on the rations they had with them until they reached San Fernando, so no efforts were made to feed the men. "Your own forces didn't feed you adequately," said one Japanese major in response to pleas for food, "and I don't choose to feed you any

104

more than you've been receiving."

Inevitably men began to drop from hunger, exhaustion, and the blazing heat. Those who fell were beaten, kicked, prodded with bayonets until those who could scrambled to their feet for a few more tottering steps. Those who could not rise were beaten to death, shot, or bayonetted.

Under the merciless sun and the choking dust of the road, water became an obsession. Some Filipino civilians tried to offer a drink to the men. Some guards allowed it; others beat the benefactors and tossed the water onto the ground. A few calmly killed the men and women whose only crime was an act of charity.

A few Filipino prisoners were forced to kill Americans who had fallen and could not rise. If they refused, they were shot, and the Americans were disposed of, anyway. One group, forced to kill and bury an American, looked back, helpless, as a hand came out of the shallow grave. The fingers moved weakly, then stopped.

After nine days of brutality, the survivors arrived at San Fernando. Here they were told they would go by train to Camp O'Donnell, their prison. The train ride was almost as bad as the march. Into boxcars, the size of the famous "forty men or eight horses" of World War I, were loaded a hundred or more wretches. They were so tightly packed there was no room to stand. With the doors closed, those at the ends could scarcely breathe. Guided by common humanity, the stronger men moved to the ends, allowing the sick and weak to be near the air seeping in around cracks in the door.

Even so, many died. But the dead had no room to fall. Propped up by their living comrades, they rode on, past all caring, to find rest at last in unmarked graves. Their surviving companions at length emerged into the light at Camp O'Donnell.

Any hopes they had for better treatment vanished when the Camp Commander told them that since they did not look and act like soldiers, they would be treated not as prisoners of war, but as captives.

The only way out of their sufferings was death or an Allied victory. Victory came, but it was too late for most of the survivors of the Bataan Death March after their years at Camp O'Donnell.

* * * * *

"The weather is uniformly bad," noted the Oberkommando der Wehrmacht War Diary on December 19, 1941. On that date Hitler personally took over the high command of the German Army, sending into obscure retirement its former head, Field Marshal von Brauchitsch, the man who had commanded in the victories over Poland, Norway, France, and Greece. But now, over-contemptuous of the professional General Staff officer, Hitler believed he could stem the tide of the Russian counterattack.

> Anyone [said Hitler] can do the little job of directing operations in war. The task of the Commander in Chief is to educate the Army to be National Socialist. I do not know any Army General who can do this as I want it done. I have therefore decided to take over command of the Army myself.

Von Brauchitsch was by no means the only one to go. Hitler made nearly a clean sweep of his former victors—von Rundstedt, von Leeb, Hoeppner—even Guderian, commander of his Panzer armies, to whom he owed so much.

Not a foot of ground must be given up! Such was Hitler's first command to his troops. In face of the Russian pressure, it was a command impossible of execution, the greatest folly in concept. In trying to obey rather than fall back to well-prepared defensive positions, the Germans suffered heavy, needless casualties. Russian attacks in January and February eroded German strength and made position after position untenable. To attempt to hold them resulted in useless loss of life. In thousands, German soldiers fell, victims of their Führer's stupid pride.

At length, on February 15, Hitler gave permission for "dignified withdrawals" to prepared positions. For the next two weeks these retreats were carried out by Army Group Center, and by the end of the month, the troops were well established. At the same time, the Russian drive ran out of steam, and the front stabilized. The greatest Russian advance was some three hundred miles. In other places there was no advance at all. The average was more than a hundred miles.

Hitler gave himself great credit for personally having stopped the great Russian counterattack. The irony of the situation was that the positions finally occupied were those prepared and planned as a winter defense line by the very commanders he had so summarily dismissed. That made no difference. Henceforth and forever more, in his own reckoning, Hitler considered his military intuition infallible.

With minor skirmishing, the Russian front remained static until May 8, 1942, when the Germans mounted their great summer offensive.

The British Home Fleet based at Scapa Flow was stretched to the breaking point. Losses, heavy demands for operations, troop convoy escort, and the need to guard the *Tirpitz*, based in a Norwegian fjord, meant that nothing was available to keep guard over the Channel. At the mouth of the Channel, in the French port of Brest, were poised three German heavy ships, the battle cruisers *Scharnhorst* and *Gneisenau* and the heavy cruiser *Prinz Eugen*. They might break out into the North Atlantic to attack the vital convoys. They might make a break for home. So long as they were there, the British connections with the world were imperiled. The RAF had made many attempts to knock them out, but all in vain.

Hitler, however, did not intend to use them against British shipping. He was obsessed with the idea of a British landing in Norway and felt that these ships would be strong protection as floating fortresses in the fjords. He ordered them to proceed to Norwegian ports and to make their way by the English Channel rather than north about Scotland.

The three ships departed Brest on the evening of February 11. Because of inadequate British air scouting, they were not spotted until 1042 the next morning. The Luftwaffe and all available German light naval forces were covering their passage. Hastily organized British opposition both by the RAF and by the slender Channel light naval forces was completely unsuccessful, and the German ships reached Germany in the early morning hours of February 13. The *Scharnhorst* had hit two mines and the *Gneisenau* one, but neither ship was damaged beyond repair.*

* The *Gneisenau* never was repaired. She received further damage during air raids on Kiel; thereafter her refit was abandoned, and she decayed into a useless hulk.

Six weeks later, British naval morale, at a nadir from the impudent passage of these ships past the White Cliffs of Dover, received a boost in one of the most successful Command raids of the war.

* * * * *

St. Nazaire on the Loire estuary in western France had been converted by the Germans to a U-boat base. But more significant in Admiralty fears was the huge dry dock built before the war to service the liner *Normandie*. The dock was the only one under German control where the *Tirpitz*, formidable sister of the sunken *Bismarck*, could be accommodated. Comparatively impervious to bombing, it became the target of British Commando attention.

"Of all the operations with which I was concerned in the late war," wrote Lord Louis Mountbatten, "the successful raid on the battleship dock at St. Nazaire is perhaps the one I am most proud to have been associated with." Admittedly almost suicidal in concept, the raid had first been considered as early as the fall of 1940, but nothing had come of the early scheme. When then Captain Mountbatten, RN, took over Combined Operations (Commandos), the problem was revived.

Any raiding force attacking St. Nazaire would be sailing into a lion's mouth. The 1,148-foot-long dock lies in the town of St. Nazaire, six miles up the Loire. Both banks were lined with German guns, well sited over the narrow, twisting, deep-water channel. The rest of the estuary consists of shoal water; no vessel drawing more than about ten feet could hope to reach St. Nazaire except by the main channel.

Because surprise was absolutely essential for the success of the operation, the RAF was requested to make an attack on the port at the time the raid was scheduled. During a raid, all attention, as the British well knew from the bombing of London, was directed to the skies. While the bombs were dropping, "you could," said one of the planners, "go into any house, commit any crime, do anything you liked, and no one would take the slightest notice of you."

As plans developed, a naval force would carry Commando troops to attend to demolition of key machinery and equipment, while an expendable destroyer, her bows laden with explosives, would crash into one of the caissons forming the entry to the *Normandie* dock.

Perhaps "naval force" is too strong a term. The Admiralty, having suggested the operation in the first place, jibbed at supplying the vessels the attack would require. A major naval force simply could not be diverted from other duties. The operation would have to be done with makeshifts.

The destroyer finally selected for immolation on the caisson was H.M.S. *Campbeltown*, one of the fifty over-age U.S. four-stackers given the British in exchange for ninety-nine-year leases on a series of bases in the Western Hemisphere. Built in 1919 as U.S.S. *Buchanan*, this 1,090-ton vessel had seen hard service and was deemed by the Admiralty suitable for the sacrifice.

The rest of the naval group consisted of sixteen motor launches with a maximum speed of 18 knots, one motor torpedo boat (PT), and one motor gunboat, to serve as command ship. Totally unsuited for such an operation because of low speed and short range, the motor launches were a hundred twelve feet in length and built of two thin skins of mahogany plywood with a layer of cloth between. The wooden construction offered no protection whatever from enemy guns. Worse, the vessels were floating tinderboxes, the danger of fire increased by their gasoline drive. To give them the range for the eight-hundred-mile voyage from Falmouth to St. Nazaire, the motor launches were fitted with an exposed extra five-hundred-gallon gasoline tank. Since these tanks were especially hazardous, they were to be used first and then filled with seawater.

Commander R. E. D. Ryder, RN, whose initials made the nickname "Red" inevitable, stood on the bridge of H.M.S. *Atherstone*, one of two Hunt-class destroyers assigned to escort the little force to the vicinity of St. Nazaire. Commander Ryder, on whose shoulders rested responsibility for the success of the raid, looked over his little command. Astern was the *Tynedale*, another escorting destroyer. In her wake plodded the doomed *Campbeltown*, altered so that her builders would not have recognized her. Her four funnels had been taken off and replaced with two sharply raked ones of an unequal size. Her guns had been removed and her silhouette changed to make her resemble the *Möwe* class of German destroyers.

Below decks her magazines had been emptied, stores and equipment removed, fuel and feed-water reduced to the amount needed to reach the objective. Riding light as she was, she was crank and difficult to handle, but she would be able to cross the estuary without having to keep to the main ship channel. In her bows were three and a half tons of explosive fitted with delayed-action fuses and surrounded with concrete and steel.

At Ryder's side was Lieutenant Colonel A. C. Newman, in command of all the Commando forces embarked in the nineteen vessels of the raiding force. For weeks he had tirelessly drilled and rehearsed his men, practicing on the *King George V* dock at Southampton, almost a duplicate of their target. Ninety-one of his men had the sole purpose of blowing up dockyard fittings, lock mechanisms, pumps and motors of the *Normandie* dock. Another hundred and sixty-six combat troops were to take out gun emplacements and protect the demolitioneers as they worked. Every man a volunteer, superbly trained, these Commandos lived for their work. No punishment was necessary in these groups. The threat "RTU" was enough. Being "Returned to Unit" was the ultimate disgrace for a Commando.

As they made their way from Falmouth on the afternoon of March 26, most of the six hundred eleven men of the expedition were having an uncomfortable time. Cramped and seasick in the motor launches and in the torpedo boat, the men made the best of it. The motor gunboat (MGB), which was to be Ryder's command ship, was in tow of the *Atherstone* to conserve her fuel. Ryder and Newman would embark in her forty miles off the entrance to St. Nazaire, where the two Hunt-class destroyers would peel off and set up a waiting patrol.

In the *Campbeltown*, life was more comfortable. Her normal crew had been reduced to seventy-five, just enough to take her on her last voyage. Approximately a third of the Commandos were embarked in the old destroyer, and even though their time on deck was limited, they lived well while they could. The ship's canteen and food stores had been provisioned normally at Falmouth for security reasons, and there was plenty for everyone. The men reveled in the delights of foods long since vanished from home—eggs, ham, butter, sausage. For a time they paid regular prices at the ship's canteen for candy, ice cream, and the like, until someone said, "Hey, the ship's going to be blown up tonight—accounts and all. What are we paying for?" After that, it was all "on the house."

More than all else, Ryder feared being spotted while at sea and thereby ruining the success of the expedition through loss of surprise. Therefore he set the course well to the westward to pass at least fifty miles from the coast of France before beginning the run-in. Also he adopted a formation to make any snooper aircraft believe the vessels were on a normal antisubmarine sweep in the Bay of Biscay.

In justification of these precautions, the next morning the destroyers spotted *U-593*. While Ryder turned his formation onto a westerly course, the destroyers attacked, forcing the U-boat to dive. She was not damaged, and five and a half hours later she reported the sighting without giving the nationality of the ships and reporting the course as west. The German Naval Group West believed they might be ships on passage to Gibraltar or perhaps vessels withdrawing from a minelaying operation. They "never anticipated," as recorded later, an attack on a French port.

At 2005 on March 27, in position 46° 25' North, 3° 20' West, Ryder and Newman boarded the MGB, the *Atherstone* and *Tynedale* turned away, and only the assault force pushed on. There was but one more checkpoint, where the submarine *Sturgeon* waited to give them a final fix. At 2215, they picked her up, dead ahead.

"Goodbye and good luck," her skipper called to Ryder.

Forty miles to go.

The wind was calm, and a faint, thickening haze lay over the water. The darkening clouds became denser, and the rain began to fall softly. Ryder noted these signs with satisfaction; he could have asked for nothing better to cover the approach to the port.

He might not have been so pleased if his thoughts had turned to the bombing attack that was supposed to provide a diversion for the operation. The RAF bombers were experiencing great difficulty in making their attack. From above a few hundred feet, the cloud cover was complete. The bombardiers had nothing to aim at. Having been briefed on the importance of staying over the area, they cruised aimlessly back and forth, dropping single bombs on a run until their strange behavior aroused suspicion. "Some deviltry is afoot," said Kapitän zur See Mecke. Then he ordered his gun positions to keep an alert against paratroopers or an attack from the sea.

About 0115 on March 28, a lookout reported the approach of a group of some seventeen vessels. Five minutes later came the alert: *Achtung Landegefahr!* (Beware landing!)

By this time Ryder's little group was well within the estuary, the precious five minutes between the lookout's report and the alert having brought them nearly a mile closer to their target.*

With only two miles to go, they could not believe their own good fortune.

Two minutes later, the whole force was brilliantly bathed in light. A few small guns opened up, but most held their fire while two signal stations challenged at the same time.

Ryder nodded to Leading Seaman F. C. Pike, who sprang to the signal light in the MGB. Making the call sign of the *Möwe*, and asking one station to wait, he flashed in German to the other a confusing signal: "Proceeding up harbor in accordance with orders. . . ."

To the amazement of the British, the firing stopped. Four more minutes had been won. They were nearly home. In six minutes the *Campbeltown* would ram the dock caisson.

With five minutes to go, deception was at an end. At 0128 the German batteries opened together. Down came the German colors from the mast of the *Campbeltown*. On all vessels of Ryder's force the White Ensign soared to the peak, shining valiantly in the glaring beams of the searchlights. Lieutenant Commander S. H. Beattie, taking the *Campbeltown* on her last voyage, ordered the automatic weapons—all that remained of the destroyer's armament—to reply to the German fire.

In a blaze of gunfire from both sides, the *Campbeltown* steamed on, Beattie trying to work her up to 20 knots to smash hard into the caisson. On deck, men were dropping from the German gunfire. The coxswain at the wheel fell dead. The

---

* The force had slowed to 10 knots on entering the estuary because the *Campbeltown* had a tendency to settle by the stern at higher speed, which would increase her danger of grounding. At 10 knots a ship travels 333 yards a minute. Two thousand yards is one nautical mile.

quartermaster sprang forward, only to be hit himself. An officer took over quietly.

There were now fifteen hundred yards to go.

Three minutes passed.

"Port twenty-five," ordered Beattie.

"Twenty-five degrees of port wheel on, sir."

"Steer three four five degrees."

"Three four five degrees, sir."

Two minutes to go.

Every German gun that could bear was concentrated on the *Campbeltown*. She was well up to 20 knots. The Commando party was lying on the decks behind protective steel plates.

Beattie made a last-minute course correction.

"Steer three five oh degrees."

Seven hundred yards—one minute—to go.

Every man braced for the shock.

On sped the *Campbeltown*, the white water flaring from her bow. A slight jerk. They had gone through the antitorpedo net.

Fifty yards to go.

Her luck had held. She had not been hit in any vital spot. Nothing could stop the *Campbeltown* now.

At 0134 the tired, gallant old destroyer smashed squarely into the center of the caisson. With screeching of metal she came to rest, thirty-six feet of her bow crumpled back.

Springing to their feet, the Commandos leaped from the decks and sprang onto the caisson, rushing toward their goals, the pumping machinery forty feet below the lip of the dock. The motor launches were coming up now, and men rushed ashore, each knowing precisely what to do.

It is not possible to recount the valor of the individual Commando parties ashore. Fighting like demons, they pressed on, destroying guns and vital machinery, and killing Germans. At length came the time to withdraw. They reached the sea wall, prepared to embark in the motor launches.

The river was literally a river of fire. Many of the motor launches had been knocked out, spilling their flaming gasoline on the surface of the water. It was a scene from hell. The screams of men burning to death in the river pierced the night. The more fortunate drowned before the flames could reach them.

A few made it to shore, where sooner or later they were picked up by German patrols.

Looking at the scene, Colonel Newman said to his second in command, Major W. O. Copland, "Well, Bill, there goes our transport."

Quickly revamping his plans, Newman ordered his Commandos to try to break through the town and then in pairs to make their way to Spain and Gibraltar. After a stubborn effort, they were pinned down by the Germans and taken prisoner. Sixty-four men had been killed. Over two hundred were captured, including Navy men. Five fortunate Commandos did manage to reach Gibraltar after an incredible journey.

The naval forces suffered even higher casualties than did the Commandos. Most were lost to gunfire or met death in the blazing river. Three of the motor launches, miraculously escaping crippling damage, filled with wounded and injured men. Finding no one to give orders, they set out on the long voyage home. They arrived at Falmouth on the morning of March 29.

Ryder in the MGB saw that the vital objective of the operation had been won. Sickened by the loss of his motor launches, he gave the order to withdraw, knowing that he was condemning his friend Newman and his Commandos to death or capture. Before Ryder gave the order, he scouted the mole for all possible passengers, cramming them into the MGB and three damaged motor launches he had rounded up in the process. When the boats could hold no more, they pushed off, Ryder bitterly staring back to where Newman and his little band were fighting for their lives.

The torpedo boat also survived to make a break for the sea, but as she tore out at 33 knots, she rammed an underwater obstruction and sank. Almost all hands were lost.

The MGB finally left about 0300, the last of the British vessels to leave. Using all her speed of 24 knots, twisting and turning, she evaded the worst of the storm of fire from the German guns and made her way to the open sea. At dawn Ryder and his men spotted the *Tynedale* and *Atherstone*, who had taken under their wing three of the motor launches. The men of the raiding party transferred to the destroyers for food and sleep, and the motor launches and MGB were scuttled. The three motor launches that made Falmouth were the only vessels to survive of the nineteen that had sailed three days earlier.

When morning broke over the city of St. Nazaire, the Germans felt quite relieved. The apparent damage was minor, most of the Commandos were rounded up, and the impudent raiders had been either destroyed or driven off.

Looming up over one end of the *Normandie* dock was the wreck of the *Campbeltown*. Her crumbled bow extended through the caisson; her stern had been scuttled, extending downward at a crazy angle.

Their first problem, as the Germans saw it, was to remove the wreck. Shortly before noon, a large party of German officials went aboard to inspect her. With never a thought of delayed-action fuses, they allowed some sightseers, including several women, to come aboard at the same time. Most of these sightseers, on finding the canteen stores still available, had descended to take advantage of the unexpected bounty. Cigarettes and candy quickly disappeared into pockets and handbags. Below the tortured plates of the bow, acid was steadily eating through the copper wire of the fuses.

Meanwhile, Commander Beattie was being interrogated nearby.

"You people obviously did not know what a husky thing that lock gate is," said the German officer. "It was really futile to try to smash it with a flimsy destroyer."

Just at that moment the three and a half tons of explosive went off.

The inspection party and the foragers on the *Campbeltown* were instantly wiped out. No one ever discovered how many were killed in the explosion, but estimates run to well over a hundred.

"That, I hope, is proof," said Beattie, when he could be heard again, "that we did not underestimate the strength of the gate."

Peace descended on St. Nazaire. Two days passed, and German control reasserted itself. Then, on Monday afternoon, March 30, a delayed-action torpedo blew up. An hour later, a second exploded.

The Germans panicked. Search parties combed the dock area looking for saboteurs. They shot at anything that moved, killing many innocent Frenchmen and not a few of their own troops. It was not until after midnight that order was finally restored. This tragic aftermath did not seriously affect the spirits of the French. In this, the first raid on French soil since the surrender in June 1940, Frenchmen saw that they had not been forgotten, that the long night of German occupation would have an end at last.

No fewer than five Victoria Crosses, Britain's highest medal, were given for this operation. Never before had so large a proportion been given. It was, as Winston Churchill wrote, "a deed of glory intimately involved in high strategy."

* * * * *

To complete their control of the Southern Resources Area, the Japanese needed to win Burma. Burma was vital not only for the protection of the Japanese flank on the Indian Ocean, but also for the oil and rubber readily available there. Land of Kipling's "Road to Mandalay," Burma is a country of rich tropical jungle, divided north and south by mountain ranges. The central plains of the Irrawaddy and Sittang river valleys afford the country most of its arable land and its only good road and rail systems. A rail line runs north from the principal seaport of Rangoon to Mandalay, thence northeastward to Lashio, starting point of the Burma Road. This famous highway twists and climbs its six-hundred-eighty-one-mile length over the lower Himalaya Mountains to Kunming, and then on an approximately equal distance to Chungking in China. It remained the only land link by which the Allies could send aid to Chiang Kai-shek, although its limited capacity of under six thousand tons a month provided slim rations for China's war needs.

As early as December 1941, the Japanese began bombing Rangoon. The raids did little damage, but the Burmese stevedore coolies were frightened into decamping, and the efficiency of the port dropped to near zero. Also in December the Japanese established airfields in southeastern Burma, and in January began to advance on Rangoon itself.

The defense of Burma fell to General Wavell's Indian Command, but there were few British troops available. For the most part the soldiers were Indians or Burmese, commanded by British officers. Ill-equipped and ill-trained for jungle fighting, the defenders fell back before the infiltration tactics of the Japanese. Rangoon was evacuated on March 7, as General Sir Harold R. Alexander was sent in to try to save the rest of the country.

By arrangement with Chiang Kai-shek, two Chinese armies were sent via the Burma Road to assist in the defense. These armies, as well as one in reserve, were under the command of American General Joseph Stilwell. In spite of these reinforcements, the situation in Burma rapidly deteriorated. With the seizure of Rangoon, there was no way to bring in supplies except by air or through small seaports on the Indian Ocean. Japanese naval units moving into the Indian Ocean in April effectively sealed this route, and the end became only a matter of time. On April 29, the Japanese took Lashio, effectively closing the Burma Road. The British remnants made successful retreats to the coast or into India, while the Chinese made their way back into their own country. As "Vinegar Joe" Stilwell put it, "We got a hell of a beating."

* * * * *

By the end of April the ordinary American was feeling that he, too, was taking a "hell of a beating." Not only was he reading of gloom and disaster and hearing it on the radio; he was reeling from a series of blows from Washington. It seemed that everything from his gasoline tank to his coffee cup was being sacrificed to the insatiable demands of war.

In Washington, the machinery for war was being refined and prepared for the offensive load to be placed on it. To centralize naval control further, the office of Commander in Chief, U.S. Fleet, and that of Chief of Naval Operations (CNO) were vested in one man, Admiral King. The former CNO, Admiral Harold R. Stark, who had some of the stigma of Pearl Harbor surrounding him, was sent to London as a special U.S. representative with the Royal Navy.

Admiral "Ernie" King has become one of the legendary figures of the U.S. Navy. His cold, piercing brown eyes and his chill, forbidding demeanor promised short shrift to subordinates who presented sloppy or ill-considered staff work for his attention. All the old sailors' tales were told about him: He breakfasted on brash young ensigns, and picked his teeth with a marlinspike. His reputation, combined with his almost total lack of a sense of humor, made him a figure of mystery and no little awe.

The real story of the man is quite different. Born in Lorain, Ohio, on November 23, 1878, he was graduated from the U.S.

Naval Academy in Annapolis, fourth in the class of 1901. His career was varied and distinguished, including experience in a variety of ship types from submarines to battleships, with staff duty and teaching assignments as well. He entered naval aviation when he was a Captain, winning his wings in 1927 at the age of forty-eight. Soon afterwards he assumed command of the aircraft carrier *Lexington*.

To his dedicated subordinates, King was a model of fairness, rectitude, and brilliance. He drove his staff hard and himself even harder. He had no use for slovenly work and did not suffer fools gladly. He kept a constant rotation among his staff officers to prevent empire building and to ensure that the voice of sea and combat experience received a hearing at the highest level of the Navy Department.

His reputation is as varied as are the accounts of him. His admirers state that he had a wider, sounder, more comprehensive view of the war than any other man. He was a continual thorn in the side of the British leaders. Lord Alanbrooke, who was British Chief of the Imperial General Staff, wrote so caustically of him in his diary that those sections almost should have been put on asbestos pages. Churchill disliked him intensely, as did Sir Andrew B. Cunningham, later Britain's First Sea Lord, and hence King's opposite number in the Royal Navy.

On the other hand, King had the friendship and admiration of President Roosevelt and the respect, if not the friendship, of the American Army Chief of Staff, General George C. Marshall. King's character had little in it of the diplomat, little of the practical politician. He forced his views on others, and by the power of his personality and by the unerring correctness of his strategic views, he made those views prevail without regard to the sensibilities of those he trampled in the process.

Almost single-handedly, King kept his colleagues on the Joint Chiefs of Staff and the Combined Chiefs of Staff from forgetting the war in the Pacific. While he agreed with the overall decision that the war in Europe must come first, he could not and would not accept the view that no effort could be expended in the Pacific area. The British, especially, begrudged every man, every gun, every plane, and every ship which was directed into the Pacific. In a postwar comment in his diary, Lord Alanbrooke complained bitterly:

The American departure from our basic strategy was mainly due to Admiral King. . . . For him the main theatre lay in the Pacific where the bulk of the American Naval Forces were . . . employed. As a result, precious shipping, landing-craft and equipment were finding their way to the Pacific instead of being allotted to the main front in Europe. It was easy enough to lay down, and to accept, the concept that Germany must be defeated first. Where the difficulty rested, however, was to decide how much effort should be devoted to hold Japan. The holding of Japan provided all the excuse necessary for a continual diversion of effort not truly required for a holding role. I still feel that, if at that stage . . . our basic strategy had been more strictly adhered to, we should have finished the war a few months sooner.*

In early April, the ABDA command having long since vanished, the British and Americans agreed to continue the system of area or theater commands exemplified in the ABDA arrangement. The British had two commands, South Atlantic and East Indies (including India), while the United States had three. One, the Southwest Pacific Command under General MacArthur, included Australia and most of the East Indies and the Philippines. The rest of the Pacific, or Pacific Ocean Area Command, fell to Nimitz, who added to his title of CINCPAC that of CINCPOA. His area was divided into three sub-areas, South Pacific, Central Pacific, and North Pacific.

The difficulty with this otherwise sensible arrangement was that trouble might well occur on the boundaries. Forces from one area might be operating in someone else's backyard. This is precisely what happened in the Battle of the Coral Sea. The American carrier forces, under Nimitz, fought the entire action in waters ostensibly belonging to MacArthur.

Even with these drawbacks, the arrangement was the most satisfactory one possible. In their respective areas of responsibility, MacArthur and Nimitz commanded all armies, air forces, marines, and naval forces of whatever Allied nationality. The ability to use multi-service and multi-national forces as weapons of a single commander's will outweighed all disadvantages that might be brought against the system. The

* Arthur Bryant, *The Turn of the Tide*, Doubleday & Sons, New York, 1957, p. 501.

resolute adherence to this principal of area command and the minimizing of international and inter-service rivalries led the way to victory.

The ordinary American knew little and cared less about such organizational niceties. He sat back appalled at the ravages the war was making on his daily life. On March 7 he learned he could no longer buy his secretary a new typewriter; two days later, that he would have to make his old radio and phonograph do for the duration.

Already aware that new tires were things of the past, and that the old family car and the bits of rubber now on its wheels would be all that they would get until the war was over, Eastern drivers found gasoline increasingly difficult to obtain. On March 19, gasoline stations in seventeen states,* the District of Columbia, Oregon, and Washington were cut twenty percent in gasoline deliveries. Three weeks later another reduction cut all filling stations to two-thirds of their average deliveries in December, January, and February. It was a time when it paid to know your friendly gas dealer. With short supplies of a highly desirable commodity, the inevitable happened in a few cases. Service declined; windshields remained dirty; oil and tires were not checked. A few dealers accepted bribes to "fill 'er up." Some expected women drivers "to be nice to them." By far the majority of filling station operators met the situation by continuing to serve regular customers as before. The stranger was often out of luck.

These cutbacks, of course, were a result of the U-boat depredations along the East Coast, particularly the losses in tankers. Already, to save both machinery and oil, the installation of new oil furnaces for homes in those same states had been banned by WPB edict. Householders who had expected to convert to oil burners shrugged their shoulders and ordered a few more tons of coal.

Homeowners had still another blow in April when the WPB called a halt to all "non-essential" home building. Practically no new homes were "essential," so the price of the older ones rose and rose. The story is told that a family living in

* Maine, New Hampshire, Vermont, Rhode Island, Connecticut, Massachusetts, New York, New Jersey, Pennsylvania, Delaware, Maryland, Virginia, West Virginia, North Carolina, South Carolina, Georgia, and Florida.

Washington had purchased a home in 1939 for $7,000. In 1942, the husband being then in the service, they sold it for $11,000. Eighteen months later, on being ordered back to Washington, they found the same house on the market and bought it again for $15,000. At the end of the war they sold it once more, this time for $18,000.

Washington was becoming a crowded city. Businessmen, dollar-a-year men, expediters, lobbyists, civil servants, clerks, typists, diplomats, soldiers, sailors, knaves and fools, heroes and heroines, inventors, press agents, patriots, grafters, prostitutes (both professional and amateur) descended like starlings and cried for food, drink, lodging, and recognition. Official Washington's pecking order, never stable at best, became a chaos. The man who shared a room with you at a modest hotel might be a nobody or the head of a large corporation. The "Battle of Pennsylvania Avenue" was as fiercely contested as most battles in the war. Its victories were good rooms, a table in a good restaurant, recognition by the *maître d'hôtel* at the Mayflower or Shoreham, or an appointment with a big Governmental official. Its defects were fleabag accommodations, dinner in a quickie restaurant or a drugstore, and a dismal trip home by bus or day coach, sleeping car and airline reservations, like other spoils, going to the victors.

War production was still the most vital concern in the nation's capital. Every advance against the enemy depended on it. In the WPB, Donald Nelson was at last beginning to see the fruits of his decisions taken on his assuming office. Three fundamental problems faced him, although only two directly concerned his office: (1) the equitable distribution of production contracts (primarily a function of the armed services) with the assignment of necessary priorities, (2) the maintenance of labor peace, and (3) the maintenance of stable prices.

At the end of March, Congress gave WPB the necessary authority to assure orderly production by passing the Second War Powers Bill, which established criminal penalties for violation of priorities orders. At the same time, it gave the President vastly greater powers of seizure of industry whenever management or labor proved recalcitrant.

A few days earlier, Nelson, had helped to ensure labor stability by urging Congress to keep the wage and hours bill intact. Amendments had threatened to antagonize both the workers and the factory managers. Nelson, meeting with Philip

121

Murray, president of the C.I.O., and William Green, president of the A.F. of L., won their concurrence to a forty-hour week at base pay with time-and-a-half for any sixth consecutive day or for work over eight hours on any given day. In return, these two major labor leaders gave Congress a pledge that no strike for any cause would be called or tolerated for the duration of the war.*

The third item of concern, prices, was not the responsibility of WPB, but of Leon Henderson's Office of Price Administration. In January the OPA had been given authority to take the necessary steps to combat inflation. On April 28, the office acted. In a sweeping order it froze prices of every major item, including rents, affecting the cost of living.

The base price set was that of March. It became effective at the wholesale level on May 11, and at the retail a week later. It included everything—shoes and sealing wax and cabbages, if not ships and kings, the two last being subject to government negotiation.

"Each and every one of us," said Mr. Roosevelt in a broadcast to the nation, "will have to give up many things to which we are accustomed. We shall have to live our lives with less."

With more money in workers' pockets than ever before and less to spend it on, stern anti-inflation measures became essential. It was estimated that the cost of living had risen at least seven hundred million dollars in January and that the rate was increasing. The Government urged increased taxes to siphon off earnings,** and Victory bonds became weapons in using up loose funds.

Victory Bonds came in all shapes and sizes. There were some priced at $10,000 for the big investor and others down to $500. The most widely sold was the Series E, priced at $18.75,

---

* In March the Department of Labor reported that forty percent of the nation's war plants were operating over a hundred and sixty hours a week, seventy-five percent a hundred and twenty hours or more, and only ten percent sixty hours or less. Further operations were held back by shortage of raw materials in many cases. For that reason one aircraft factory had to cut down to a forty-hour week. The average worker was on the job forty-eight to fifty hours a week.

** On March 15, General Motors sent the Bureau of Internal Revenue what was believed to be the largest check ever written up to that time: $71,800,000, for their first quarterly installment.

$37.50, and $75. They would mature in ten years and have then a value of $25, $50, and $100. They could be bought at any bank or post office or through payroll-savings plans. The interest rate was low, but the loyalty appeal was high.

To stimulate sales, bond rallies became widespread. Often these featured notables from show business: Bob Hope, Bing Crosby, Jack Benny, Carole Lombard (before her tragic death), Jimmy Durante, Jimmy Dorsey, to name only a few. Hostesses featured "Bond Dances," where the purchase of a bond was the ticket of admission, with a further purchase required for each dance.

Schoolchildren were urged to buy bonds through Bond Stamps available at post offices. They cost a dime, a quarter, or half a dollar. You pasted them in a booklet supplied free with the first stamp, and when it was full, the booklet could be redeemed for an $18.75 bond with a maturity value of $25.

On one festive occasion, an enterprising young lady featured a "Bond Stamp Strip Tease." Pasting War Bond Stamps all over her otherwise nude body, she allowed delighted patrons to pull them off one by one at fifty cents a pull.

The average citizen bought his bonds and was less disturbed by shortages than by uncertainty. He knew he could buy no new tires. So he would recap those he had. No, said OPA—there was a shortage of recapping materials. At least, then, he had the present tires. Yes, but—said OPA. Private tires might have to be requisitioned for doctors, policemen, firemen. Take a taxi? They might not last much longer. Do you need a new suit? Get one, but with only one pair of trousers, and no patch pockets, no vest, no cuffs, no pleats. Does milady need new stockings? There were no silk ones to be had, and nylons were selling for up to twenty dollars a pair. Later the price went up, for they were available only on the black market. Should you grow a victory garden? Yes, said WPB. No, said the Agricultural Administration. The only thing to do was to stay home, have a drink (not too much, for alcohol was going into war service, too), read, or write a letter to a son in the service (if you don't use too much electricity for lights).

If you wanted to buy a used car, you could expect to pay at least a hundred dollars over the "book" price—much more if the car had good tires. Chevrolets of 1939 vintage were fetching $595 on the average; a year earlier, the same car could have been had for a hundred dollars less. Cars of the 1941 line were selling at or above the new-car list price. Even jalopies were in demand; they might have good tires on them. Said a Detroit used-car dealer, "You would think this salesroom was a mosque to see all those guys down on their hands and knees looking at tires."

The latest thing in writing was the "V-letter." Written on one side of one sheet, the letter was microfilmed and the film sent by air to posts overseas. There an enlarged print was delivered to the addressee. Reason? To save cargo space and handling en route. Also, if the roll of film was lost in transit, another could be sent. "V-mail" was never very popular with the soldiers and sailors. It lacked the personal touch; there was no way of microfilming the perfume many girls were accustomed to sprinkle on the letters they sent to their men overseas.

Men—more men. The demands of war were insatiable. On farms, in factories, in the services, the needs grew, but the supply was shorter. Already all men from twenty to forty-four had been registered. Soon the age would be extended to sixty-five. Those who had received deferments were reviewed. Men with new wives or wives capable of supporting themselves heard the summons of their draft boards. The Army lowered its physical requirements. Vision as poor as 20/200 was acceptable if correctable to 20/40. The rule was: if, in preliminary examinations, men seemed sound they would go to be given complete physicals by the Army. Even men with no teeth might find themselves in khaki.

In hope of winning commissions or being taken by the Navy, many volunteers tried to beat the physicals. To lower blood pressure, take a bromide. To gain weight, eat bananas and drink a lot of water just before the examination; if the examination was too protracted, these volunteers found themselves in considerable discomfort. Memorize the eye chart and drink carrot juice to pass the eye examination. One enthusiastic applicant had memorized the eye chart, which was mounted on the back of a door. As he was happily reading it, a nurse opened the door. He went right on reading.

War demands brought job opportunities on a scale never known before. The rich got poorer through higher taxes, and the poor got richer—especially blue-collar workers. Caught in the middle, as usual, were white-collar employees, clerks, typists, middle-grade executives. Maids and houseworkers disappeared; they had become riveters or welders or truck drivers.

In April, in an attempt to bring some order into the manpower mess, the President established the War Manpower Commission under the former Federal Security Administrator, Paul V. McNutt. The Commission, a nine-man board, resembled a directorship of a holding company, including in its membership WPB Director Nelson, the Secretaries of War, Navy, Agriculture, and Labor, as well as representatives of Selective Service and the Civil Service. The Commission was supposed to have the power to govern the manpower policies for everyone except members of the armed forces, to train workers, and to move them from non-essential to essential jobs. It also included womanpower in its purview, although officials shrank from the idea of compulsion in dealing with women.

That same week the Bureau of Economic Warfare under Vice President Wallace and Milo Perkins was given full powers for control of stockpiling. This activity, a stepchild of WPB, had gravitated to Jesse Jones's Reconstruction Finance Corporation. The RFC had moved too slowly for the President, and he removed stockpiling authority from Jones's too conservative hands.

By this time the major organizations for production and for the economy had been established. Dubbed "Roosevelt's War Cabinet," the chairmen were the virtual dictators of nearly every phase of the nonmilitary side of American life. If they had ever met as a "cabinet," President Roosevelt would have seen gathered around the table Donald M. Nelson, Chairman of WPB, Leon Henderson of OPA, Henry A. Wallace and Milo Perkins of BEW, and Paul V. McNutt of WMC. In the wonderful world of Washington, these men controlled not only the economy of the country but also each other, for in almost every case each man was a member of someone else's commission, board, bureau, or office. It was a very companionable system, but, strangely enough, it got the work done.

At the end of April the United States had taken most of the steps necessary for waging war. The commissions, offices, bureaus were in being. The legislation was on the books. Industry was well on its way to conversion to total war production. Consumers were learning to get along without safety pins and typewriters, rubber bands and tires, metal-tipped shoe laces and new oil burners, gasoline and new radios.

Yet, behind it all, a level of malaise existed. No one was satisfied with the way things were going. War news was the story of defeat succeeded by disaster. People felt that Washington was indulging in politics as usual, afraid to get on with the job. They called for leadership and got another alphabetical creation. The peak was reached at the end of the month with the establishment of PWPGSJSISIACWPB.* At the same time, Washington officials feared that the public was not ready for hard truths, did not know "that there was a war on," needed to be spoon-fed. If the mutual distrust continued, it could vastly hurt the progress of the war.

The nation turned a psychological corner on April 18 when Army bombers under the command of Lieutenant Colonel Jimmy Doolittle made the first attack on Tokyo. President Roosevelt announced that they had come from "Shangri-la," the mythical monastery in James Hilton's novel *Lost Horizon*. The raid revived flagging morale in the country. At last, at long last, something positive had been done.

CHAPTER FIVE

Westward to the Rising Sun

> *This battle fares like to the morning's war,*
> *When dying clouds contend, . . .*
> Shakespeare,
> Part Three of King Henry the Sixth

That runway's only five hundred feet!" yelled Captain Charles R. Greening, USAAF.

There was no mistake, Lieutenant Colonel James H. Doolittle assured him. The twenty-four crews, volunteers for an unknown, dangerous mission, would have to get used to quick, short takeoffs.

---

* Pipe, Wire Products and Galvanized Steel Jobbers Subcommittee of the Iron and Steel Industry Advisory Committee of the War Production Board.

Actually, the runway was eight hundred feet in length, marked with flags at the four-hundred-fifty-foot mark and every fifty feet thereafter. Colonel Doolittle drove his crews to get them used to lifting a B-25 medium bomber in the shortest possible space, to take off and fly to an "unknown destination." No word could be allowed to leak. A single careless statement could imperil the mission. Until the last moment, only a handful of men knew. Target? Tokyo.

The inspiration for the raid was born as a result of a casual remark of President Roosevelt a day or so after Pearl Harbor. Roosevelt said he wanted to bomb Japan as soon as possible to pay back in some small measure for the sneak attack.

On January 10, Admiral King and some of his staff were discussing how the Navy might retaliate after its recent humiliation. A carrier raid on Japan could not be considered. With the range of carrier planes limited to about three hundred miles, the risk of taking the precious flattops close to Japan was insupportable, especially in view of the sinking of the *Prince of Wales* and *Repulse*. The gloom was thick.

Then Captain Francis Low, the operations officer, had a flash of inspiration. Why don't we fly long-range Army bombers from the deck of a carrier?

Could it be done? No one knew.

Then find out, ordered King.

The next day Captain Donald W. ("Wu") Duncan, USN, King's air officer, grappled with the problem. What kind of plane had the right capabilities? Could it fly far enough with a heavy enough bomb load? If so, could it be fitted to a carrier's deck? Would its right wing clear the island without the left wheel running off the edge of the flight deck? Could it lift into the air in the length of deck available? Could it land back aboard?

These were some of the problems Captain Duncan grappled with. Since he planned for the carrier to approach no closer than five hundred miles to Japan, he needed a plane with more than twice that range. Twenty-four hundred miles, he decided, was the minimum, especially if, as he was sure, no Army bomber could land on a carrier. In that case they would have to bomb Japan and then fly on to China. Twenty-four hundred miles was none too much range. Some of the planes would have to fly at least two thousand miles, as it was. And if the force was discovered before they got within five hundred miles of Japan, the planes would have to go early. The alternative was to scrap the mission.

By this time Duncan had decided there was no chance at all of getting the planes back aboard, especially as he had no intention of keeping the carrier waiting near the Japanese coast for the planes to get back. The carrier would launch the planes and then clear out. China it would be. Or perhaps the Russians could be persuaded to accept sixteen Lend-Lease aircraft delivered in a somewhat used condition via Tokyo. The trouble with this idea was that Russia was not at war with Japan.

The twin-engined Army B-25 seemed to Duncan the only aircraft with both the range and bomb capacity suitable for the mission. These aircraft had a gross weight of fifty-six thousand pounds, with a sixty-seven-foot-six-inch wingspread. They had a top speed of over three hundred miles an hour. In their normal condition, they could carry a ton of bombs.

At this point the Chief of Staff of the Army Air Forces, General Henry H. Arnold, was brought into the picture. He enthusiastically supported the project and agreed to provide the aircraft and see to the pilots' training.

The man picked to head the mission was Jimmy Doolittle. An aviation pioneer, Doolittle had been a stunt man, a test pilot, an all-round expert in every kind of plane. He had supplemented his practical experience with a scientific education at Massachusetts Institute of Technology. From every point of view, he was the man for the job.

When Doolittle reported to Arnold's office, wondering about the sudden summons, the General wasted no words.

"Will you bomb Tokyo?" he demanded.

"Yes, sir."

Arnold then revealed the basic plan and told him to get going on it. After reviewing Captain Duncan's ideas, Doolittle began to add details of his own: how to lighten the plane, how to increase its fuel capacity. At Wright Feld, Ohio, Doolittle managed to lift a modified, fully loaded B-52 off the runway in the space of five hundred feet.

That done, he set about recruiting his crews. Although the deck capacity of the *Hornet*, the carrier assigned to the mission, limited the strike to sixteen aircraft, he decided to train twenty-four crews, to allow for illness, accident, and the thousand other things that might go wrong. The volunteers were drawn from the 17th Bombardment Group and from the 89th

Reconnaissance Squadron. There were far more volunteers than Doolittle needed, even though they could be told nothing about the mission other than that it was dangerous, important, and interesting.

In a few days, the twenty-four volunteer crews reported with their B-25s at Eglin Field, Florida, for intensive training. Mystified, the men watched their planes being modified for the mission. All nonessential gear was removed, including many things that seemed quite essential to the pilots. Additional gas tanks filled much of the fuselage space, bringing the capacity of the plane up from 646 gallons to 1,141. Dummy tail guns were installed to discourage pursuers. The bombload was to be two thousand pounds.

"Drop the landing flaps and pour on the coal." This was the gist of the takeoff instruction given the pilots by naval Lieutenant Henry Miller, assigned as special instructor in carrier operations. Time after time they practiced taking off from the short runway with ever increasing loads. Two planes were lost in the exercises, but there were no losses among the air crews. Eventually every one of the pilots was able to lift his protesting plane into the air within five hundred feet when aided by a 30-knot head wind. This amount of wind would be provided by the carrier's speed.

The training went on. Navigation, bombing, cross-country, night flying, gunnery, bombing, more bombing, minimum-altitude approaches and minimum-altitude pull-outs. On the ground they studied carrier procedures, celestial and dead reckoning navigation, first aid. They got shots against every disease they had ever heard of and some they hadn't. One sergeant complained that if he was hit in action he would bleed serum.

Four weeks was all the time the rigorous schedule would allow them. Then came the orders to fly their stripped B-25s to McClellan Field, Sacramento, California, for a check on their planes and final liberties, the last nights Stateside.

A few days earlier, Admiral Halsey had received a summons to Admiral Nimitz's headquarters. Captain Duncan was waiting and gave Halsey a rundown on the proposed operation, including the Navy's role.

"Do you believe it would work, Bill?" asked Nimitz.

"They'll need a lot of luck," replied Halsey.

"Are you willing to take them out there?"

"Yes, I am."

"Good," said Nimitz. "It's all yours!"

On April 1, with the *Hornet* tied up to a dock at Alameda Naval Air Station, the planes landed nearby and, one by one, were picked up by cranes and hoisted aboard. Only sixteen of them were to go. Disappointed plane crews looked on in envy. Some boarded the *Hornet* as standbys, hoping they would get a chance later.

After she was loaded, the *Hornet* moved out into San Francisco Bay and anchored. The sixteen Army planes were parked in takeoff position, the tails of the last two extending out over the water. The skilled deck crews lashed them down and covered their vital parts with canvas to protect them from the salt spray. After being shown their quarters, most of the Army personnel and ship's company went ashore for one last night on the town. They visited families, those fortunate enough to have them living near. Others ranged from the Top of the Mark on Nob Hill to the fleshpots of the Embarcadero and lower Market Street. Some saw the movie *Joan of Paris* at the Golden Gate Theater; the stage show featured Dick Powell and Jack Teagarden's orchestra. Some watched strippers in nightclubs and at the Liberty Follies at Broadway and Stockton.

San Francisco was giving the boys a typical send-off.

The next morning, men still somewhat bleary-eyed from the night before heard the wail of the boatswain's pipe and the word on the loudspeakers. "Now go to your stations, all the special sea details! All departments make all preparations for getting underway! Make your reports to the Officer of the Deck on the bridge!"

On the *Hornet*'s bridge, Captain Marc A. Mitscher looked down on his strange-appearing flight deck. To make room for the B-25s, the *Hornet*'s own planes had been sent below to the hangar deck, where they occupied every available bit of space, some even being suspended from the overhead. Until she was rid of her strange deck load, she would be helpless to defend herself. This was the reason Halsey and the *Enterprise* were going along—to provide air cover on the way.

At 1130, the *Hornet,* accompanied by the heavy cruiser

Vincennes, the light cruiser *Nashville*, the oiler *Cimarron*, and the destroyers *Gwin*, *Grayson*, *Meredith* and *Monssen* passed under the Golden Gate Bridge. Two hours later they had cleared the Farallon Islands and set course 294°, speed 16 knots.

The bullhorn blared.

"Now hear this," called the executive officer. "This force is bound for Tokyo."

Cheers rang through the ships. Navy men looked with respect at their Army passengers. Some decided to see if they could figure out a way to go in one of the planes.

On the way northwest, the pilots and crews received indoctrination lectures: target assignments, contingency plans, Japanese customs, a few words of Chinese to identify them as American fliers. There was review of navigation, of target identification, of carrier procedures.

On April 13, in latitude 38° North, 180° West, the *Hornet* group rendezvoused with Halsey's *Enterprise*, accompanied by the cruisers *Northampton* and *Salt Lake City*, the oiler *Sabine*, and the destroyers *Balch*, *Benham*, *Banning* and *Ellet*. Task Force 16, now complete, set a westerly course through worsening weather. *Enterprise* planes provided a combat air patrol and sent scouts ahead to watch for Japanese pickets. As the ships drove toward Tokyo, the radios were no longer able to pick up Stateside broadcasts and the off-duty men amused themselves by listening to Tokyo Rose and other English-language propaganda broadcasts. On April 16 they listened open-mouthed as Radio Tokyo announced: "Reuters, British news agency, has announced that three American bombers have dropped bombs on Tokyo. This is a laughable story. They know it is absolutely impossible for enemy bombers to get within five hundred miles of Tokyo. Instead of worrying about such foolish things, the Japanese people are enjoying the fine spring sunshine and the fragrance of cherry blossoms."

The ships sailed on westward. On April 17, when they were a thousand miles east of Japan, all ships fueled from the *Sabine* and *Cimarron*. Then, at 1400, leaving them and the eight destroyers behind, the carriers and the cruisers set speed at 23 knots for the final run-in.

All went well until early on the morning of April 18, when the radars on the carriers began picking up Japanese fishing vessels doing double duty as pickets. Avoiding the first few by

131

radical changes of course, the force was finally spotted by a vessel that loomed up only six miles ahead. Before the *Nashville* was able to sink her, she got off a warning.

This was it.

The raid was compromised. Halsey had to decide whether to launch at once or to scrub the attack. The force was still six hundred and fifty miles from Tokyo.

Fifteen minutes after the discovery, at 0800, Halsey sent a signal to the *Hornet:* LAUNCH PLANES X TO COL DOOLITTLE AND HIS GALLANT COMMAND GOOD LUCK AND GOD BLESS YOU.

Alerted by the earlier sightings, the B-25 crews had already had breakfast and assembled in the ready room. Doolittle hastened in with last-minute orders: fly low to avoid detection; hit military targets only; avoid the Emperor's Palace at all costs; save gasoline—you will be taking off beyond the limits of safety. Head for Chuchow in China. Fly as far as you can, and walk the rest of the way. Check your pockets for all items that might reveal where the raid came from. Name, rank, and serial number, if captured.

"Army personnel, man your planes." The bullhorn blared its summons. Gathering up their flight packs, the crewmen dashed topside.

On the windswept flight deck, their clothing flapping, the men made their way to their planes. One member of a relief crew offered a buddy $150 to let him go in his place. The offer was refused.

Every man in his station, the pilots kept their eyes on the yellow-jerseyed plane controllers, men who would guide each one to his takeoff spot.

The *Hornet* turned into the wind. Men exposed on the flight deck leaned into it as the *Hornet*'s speed and the wind combined to take nearly 45 knots off the speed the planes would have to make on the flight deck.

"Stand clear of propellers!" roared the bullhorn. Then— "Start engines!"

Propellers turned over, engines coughed, and black smoke poured from the exhausts. Soon thirty-two propellers were flashing over smoothly, glinting in the morning light.

The red flag in the air control station changed to green. The first plane control petty officer raised his arms and beckoned. Doolittle slowly advanced his throttles. His plane moved forward. The plane controller passed him on to the next and signaled to Lieutenant Travis Hoover, then in turn to Lieutenant Robert M. Gray, Lieutenant Everett W. Holstrum, and the rest.

Colonel Doolittle's plane reached the flight deck officer. He checked the alignment of the plane, saw that the nose wheel was exactly on the stripe painted as a guide on the *Hornet's* deck, and raised his hand, the fist clenched. Doolittle set his brakes harder. The flight deck officer made a whirling motion with his right hand. Doolittle advanced to full throttle. The roar of engines made it impossible to hear anything else. Doolittle checked his gauges and gave a thumbs-up signal. Choosing his moment so that the pitching bow would be on the rise just as the plane got there, the flight deck officer swept his arm toward the bow. Doolittle, holding his throttles jammed full, released his brakes. The freed plane sprang forward. Faster and faster the B-25 rolled down the deck.

"He'll never make it!" yelled a Navy pilot.

As Admiral Halsey wrote later, "There wasn't a man topside in the task force who didn't help sweat him into the air."

At the end of the run, the *Hornet's* bow slammed down, falling away from Doolittle's plane. The B-25 hung in the air, seemed to hesitate, and then flew on. Doolittle was airborne.

The time was 0825.

There was no time for congratulations. Hoover's plane was poised at the flight deck officer's station. Down swept the relentless arm. Hoover rolled down the flight deck. He was off. Then Gray. And Holstrum. And Captain David M. Jones. And Lieutenant Dean C. Hallmark. And Lieutenant Ted W. Lawson. And Captain Edward J. York. And Lieutenant Harold F. Watson. And Lieutenant Richard O. Joyce. And Lieutenants Charles R. Greening, William M. Bower, Edgar E. McElroy. And Major John A. Hilger. And Lieutenants Donald G. Smith and William G. Farrow.

The entire launch took fifty-nine minutes, an average of one plane every three minutes and forty-one seconds. This was slow by Navy standards for naval aircraft, but it was remarkable considering that none of the pilots had ever taken off from a carrier before.

At 0925 Halsey ordered a change in fleet course and axis to 090 (due east) and began his retirement at 25 knots. On the way out, the task force spotted and attacked a total of sixteen more picket vessels. A prisoner taken from one told a grim story. He had summoned his captain to report, "Two of our beautiful carriers ahead, sir."

The captain came on deck and looked at them a long time through his binoculars.

"They're beautiful," he said, "but they're not ours."

Then he went below and put a bullet into his head.

Doolittle and his men sped westward, skimming the wave tops. The farther they flew, the more the weather improved. There was nothing to hide them as they sped over fishing boats by the hundred. At any moment they expected fighters to jump them.

The Japanese had scheduled a practice alert for that morning. It ended just as the first of Doolittle's raiders came, so most people thought his attack was a part of the drill. Thus the psychological impact of the raid was much weakened as far as the Japanese people were concerned.

Although the picket's warning was picked up in Tokyo, Doolittle and his men gained complete surprise. Naval officials believed that it would be the next day before the carriers could launch, if they were foolhardy enough to come on in the face of the alert.

Thirteen of the planes attacked Tokyo. Their bombs began dropping at 1215 as the Japanese responded with only feeble defenses. Radio station JOAK suddenly went off the air. The bombers dropped their load and went on, pilots anxiously watching their gas gauges. The other three planes were assigned to Nagoya, Osaka, and Kobe. They carried out small incendiary bombs, which did considerable fire damage. Although all bombs were aimed strictly at military targets, inevitably some fell on civilian installations. For this, three of the fliers paid with their lives.

All of the planes left the coast of Japan safely. Then they began running into difficulties. Fuel consumption was higher than anticipated, and the coast of China looked farther and farther away. Flying on into the night, the pilots looked for signs of the shore—lights, fires, the radio beacon from Chuchow airfield. But something had gone wrong. The Chinese had not been alerted, and when a few bombers actually got that far, the Chinese thought it was an air raid and put out the lights.

All sixteen planes were lost. One landed safely at

Vladivostok, where the Russians, who were not at war with Japan, interned the plane and crew. Fifteen months later, the men made their way to Persia and freedom.

Five men were killed in parachuting from their planes; others with broken bones and other injuries were cared for and passed on to points whence they could be sent home. Eight men in all were taken prisoner by the Japanese. After merciless interrogations, torture, medical neglect, and a mock trial, all eight were condemned to death. The Emperor "graciously" commuted the sentence of five to life imprisonment. They spent all but seventy days of the next forty months in solitary confinement. One died.

On the afternoon of October 15, 1942, in a cemetery near Shanghai, Lieutenant Dean E. Hallmark, Lieutenant William G. Farrow, and Sergeant Harold A. Spatz were tied to crosses and executed by firing squads. Their supreme sacrifice was a result of the panic experienced by high Japanese officials because of the raid. Although they kept the Japanese people from knowing of the attack, they could not keep it from affecting their thinking. Several bad decisions grew from their panic.

The retiring task force was pursued by Japanese planes and ships, but got away unscathed. The *Hornet,* her flight deck freed, was able to share normal combat air patrol and search duties with the *Enterprise.* The trip back passed uneventfully. On April 25, one week after the launch, the force entered Pearl Harbor. All hands were looking forward to a rest. But it was not to be. Trouble was brewing in the South Pacific. Five days after they arrived, the *Enterprise* and the *Hornet* sailed for the Coral Sea.

They were too late. While they were still a thousand miles away, the first real carrier battle in the history of the world took place.

* * * * *

The Coral Sea. The very name suggests the romance of the South Seas, of the explorations of Cook and Bligh, Bougainville and Mendaña. Visions of nodding palm trees in the moonlight where bare-breasted maidens dance languorously vie with glimpses of the perfect blue of the tropical sea unbeset by the violence of nature's moods. South of the Solomon Islands and down to the reef-fringed coast of Australia extends this beautiful sea, hemmed in on the east by the Santa Cruz and New Hebrides Islands and by New Caledonia. It was into this, one of the most heavenly areas of the world, that the violence of war was about to intrude.

Two lines of action presented themselves to the triumphant Japanese. Their advances into the Resources Area had been made with so little cost to themselves that it was easy to imagine that no matter what they tried, they would accomplish it with ease. The "victory disease," as Japanese critics later called it, infected everyone, from private to general, from seaman to admiral, from peasant to Prime Minister.

The Japanese had estimated that it would take six months to complete the conquest of the Philippines, Malaya, and the Netherlands East Indies. In the event, this time had been cut in half, and rather than accept a mere passive, defensive role, the Japanese believed that additional expansion would extend their defensive perimeter and further discourage the United States to the point of accepting a peace proposal that would leave Japan with her war objective intact.

Debate over future moves by Japan was extensive and sometimes bitter. Since any operations into the South or Southwest Pacific were largely Navy shows, it was in the Navy that the argument became hottest. Theoretically, the Naval General Staff planned overall naval strategy, but the practice at this time was otherwise. Because of his immense prestige, Admiral Isoroku Yamamoto, Commander in Chief, Combined Fleet, exerted much influence in determining future plans. It had been his determination that brought about the Pearl Harbor attack. The success of the opening months of the campaign further enhanced his power, and his headquarters arrogated to themselves strategic planning normally the duty of the Naval General Staff.

As Combined Fleet Headquarters saw it, Japan's next move should be to the east. The seizure of bases in the Aleutians and the capture of Midway Island, they felt, would bring about a decisive fleet engagement with the remnants of the American Navy in the waters west of Hawaii.

Yet, when Yamamoto's representatives presented this plan at Naval General Staff Headquarters, it met with considerable—even vehement—opposition. The eyes of General Staff planners were turned south, not east. Australia was the target. At first they had considered actual invasion of the subcontinent, but the Army would have none of it. Accordingly, the Naval General Staff planners looked to means of isolating Australia, for they feared it would be used by the Allies as a springboard for future advances against Japan. To accomplish Japanese purposes would require the capture of eastern New Guinea, the Solomon Islands, New Caledonia, and the Fijis. They could see no point in wasting energy in the northern and central Pacific areas, particularly to seize bases that probably could not be held.

The dispute between Combined Fleet and Naval General Staff became acrimonious. Neither side would budge. Then two events took place that forced the decision. The first: Admiral Yamamoto threatened to resign unless his Midway operation was carried out. The second: the Doolittle raid convinced the Naval General Staff that the Americans must be driven as far east, as far from Japan, as possible. They, therefore, gave a reluctant approval to the Midway plan. But, since two months must elapse before it could be put into effect, they decided to have their cake and eat it too by taking on the first phase of the southern plan before the Midway operation. They would seize Tulagi in the southern Solomons and Port Moresby on the southeastern coast of New Guinea.

The island of New Guinea looks something like a misshapen sea bird swimming westward north of Australia. The western end the Dutch have named Vogelkop—bird head. The island, almost twelve hundred miles in length, is even to this date largely unexplored. Many of the natives still live in the Stone Age. A few civilized villages cling precariously to its perimeter, but inland all is jungle or mountain. The Owen Stanley Mountains form the bird's spine and extend up to nearly seventeen thousand feet. In the tail of New Guinea, the Papuan peninsula, the Japanese had already taken Lae and Salamaua. Conquest of Port Moresby would place northern Australian cities within bombing range, while a Japanese base in Tulagi would threaten American establishments in the New Hebrides.

With smug complacency, the Japanese set out on these two ventures, to the south and to the east. The thought of failure never entered their minds. Yet fail they did. In both ventures.

After his successful attack on Pearl Harbor and a period of support operations in the Resources Area, Admiral Chuichi Nagumo had led his carrier forces into the Indian Ocean, where they played havoc with British installations and sank the cruisers *Cornwall* and *Dorsetshire* and the carrier *Hermes*. On leaving the Indian Ocean, Nagumo detached two of his carriers, *Shokaku* and *Zuikaku,* to proceed to Truk. The other four returned to Japan to prepare for the Midway operation. The *Shokaku* and *Zuikaku* would provide the muscle in the forthcoming MO operation against Tulagi and Port Moresby.

In overall command was Vice Admiral Shigeyoshi Inouye, who established his headquarters at Rabaul. With typical Japanese fondness for the complex, no fewer than six naval forces and a naval air force were assigned. It was as delicately balanced a plan as is a child's sand castle. An unexpected blow could bring it down in ruins.

The first target was Tulagi. A small force of transports, destroyers, minelayers and lesser naval types under Rear Admiral Kiyahide Shima made an unopposed landing on Tulagi across from Guadalcanal on May 3 and began to establish a seaplane base. Meanwhile, the Port Moresby Invasion Group from Rabaul headed for the Jomard Passage between the tail of New Guinea and the Louisiade Islands to the east. This group was covered by land-based air from Rabaul, by a Support Group, which also had the job of establishing a seaplane base in the Louisiades, and a Covering Group under Rear Admiral Aritomo Goto. A powerful Striking Group, commanded by Vice Admiral Takeo Takagi and built around the two carriers *Zuikaku* and *Shokaku,* was to sweep around the eastern end of the Solomons and enter the Coral Sea by the back door.

D-day for Port Moresby was May 7.

The Japanese never made it.

In Pearl Harbor, Admiral Nimitz was keenly aware that something was brewing in the Coral Sea. As early as April 17, he had received intelligence that an invasion force would head for that area around May 3, protected by three carriers. That the intelligence was firm he had no doubt, for it was based on the reading of the code of the Japanese High Command's own messages.

Even when you know your enemy's intentions, it is not always easy to stop him, especially when your resources are limited and when the same intelligence tells you that the enemy is also brewing up something for the Central Pacific a month later.

Part of the problem would be one of command. Most of the Coral Sea lies in the area set aside as MacArthur's Southwest Pacific (SOWESPAC). However, agreement by the Joint

Chiefs of Staff had provided that any fleet action in MacArthur's area would come under the strategic control of Nimitz as Commander in Chief of the Pacific Fleet (CINCPAC). On the other hand, Nimitz would not have control of the land-based air from Australia; he could only request attacks or searches. He might or might not get them.

Ruefully thinking of the two fine carriers even then approaching Tokyo, Nimitz cast about for forces to stop the Moresby thrust. Already in the South Pacific were the *Yorktown* with five cruisers and five destroyers and the *Lexington* lightly escorted by four destroyers. These two groups he ordered to rendezvous with Rear Admiral Frank Jack Fletcher in the *Yorktown* in overall command. From Australia, "MacArthur's Navy" contributed the Australian cruisers *Australia* and *Hobart* under the brilliant British Rear Admiral J. C. Crace. The American cruiser *Chicago* and two destroyers were also with Crace's force.

There was little else that Nimitz could scrape together. A fueling group built around two oilers, a seaplane search group at Noumea, a handful of submarines that might be useful, and more or less cooperation from SOWESPAC land-based air— these were the limits of Nimitz's resources. The *Saratoga* was still at Puget Sound undergoing repairs from her torpedoing in January. At one point Nimitz even considered ordering the repaired Pearl Harbor battleships out to lend their weight. He quickly discarded the notion, since the vulnerable battlewagons could no more keep up with the *Yorktown* and *Lexington* than a boy on a bicycle can keep up with Le Mans racer. Halsey's *Enterprise* and *Hornet*, Task Force 16, would make all the difference if they could get there in time. They left Pearl Harbor on April 30, with thirty-five hundred miles to go. If his force could make it in time, Halsey would take over command. But the battle was ended long before Task Force 16 arrived.

It was on these slender forces that Nimitz was able to collect that the American position in SOWESPAC must stand or fall.

On May 1, the *Lexington* and her consorts joined Fletcher's *Yorktown* group and came under his tactical command. They were some three hundred miles south of the eastern Solomons. Fletcher ordered both groups to fuel from the two oilers available. Crace, when he joined a little later, received the same orders.

Fueling at sea in those days was a slow and cumbersome

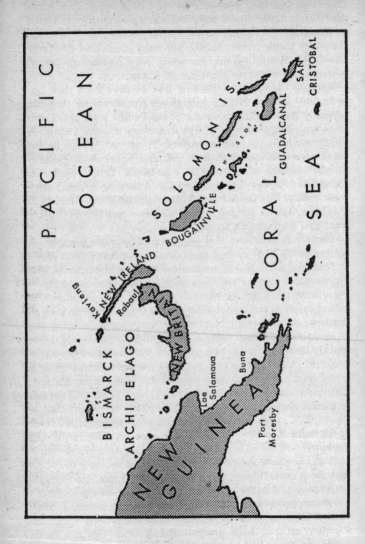

THE SOLOMON ISLANDS
AND THE BISMARCKS

140

practice, and this occasion was no exception. Rear Admiral Aubrey W. Fitch in the *Lexington,* given a bad estimate by his staff, informed Fletcher that he would not be done before noon on May 4. This information did not bother Fletcher unduly, for he had finished his own fueling on May 2, and he felt that the *Yorktown* could use the time scouting for the enemy while the *Lexington* finished up. Just about sunset on May 2, he pulled out, leaving Fitch to rendezvous with him at sunrise on May 4.

The Japanese landing at Tulagi at 0800 on May 3 surprised Fletcher, although it was eleven hours before he heard about it. Meanwhile the *Lexington* group had completed fueling a little after noon on the same day, almost twenty-four hours ahead of schedule. Feeling no urgency, and unable to break radio silence, Fitch decided to keep the rendezvous the next day without making any attempt to inform his superior. Why did he not send a plane to drop a message is one of the unanswered questions of the war.

When Fletcher learned that Japanese troops were landing troops at Tulagi, he set off to do something about it. He might have directed the *Lexington* to break off fueling and join him in the attack he proposed. He might have waited until the rendezvous and made the attack with both carriers. He did neither.

He sent the oiler *Neosho* and a destroyer to keep the rendezvous and tell Fitch to meet him at sunrise on May 5 at a point some three hundred miles south of Guadalcanal. Then, with these preliminaries attended to, the *Yorktown* group set off at high speed to the north to try to knock out the Tulagi landing.

The morning of May 4 came in drizzling and cold for the *Yorktown* group. A rare cold front had moved into the Coral Sea, bringing with it leaden skies, frequent rainsqualls, and southeast winds of up to 35 knots. At 0630, the *Yorktown* began launching a strike of twenty-eight SBD (Dauntless) dive bombers and twelve TBD (Devastator) torpedo planes. No fighters could be spared to accompany the strike, for the *Yorktown* carried only eighteen; all of them were needed to maintain a CAP (combat air patrol) over the formation.

After an uneventful run-in to the target, passing on the way over the jungle-filled wastes of Guadalcanal, the air squadrons broke out into clear weather over Savo Sound south of Tulagi. Attacking by squadrons as they arrived, the pilots smashed into everything they saw. Repeated strikes during the day raised the score in the pilots' minds, for they reported successes far beyond the fact. The tendency of pilots of all nations to overestimate their accomplishments was never eradicated during the war. Later, intelligence officers became more wary in accepting pilots' claims. But let only those who have known air combat criticize. None else can know the confusion, the speed, the shooting and being shot at, the kaleidoscopically changing picture. A split-second glimpse becomes tomorrow's headline and an entrenched national myth until corrected by skeptical historians years later.

"We found that harbor a busy place," reported an SBD pilot. "Everything was there, from cruisers to rafts. Lighters were carrying troops and equipment from the troopships to the shore. One of those troopships was at least a twenty-thousand-tonner, and the others in the six- to eight-thousand-ton class."

Only one transport, an 8000-tonner, was present. Minesweepers were called transports, and Shima's flagship, the minelayer *Okinoshima*, of 4400 tons, a light cruiser. The upshot of the battle was that three small minesweepers and four landing barges were sunk and two destroyers damaged. "The Tulagi operation was certainly disappointing," said Admiral Nimitz, "in terms of ammunition expended to results obtained."

Nevertheless, Fletcher's pilots were jubilant as they returned to the *Yorktown* and the carrier headed south to rejoin the *Lexington*.

Admiral Takagi's Striking Force with the two big carriers was racing to help out at Tulagi, but it was too far away. By the time Fletcher broke off the attack, the *Shokaku* and *Zuikaku* were still far out of range. Thus Fletcher got away with it.

The next morning the two American carriers were reunited in latitude 16° South, longitude 160° East. But they were not ready for operations, for the *Yorktown* now had to fuel, and Fletcher spent most of the day in this operation, the *Lexington* spending her sixth consecutive day in idleness. All this time she had steamed back and forth in a relatively small area of ocean south of the Solomons—a tempting of fate, in view of possible submarine or air attacks. The ships were south of the cold front, in perfect weather, affording excellent visibility to any would-be attacker.

As if on cue, a Japanese four-engine patrol plane from Rabaul flew near the formation, only to be shot down by the CAP.

When the plane failed to return to base, Admiral Inouye knew something was brewing, but he did not know the location of the American carriers, so he was helpless to act. Fletcher, meanwhile, continued fueling, completing the operation at 1930 and reversing course to the northwest to close the distance to Rabaul, whence he assumed the next Japanese moves would be coming.

While these events were transpiring, unsuspected by either Fletcher or Fitch, the Japanese Striking Force, half an hour earlier, had rounded the tip of San Cristobal Island and entered the Coral Sea.

The morning of May 6 found the American carrier force, now designated Task Force 17, steaming westward, while Takagi, having reached a position south of the central Solomons, turned south, directly toward Fletcher's track. But neither side knew of the other's presence.

Meanwhile, Fletcher, topping off his ships once more, was receiving reports from MacArthur's search planes of Japanese troopship movements toward the Jomard Passage, so in midafternoon he broke off fueling and headed northwestward once again to be in range of these new targets at dawn on May 7.

Takagi, too, had to fuel, which he did expeditiously on the afternoon of May 6. At this time the Japanese and American carrier forces were only seventy miles apart. Search and communication failures cost each side golden opportunities to catch the other with its planes down. A Japanese search plane had correctly reported Fletcher's position at 1100 that morning, but since the report went through Rabaul, Takagi did not receive it for twenty-four hours. Two search flights from the American carriers missed seeing Takagi. The morning patrol turned back just short of making contact, while the afternoon search saw nothing, for Takagi's force was now in the overcast that had sheltered the *Yorktown* two days earlier.

To the westward, the Japanese forces continued their advance toward Port Moresby, in spite of two fruitless bombing attacks by Army planes from Cloncurry, Australia. On the evening of May 6, all Japanese Port Moresby forces were poised for entry into the Jomard Passage.

That same day, May 6, over two thousand miles to the

northeast, the American flag was being hauled down. That date, the low point of the Pacific war, marked by missed opportunities in the Coral Sea, saw General "Skinny" Wainwright surrender the island fortress of Corregidor to the Japanese.

Fueling finally completed, Fletcher detached his remaining oiler *Neosho** with the destroyer *Sims* as escort to await the combatant ships at a rendezvous on the disengaged side. On arrival at "Point Rye" the next morning, May 7, the *Neosho*'s lookouts spotted carrier planes nearby. Hoping they were friendly, the crews of the *Neosho* and *Sims* awaited developments.

Unfortunately for the two American ships, the planes were Japanese. Their pilots were no better at recognition of ship types than the Americans had been over Tulagi. They promptly radioed back that they had spotted a carrier and a cruiser.

Poor *Neosho*. Poor *Sims*. Theirs was the unwelcome role of sacrificial victim. On them the full fury of the Japanese attack would fall.

Commander Carrier Division Five, Rear Admiral Tadaichi Hara in *Zuikaku*, made the actual decisions for the conduct of air operations under the general direction of Takagi. When the search plane report of sighting a carrier and cruiser came in, Hara accepted it completely and ordered an all-out attack with both bombers and torpedo planes.

A single plane went by the *Neosho* and *Sims* about 0900 followed by fifteen high-level bombers half an hour later. So far, no damage. An hour later another attack developed, and the *Sims* barely eluded a stick of bombs. Still no damage.

Toward noon their luck ran out. Thirty-six dive bombers made an attack on the "carrier" *Neosho*. The *Sims*, trying to guard the sluggish oiler, took three quarter-ton bombs. Two exploded in her engine room. She jacknifed and sank stern first in a matter of minutes.

While the pitifully few survivors of the *Sims* struggled in the water, the *Neosho* received the undivided attention of the aircraft. Soon she had been near-missed eight times and had taken seven direct hits. A plane crashed into her, and flaming

---

* The *Tippecanoe*, the other oiler, had been emptied by the *Lexington* group on May 3 and was detached then.

gasoline spewed over the decks. At this her skipper, Captain John S. Phillips, ordered, "Make preparations to abandon ship and stand by."

This was not an order to leave the ship. But, with shameful lack of discipline, many of her crew waited no longer. Cutting rafts and boats away, they scrambled to leave the stricken vessel, heedless of orders. Many of the men were brought back aboard by steadier crew members. Others of the fugitives were doomed to die in the water or from exposure in the rafts.

No further Japanese attacks developed that day. Her engines dead, her interior gutted, the *Neosho* remained afloat. For four days she drifted with the trade winds, a battered hulk, until she was sighted about noon on May 11 by a patrol plane. (The sighting might have come earlier if the *Neosho's* navigator had not made a fifty-mile error in plotting her position on the day of the attack. That afternoon the destroyer *Henley* found her and removed a hundred and twenty-three survivors, including some from the *Sims*. After searching for more than twenty-four hours for other survivors, the *Henley* gave up and went to Brisbane.*

Admiral Fletcher in the meantime had continued his north-westerly course throughout the night. On the morning of May 7, at sunrise, he turned north, at the same time detaching Admiral Crace's Support Group to close Jomard Passage and block the Japanese headed for Port Moresby.

This decision has been much criticized. By detaching three cruisers and three destroyers, Fletcher weakened an already minimal screen. If the firepower of Crace's six ships had been with the carriers, the tragic events of the next day might have been averted.

Fletcher afterwards stated that he had sent Crace on ahead so that even if he and his carriers were wiped out, there would still be a surface force ready to block the Japanese from their objective of Port Moresby. Perhaps Crace's ships drew attacks that might have been directed against the *Lexington* and *York-town*.

For draw attacks they did. The Japanese threw as much air power at them as they had against the *Prince of Wales* and

---

* Two days later the destroyer *Helm* found four more survivors of the *Sims* in four rafts. Sixty-four men who had been with them had died.

Repulse, but the result was the exact opposite. Not a ship was hit, as a result of Crace's brilliant maneuvering. Intense antiaircraft fire shot down five torpedo planes.

Scarcely had they beaten off the last Japanese attack when three more bombers appeared. Their bombs narrowly missed the destroyer *Farragut,* and as the planes sped away, the crew of the *Farragut* stared after them in amazement and rage. They were not Japanese. The attackers were B-26 Marauders of the U.S. Army Air Force from Townsville, Australia. There can be no possible doubt of it. Not only were they recognized from the ships, but photographs taken by the planes themselves reveal that it was Crace's force they attacked. But air officers on MacArthur's staff refused to admit it. They even refused to discuss plans for preventing such errors in the future. This is service rivalry with a vengeance!

No more attacks developed. Crace continued to move westward until midnight, when he learned that the Port Moresby Invasion Force had reversed course. Receiving no further instructions from Fletcher, Crace decided to head for Australia.

The Japanese Port Moresby Invasion Force had turned back. It was almost unbelievable. How—why—had it happened?

After he had detached Crace and turned north on the morning of May 7, Fletcher sent out search planes. At 0815 a report came in from a *Yorktown* plane of "two carriers and four heavy cruisers in position 10° 03' South, 152° 27' East." This position was about two hundred twenty-five miles to the northwest of the Americans. Fletcher assumed that this was the main Japanese striking force. Actually Takagi and Hara were about two hundred miles to the southeast of Fletcher, exactly in the opposite direction from the force just reported. Wasting no time, Fletcher pressed on to close the distance and by 1030 had launched a full strike of ninety-three planes from both carriers, retaining only forty-seven for CAP and reserve. The American carriers were once again in the overcast, but it was not bad enough to hamper flight operations.

As soon as the strike group had left, the search planes returned. A possibly disastrous error came to light in debriefing. The coding grid for the pilot's contact reports had slipped. His report of two carriers and four heavy cruisers should have read "two heavy cruisers and two destroyers."

Now Fletcher was in a quandary. Had he but known it, he had made the same error Hara had made of sending a major strike to attack an insignificant force. But where Hara's pilots had found only the *Neosho* and *Sims,* Fletcher's airmen hit pay dirt.

The pilot's report had actually been on a sighting of a small splinter force assigned to set up a seaplane base in the Louisiades. It was an insignificant target, not worth the strength thrown at it. However, after receiving the corrected sighting report, Fletcher made the courageous decision not to recall the strike. His primary job was to prevent the invasion of Port Moresby. If the puny force he knew about was in the area, it stood to reason that there must be more nearby. He gambled that his fliers would find something.

They did.

At 0900, Admiral Inouye, knowing of the presence of American carriers in the Coral Sea, ordered the Port Moresby Invasion Group to reverse course and wait until the situation became clearer. This turn-away point between Misima and the Deboyne Islands at 0900 on May 7 marks the farthest limit of Japanese advance into the Southwest Pacific. With the surrender at Corregidor not twenty-four hours old, the Japanese tide had ceased to flood.

Spoiling for a fight, Admiral Goto brought his Support Group down toward the Jomard Passage as the 12,000-ton carrier *Shoho* accompanying him prepared to launch a strike against Task Force 17. He knew exactly where Fletcher was and meant to capitalize on that knowledge. The weather was clear and all was in readiness. Then—

At 1100, Japanese lookouts report enemy aircraft. The hunter has become the hunted.

Lieutenant Commander W. B. Ault, leading the *Lexington*'s attack group, at that very moment looked down on the sea and spotted a carrier, heavy cruisers, and destroyers. It was Goto's Support Group. Soon all aircraft had driven in for the attack. In the absence of a strike coordinator to designate targets, as would be the practice later in the war, all ninety-three aircraft smashed at the hapless *Shoho*. Commander Ault's initial attack near-missed and merely blew five of her planes over the side. Subsequent attacks placed thousand-pound bombs on her, and she shuddered to a stop, flames spouting from her entire length. At 1136, she yielded to the merciless pounding and slipped into the depths.

Aboard the American carriers the voice of Lieutenant Commander R. E. Dixon crackled through the radios:

"Scratch one flattop! Dixon to carrier. Scratch one flattop!"

It is perhaps too critical to note that in their enthusiasm to knock out the *Shoho,* the American pilots left the rest of Goto's force unscathed. Goto retired to the Deboyne Islands to lick his wounds.

So far in the Coral Sea action, the main participants had not yet come to grips with one another. Each had sent a main strike against a small segment of the enemy. Each had decisively routed the target force, but Fletcher had been luckier than Hara, for he had sunk a carrier and turned back the essential cover for the Port Moresby invasion.

But the preliminary bouts are over. The main contestants, the feature attractions, are about to enter the ring.

By late afternoon on May 7, Fletcher wisely decided not to send another strike after Goto's force. With the *Shoho* gone, it was a relatively insignificant group. He knew he had not yet located the major Japanese carrier strength, and he also was well aware that the Japanese knew where he was. He was still protected by the overcast and poor visibility, so it seemed unlikely he would be spotted. Rather than seach for the Japanese carriers when it was too late to get off an attack that day, he decided to continue his westerly advance to be in better position to block the Port Moresby Invasion Group on the morrow. He had no way of knowing that the cautious Inouye had already recalled it.

Hara, however, had other ideas. He launched a twenty-seven plane search and attack group at 1630 to hit the American carriers if his pilots could find them. Because of the poor visibility, they failed to make contact. On their way back, they happened to pass over the *Lexington* and *Yorktown* fighters. In the ensuing dogfights, the Japanese lost nine aircraft and the Americans two. Shaken by this experience, the Japanese made for home, and, as luck would have it, some of them passed right over the American carriers. They thought they had found their own. Six of them attempted to join the *Yorktown's* land-

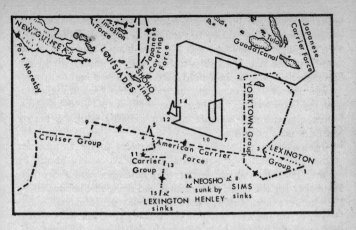

BATTLE OF THE CORAL SEA, MAY 4-8, 1942

1. May 1, 0623 *Yorktown* and *Lexington* rendezvous.
2. May 4, 0701 *Yorktown* sends air strike against Tulagi.
3. May 5, 0846 *Yorktown* rejoins *Lexington* and refuels.
4. May 7, 0725 Crace's Cruiser Group detached to cover Port Moresby.
5. May 7, 1000 Fletcher launches strike against Japanese Covering Force.
6. May 7, 1150 Light carrier *Shoho* sunk.
7. May 7, 0815 Japanese launch air strike against *Neosho* and *Sims*.
8. May 7, 1230 *Sims* sunk; *Neosho* disabled and drifting.
9. May 7, 1425 Japanese planes attack Crace's Cruiser Group.
10. May 7, 1615 Japanese launch night air attack group.
11. May 8, 0900 U.S. carriers launch air attack on Japanese carriers.
12. May 8, 0915 Japanese carriers launch air attack on U.S. carriers.
13. May 8, 1118 U.S. carriers under air attack; 1120 *Lexington* hit.
14. May 8, 1058 Japanese carriers under air attack; 1058 *Shokaku* hit.
15. May 8, 1956 *Lexington* sunk.
16. May 11, 1550 *Neosho* sunk by *Henley* after removal of crew.

ing circle to come aboard, but they were recognized and fired on. One was shot down.

The others headed north and were observed by the *Lexington*'s radar, orbiting in a landing circle only thirty miles away. A delay in communications kept this knowledge from Fletcher for two and a half hours, until 2200. By that time, any opportunity to catch them so close at hand was lost. They could have moved as much as seventy-five miles since the radar observation. Besides, Fletcher found that the *Yorktown*'s radar had shown no such picture. It was better to wait.*

Briefly Fletcher considered sending a night surface force to try to knock out the Japanese. He gave it up because of uncertainty of the enemy's position. The waning moon would not give much light, and he would need his cruisers and destroyers for antiaircraft protection the next day. "All things considered," he wrote, "the best plan seemed to be to keep our force concentrated and prepare for a battle with the enemy carriers next morning."

Inouye, too, had similar ideas. He went so far as to order Goto and a destroyer squadron to rendezvous and attack by night. Then he thought better of it and canceled the order, probably for the same reasons that had decided Fletcher.

The next day, May 8, would be the day of decision.

On board the *Lexington* on the last night of her life—that is not pathetic fallacy; to a seaman, a ship lives—the quiet, orderly routine went on, in spite of tenseness over the expected battle on the morrow.

The *Lexington* had been a happy ship. Originally she was laid down as a battle cruiser. After the Washington Naval Treaty of 1921, when she was about one-third done, she and her sister *Saratoga* were saved from the scrap heap by Admiral William A. Moffett, Chief of Aeronautics, who urged that the two ships be converted to aircraft carriers. The "Lady *Lex*," as she was known in the Navy, had been built by the Fore River Ship Building Company. Her keel had been laid in 1921, but it was about seven years before she was commissioned, as a result of the change in her design. Nearly nine hundred feet in length, she officially displaced 33,000 tons, although fully loaded she was over 40,000. Originally equipped with eight 8-inch guns, she had been stripped and lightened when the main battery was replaced with 5-inch dual-purpose guns. Her hundred and eighty thousand horsepower turbo-electric engines could drive her through the water at better than her 34-knot designed speed.

She had been commanded by some of the most distinguished officers in the Navy. Every one of her captains had gone on to reach flag rank including her third, Ernest J. King. At the Battle of the Coral Sea a few members of her original

* By 2200 the Japanese carriers were ninety-five miles to the east.

crew were still on board—"plank owners" the Navy called them. These men had ridden her some three hundred forty-five thousand miles, had known fifty-seven thousand seven hundred landings on her flight deck, had sailed her through fair weather and foul to meet her destiny far from home on May 8, 1942.

The morning of her last day dawned fair and lovely. The tropical front that had sheltered Task Force 17 for two days had moved northward and was now covering the Japanese carrier force.

Both Admiral Fletcher and Admiral Hara rose early that morning. Each knew he had to get in the first blow if he was to be successful. But neither knew the location of the other. "It's likely," said the *Lexington*'s skipper, Captain Forrest C. Sherman, "that the position will be similar to that of two boxers, both swinging a knockout punch at the same time and both connecting." Perhaps a better comparison would be with the *andabates* of the ancient Roman arenas. Those unfortunates were fitted with helmets with no eye slits, given swords, and forced to fight each other blindly. The crowds loved them, laughing themselves sick as they watched the miserable wretches hack each other to pieces.

In the Coral Sea it was no laughing matter. No spectators watched the ensuing battle on which the safety of the Southwest Pacific rested.

In many ways the two forces were almost exactly evenly matched. Each side had two carriers. Fletcher had radar, but his carriers had operated together for only a few days. Hara had no radar, but *Zuikaku* and *Shokaku* had been working as a division for more than six months; each understood the other's ways. Fletcher had a hundred twenty-two planes and Hara a hundred twenty-one. Perhaps most important of all, Hara had the cover of the overcast weather.

At 0600, Admiral Hara launched a search mission covering an arc from 145° to 235°.* He was pretty sure that Task Force 17 was somewhere to the south of him. An hour later, at sunrise, he launched a strike of ninety aircraft on the median line of the search, i.e., 190°, ten degrees west of south and followed the route of the planes at 30 knots.

Admiral Fletcher had by this time turned tactical command

---

* Roughly SE by S to SW by W.

over to Admiral Fitch, the most experienced carrier officer in the Navy. Having no real idea of where the Japanese Striking Force was, Fitch had to send out a 360-degree search of eighteen planes, beginning at 0625. At 0815, peeking through a hole in the overcast, Lieutenant (jg) J. G. Smith made contact and reported the composition, speed, and course of the Japanese Striking Force, a hundred seventy-five miles away to the northeast of the American carriers. The *Lexington*, meanwhile, had intercepted a Japanese search plane report accurately giving her own position, so something was bound to happen soon.

As soon as Smith's amplifying report was received, both American carriers launched aircraft, a total of eighty-two planes. An hour later, Lieutenant Commander R. E. Dixon verified the contact, but reported that the Japanese were some twenty-five miles north of the previously given position. Dixon remained over the contact for another hour or more to assist the strike in finding the enemy. At 1045, low on fuel, he had to break off and return to base.

But his job was done. *Yorktown* pilots had spotted the two carriers by this time. They were in two groups about ten miles apart, each screened by two cruisers and two or three destroyers. While the dive bombers waited for the slower torpedo planes, the *Zuikaku* and her escorts scuttled into a rainsquall. All aircraft therefore concentrated on the *Shokaku*. The torpedo planes led the way. Skimming low over the water, jinking and swerving to avoid antiaircraft fire, they dropped their "fish" and turned away. They believed they made three hits, but actually the torpedoes, too slow and launched at too great a range, all missed. The dive bombers, attacking right after the TBDs, had better luck, getting two hits, although they reported six.

Unable now to launch aircraft, the *Shokaku* appeared to the departing pilots to be "burning furiously."

It was nearly another hour before the *Lexington*'s planes got there. They had gone to the position originally reported by Smith and, finding nothing there, had begun a box search. It was not until 1140 that they reached their targets. By this time some of their planes had fallen by the wayside, having strayed out of formation, so there arrived over the target only eleven TBDs, four SBDs and four F4F Wildcats. Attacking through a hole in the overcast, they had no better luck than had the

Yorktown planes. All torpedoes again missed. They were too slow. "We could turn and run away from them," one Japanese officer remarked. Three F4Fs were shot down, but the dive bombers landed another bomb on the burning *Shokaku*. Jubilant pilots' reports that she "was settling fast" were grossly exaggerated. She was quickly brought under control, and her planes were sent over to the *Zuikaku*. Her fires were extinguished by 1300, and Takagi ordered her to return to Japan. She made it after nearly sinking on the trip and lived to fight another day.

The Japanese commander was not upset at cutting his carrier strength in half. By this time his pilots had informed him that both American carriers were on the bottom.

The American attack had been partially successful, but now the *Lexington* and *Yorktown* faced a fight for their lives.

The Japanese strike group must have passed near the American planes on their way to hit the enemy.* Better guided and in better formation than the American planes, the Japanese found the *Lexington* and *Yorktown* about 1100, just the time predicted by Captain Sherman. The American carriers were about a mile apart in the middle of a circular formation of cruisers and destroyers. Changing course back into the wind, the carriers stepped up to 25 knots, then 30, and began to scramble all fighters. Some of the CAP had to be landed at once, since they were low on fuel. It seems incredible that in view of Captain Sherman's prediction that the attack would come at 1100, the air officer should have planned a recovery at that very time. As it was, dive bombers had to be pressed into service as fighters. Far too slow for the job and inadequately armed, the Dauntlesses responded nobly. They shot down four torpedo planes at an equal cost to themselves.

The Japanese, twenty miles from Task Force 17, split into three groups, two of torpedo planes and one of bombers. Streaking low along the water, the first torpedo group came in on both bows of the *Lexington*. One plane was blown to bits by antiaircraft fire, but the others kept coming. The other torpedo group, meanwhile, made for the *Yorktown*, and the dive bombers remained orbiting high in the sky awaiting their moment.

* The story that the two groups saw each other and waved greetings on the way to the attack is apparently a newspaperman's fancy.

Both Captain Sherman and Captain Buckmaster of the Yorktown maneuvered their ships independently in an effort to dodge the attacks. The inevitable result was to spread the formation out at the expense of concentration of fire. Eventually the two carriers separated several miles, and the skippers of the five cruisers and seven destroyers had to make quick decisions as to which to follow. The majority stayed with the Yorktown.

About 1118, the Lexington, victim of an "anvil" attack, with planes coming in on each bow, received her first torpedo hit. It was impossible to turn away from one set of torpedoes without presenting the beam to the others. Eleven torpedoes missed before one plowed into her port side forward; seconds later, another one hit, portside, opposite the island. Within a few more seconds, two bombs hit aboard and several near-misses shook her violently. Reporters aboard believed the near-misses were additional torpedo hits.

The Yorktown, smaller and more maneuverable than the "Lex," was by no means ignored. The torpedo plane attack failed, largely because the Japanese did not use the "anvil" method on her. She managed to dodge all torpedoes, only to fall victim to the dive bombers five minutes later. After dodging many of the bombs, she took an eight-hundred-pound bomb that hit the flight deck near the island and penetrated deep into the ship, killing or seriously injuring sixty-six men. The fires, however, were quickly controlled. By 1140, the attack was over, and so, though no one knew it, was the Battle of the Coral Sea.

On recovery of aircraft, each side felt jubilation. The Japanese had lost forty-three aircraft that day and the Americans thirty-three. The returning American pilots reported both Japanese carriers were afire and sinking. It is obvious what happened. The Shakaku was first attacked by Yorktown planes and left as a goner. When the Lexington attack came in a few minutes later, the Zuikaku was still hidden by a rainsquall; the pilots, however, believing one carrier already sunk, attacked the "remaining" one and believed they had sunk her as well.

The Japanese pilots were merely victims of their overoptimism. They reported a large carrier sunk—it was identified as the Saratoga—and a "medium carrier," either the Enterprise or Yorktown, also sunk. They also reported a "battleship" left

154

burning. The hit on the "battleship" was as mythical as the ship.

The *Yorktown* quickly patched the damage to her flight deck and recovered her aircraft. The *Lexington* had taken a seven-degree list, but had partially corrected this by pumping fuel oil to the high side. The fires still blazing below decks were not visible from the air, and returning pilots were unaware she had been hit until they were told as they stepped out of their aircraft onto the flight deck.

The *Lexington* seemed to have survived her first battle damage very well. Patching and shoring up weakened bulkheads, the damage control officer, Commander H. R. Healy, and his men had confined the flooding to only a few of the *Lexington*'s six hundred watertight compartments. By telephone he reported to Captain Sherman, "We've the torpedo damage temporarily shored up, the fires out, and soon will have the ship back on an even keel. But I suggest, sir, that if you have to take any more torpedoes, you take them on the starboard side."

Even as he spoke, disaster struck. Insidious, unseen, deadly, gasoline vapor from ruptured fuel lines seeped along the decks. Inevitably it found a spark. Someone had left a motor generator running. Confined below decks, the vapor exploded at 1247 in a cataclysmic roar. The carrier shook and shuddered. More explosions followed.

Even then the "Lady *Lex*" might have lived, except that the explosion struck at the heart of her defenses. It wiped out damage control central and killed Commander Healy and most of his men. Telephone lines began to fail as the fires spread rapidly. Flames jumped from one compartment to another, the paint on one side catching fire from the heat on the other. Over the years, industrious seamen had built up coats of paint as much as a quarter of an inch thick.

A second major explosion came two hours later. Now ventilation could no longer be supplied to the engineering spaces. The temperature began to mount from the customary hundred degrees. Up and up—120, 130, 140, 150, and even more. Captain Sherman ordered magazines flooded and engines spaces abandoned. Slowly, slowly, the "Lady *Lex*" came to a stop.

The destroyer *Morris* came alongside to assist in fighting the fires. It was no use. Captain Sherman ordered the sick and wounded evacuated to the destroyer.

The last hour had come.

At 1707 Admiral Fitch called down from the flag bridge to Captain Sherman, one deck below.

"Well, Ted, let's get the men off."

As he gave the order that broke his heart, Captain Sherman at least had the satisfaction of watching an abandonment superbly done. There was no confusion. Boats and life rafts were put in the water. Men quietly descended the lifelines and dropped without fuss into the sea, where the waiting craft picked them up. Three destroyers assisted in the rescue work, emptying the rafts and boats as fast as they were filled.

Search parties aboard the *Lexington* hunted below decks to make sure no one was left behind. Even the Skipper's dog, Wags, was saved. Admiral Fitch and his staff transferred to the *Minneapolis*.

The last three men remaining aboard were the executive officer, Commander M. T. Seligman, the Captain's Marine orderly, and, naturally, the Captain. They made one last search for anyone left behind. There was no one.

Another violent explosion shook the dying ship. Yet the three men were reluctant to leave. Captain Sherman went into his cabin a moment and reappeared with his best hat.

"I hear there's not to be any more gold braid till after the war, and I wouldn't like to have to use that yellow cotton substitute. Thought I'd better save my best one."

The three men made their way aft. Commander Seligman urged haste, for he feared a last, massive explosion. First to go down the lifeline was the orderly, then the executive officer. As the Captain still hesitated, the thought ran through his head, he confessed later: "Wouldn't I look silly if I left this ship and the fires went out?" Then he went down.

The *Lexington,* a dead ship, now held only the dead.

Not a man was lost in the abandonment. Every man who was still alive when the order was given reached safety.

At length Admiral Fletcher sent the destroyer *Phelps* in to put the old "Lady Lex" out of her misery. Firing four torpedoes into the starboard side, the destroyer pulled away and watched with the rest of the force.

The *Lexington,* burning and exploding, shook more violently, settling lower and lower in the water. At about 2000, the tormented ship committed her body to the deep, still on an even keel, disdaining to bow to her enemies. There she will rest with her dead, fifteen thousand feet down, until the end of time.

Who won? On sober evaluation, it seems the Japanese did. The 12,000-ton carrier *Shoho* and a few small ships were a small price to pay for the *Sims, Neosho,* and *Lexington.* But the Japanese drive on Port Moresby had been turned back. Admiral Inouye, learning that Takagi's Striking Force had only five operational aircraft remaining, "postponed" the invasion indefinitely. Admiral Yamamoto countermanded this order and sent every ship he had left out to catch Fletcher's survivors. Failing to make contact, he canceled the order. All forces retired to Truk or Rabaul.

Fletcher was not there to be caught. Sensing that Port Moresby was safe, Nimitz ordered Task Force 17 to return to Pearl Harbor at its best speed.

Big things were brewing in the Central Pacific.

CHAPTER SIX

May-June: Three Gallons a Week!

> *Feet have they, and walk not.*
> Book of Common Prayer

Twenty-one Ships Sunk or Disabled in Coral Sea Battle!" trumpeted the headlines. "Americans Repulse Japanese in Massive Sea Victory!"

There was rejoicing in the country, in the cities, in the villages. The Japanese, rapidly gaining a reputation for invincibility, had now, at long last, been stopped. The Navy communiqué, coming only a few days after the news of the loss of Corregidor, raised the spirits of men; it answered the question, "Where is the Navy?"

Officially the Navy Department announced that the Japanese had lost an aircraft carrier, a heavy cruiser, a light cruiser, two destroyers, a seaplane tender, four gunboats, three submarines, and three transports. Heavily damaged were another carrier, a heavy and a light cruiser, another seaplane

157

tender, and two cargo carriers. Nothing was said of the U.S. losses. The news would not be released for weeks.

In sinkings alone, the claims were exaggerated by two and a half, for actually only six Japanese ships were sunk in the battle, a minelayer, three minesweepers, a destroyer beached, and the light carrier *Shoho*. In addition, as had been noted, the *Shokaku*, heavily damaged, was out of action for some months. The Navy had simply accepted the overoptimistic reports of the pilots. The country needed good news, and no one had any disposition to belittle it.

John Citizen Backhome needed all the reassurance he could get, for he was being dealt heavy blows to his way of life. Things he had taken for granted, the immutable truths of existence, now no longer had any reality, it seemed. Already grumbling over restrictions, with no new car, no new tires, no new typewriter, he now learned that war is hell. He would have to restrict the use of sugar in his coffee, limit his credit buying and probably walk downtown to buy either sugar or anything else. On May 4, 1942, he or his wife went to an appointed place to register for rationing and receive War Ration Book No. 1. It contained coupons entitling the holder to one pound of sugar every two weeks. Every man, woman, and child in the country was entitled to a ration book, but not unborn children as several expectant mothers hoped. If someone died, his family had to turn in his ration book within ten days or face heavy penalties. Some enterprising housewives had tried to beat the game by hoarding, only to be foiled by having coupons detached for sugar at home. Most dared not lie about it, under penalties of perjury. One man had no coupons left, for he had in his pantry a 577-year supply at rationing rates!

Sugar bowls vanished from restaurant tables. In cafeterias a scant teaspoonful of sugar might be doled out to a coffee or tea drinker. Icing on cake became thinner and more stretched with starch or flour. If you wanted to get a birthday or wedding cake from your bakery, you had to take in enough sugar for the icing and hope you would get it all back on the cake. Sales of saccharine and other sugar substitutes soared, and children wistfully bemoaned the loss of candy bars and lollipops.

If sugar rationing hit America's sweet tooth, gasoline rationing in the Eastern Seaboard hit Mr. Backhome where it hurt, in his feet. Earlier restrictions had cut him down to such an extent that his life seemed crippled. Now, on May 15, all other pleasures vain, he longed for a spin in the old family car. But it was scarcely to be. The holder of an A card, the one reserved for those who were unable to think up reasons convincing to the ration board, was able to buy only three gallons a week. *Three gallons a week.*

A whole way of life had to be changed. Then, as now, America moved by automobile. The countless carefree trips to the store, to school, to the office, to the golf course, to the bowling alley, to dances, to the movies were endangered. "Pop, can I have the car tonight?" was now a meaningless question, because Pop had better not take the car tonight, either. Must America become a nation of stay-at-homes? The answer was *yes,* unless you cared to battle the throngs fighting for places in public transportation or—walk.

The first gasoline registration was less than a glorious success. Far too many people demanded B or X cards. B cards came in various degrees, from B-1 to B-12, allowing limited business use of automobiles. But best of all was the X card. This permitted unlimited purchases. It was supposed to be issued only for essential uses—in defense industry, ambulances, fire engines, police cars, and other emergency vehicles. How well you could do depended on how good a story you could tell the ration board. Some boards were stony-hearted, while others were quite susceptible to a sad tale. All sorts of yarns were spun to make up whole cloth to convince ration boards. Station wagons were declared to be ambulances or trucks. One man declared he was allergic to buses and trolley cars. The upshot was that in some districts A-card holders were as few as twenty percent of the number of drivers. The average for the seventeen-state area was twenty-five percent. OPA head Leon Henderson had expected the percentage to be thirty-three.

Those who had been unable to achieve anything better than an A card were outraged to learn that all members of Congress got X cards. Wrote one irate taxpayer to her Senator:

It is a humiliating disappointment to many of us . . . that you should be one of the overwhelming majority of Senators who refuse to give up your special privileges in the gasoline rationing.

If the so-called leaders of our country set such an example of selfish lack of public spirit in this crisis, what can be expected of the people they are supposed to represent! Is it any wonder that so many are claiming X cards?

It really looks as though there is less real patriotism and willingness to go all out to win the war in Washington than anywhere else in the United States.

The Senator, stung by the letter, telegraphed his reply:

APPRECIATE THOUGHTS GAS RATIONING. SOLUTION DUE SHORTLY TRANSPORTATION PIPELINES.

The Senator's reply did not satisfy his constituent. Nor were the pipelines soon forthcoming. Instead, it would not be long before gasoline rationing spread all over the country. The problem was not only gasoline; it was rubber.

The American rubber supply came mainly from the Far East, approximately ninety-seven percent of it. The small trickle from Brazil and other places would serve only to whet the appetite; it could not satisfy the increased demands for war. The only way out was to build a huge synthetic rubber industry. Men in Washington were beginning to grapple with this problem, but the solution was not yet. Meanwhile Mr. Backhome and his friends would have to stay home or walk.

The gasoline shortage was having distressing by-products. Many filling station operators locked their doors and went into the service or took another job. The loss of gasoline tax revenues threw the budgets of many states out of kilter. Until they could find some subsitute kind of revenues, states had, in some cases, to operate on deficit budgets.

Price control, too, caused hardships; with the prices frozen at the highest selling point in March, it prevented a great rollback of the cost of living to the consumer. Shopkeepers were sometimes caught in a squeeze; if they had postponed raising prices until April, higher wholesale costs hurt them severely. The more patriotic retailers, who had obeyed the President's injunction to hold the line on prices, now found themselves caught. Prices were frozen at what *they* had been charging in March. Others, who had cashed in on the bonanza of more ready cash, were sitting pretty. *Their* profit margin remained the same. It took a long time for adjustments to be made to bring some sort of equity into the situation.

160

Charge-account buying came under fire early in the month, and on May 6 a regulation came out stiffening credit terms. A man who made charge purchases was required to make full payment within forty days after the end of the month in which the purchases were made. If he did not, then the outstanding sum would be treated as installment buying, becoming subject to service charges and requiring payment in full in no less than six months. Also requirements for installment buying were stiffened, with a third of the cost demanded as down payment.

Still, taking it all in all, the people at home were far better off than those who were called to the services or the civilians in other countries who had known rationing so long that it had become a way of life. Black markets would be born in the United States, but they never flourished to the extent that they did overseas. Eventually the American people would become accustomed to these shortages and would have to face up to others yet undreamed of.

More and more men and women were going into the services. On May 16, Mrs. Oveta Culp Hobby was sworn in as a major in the Army, head of the Woman's Army Auxiliary Corps and authorized to begin recruiting. Mrs. Hobby was somewhat relieved when she discovered that the uniform the women would wear had not been designed by the Army, but by Lord & Taylor of New York. It must be admitted that the uniform was not one of Lord & Taylor's most inspired creations. The heavy khaki cloth specified simply could not be tailored to be attractive, and as the recruits tended to approximate the shape of the average woman, not the fashion designer's glamorization of her, the girls simply looked dumpy. In spite of these drawbacks, the girls responded, releasing many men for combatant jobs elsewhere.

The Navy's V-7 program was by this time getting into high gear. Initially, facilities were set up to turn college graduates into officers in the space of three months at Municipal Pier, Chicago, and on the U.S.S. *Prairie State* in New York. As the program expanded, college facilities were taken over, and college campuses echoed to the sound of marching feet, while in the classrooms the aspiring officers pored over such subjects as ordnance and gunnery, tactics, and communications, and contemplated the magic phrases "Can Dead Men Vote Twice" and

"True Virgins Make Dull Company."* Competition was keen and bilging** was frequent. Those who bilged were sent with the Navy's compliments to their draft boards, whence they went to put on Army khaki rather than Navy blue.

The Navy recruits, both officer and enlisted, were generally better off than those taken by the Army. In the first place, Navy training stations tended to be near the water or near large cities—San Francisco, San Diego, Long Beach, Chicago, Boston, New York, Norfolk, Charleston, Jacksonville. Here their families could find accommodation, even though at exorbitant cost when landlords gouged. But most Army camps had been set up far from civilization, where land could be had cheap. Wives loyally trying to be near their men found no place to stay within miles, and what they could find was generally substandard at high cost. Trailer camps rose near the Army establishments, and the vultures moved in—gamblers, pimps, prostitutes. They vied for the money and the time of the men who sought relief, any kind of relief, from the drudgery and exactions of basic training.

As men graduated from recruit training, they were formed into divisions, ready to go overseas. Under agreement between Britain and the United States, a buildup in the United Kingdom was to begin when American troops were ready. Here they would receive further training and would be ready to go into battle when the time came.

After a few short days home on leave, the graduate of basic training would report to one of the embarkation stations in the country—most usually Fort Dix, New Jersey. Here he would be checked for shots and for complete outfit and be assigned to a transport to carry him across the Atlantic to the British Isles.

Let us go aboard a transport with him.

Transports came in all sorts and conditions of ships. Some were operated by the Army, some by the Navy. Some such as the *West Point* (née *America*) and *Wakefield* (née *Manhattan*) had been luxury liners. Others had been dingy cargo carriers. Some were new Liberty Ships modified to handle troops. It

* Mnemonic devices for converting magnetic compass reading to true directions: Compass + Deviation = Magnetic + Variation True. The second is used for going from true to compass heading.
** Bilge—Navy slang for flunking or failing.

made little difference. The troops were jammed together and the conditions miserable. No stewards came to serve breakfast in bed. No one lolled easily in deck chairs or played deck tennis. There was no room. Ships that in peacetime had carried eight hundred pampered passengers now crammed four thousand miserable troops aboard.

Up the long gangway, carrying full pack, all personal possessions—everything he thought he would need and everything the Army thought he would need—staggered the soldier-passenger. As he stepped aboard he received a tag indicating his berthing space and his bunk. Number Two hold. Urgently urged forward by the transport's crew, he found Number Two hold and the companionway leading down into it. Here, dimly lit by a few reluctant electric light bulbs, rose tier on tier of bunks, eight, ten, twelve soaring one above the other to the top of the space. No innerspring mattresses existed here. The bunks were merely canvas fastened to a frame of steel piping and covered with a treated flash-proof covering. To a nearby stanchion the soldier affixed his pack and his worldly possessions, and then turned in. There was nothing else to do. No troops were allowed on deck during loading. He pored over the regulations and the daily routine that had been given him with his tag when he stepped aboard. No smoking in the berthing spaces. No smoking on deck after dark. Use the butt kits. Exercise periods allowed on deck. The day's routine.

PLAN OF THE DAY: U.S.S. SARDINE BOX

0430	Call troop IPs and cooks.
0500	Call cooks, mess cooks, and bugler.
0500	REVEILLE FOR TROOPS.
0600	Breakfast for troops.
0165	Pipe sweepers. Take trash to incinerators after daylight.
0700	Breakfast for crew.
0724	Sunrise. Light ship.
0800	Turn to. Commence ship's work.
1000	Routine inspection of all crew and troop berthing spaces and heads by designated ship and troop officers.
1100	Dinner for sentries, working details, and watch standers.

1200	Dinner for the crew.
1300	Turn to. Continue ship's work.
1330	General Quarters. Troops not assigned stand clear of passageways and ladders. Troops then go below to assigned compartments until normal routine is resumed.
1400	Secure from General Quarters.
1400	Signal drill.
1500	Supper for troops.
1600	Knock off ship's work.
1700	Supper for crew.
1819	Sunset. Darken ship. NO SMOKING ON THE WEATHER DECKS. (The glow of a cigarette can be seen from an enemy submarine at a distance of over two miles.)
1915	Dump all trash and garbage.
2200	Taps. Lights out in all berthing spaces.

At last the ship's engines began to throb. A long blast on the whistle. They were off! But were they? Later, arriving on deck, Private G. I. Homesick looked out and saw the ship was stopped. Far in the distance could be seen the glow of city lights. Close at hand were other ships, transports and their escorts. The thickening night yielded no clue of where they were. It was some anchorage, somewhere near where they had started. They were waiting for the troop convoy to assemble.

Later, often much later, the ship's engines throbbed once more. She put her bow toward the harbor entrance and started off, passing the sea buoy and finding her place in the formation. Ahead and around, destroyers snuffled importantly, probing with their sonars for any lurking U-boats. Slowly, slowly, the formation took shape. The guardian destroyers took their assigned stations in a bent-line screen, and the convoy moved off.

Few of the troops could see the departure. They lay in their bunks dreaming of home, or apprehensively turning their minds to the perils of the sea. They could hear nothing except for the beat of the engines, the whir of the ventilators, the soft swish of the water against the skin of the ship, and desultory conversation among themselves. There was little to discuss. There are moments when men are happiest alone with their thoughts.

The bow rose. Then it plunged down. The ship had reached the first easy rollers of the Atlantic. A few men grinned at the odd sensation. Others turned pale or turned green. A noise of retching. "Keep it off the deck!" Soon the odor of vomit was added to the miasma of sweat from unwashed bodies. At the end of an hour, nearly every one was more miserable than he had ever been in his life.

The hatch opened. A sergeant, a little green himself, but manfully controlling it, appeared.

"All right, you guys! Outta those racks! Get it cleaned up! Ya wanna live like pigs?"

Groaning, those who could set sullenly to work. After an eternity some semblance of order was restored to the compartment. The wretched men turned back into their bunks. Sleep could ease their misery. They slept.

As the days passed and the men found their sea legs, there was boredom to contend with. There was literally nothing to do. Some men spent the day standing in line. As soon as they finished breakfast, they fell in again to wait for the second—the only other—meal of the day. Poker games went on surreptitiously in odd corners of the ship. Some games lasted for the entire crossing. Or perhaps it was craps. "Ten's the point—I'll fade you—"

A sudden muffled explosion in the distance. A thud on the ship's hull as though she had been hit by a giant hammer. God! What was that? U-boats! Panic began to rise, only to be quelled by the officers. Those on deck could see a destroyer charging about in a seemingly aimless manner. Every so often, towers of water would rise from her wake, and the thud would come again. She was dropping depth charges on something. Would it attack again?

Finally, when nothing seemed to have happened, the destroyer would break off and resume her station in the screen. Had the U-boat been sunk? No one knew. But the rumors did. From one man to another, the stories spread. We have been attacked by two U-boats, and they were sunk. No, it was seven. These eleven U-boats got three ships in the convoy. Like Falstaff's men in buckram, the stories grew, until the Battle of Jutland would not have equaled the story bruited about the ship.

At long last the coast of England loomed up ahead. A few dreamed of the historic sights, thrilling to their first glimpse of the Old World. Most looked ahead to passes to town where they could find liquor, beer, women, or fun.

It was quite a while before they could enjoy these delights. It took an interminable time to get the ship in to its berth, to get it unloaded, to get the men loaded into buses or trains to take them to the camps where they would review their training, drill, and try to work themselves back into combat shape. The joys of London, of Newcastle, of Hull, of Bristol were far away.

It took a long while for the men to learn to get on with the British and the British to accept them. They were more highly paid than their United Kingdom counterparts, and were readier to spend money in the pubs and on the girls. A British complaint was that the Yanks were "over-paid, over-sexed, and over here." The American G.I. had his complaints, too. No one could understand British money—those tanners and quids, those half crowns and guineas, those bobs and florins. The beer and whiskey were warm, and British food cold and tasteless. Those who were invited to British homes complained of the poor and skimpy food, little realizing that their hosts were using up several days' rations entertaining their American guests. It took a long time before the G.I.s and their British hosts learned to live without friction.

* * * * *

The British had known war in a way Americans could not appreciate. They had suffered the humiliation of Dunkirk, the blitz of the Battle of Britain, the hard fighting in the Western Desert, the loss of Norway, Greece, and Crete. They had seen their sons go off aboard ships of the Royal Navy, never to be heard of again, their soldiers find unmarked graves in distant places of the world, their fliers sacrifice their lives against the Luftwaffe and the Italian Air Force. When Japan attacked the United States, the British, faithful to their promises, had promptly declared war, only to suffer the disasters in the Far East already recounted.

A natural meeting place for their enemies was in the Indian Ocean. British India offered untold wealth for either Japanese or German conquerors, and the British base at Trincomalee on Ceylon was vulnerable to Japanese raids. The exiguous naval forces Britain could spare for the Indian Ocean needed a more secure base than Ceylon could afford. Hence, early on in the war, they had established a secret operating base, known as Base T, never discovered by the Japanese during the war. It was Addu Atoll, in the southern Maldive Islands, over five hundred miles south of India.

Although the British had no way of knowing it, the Japanese had no further plans for operations in the Indian Ocean after the January raid by Nagumo's force. Except for submarine operations, they intended to devote their attention to the Pacific.

Even submarine operations could be serious enough, especially as the Germans has assigned U-boats to that part of the world. Since at that time it was absolutely impossible to send supplies through the Mediterranean to maintain the British forces in the Western Desert, supplies for the forces opposing Rommel had to come the long way around Africa, a distance of over ten thousand miles. Before Japan entered the war, the trip from Freetown on south to Cape Town and then up through Mozambique Channel between Africa and Madagascar, past Aden, and through the Red Sea to Suez had not been particularly hazardous. But in the spring of 1942, the very life line of the British position in the Near East was imperiled.

On the northern end of the huge island of Madagascar is the magnificent harbor of Diego-Suarez. In enemy hands it would afford a base that could make it impossible to send supplies through the Indian Ocean and Red Sea. Madagascar was nominally neutral, belonging to France, but neither Prime Minister Churchill nor President Roosevelt was of the belief that the Vichy Government would resist a German or Japanese demand for its use.

The Japanese [telegraphed Churchill to Roosevelt] might well turn up at at the former [Madagascar] one of these fine days, and Vichy will offer no more resistance to them than in French Indo-China. A Japanese air, submarine and/or cruiser base at Diego Suarez would paralise our whole convoy route both to the Middle and the Far East. We have therefore for some time had plans to establish ourselves at Diego Suarez by an expedition either from the Nile or from South Africa.

167

The decision to take Diego-Suarez by amphibious assault was made on March 18. Since the British were stretched thin, it would require weakening something, unless the United States could be of assistance. Churchill proposed to use Force H, a heavy force stationed at Gibraltar, as the backbone of the assault force and suggested to President Roosevelt that the U.S. Navy send an equivalent force to the Rock while Force H was so engaged. Roosevelt, however, preferred to send American ships to relieve elements of the Home Fleet at Scapa Flow, so that it could, in turn, form another striking group at Gibraltar. Accordingly, the U.S.S. *Washington*, one of America's newest battleships, and several other ships became temporarily a part of the Home Fleet. Their adventures will be recounted later.

The striking force for Operation Ironclad, as the Madagascar assault was known, comprised a battleship, *Malaya*, two aircraft carriers, *Illustrious* and *Indomitable*, two cruisers, nine destroyers, six corvettes, and six minesweepers. Another battleship, the *Ramillies*, joined later.

Since the approach to Diego-Suarez harbor was through the heavily defended Oranjia Pass, the actual assault was made on May 3 from the other side of the island, across a narrow isthmus. Although the Vichy French defenders were given ample opportunity to surrender, their notions of "military honor" demanded that they resist. Their opposition was short-lived, for the capture of Diego-Suarez took in all only three days. The troops working their way from the west to the back door of the city were temporarily held up, so the proposal was made of sending a small party around to the front to divide the defenses. Fifty Marines were placed on board the destroyer *Anthony* for the trip. Shortly after 2000 on May 6, the *Anthony* arrived at Oronjia Pass and entered the harbor without difficulty, being fired upon only at the last moment. Under heavy gunfire, she put her stern to a dock and the Marines leaped off.

Their difficulties were only beginning. They had expected a hard fight, but their problems were of a quite a different sort. They seized the house of a general, and the naval commandant quickly surrendered. After that, units surrendered so fast that the Marine commander, Captain M. Price, was distressed to know what to do with them. Before his problem could get out of hand, the troops from the west made their way into the town, and it was all over.

Resistance continued for some months on other parts of the island, but the vital base of Diego-Suarez was kept from the enemy.* The vital convoys to India and Egypt could keep coming.

* * * * *

If the long way around to Egypt was secured, the short way through the Mediterranean remained tightly barred. Force H guarded the Strait of Gibraltar. The Mediterranean Fleet at Alexandria supported the Western Desert Forces and held the Italian Navy at bay. Halfway between these two forces stood the island of Malta. Here the gallant defenders eked out a precarious existence under the worst bombing attacks ever thrown at any spot in the world—the worst, that is, until the advent of atomic weapons.

At the crossroads of the Mediterranean, nearly equidistant from Gibraltar and Alexandria, and nearly equidistant from Italy and Africa, Malta had long been a British base. Napoleon had made it a pretext for resuming war in 1803. In 1942 it sent forth submarines and aircraft to prey on Axis shipping supporting Rommel in North Africa. When Malta was strong, the Afrika Korps went on short rations, for few ships could get through. When it was weak, Rommel was able to advance far to the east, driving the British back to the shadows of the pyramids.

To keep Malta supplied was an almost unbelievably difficult task. Each time the British tried it, they had to fight a major sea and air battle. The losses were enormous, the cost in blood and lives immeasurable. Yet Malta never gave in.

Both sides recognized the vital importance of Malta. As early as February, Admiral Raeder, Commander in Chief of the German Navy, urged its capture. But Hitler, his attention focused on the Russian front, had little to spare for the Mediterranean theater. He never did understand its vital importance and begrudged every plane, every man, every vehicle assigned to that region. A Luftwaffe unit, Fliegerkorps II, was stationed in Sicily, and under the leadership of Field Marshal

---

* Diego-Suarez was not quite safe. A Japanese seaplane launched from a submarine bombed and sank a tanker and damaged the *Ramillies*. Midget submarines also penetrated the harbor.

Albert Kesselring as Commander in Chief, South, German aircraft pounded Malta. Air reinforcements poured into Sicilian bases, and soon the beleaguered island was enduring up to ten air attacks a day. Any ships approaching the island also received the attention of the Luftwaffe as well as of the Italian Navy.

Because of extreme British naval weakness in the Mediterranean at the beginning of 1942, Axis convoys were getting through to Tripoli with little interference. Meanwhile, the men and women of Malta were near starvation. They had to get supplies, or the island would fall. A single ship got through in early January and a small convoy toward the end of the month. One more trip was made by a single ship in early February, and then it was another story. Rommel began an offensive, depriving the British of the key harbor of Benghazi.

Early in February, Admiral Sir Andrew B. Cunningham at Alexandria sent out a three-ship convoy to attempt the run to Malta, escorted by three cruisers and sixteen destroyers. The Luftwaffe spotted the convoy, and two of the ships were sunk; the other, disabled, had to be sent to Tobruk. Malta received nothing at all.

In early March, fifteen Spitfire fighters arrived at the island, being flown from the carriers *Eagle* and *Argus*, but these could only help ward off air raids and attack Axis convoys; they could not alleviate the shortages of food and fuel.

On March 20, the British tried again to send a convoy through. This time four cargo ships were sent, escorted by four cruisers and sixteen destroyers under the command of Rear Admiral Sir Philip Vian. On the 22nd, another light cruiser and a destroyer joined up. All went peacefully until shortly after noon on the same day, when a submarine reported that major units of the Italian fleet had left their base at Taranto about 0130.

Admiral Vian was determined that the convoy should reach Malta. He left the antiaircraft cruiser *Carlisle* and six small Hunt-class destroyers to guard the convoy and turned to face the major threat.

A major threat it was indeed. The Italians were in two groups. One consisted of two heavy cruisers and one light, with four destroyers. The other contained six destroyers shepherding the battleship *Littorio*.

The first brush with the cruiser group was comparatively inconsequential. But the convoy came under heavy air attack, and Vian brought his force back to lend a hand. As "we closed [he wrote], the sky above it was obscured by the shell bursts of *Carlisle* and the Hunts, and the rumble of their guns was unceasing." With the return of Vian's ships, the attack was soon beaten off, but Vian knew worse might follow.

After their repulse, the three Italian cruisers joined the *Littorio*, and the combined force attempted to work around past Vian's defenders to get at the convoy. For the next several hours, the Italians tried first one side and then the other, while Vian with his light forces moved to parry each thrust. Since the Italians were faster than their enemies, they would have been bound to win at the game had they persevered, but by 1855 they had broken off the action and were retiring to the northwest. Since the *Littorio* could have blown all the British ships out of the water, the Italian retreat is difficult to comprehend. Three of the British cruisers and two destroyers were damaged in this, the Second Battle of Sirte. But the convoy was not hit.

The weather was worsening into gale conditions, and the convoy dispersed in an effort to escape detection. They were not so fortunate thereafter, for one of the ships was sunk the next morning twenty miles short of her destination. Another only eight miles from Malta was hit badly and could not be towed because of the heavy seas. Three days later she was pulled into Malta and beached. Only half her cargo could be salvaged. The other two ships got in safely, to the rejoicing of the Maltese.

Their joy was premature, for fearsome air attacks were directed against both ships, and they soon sank. In all, only a little more than five thousand tons of the twenty-six thousand sent out reached the defenders.

More would have to be done.

The air attacks on Malta increased in fury as March gave way to April. At the same time, the strength and morale of the Mediterranean Fleet were at their nadirs. First one ship and then another was lost or damaged, most of them victims of the vastly increased Axis activity. Dockyards were crammed, and men were existing in unfit conditions. At the end of March, the beloved Commander in Chief, Admiral Cunningham, was ordered home to be reassigned to Washington as the First Sea Lord's representative with the Combined Chiefs of Staff. His departure depressed everyone from seaman to admiral. His successor, Vice Admiral Pridham-Wippel, held only an interim appointment pending the selection of a new Commander in Chief.

During this time the Chiefs of Staff in London decided it was impossible to send another convoy through to Malta in May. The naval strength simply was not available. Malta would have to tighten its belt.

Malta was not completely abandoned during April. Other than food, her greatest need was for air strength to combat the Luftwaffe. Yet there was little chance of getting aircraft out to her. The only British plane that had any chance against the German fighters was the famed British Spitfire, the hero of the Battle of Britain. Yet this plane did not have the range to fly out from Britain, for it could not reach Gibraltar from the United Kingdom nor Malta from Gibraltar. The only way was to bring them in by carrier. This had been tried, but the two British carriers sent in March had been able to fly in only fifteen aircraft.

At the request of Churchill, President Roosevelt made the new American carrier *Wasp* available for a Spitfire run to Malta. Loading forty-seven of them on board at Glasgow, she sailed on April 14, escorted by British warships, for the Mediterranean. The trip down was uneventful, and the ships passed through the Strait of Gibraltar on the night of April 18/19 unobserved. At 0400 on April 20, the *Wasp* began to launch planes, eleven of her own for a combat air patrol, and then all forty-seven Spitfires. The entire launch was over at 0501, and the *Wasp* and her escorts headed back for Gibraltar. All hands were elated when they received word that all the Spitfires had arrived safely.

They rejoiced too soon. When the Germans learned of the aircraft, which was almost immediately, they threw everything they had into the attack and destroyed a good number of the planes on the ground before they could even be refueled. By the end of the month, Malta's air defense was practically impotent.

But help was on the way, for the *Wasp* was making another trip. She went straight back to Glasgow and loaded on another forty-seven Spitfires and turned her bow once again toward the Mediterranean. On the night of May 7, she joined the carrier *Eagle* off Europa Point in the Strait of Gibraltar, and the two carriers sped in company to the launching point. In the early morning hours of May 9, both carriers launched their planes, and sixty of them reached Malta safely.* This time, the arrangements for their care were much improved, and they mauled the Luftwaffe severely. In fact, some authorities say this was the turning point in the Air Battle at Malta.

The jubilant Churchill telegraphed President Roosevelt: WHO SAID A WASP COULDN'T STING TWICE?

But Malta needed more than planes. Rations were near the starvation level, and the planes could not long fly if no new supplies of aviation gasoline arrived. Before any convoys could be run, the Mediterranean Fleet at Alexandria and Force H at Gibraltar had to be strengthened. Soon ships began to arrive from home waters, from the Far East, where the British were abandoning the scene to the Americans, and from Madagascar, where the operations were nearly completed.

This time, the effort was to be a massive one. It consisted of two parts: Operation Vigorous, to send eleven supply ships through from Egypt; and Operation Harpoon, to send six more in from the west. These were to arrive in Malta on successive days so as not to cramp the harbor facilities and also to deceive the enemy.

Ships destined for Operation Harpoon sailed from England and Scotland on June 5 and entered the Mediterranean a week later. The muscle for their escort was provided by the battleship *Malaya* and the carriers *Eagle* and *Argus*. They were to support the convoy until they reached the Sicilian Narrows between that island and Tunisia. Then they would leave the convoy to a light escort while they waited, not daring to expose such valuable ships to the Luftwaffe and Italian air force.

At the other end of the Mediterranean, Admiral Vian was again preparing to sail to cover Operation Vigorous. He had no heavy ship with which to face an incursion of the Italian fleet. He had in all only seven cruisers, an antiaircraft cruiser, and twenty-six destroyers as combatant ships. In a forlorn attempt to deceive the enemy, Admiral Sir Henry Harwood, who had taken over as Commander in Chief, Mediterranean Fleet, sent the venerable *Centurion* to pretend she was a battleship. This tired old ship, a veteran of Jutland, had long since had her

---

* One of the planes returned to the *Wasp* with a malfunction, and three failed to reach Malta.

173

guns removed and had acted in prewar years as a radio-controlled target ship. She may have lifted her bow a little more proudly as she stood out of Alexandria, acting after all these years once more as a combatant ship. Unhappily the Germans soon discovered that she was only acting.

The Luftwaffe soon spotted the movements of both operations. The ships of Operation Harpoon were well inside the Mediterranean by June 12, and those who needed to had fueled. The next day, Saturday, the force was spotted by both submarines and aircraft. No attack developed until Sunday, when Italian planes appeared about 1030. The two carriers were handicapped, for they had to turn back toward Gibraltar to launch or recover aircraft, and as they were comparatively slow, this meant it took a long time to catch up. In contrast to their usual performance, the Italians were highly accurate in their bombing. The cruiser *Liverpool*, hit in the engine room, had to retire to Gibraltar in tow of a destroyer. A merchant ship was sunk. By evening, the convoy was within range of airfields on Sardinia, and it was attacked by both Italians and German aircraft, which inflicted no further damage, although the defenders lost seven aircraft while shooting down eleven of the enemy.

Shortly after the air attack was beaten off, the convoy reached the Sicilian Narrows. Since he had lost the *Liverpool*, Vice Admiral A. T. B. Curteis had no cruiser to spare to send with the merchant ships, and so the convoy was left to the escort of the antiaircraft cruiser *Cairo*, nine destroyers, and four fleet minesweepers.

The next morning, when the convoy was some thirty miles south of Pantelleria, they received a rude shock. A Beaufighter from Malta reported that two Italian cruisers and four destroyers were only fifteen miles away. Five of the larger destroyers sped to attack this force, while the *Cairo* and the four small Hunt-class ships laid a protective smoke screen. Then they hurried north to join in the fray.

Left unprotected except for the minesweepers and the exiguous smoke, the convoy was set on half an hour later at 0700 by dive bombers. One ship was sunk, and another hit and disabled, but taken in tow. While the convoy turned south, the Italian forces tried to sweep around the destroyers but were foiled by the gallant action of the destroyers and by another smoke screen. Two of the British destroyers were badly hit during the action, the *Bedouin* and the *Partridge*.

About 1120 another air attack developed, and another ship was hit. In this crises, the senior naval officer, Captain C. C. Hardy of the *Cairo*, decided to sink the two crippled merchant ships as the best hope of getting the last two survivors through to Malta.

By this time the Italian squadron had given up and gone back to base, but the air attacks continued. The unfortunate *Bedouin*, in tow of the *Partridge*, was hit and finally sunk, but the latter ship eventually reached Gibraltar. Since the convoy was by now under an umbrella of fighters from Malta, no more damage was done to the ships by enemy air attack, but the incessant attacks on the island had disorganized the minesweeping arrangements, and the channel was not clear. Three destroyers, a fleet minesweeper, and one of the two remaining merchant ships were mined; although four of the five managed to reach port, the Polish destroyer *Kujawiak* went down near sight of her goal. Having delivered two of the six merchantmen, the escort turned back and rejoined the battleship and carriers, whence they made their way safely to Gibraltar. The cost for delivering two merchant ships: four merchant ships and two destroyers sunk; a cruiser, three destroyers, and a minesweeper badly damaged.

Operation Vigorous, the companion attempt from the east, was also having its vicissitudes. Eleven heavily escorted merchant ships sailed from Haifa and Port Said on June 11. Their movements would be covered, they hoped, by a diversionary convoy. But it did not work out that way. The enemy aircraft quickly spotted the real convoy. Two ships were heavily damaged on the next day; one reached Tobruk, but the other was lost on the way to Alexandria.

From June 13 on, the convoy was snooped day and night by aircraft, flares turning the night sky into, in Milton's phrase, a "darkness visible" that offered no shelter for the ships. Fighters from the Western Desert gave their support, but even so, two more ships fell by the wayside, one sunk and one damaged. Just before midnight on June 14, Admiral Vian knew than an Italian fleet had sailed to attack him and that it contained two battleships, the *Littorio* and the new *Vittorio Veneto*. The convoy reversed course several times to confuse the enemy, but to no avail, since Axis aircraft were overhead almost continuously. The number of merchant ships remaining by this time was six. Shorebased British aircraft joined in the battle, as the enemy threw, in Admiral Vian's words, "all known forms of attack" against the convoy. The Italian cruiser *Trenton* was damaged and eventually sunk, and the *Littorio* was damaged. But, before the operation was over, the British lost the cruiser *Hermione,* three destroyers, and a merchant ship, in addition to four damaged.

By evening of June 15, less than a third of the antiaircraft ammunition remained aboard Vian's ships, and the air attacks showed no signs of abating. With many regrets, he ordered the operation abandoned and the convoy to return to Alexandria.

Two out of seventeen merchant ships had reached Malta. *Parturient montes.* . . .

* * * * *

The Western Desert is a brown waste of sand, tumbled rock, heat, and flies that come not as single spies, but in battalions. During the day the temperature rises into the hundreds, while at night it may drop to as low as twenty. Over the centuries the Arab has learned to live with its heat, its sand, its lack of water. He remains a figure of romance, perched on his camel, clad in his *serd* and *jubba*, his *kaftan* and *hezzam*, his *jelabia* and *sirwal*, his head adorned with the *ma-araka* cap and *kafiya* headdress bound with *agals*.

This picturesque garb, so ancient it was worn by Abraham as he came out of the city of Ur, formed no part of the dress of the soldiers on either side in the Second World War. The British Tommy wore a short-sleeved shirt and short trousers. The German and Italian uniforms were often similar. Men's skin tanned almost black, and they needed more water than the natives, whose clothes trapped the body moisture.

Water and gasoline were two keys to success in the desert. These two fluids by their presence or absence decided who would live and who would die. In the British Eighth Army, men were allowed a gallon a day for all purposes—drinking, making tea, and washing. Most of the washing, especially of clothes, was often done in gasoline, which was generally in more plentiful supply than was water. Some of the hardened Desert Rats claimed they could tell which oasis had furnished their drinking supplies—Sidi Barrani, El Adem, Buqbuq. It was the last place civilized men should have had to fight one another, if civilized men must be called upon to fight.

It was under these conditions that Britain staked her survival as an empire. If the British position in Egypt should fall, then all the Near East would go with it, and the way to the Persian Gulf and its oil riches would be available to the Germans for the taking. Iran and Iraq would be able to offer little resistance, and then Turkey would have to join with the Axis or be overrun. The whole southern flank of Russia would be exposed, and at the same time, the way to India would lie open.

General Sir Claude Auchinleck, Commander in Chief of the Middle East, well understood the stakes. So did his principal opponent, Colonel General Erwin Rommel. It was fortunate for the British that Hitler and the German High Command understood them little or not at all. If they had, they would not have denied Rommel the pitifully few men and tanks he needed for his triumph. A tiny fraction of the men and equipment they lavished on the Russian front would have turned the tide in the desert. As it was, Rommel came within an ace of winning these priceless goals.

Since February, the Afrika Korps and the British Eighth Army had faced each other in eastern Libya at El Gazala. Each side was building strength for a looked-for offensive; each side prepared to oppose the other's attack if it came first. The intensified air assaults on Malta had aided the Axis buildup, for the Malta-based aircraft and ships were too weak to interfere seriously with shipping coming across the Mediterranean from Italy. Scarcely a ship was lost by the Italians and Germans during this period, but unfortunately for Rommel, not enough was shipped to ensure success.

In April, Hitler and Mussolini agreed that the capture of Malta in July would be a cheap way of winning the war in the Mediterranean. Hitler was never wholeheartedly behind the project, but he could not afford to let the Italians do it alone, since he had no confidence in their ability to bring it off, and failure would be worse than not trying it at all. Accordingly, Rommel received instructions to launch an offensive in May, capture all of Libya, including Tobruk, and advance as far as the Egyptian border. Then, his air arm would lend support to the Malta invasion, which was to be done by air drop, mostly by Italians. After Malta had been seized, then Rommel could resume his advance toward Alexandria and the Middle East.

177

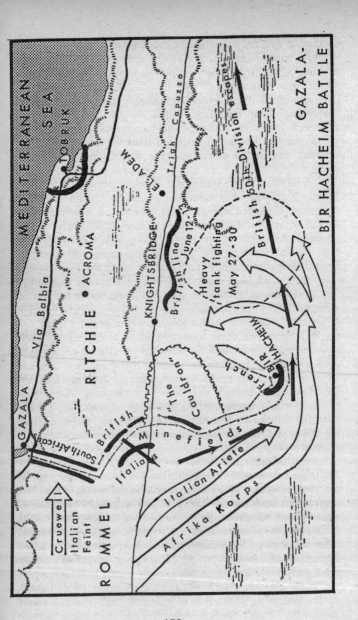

BIR HACHEIM BATTLE

In anticipation of a probable German offensive, the Commander of the Eighth Army, Major General Neil M. Ritchie, constructed a defense line extending from El Gazala on the coast to Bir Hacheim, forty-odd miles to the south. A continuous minefield containing over half a million mines stretched between the two anchors. Within the area between Gazala and Bir Hacheim were various "boxes," as the British called them, which were manned by anything from a brigade to a division.

In this prepared defense, Ritchie revealed himself to be a soldier of the old school, tutored in the World War I ideas of static defense. The fundamental requirement for such a defense is that it rest on flanks which cannot be turned. The northern end of Ritchie's line was secure enough, for it rested on the sea, but to the south it was a different story. South of Bir Hacheim, the desert extends another thousand miles of characterless monotony. Ritchie's dispositions might have been sound enough had there been another army on his left, and another on its left, to the end of the desert. As it was, south of Bir Hacheim there was nothing. Ritchie's left flank, literally, was built on sand.

British intelligence predicted that Rommel's attack would be a direct thrust against Gazala in an attempt to win through to Tobruk along the Via Balbia, a hard-topped road parallel to the sea. For that reason, Ritchie stationed the First South African Division from Gazala southward some six miles to hold the line. His reserve he stationed in easy range of reinforcement. His armor he placed in an ambiguous position, well behind the line to the south from "Knightsbridge" to a position directly east of Bir Hacheim. The armor he expected to fall on the flank of Rommel's direct thrust; if by chance Rommel attempted to sweep around Bir Hacheim, then the armor would intercept him in that area.

Unfortunately for the British, Ritchie compromised, and instead of maintaining his armor intact as a mobile spearhead, he distributed much of it to his infantry divisions, so that when the time came, the British tanks never met Rommel's panzer units as an organized force. Instead, they were expended piecemeal to no purpose.

Auchinleck, as Commander in Chief of the Middle East, could only give advice to Ritchie in his dispositions. To have done more would have shown no confidence in his subordinate; he would have had to relieve him. The Commander in Chief was concerned over Ritchie's proposed use of his tanks. "They have been trained to fight as divisions, I hope [he wrote on May 20], and fight as divisions they should. Norrie must handle them as a Corps Commander, and thus be able to take advantage of the flexibility which the fact of having two formations gives him."

Ritchie saw fit to ignore this advice, and it cost him the battle.

At 1530 on the afternoon of May 26, the Afrika Korps struck. Under German General Cruewell the Italian infantry made a frontal assault on the Gazala position, just as Ritchie expected. Two panzer regiments lent their assistance to this attack.

But the main thrust was elsewhere. Cruewell's attack was only a feint and a holding operation. During the afternoon, Rommel's main forces had assembled in an area a little behind Cruewell, and some of them started off as though to support the Gazala attack. After dark, however, all this changed. The panzer regiments left Cruewell, and the pretended reinforcements whirled about and made top speed toward the south. Ten thousand vehicles began to roll through the moonlit night toward Bir Hacheim and an expected armored battle.

By daybreak the Axis striking force was some ten or twelve miles southeast of Bir Hacheim, and after an hour's rest drove on toward their objectives.

Rommel's plan had been to drive around the British defenses and reach Tobruk, trapping the Eighth Army behind him. Rommel had five hundred sixty tanks for this battle, the British about seven hundred, with two hundred more brought in before the battle ended. Because of heavy fighting, Rommel's men were unable to attain their objectives on the first day. Although the 90th Light Division reached El Adem by noon, the main thrust toward Knightsbridge was held up by the British Seventh Armoured Division, and it was able only to reach the Trigh Capuzzo, an ancient caravan trail running parallel to the coast and about twenty miles from it. Both sides suffered heavy losses in the tank battle, but Rommel received an unpleasant surprise when the British used for the first time the American Grant tank, which outranged the German tanks and had a heavier gun. As for the two hundred forty Italian

180

tanks Rommel had with him, the men who manned them called them traveling coffins.

At the end of the day, the German-Italian force was in some difficulty, for the 90th Light Division was cut off at El Adem and under heavy attack. Farther west the panzers were pinned down in the Knightsbridge area. The British Seventh Armoured Division was severely mauled by the day's actions, while the First Armoured Division farther north had not come into action at all.

However, in spite of the precarious situation [wrote Rommel in his diary] and the difficult problems with which it faced us, I looked forward that evening full of hope to what the battle might bring. For Ritchie had thrown his armour into the battle piecemeal and had thus given us the chance of engaging them on each separate occasion with just about enough of our own tanks. This dispersal of the British armoured brigades was incomprehensible. In my view the sacrifice of the 7th Armoured Division south of Bir el Harmat served no strategical or tactical purpose whatsoever. . . . They should never have allowed themselves to be duped into dividing their forces before the battle or during our feint attack against the Gazala line. . . . Mobile warfare in the desert has often and rightly been compared with a battle at sea—where it is equally wrong to attack piecemeal and leave half the fleet in port during the battle.

After heavy fighting the next day, Rommel decided to withdraw his forces into a bridgehead in the center of the line while he brought up supplies and while the Italian Ariete Division was investing Bir Hacheim. To speed up the conquest of that strongpoint, Rommel ordered the 90th Light and the Trieste divisions to lend a hand.

The defenders of Bir Hacheim, the First Free French Brigade and a battalion of Jewish volunteers, had held the Italian Ariete Division to a standstill before Rommel's arrival in the area on June 2. He took personal command of operations against the strongpoint, because so long as it held out, it would be a threat to any advance eastward. In spite of his leadership, it took eight days of hard fighting until the fortress capitulated. A few survivors made their way out and rejoined

181

the Eighth Army. The rest, including the gallant French General Pierre Koenig, were taken prisoner.

Ritchie, meanwhile, had lost control of the battle. His great opportunity would have been to attack the Italian 21st Corps on the Gazala line with all his armor and drive into Rommel's rear. Instead, fearing a trap, he continued to expend his armor piecemeal in futile attacks on the "Cauldron," as Rommel's fortified position in the center was called.

In the Cauldron the Afrika Korps had been making good use of the time it took to subdue Bir Hacheim. Reinforcements came in, and Rommel's line of communications was established. By June 10, Rommel made his next attempt and fought against the weakened Eighth Army for two days along the Trigh Capuzzo between Knightsbridge and El Adem. At the end of June 13, his forces reached the sea, and Ritchie's troops on the Gazala line were threatened with entrapment. Many had already withdrawn during the hard fighting. The rest fought their way out and withdrew all the way to the Egyptian frontier, in spite of the fact that this meant leaving Tobruk to its fate.

About this time, the Prime Minister intervened. To him, Tobruk was a symbol of British resistance. The previous year it had held out during a siege of two hundred forty-two days. It must not fall now.

Presume [cabled Churchill to Auchinleck] there is no question in any case of giving up Tobruk. As long as Tobruk is held no serious enemy advance into Egypt is possible. . . .

By the time Auchinleck had passed this order on to Ritchie, it was too late. Most of the Eighth Army had already gone by. Tobruk would have to endure another state of siege.

Unknown to Ritchie, who did not ask, and to Auchinleck, who was too busy to be concerned with details, the defenses of Tobruk had fallen into a sad state of disrepair. Tank traps had filled with sand so that they would no longer stop a baby buggy. Ammunition was scarce, and the troops in the city were garrison troops, not combat-seasoned men as had been the case a year earlier. The commander, Major General Klopper, had been a general for only a month, and his previous experience had been largely administrative.

Ritchie in a conference on June 16 warned Klopper to be

particularly concerned with the southwestern approaches, although the southeast route was much more vulnerable. The British should have known, for they had used the latter way themselves twice in capturing the city, and Rommel had planned to use it himself a year earlier before he decided to bypass. The southeast would be no danger, assured Ritchie, so long as the fortress of El Adem held out.

At that very moment El Adem was falling. Ritchie must have learned this fact as soon as he arrived at his headquarters near the border. But he seems to have made no effort to inform General Klopper about this interesting fact. The southeastern approaches remained the weaker ones.

And it was through the southeast that Rommel attacked. Heavy air attacks pounded the city while the triumphant Axis forces ostentatiously marched past it on the Via Balbia toward the Egyptian border. Then on the morning of June 20, picked forces turned back and invested the city. The attack began at 0520 and continued throughout the day; by evening the town and harbor had been captured, and two-thirds of the fortress. The next morning General Klopper surrendered.

> This was one of the heaviest blows I can recall during the war [wrote Churchill]. Not only were its military effects grievous, but it had affected the reputation of the British armies. . . . Now in Tobruk a garrison of 25,000 (actually 33,000) seasoned soldiers had laid down their arms to perhaps one-half of their number. If this was typical of the morale of the Desert Army, no measure could be put upon the disasters which impended in Northeast Africa.

This statement is perhaps more eloquent than accurate. As noted, the men were not seasoned veterans, nor was their commander. They had been abandoned, given faulty advice and misleading intelligence reports. They had no firm leadership, for their officers always seemed to be reacting to the situation just past rather than to the present emergency. They had no adequate defense against tanks. They were symbols, but not the disaster the Prime Minister states. The graver disaster lay just ahead.

When the delighted Führer heard of the capture of Tobruk he telegraphed congratulations to Rommel and promoted him to Field Marshal. "I would rather [Rommel grumbled in a letter to his wife] he had given me one more division."

183

The next possible strongpoint in the desert was Mersa Matruh, and it was here that Ritchie planned to make his last stand. He disclosed these plans to Auchinleck when the latter flew to Eighth Army headquarters on June 22. He proposed to repeat his dispositions before Gazala, except that he had far less to do it with and again no firm fortress at the southern end. He posted the 10th Corps in Mersa Matruh itself, and thirty miles to the southwest the First Armoured Division—rather what was left of it. Behind them the New Zealand Division would act as a reserve. Minefields extended south from the 10th Corps perimeter and northeast from the First Armoured Division's position. They did not meet. To plug the gap two small forces were stationed, but in effect, Ritchie's line had no center.

Flying back to his headquarters in Cairo, General Auchinleck was very thoughtful. From his demeanor, it was obvious that General Ritchie meant the Eighth Army to stay at Mersa Matruh, if not alive, then dead. There would be no more retreating. Ritchie seemed to be accepting the destruction of the Eighth Army and his own death with complete equanimity.

Auchinleck knew he could not permit the Eighth Army to be destroyed, for it was the only fighting force that could hold the Near East. Ritchie's plans meant the loss, perhaps, of the war.

It was obvious that Ritchie would have to go. Before the plane touched down at the Cairo airport, Auchinleck had made this decision. Mersa Matruh must be evacuated and the Eighth Army moved back to El Alamein where a more suitable terrain would aid the defense. If El Alamein could not be held, then the Eighth Army would retreat further; it could not be sacrificed.

In view of the enormous stakes, Auchinleck decided that there was only one man who could be asked to take charge of the Eighth Army at that moment—himself. Since he had kept Ritchie perhaps too long in command, he, the Commander in Chief, would have to accept the consequences.

On the afternoon of June 25 Auchinleck flew back to Ritchie's headquarters and relieved him of his command. Immediately he set about trying to dispel the atmosphere of defeatism that hung over the Eighth Army. Also he set about drawing up orders to move the troops to the El Alamein line.

He had no opportunity to carry out his intentions. Before he could move, Rommel struck. Auchinleck was faced with fighting the battle he had hoped at all costs to avoid.

After the success of Tobruk, Rommel advanced toward the Egyptian border, where his orders bade him stop while his air detachments helped out in the Italo-German airborne invasion of Malta. But Rommel was in no mood to stop. As well as Auchinleck, Rommel understood the magnificent opportunities the conquest of Egypt would give to Germany. Accordingly, he telegraphed his superiors in Germany for permission to continue. After winning Mussolini's concurrence, Hitler personally gave the order for Rommel to drive on.

Auchinleck's command of the Eighth Army was little more than twenty-four hours old when the Afrika Korps struck. Since there had been no time to implement a reorganization, the "Auk," as he became known, had to fight with Ritchie's battle plan. But there was a difference. The "Auk" was concerned with saving as many of his men as possible, together with their equipment, to take up their positions on the El Alamein line.

Both British and German intelligence was faulty. The British thought the Germans had far greater strength than was actually left from the hard fighting of the past few weeks. Rommel believed that the central part of the British line was the strongest, and it was here that he thrust his armor. On the morning of June 26, Rommel sent his tanks through the center and the 90th Light Division around the north. By the next morning, the position at Mersa Matruh was enclosed. For Auchinleck it became a matter of extricating what he could. The Seventh Armoured Division in the south and the New Zealand Division, both severely battered, managed to pull back, while the 10th Corps to the north, the order to fall back delayed by communication difficulties, had to fight their way out. Most of them made it, but had to leave behind most of their equipment, while some six thousand of their men were captured by the Germans.

Auchinleck counted himself fortunate, in the circumstances, that he had been able to preserve as much of the Eighth Army as he had. The position at Mersa Matruh had been unsound from the first, and Ritchie's dispositions had not helped. At El Alamein it would be a different story.

The small village on the coast of the Mediterranean called

El Alamein has become as famous in history as Antietam, Bunker Hill, Gettysburg, Belleau Wood, Waterloo, or Philippi. Here at last in the desert war was a place that could be defended. Forty miles south of the coast lies the notorious Qattara Depression. This is a torment of twisted rock formation, so convoluted that no man, beast, or vehicle can cross it. Seven-hundred-foot cliffs separate it from the desert to the north. Here was a solid anchor for the British left flank.

The few days remaining, before Rommel's assault on the El Alamein position, the "Auk" spent in reorganizing the Eighth Army. His most vital innovation was to establish a series of battle groups, built around motorized infantry with twenty-five-pounder guns. This gave a mobility that had not existed before, when the trucks were in one organization and the infantry in another. Henceforth the Eighth Army would be able to move and to hit. Rommel had used battle groups for months.

The "Auk" drew up his positions on the El Alamein line with the infantry lightly holding the front positions. Behind them were the mobile artillery and the armored divisions newly equipped with the few remaining tanks available. He intended to use his artillery to support his tanks, so that the fancied German superiority might be overcome.

These plans worked. Rommel had had fewer men and tanks than the Eighth Army from the beginning of the offensive, but his audacity had been met only with a lack of imagination on the part of the defenders. Now he faced a commander who could call his bluff successfully.

On July 1, Rommel made his attempt on the El Alamein line, but he was stopped cold. For three days he attempted to force his way through, but in the end he had to give it up. If he had received the material support he required, he might well have made it, but he did not. Of the sixty thousand tons he estimated he needed, he received three thousand. As he advanced toward Mersa Matruh, eighty-five percent of his vehicles were captured British ones, running on abandoned British gasoline.

By July 4, the battle was decided; it was to be a stalemate. Neither Rommel nor the "Auk" was able to make any progress against the other. But Egypt was saved, and the Eighth Army was saved. The panic in Alexandria and Cairo subsided, and the Mediterranean Fleet, which had evacuated its base at Alexandria, returned, a little sheepish over the whole thing. Rommel made his last attempt on July 17. It was in vain.

The stand of the "Auk" and the Eighth Army at El Alamein was as decisive in its way as the Battle of Midway in the Pacific. It is an unhappy quirk of fate that the name of El Alamein should be forever associated with another, less gifted, more colorful commander and another battle that took place three months later. The First Battle of El Alamein stopped the Germans; the second was a part of the great offensive to drive the Axis out of Africa.

* * * * *

Far to the north, Russian and German soldiers faced one another across the winter line. With the coming of spring, the fighting would break out again in all its bitter fury. It would be the great opportunity.

The German army in 1942 was not what it had been the previous year. Too many men had fallen; too much equipment had been destroyed. The time was at hand, and the opportunity now; if Germany was to win the war with Russia, there could be no delay.

For the 1942 campaign, Hitler planned to concentrate everything on the south, to win the Caucasus region with its oil, and to link with Rommel in Persia. The operation plan, "Case Blue," grew out of the Führer Directive 41. Leningrad and Moscow would be spared; Voronezh, Sevastopol, and Stalingrad were the objectives.

The Soviets, too, had plans for an offensive, and theirs jumped off before the Germans were ready. During the winter, the Russians had established a salient near Kharkov that extended like a dagger into the German positions and threatened the supply to the whole southern position by reason of the rail lines it controlled. The Russians hoped, on the other hand, to retake Kharkov and drive a gap between the two arms of Army Group South. On May 12, the Red Army broke through on either side of Kharkov. Marshal Timoshenko hoped to trap a large segment of General Paulus's Sixth Army and exterminate it in the pincers movement. The Germans, fighting ferociously, managed to break from the trap and cut off Timoshenko's penetration, but the fighting was sickening to the end. The Russian plan to cut off a German army had backfired; instead,

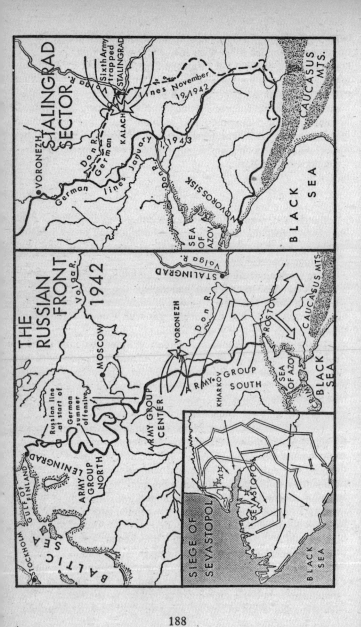

STALINGRAD SECTOR

Sixth Army Trapped STALINGRAD

KALACH

German lines November 19, 1942

German lines January 1, 1943

VORONEZH

Don R.

Don R.

German lines January 1, 1943

CAUCASUS MTS.

NOVOROSSISK

SEA OF AZOV

BLACK SEA

THE RUSSIAN FRONT 1942

Volga R.

STALINGRAD

Volga R.

MOSCOW

VORONEZH

Don R.

ROSTOV

CAUCASUS MTS.

Russian line at start of German summer offensive

KHARKOV

ARMY GROUP SOUTH

SEA OF AZOV

CRIMEA

BLACK SEA

ARMY GROUP CENTER

ARMY GROUP NORTH

LENINGRAD

GULF OF FINLAND

BALTIC SEA

STOCKHOLM

SIEGE OF SEVASTOPOL

SEVASTOPOL

BLACK SEA

188

twenty-two Russian divisions were cut off, annihilated, or captured, with 239,000 Russian soldiers taken prisoner, and 1,250 tanks and 2,026 guns captured or destroyed. The way was ready for the main German drive to the south. It had taken over a month to rout Timoshenko's forces, and the drive on the Caucasus could not begin until it was over. The battle around Kharkov ended on June 27, and the next day the German Army Group South jumped off to their rendezvous with victory, as they thought. Ahead of them lay Stalingrad.

Before these events took place, another large Russian force had been destroyed in the south. The German 11th Army under General Manstein on May 8 attacked in the Kerch peninsula, driving the Russians back and into the sea. Then, wheeling about, Manstein opened an attack against Sevastopol, the fortress city of the Crimea and the principal Russian naval base in the Black Sea.

In 1854-55, French, British, and Turks had laid siege to Sevastopol. The Crimean War is chiefly remembered for the work of Florence Nightingale in bringing relief to the wounded and sick soldiers of the allied forces, and for the futile Charge of the Light Brigade, immortalized by Tennyson. The siege then had lasted three hundred forty-seven days before the Russian surrender.

It was to be a different story in 1942.

The Russian garrison at Sevastopol, cut off since the previous year from support by land, had received supplies and reinforcements by sea. They had taken full advantage of the time and materials gained then by erecting a series of defenses in depth designed to keep out any attacker. The city stands at the tip of a peninsula, its southern and western sides on the sea. A semicircle of defenses faced the landward side. The outer defense was a line of trenches, tank traps, and mines, supported by barbed wire, concrete gun emplacements, and observation posts. This outer ring was from one to two miles in depth. The second row of defenses was a series of concrete fortifications, especially heavily constructed and each completely equipped with its own magazines, food stores, barracks, hospitals, and heavy guns. At least two of these fortifications had 12-inch guns. The attacking Germans named these forts with easy-to-remember names: Stalin, Volga, Siberia, Molotov, GPU, Maxim Gorki I, and Maxim Gorki II. The third row of defenses was mounted on the old city walls themselves, the fortifications that had withstood siege nearly a century before. But the Russians had greatly strengthened the old masonry walls, had mounted modern weapons on them, and had constructed under them a veritable rabbit warren of passageways, food and ammunition storage areas, and hidden strongpoints. Seven Soviet divisions, plus several other unattached units—a total of over a hundred thousand men—were prepared to defend the city and their lives.

It was indeed a formidable task for General Manstein.

He set about it with a grim determination and a Prussian thoroughness fantastic in its effects. On June 3, German artillery, which had been moving up into position for weeks, opened up with a resounding roar. From the skies, Stuka aircraft from General Freiherr von Richtofen's Seventh Air Corps screamed down on the city. Thousands of rounds of shells fell upon the defenses, on both the outer rings and the city itself. German mortars lobbed their huge projectiles onto the fortifications, while fighters screamed down, their guns hunting down anyone who moved. The Seventh Air Corps flew up to two thousand sorties a day, and the shells never let up, night or day. For five days this went on, this ghastly overture to the main attack. For five days the defenders died from shells, bullets, bombs, or the unendurable shock of the assault.

For the particular assault, the Germans had brought up three giant guns, almost without precedent in war. The smallest, a descendant of the "Big Bertha" of World War I, fired a 16.8-inch shell up to nine miles. Another, known as "Thor" a 24.2-inch mortar, firing a two-and-a-quarter-ton bomb, was dwarfed by "Dora," with a caliber of 31.5 inches. Its shell weighed five tons ordinarily. Its armor-piercing shell was over seven tons, and it could hurl these projectiles twenty-four miles. On one occasion at Sevastopol, a shell from this gun blew up an ammunition dump buried a hundred feet below ground. The crew for this gun was 4,120 men.

Foot by foot, the merciless German bombardment destroyed Sevastopol's defenses. Foot by relentless foot the German troops advanced, always behind the cover of their artillery and beneath the support of the Luftwaffe. The Russian resistance was stubborn, heroic, and useless. By June 20, the Germans had reached the north shore of the harbor, where the city defenses were weakest, and eight days later, they crossed the harbor in rubber boats. Resistance ended July 1, but not before many tragic scenes were played. In one barricaded strongpoint, where over a thousand soldiers, women, and children had taken refuge, the commander refused to open the doors to the Germans. As they prepared to force their way in, the entire place blew up; the Russians had fired the magazines. They, at least, would not face German captivity.

While the Russian garrison of Sevastopol was holding out in its hopeless position, while Rommel was driving on toward Tobruk, an arrogant Japanese fleet was plowing its way through the waters of the central and northern Pacific. Its destinations: Attu, Adak, Kiska, and—Midway.

CHAPTER SEVEN

The Battle of Midway

> *Long is the way*
> *And hard, that out of hell leads up to light.*
> Milton, Paradise Lost

Far to the northeast of Hawaii lies a small coral atoll known as Midway. No nodding palm trees, no languorous Polynesian maidens entice the tourists. Only rough coral sand, scrub grass, and gooney birds characterize this featureless bit of waste real estate that was to play a key role in the Pacific war.

First discovered in 1859, Midway served variously as a coaling station and a treasure trove for Japanese feather collectors during the nineteenth century. In 1903 a cable station was established there, but it was not until 1935 that Pan American World Airways began to develop the island as a stopover point for its trans-Pacific Clippers. They established airport facilities and a small hotel for their passengers. Five years later the Navy built a small naval air station on Eastern Island, the smaller of the two habitable ones that make up ninety-nine percent of Midway's dry ground. The larger, Sand Island, was already in use for the Pan Am facilities.

"Midway Island acts as a sentry for Hawaii," wrote Admiral Nagumo. Therein lay its key role. Of little value in itself, Midway, by its location, was the key to the American position in the Hawaiian Islands. The Americans had to hold Midway.

Midway was the key to Japanese victory, as Admiral Yamamoto saw it. He knew he had to defeat the American Navy in 1942, or Japan would lose the war. Far more than most Japanese, Yamamoto had a thorough respect for the American capacity to build ships, planes, and guns enough to overwhelm the Japanese Empire. As he saw it, the only chance was to inflict such an overwhelming defeat on the U.S. Navy while it was still weak that America would lose all will to fight and would be content to permit Japan to have her way in Asia. In his mind, the capture of Midway was of far less importance than the expected battle nearby.

To review briefly the strategic reasons for the Japanese attempt on Midway: Possession of Midway and certain bases in the Aleutians would extend Japan's defense perimeter far to the east; it would protect Japan's left flank in forthcoming operations in the Solomons, the Fijis, and New Caledonia, and it would force the Americans into a naval battle. Since April 18, another reason had become plain to the Japanese planners; possession of Midway would plug the gap through which Halsey's carriers had raced to bomb Tokyo. The profound embarrassment felt by the Japanese military at their failure to protect the Emperor from such danger determined them to make amends at whatever cost.

Yamamoto did not anticipate that the cost would be very great. The Japanese fleet available for the operations outnumbered the battered U.S. Pacific Fleet in every category. Fresh from their victories in the South Pacific, the Japanese Navy men, officers and enlisted alike, believed that any meeting with the U.S. Navy would be a pushover.

Even the most optimistic American naval leaders would have to admit that the Japanese confidence was justified. In every major class of combatant ship except one, the U.S. Navy was inferior. Consider the lists on p. 193.

A lesser man than Admiral Nimitz, Commander-in Chief, Pacific Fleet, might have thrown in the sponge. But never for an instant did he lose heart. He had one enormous advantage. For some months now, the Americans had been reading the Japanese naval code, and although not all details were sent by radio, the Japanese had rather thoroughly compromised their plans. Nimitz, as early as May 10, had known pretty much that

192

SHIPS AVAILABLE FOR THE BATTLE OF MIDWAY

Type	United States		Japan	
Battleships	0·	(0) *	10	(10)
Aircraft carriers	3	(3)	4	(4)
Light carriers	0	(0)	4	(2)
Heavy cruisers	9	(7)	11	(8)
Light cruisers	4	(1)	11	(9)
Destroyers	30	(17)	57	(44)
Submarines	23	(19)	22	(16)
Totals	69	(47)	119	(93)

the Japanese were going to make a major move in the Central and North Pacific, that it would come in the first week of June, and that nearly all of the Japanese Navy would be committed. There was disagreement in the Navy Department as to the direction of the major drive, for intelligence revealed that the Japanese would be headed for both the Aleutian Islands and Midway. Nimitz resisted strong pressure that he send his major forces north to protect the barren, fogbound Aleutians, for he correctly estimated that the Aleutian operation was at worst a secondary one, or more probably a feint.

In this estimate, Nimitz was completely correct. The Japanese Combined Fleet Headquarters had their attention almost completely fixed on the Midway aspect of the operation. The primary purpose of the Aleutian move was to pull the Americans out of position; the proposed occupation of Adak, Kiska, and Attu would be convenient for weather and observation stations, but otherwise not very important.

Admiral Yamamoto began losing the Battle of Midway when he drew up his operation plan, for instead of keeping his fleet close together or in mutually supporting task forces, he scattered it all over the ocean. No fewer than five main forces, most of them subdivided several times, left Japan and other bases to carry out the attack against Midway and the Aleutians.

The spearhead of the thrust was Nagumo's First Carrier Striking Force, containing the four fleet carriers *Akagi, Kaga, Hiryu,* and *Soryu.* All four were veterans of the Pearl Harbor

* Numbers in parentheses indicate the ships present at Midway. The other ships were in the Aleutian phase of the battle.

attack and operations in the South Pacific and the Indian Ocean. Originally the *Shokaku* and *Zuikaku*, the other two Pearl Harbor carriers, had been assigned to the operation, but their battle in the Coral Sea had left both unfit for action. The *Shokaku* had been so heavily damaged that she would not be ready to fight again for months; the *Zuikaku* was in good shape, but her air group was depleted to an extent that made her useless. And there were no trained pilots ready to go aboard. So she was left behind.

The absence of the two big carriers did not worry Admiral Yamamoto. He believed that both American carriers had been sunk in the Coral Sea and that at most two American carriers, the *Hornet* and the *Enterprise* would be available to the Americans in the coming battle. To be on the safe side, the Japanese "allowed" the Americans one more carrier, for there was a "remote chance" that only one had been sunk in the Coral Sea.*

The Japanese estimate of American carrier strength, adding the generous "allowance," was right on the button. The best that Nimitz could do was to scrape together three carriers for the battle—the *Enterprise*, the *Hornet*, and the damaged *Yorktown*. The only other operational fleet carriers in the fleet at that time were both too far away to have any chance of reaching the battle zone in time. The *Saratoga*, her repairs completed, sailed from San Diego on June 1, but arrived at Pearl Harbor after the battle was over. The *Wasp*, after her spitfire deliveries to Malta, was still crossing the Atlantic while Midway was fought.

On the afternoon of May 27, 1942, the *Yorktown* limped into Pearl Harbor, ruptured steam lines leaking, boiler tubes bent and distorted, plates buckled, taking water from the near-misses that had so nearly spelled her doom in the Coral Sea battle. After receiving her damage report, Admiral Fitch estimated that it would take thirty days in a shipyard before she was ready to fight again.

That very afternoon, the *Yorktown* entered the dry dock at the Pearl Harbor Navy Yard. The caissons were closed, and

* The Japanese believed that the big carrier sunk in the Coral Sea was the *Saratoga*. It was, as we have seen, the *Lexington*. This confusion explains some of the discrepancies found in Japanese accounts of the early months of the war in the Pacific.

the water was pumped out. The big ship settled easily on the blocks. Over fourteen hundred men assailed her with cutting torches, welding gear, miles of electrical wire, replacement parts, and wood. The wood was used to make templates for plates, girders, bulkheads, and bulwarks which were then fabricated in the nearby shops and installed in the ship without reference to blueprints. Night and day these men worked, deep inside her vitals, on her flight deck, under her keel, up her mast, laboring on and on, taking only a few minutes off for a sandwich and a cup of coffee, and then picking up their tools to work on until the job was done.

At 1100, May 29, less than forty-eight hours after she had entered the dock, the *Yorktown* again felt the water under her keel and a little later moved out into the anchorage, hundreds of workmen still aboard. She took on fuel, a replacement air group and their planes, food, and ammunition. She sailed for the battle at 0900 on May 31, her scars still showing, but ready for the fight.

Her battle comrades *Hornet* and *Enterprise* had already left Pearl Harbor two days earlier. After their futile dash toward the Coral Sea they had been ordered to return at best speed to get ready for the Midway battle. On their arrival at Pearl, Admiral Halsey, worn out from six months of high-speed operations and nervous strain, had developed such a painful skin disorder that he had to be sent to the hospital at Pearl Harbor and later to the States for treatment. In his place, Nimitz assigned Rear Admiral Raymond A. Spruance as Commander Task Force 16. Spruance, a quiet, undemonstrative man, lacked the color and, hence, the press appeal of Halsey, so he has never received full recognition for his leadership during the Pacific War. He was not an aviator, but he had had a distinguished career in the Navy. His cool head and careful judgment were essential in the trying days to come.

Task Force 16, in addition to the two carriers with a hundred fifty-eight aircraft aboard, consisted of six cruisers, nine destroyers, and an oiler group of two oilers escorted by two additional destroyers. Task Force 17, with the *Yorktown*, carrying seventy-five aircraft, as flagship, was more lightly escorted by two cruisers and six destroyers. The two task forces were to operate independently during the battle, under the overall command of Rear Admiral Frank Jack Fletcher, the commander in the Coral Sea action. Although they were independent of one another, they managed to coordinate their operations far better than the Japanese did, so that the Americans were both mutually supporting and acting under the will of a common commander.

Northwest the two task forces moved to a waiting position about three hundred twenty-five miles northeast of Midway. Here they met and coordinated air searches, waiting for whatever the Japanese would throw against them.

The Japanese were throwing plenty, but it was so scattered that it gave the Americans an opportunity to defeat a part of the force and so turn back the rest. This is precisely what happened.

A key part of the Japanese plans was to station a cordon of submarines between Pearl Harbor and Midway to give advance notice of any movement of the American fleet in the direction of the battle zone. Since Yamamoto did not expect the American naval forces to sortie until after the news of the attack on Midway, he demanded no particular haste in getting the submarines into position. The result was that they were too late. By the time they arrived on station, the two American task forces were already beyond them, ready to pounce on the flank of the operation.

On May 26,* Nagumo's carrier force sortied from Hashira-jima anchorage, south of Hiroshima. Aboard its four carriers were two hundred seventy-two aircraft: ninety-three fighters, eighty-seven dive bombers, and ninety-three torpedo planes. It was escorted by two battleships, two heavy cruisers, a light cruiser, and eleven destroyers. It was the spearhead of the Japanese attack. The main body, which had left a day or so earlier, was actually to take station behind the carrier force as a mop-up brigade. The force contained three battleships, including Yamamoto's flagship, the brand-new *Yamato*, the largest warship in the world. This vessel, which had a standard displacement of 63,000 tons, carried nine 18.1-inch guns. The largest American battleships had 16-inch guns. The *Yamato* and her sister *Musashi* had been constructed so secretly that American intelligence knew little of them. They were always referred to in Japanese naval correspondence as the "special sixteen-inch battleships." With the *Yamato* there were a light

* Tokyo Time, a day ahead of Pearl Harbor. All other dates and times in this chapter have been corrected to the time of the battle.

carrier with eight torpedo planes aboard, two seaplane carriers, and thirteen destroyers. In addition, at the time of sailing, a detachment known as the Aleutian Support Force accompanied the main body. This included four more battleships, two light cruisers, and supply ships.

The Midway Occupation Force sailed in two parts, the transports and their escorts from Saipan and Guam in the Marianas, and the supporting combatant ships, called the Second Fleet, from Japan. A minesweeping group completed the forces bound for Midway.

The Japanese forces assigned to the Aleutians were almost as badly split as the Midway ones. They were divided into three seperate groups, again so widely dispersed that they could not help each other. The Aleutian operation was under the command of Vice Admiral Hoshiro Hosogaya in the heavy cruiser *Nachi*; he had two more heavy cruisers with him, and two light carriers with a total of ninety aircraft. The other forces were the Adak-Attu Occupation Force and the Kiska Occupation Force, accompanied by light cruisers, destroyers, seaplane carriers, and assorted smaller ships.

Since the local defenses of the Aleutian Islands were practically nil, except for planes stationed at the naval air stations at Dutch Harbor, Kodiak, and Sitka and Army air bases at Kodiak and Anchorage, as well as two partially completed bases at Cold Bay and Otter Point, to which no planes had been assigned, Nimitz had to deplete his slender resources to send a naval task force north. Task Force 8, under the command of Rear Admiral Robert A. Theobald, comprised only five cruisers, three of them light. Four destroyers accompanied the cruisers in their operations, while nine more, organized as a striking group (Task Group 8.4), were available in case of need.

Admiral Theobald distrusted Nimitz's intelligence reports that the Japanese objectives were Attu and Kiska; he feared it might be a ruse to draw him too far to the westward so that he could not intercept a Japanese attempt to take Dutch Harbor. He had no objection to moving air strength to the west; indeed, he persuaded the Army General to move sixty percent of his planes to the Otter Point and Cold Bay bases. However, he knew that he had to keep his small task force mobile, ready to intercept the main landing attempt at Dutch Harbor. Nimitz had informed him that the Japanese commander probably had

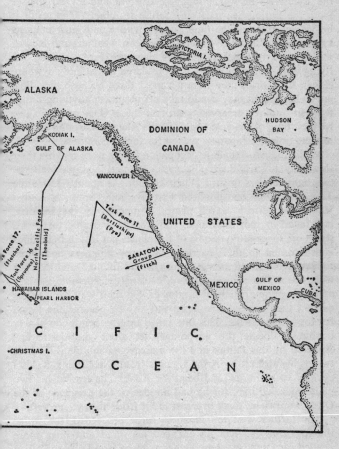

PRELIMINARIES TO MIDWAY

199

two aircraft carriers with him, and with the complete absence of any air strength in his little group except for float planes carried by his cruisers, he felt he had to remain under air support from land-based air. If he could depend on it, that is.

Aleutian weather is notorious for its unpredictability. Near the Aleutians the warm Japanese Current and icy air masses from the Bering Sea meet and refuse to mingle. The result is heavy fog much of the time, sudden wild squalls and tempests known as "williwaws," generally overcast weather, and lack of visibility so frequent that flying days are rare. In fact, the flying days would probably be considered unsuitable anywhere else in the world; they were accepted there because the pilots got so bored that they would take off in almost anything rather than sit another dreary day around the B.O.Q. or club. The foggiest time of the year begins in the Aleutians around June 1, just the time the Japanese picked for their operations.

While the two Japanese occupation forces were making their slow way toward their objectives, Admiral Kakuta took the two light carriers toward Dutch Harbor. At about 0250, June 3, he was some one hundred sixty-five miles south of Dutch Harbor. American search planes, hampered by the weather, had failed to spot this force, and Kakuta was able to get his strike off successfully. Some of the planes got lost in the clouds and returned to their carriers, but nine bombers and three fighters from the *Ryujo* got through and found Dutch Harbor wide open. The planes attacked, causing considerable damage and losing one of their own number. On their way back to the carrier, they spotted five destroyers, which became the target for the second strike. This one failed utterly, being completely unable to locate the anchorage, let alone the destroyers. Angered by this failure and the unexpected shooting down of two of his aircraft by Army fighters from Otter Point, Kakuta decided to withdraw and head for Adak. The loss of his two planes puzzled him, for he had no idea of the existence of the Otter Point field; thick overcast hid it from his own aircraft.

The farther west the Japanese force proceeded, the worse the fog grew, so Kakuta changed his mind and once more headed for Dutch Harbor. This time more blood was spilled on both sides. The thick weather that masked Kakuta's approach parted, and American search planes spotted his force. Army planes got only near-misses on the Japanese carriers and cruisers, while the Japanese did heavy damage to the Dutch

Harbor installations. On their way back to their carriers, the planes spotted the Otter Point field on Umnak and went on to bomb it, losing three of their number in the process.

Admiral Theobald, meanwhile, observing radio silence in his flagship *Nashville*, was helpless to intervene in the battle. In fact, the sparse radio reports he was receiving left him pretty much in the dark as to what was happening. Unable to endure the suspense and uncertainty, he peeled off from the rest of his task group and headed for Kodiak, arriving early on the morning of June 5. Here he found out little more about the enemy's movements; the bad weather effectively prevented anyone from knowing what the other side was doing.

The afternoon of June 4, Admiral Kakuta received a puzzling message ordering his force south to rendezvous with Nagumo and concluding: "Landing operations on Midway and the Aleutians are temporarily postponed."

Kakuta had, naturally, no way of knowing that disaster had struck the Japanese. Nor was his uncertainty relieved by the receipt of another message a few hours later canceling the rendezvous with Nagumo. Yamamoto had learned that Kakuta's force could not reach the Midway area before June 8. By that time it would be too late. As a result, Yamamoto ordered the occupation of the three Aleutian islands to continue. Admiral Hosogaya considered that Adak was too close to the newly revealed airfield on Umnak and so decided to content himself with Attu and Kiska. At the latter there was no opposition from the ten men manning the weather station. On the same day as Kiska was taken, June 7, twelve hundred troops stormed ashore on Attu. They crossed the island in full battle array through the snow and, loaded for bear, charged the village of Chichagof. By this gallant action, they took the entire population of the village prisoner—twenty-four Aleuts, fifteen children, and Mr. and Mrs. Charles Jones, American missionaries. The fierce Battle of Chichagof is not featured in Japanese accounts of the war.

Twelve hundred miles to the south, the war had already passed its turning point in the Pacific. Admiral Nagumo's force had met the American carriers and had run into a buzz saw.

By June 3, all forces on both sides were nearing the Midway area. The Japanese carrier force, six hundred miles ahead of

Yamamoto's main body, had run into a fog front, so they were often unable to see the next ship in the formation. This was an extensive blanket, extending some twelve hundred miles in a northeast-southwest direction, and was about four hundred fifty miles at its widest point. It was, however, west of the main scene of action the next day. But it did serve to cover the Japanese forces during the run-in by hiding them from the searches.

The dense fog, with its anxieties of station keeping and avoiding collision, added to Japanese apprehension. Uncertainty over the location of the American fleet disturbed them, for Nagumo's force had been given two missions, to destroy the American naval ships and to support the landing on Midway by air attack on June 5. To seek out and destroy the American fleet meant that Nagumo had to have freedom of movement in order to engage in battle on favorable terms. To send air strikes against Midway tied him to a circle within three hundred miles of that island.

Assuming that the American task forces would not be lured out of Pearl Harbor until after they were alerted by the attack on Midway, Nagumo decided to adhere to his schedule of air strikes. This mistaken assumption, that the American carriers were still swinging at anchor in Pearl Harbor, affected his decisions the next day and probably cost him the battle.

In the wardrooms of the four Japanese carriers, the pilots, not privy to these high councils, laughed and joked, knowing they had nothing to do until the weather improved. They played cards, wrote letters, and slept.

By afternoon the weather cleared, and plans were made for an attack on Midway the next day, June 4, preliminary air strikes to knock out the air strength and shore defenses in readiness for the landing on June 5.

Unknown to Nagumo or to any other Japanese commander, Fletcher's two task forces had reached a waiting position to the northeast of Midway. On his way to the rendezvous, Spruance had been giving careful consideration to Nimitz's instructions: "In carrying out the task assigned . . . you will be governed by the principle of calculated risk, which you shall interpret to mean the avoidance of exposure of your force to attack by superior enemy forces without good prospect of inflicting, as a

202

result of such exposure, greater damage on the enemy." On the day before the rendezvous, Spruance had given his instructions to the ships of his task force.

An attack for the purpose of capturing Midway is expected. The attacking force may be composed of all combatant types including four or five carriers, transports and train vessels. If presence of Task Forces 16 and 17 remains unknown to enemy we should be able to make surprise flank attacks on enemy carriers from position northeast of Midway. Further operations will be based on result of these attacks, damage inflicted by Midway forces, and information of enemy movements. The successful conclusion of the operation now commencing will be of great value to our country. Should carriers become separated during attacks by enemy aircraft, they will endeavor to remain within visual touch.

Spruance's message was basically the plan of battle. On the evening of June 3, the three American carriers were in company, about three hundred miles from Midway and about four hundred from Nagumo. During the day, American search planes from Midway had spotted a portion of the Japanese Occupation Force almost seven hundred miles a little south of west of Midway. The report was confirmed and amplified by 1100, and the commander of the Naval Air Station promptly sent out nine B-17 Flying Fortresses to attack what had been reported as the Japanese main body. Actually it was the transport group, with no ship heavier than a light cruiser. At 1624 the Forts found the force and attacked in three high runs from an altitude of eight to ten thousand feet. They made no hits, although they reported damage to "two battleships or heavy cruisers." Nine hours later four two-engine amphibians (Catalinas), each fitted with one torpedo, attacked and damaged the oiler *Akebono Maru*.

In the *Yorktown* and *Enterprise*, Admirals Fletcher and Spruance were well aware of the sightings of the Occupation Force, but unlike the Midway defenders, they were certain that there were carriers somewhere in the offing and that the force so far attacked could not be the major threat. On the evening of June 3, Fletcher ordered both American task forces to move

203

toward the southwest to a position about two hundred miles north of Midway, where he hoped to be east of the Japanese carriers. If his calculations were correct, he would be able to attack them while they were delivering their first strike on Midway.

As the ships of Task Forces 16 and 17 pushed on through the night, the watches changed in succession while officers of the deck on the bridges made the tiny course and speed adjustments necessary to keep station. Off-watch men shot the breeze, wrote letters, drank coffee, listened to the ship's service radio, or turned in their bunks and slept. Pilots in the wardrooms discussed tactics for the coming day or sat alone with their thoughts. From a phonograph came a voice singing the song, "Don't Sit Under the Apple Tree."

One by one, the men left the wardrooms. The steward's mates made fresh coffee for the oncoming watch standers and then turned out the lights, leaving only dim red lights burning. As much silence as ever comes to a big warship settled in. Tomorrow would be a busy day.

Thursday, June 4, dawned early. The sun rose at 0457, but already the ships had been humming with activity. Planes were checked, bomb and torpedo loads made ready, fuel gauges and dip sticks compared, magnetos looked at. Cooks and bakers were busy in the galleys, and the aroma of eggs and bacon was carried through the ships by ventilating systems. Additional boilers were lighted off. Unshaven, bleary-eyed skippers came out of their sea cabins, checked their positions in the formation, looked at the weather, and cast a critical eye at their own ships. Dawn General Quarters secured, and crews went back to their bunks for a few precious moments before reveille.

It was a beautiful day, with a gentle southeast wind blowing at about ten knots. The weather was cool and the visibility unlimited.

The *Yorktown* had the search duty that morning, and at 0430 she launched ten SBD Dauntlesses to sweep the northern semicircle out for a hundred miles. Search planes from Midway went out about the same time, and it was one of these that first discovered the enemy. At 0534 came the first flash: "Enemy carriers." A few minutes later, at 0545, the same plane reported: "Many enemy planes heading Midway bearing 320° distant 150." Eighteen minutes later came the message

Fletcher and Spruance had been waiting for: "Two carrier and battleships bearing 320° distant 180 course 135° speed 25."

Officers raced to their charts and plotting boards. They laid off the range and bearing from Midway as reported by the plane, and then compared the direction and distance from the American carriers. The enemy carrier force was about two hundred miles to the west southwest. This position was off by about forty miles of the actual enemy position, and this error was to be of vital importance, but Fletcher had achieved his objective. He had brought his task forces onto the flank of the enemy undiscovered, and many of the enemy planes were off on a strike.

Wishing to keep part of his force in reserve, since only two enemy carriers had been spotted, Fletcher ordered Spruance to take Task Force 16 with the *Enterprise* and *Hornet* and "proceed southwesterly and attack enemy carriers when definitely located."

Since early morning hours the Japanese carrier crews had been hard at work. Knowing the location of his target, Midway, Nagumo did not have to await the result of searches before launching his attacks. Before sunup the *Akagi*, *Kaga*, *Hiryu*, and *Soryu* began launching planes—fighters, dive bombers, and torpedo planes loaded with bombs for the first raid. He launched a total of a hundred and eight aircraft from his four carriers in fifteen minutes for his first attack wave. At 0500 he began launching the second wave, also of a hundred and eight, leaving him with only fifty-six in reserve. The excitement on the Japanese carriers was extreme. This was the first major attack that the carriers had delivered on an American base since Pearl Harbor.

The canny Nagumo did not allow himself to be completely lulled by the general belief that the American carriers were in Pearl Harbor. Failure of plans for scouting the Hawaiian Islands disturbed him. As any prudent commander would do in the circumstances, Nagumo sent out a search mission; however, in his anxiety to put the maximum number of planes over Midway, he skimped on the search. A total of seven aircraft were assigned to the mission, and their sectors did not overlap. They were to depart at the same time as the first strike wave and could not possibly reach the limits of their assigned

205

search before the second strike left. Thus, if they did spot anything, Nagumo would have nothing left to send after the Americans. He could, of course, divert the second strike wave, but they were armed with bombs intended for shore installations, not with torpedoes for use against ships.

Even at best, the search plan was minimal, assuming that everything went well. And everything did not go well. The *Akagi* and *Kaga* each contributed a plane to the search in the southern sectors. The battleship *Haruna* sent a float plane only to a distance of a hundred and fifty miles, while the search plan called for three-hundred-mile searches. The two cruisers *Chikuma* and *Tone* sent out two scouting planes each, but all four of these launches were delayed, and Admiral Nagumo was not informed of it so he could assign other planes to the missed sectors. One of *Chikuma*'s planes turned back with engine trouble; the other flew directly past the American force without spotting it. It was not until the *Tone*'s second plane, half an hour behind schedule, neared the end of the outward leg that she sighted the Americans to the northwest. The message reached Nagumo some time after 0730, and it caused consternation. Since the *Tone*'s scout plane had not identified the type of ships, further delay ensued while he sent the obvious question: "Ascertain ship types and maintain contact."

The minutes dragged by. On the decks of the *Akagi* and *Kaga* thirty-six torpedo planes, held back at the last minute from the second attack wave, were being fitted with bombs instead of the torpedoes they had first carried. The changeover had been half completed when the contact report came in. Nagumo immediately ordered the rearming suspended and alerted his force for a possible carrier battle.

Confusing and misleading reports began to arrive from the search plane. At 0809: "Enemy ships are five cruisers and five destroyers." At 0820: "Enemy force accompanied by what appears to be aircraft carrier bringing up the rear." At 0830: "Two additional enemy ships, apparently cruisers, sighted. Bearing 008°, distant 250 miles from Midway. Course 150°, speed 20 knots."

Admiral Nagumo had to make a difficult decision. He believed that at least one carrier faced him, and he had to believe that the American commander knew of his presence, for the Japanese carrier force had already undergone one attack from Midway-based planes that morning. But most of his torpedo planes on deck were loaded with bombs; those on the hangar deck were the only ones with torpedoes still aboard, and to send them off, he would have to respot his decks. The *Hiryu* and *Soryu* had thirty-six dive bombers between them ready for launch, but so many fighters had been sent to Midway that none could be spared from the combat air patrol to accompany bombers and torpedo planes to attack the American carrier force. There was another complication. The first Midway attack wave was due back before 0900, low on fuel, and would have to be recovered immediately.

He decided to change his torpedo planes back to torpedoes, recover the strike group, and then, while he headed north to conceal himself from the Americans, he would reorganize his air strength and launch an attack against the American carriers. It was a sound decision—in peacetime. If he could have carried it out, it might have won him the battle. But it took time to recover the strike, rearm and refuel planes, get them ready for launching, and get them into the air. And time was what he did not have.

At 0702, the *Enterprise* and the *Hornet* began launching aircraft. With the news of the attack by carrier planes on Midway, Spruance and his Chief of Staff, the brilliant but sometimes mercurial Captain Miles Browning, decided that there was a good chance of catching the Japanese carriers while they were recovering aircraft or while they were being refueled. It was a long shot, both in percentage chances and in the distance the planes would have to fly, but Spruance accepted the risk. If further information came in on the enemy's movements, the word could be passed to the planes by radio.

Clearly realizing that this was his great opportunity, Spruance launched a "full strike," sending every plane he could spare from combat air and antisubmarine patrol. He sent off from his two carriers twenty F4F Wildcat fighters, sixty-seven SBD Dauntless dive bombers, and twenty-nine TBF Devastator torpedo planes, a total of a hundred and sixteen aircraft. Fletcher, some distance behind, began to launch about two hours later, sending about half his strength: seventeen dive bombers, twelve torpedo planes, and only six fighters. A hundred and fifty-one American planes were winging their way toward the enemy carriers, if they could only find them.

On the way to the target, the American planes became separated. Because of the long way to go, they had not taken time to form up over the carriers as they usually did. Instead, each squadron headed off, hoping to form up with others on the way in.

It did not work out that way. The torpedo planes were flying low, and the fighters and dive bombers high. Because the torpedo planes were the slowest, it was difficult for the planes at higher altitudes to keep from getting ahead, especially with clouds between them.

The *Hornet*'s Torpedo Squadron Eight, consisting of fifteen TBF Devastators, was the first of the American carrier groups to make contact. Under the command of Lieutenant Commander John C. Waldron, the TBFs had flown to where he expected the Japanese to be. There was nothing there. A few minutes earlier, the *Hornet*'s dive bombers and fighters had reached the same spot. Finding nothing, they had turned southeast and eventually landed on Midway. Waldron, on the other hand, turned his squadron north and soon spotted the Japanese. The ships were in a tight formation, the carriers in a box arrangement in the center, surrounded by two battleships, three cruisers, and eleven destroyers. These were pretty formidable odds—fifteen planes against twenty ships.

Utterly alone, their fighter protection off with the dive bombers, the planes of Torpedo Squadron Eight passed on to the attack. Puffs of smoke from antiaircraft shells burst in front of their eyes. The air suddenly seemed filled with Japanese Zero fighters, here, there, everywhere.

What thoughts must have gone through the minds of these men as they pressed home their attack can never be known. They knew they had no chance whatever of returning to their carrier, for the range was too great. Their fuel would be gone long before they could make it, even if the Japanese did not get them first. In a letter to his wife, Waldron had written: "I believe that we will be in battle very soon—I wish we were there today. But as we are up to the very eve of serious business, I wish to record to you that I am feeling fine. . . . If I do not come back—well, you and the little girls can know that this squadron struck for the highest objective in naval warfare—'to sink the enemy.' . . . I could not be happy ashore at this time. My place is here with the fight . . ."

Skimming low over the water, Waldron led his squadron on. A plane dropped and smashed into the sea, breaking to bits on the impact. Then another. And another. Soon, over half the squadron had been shot down. The survivors drove on, un-daunted. Ensign George Gay saw the leader's ship burst into flames. Waldron tried to climb out, but the TBF smashed into the water first. Gay kept boring in. Now he was the only one left. His radioman was dead. Alone of the men of Torpedo Squadron Eight, Gay was still alive. A carrier loomed up ahead, and Gay released his torpedo. The carrier swerved away, and Gay's plane was hit again. It pancaked into the water, and the pilot was able to climb out. Hiding under a seat cushion, he escaped the notice of the Japanese and remained in the water, the sole American spectator of the events to come.*

As soon as Gay hit the water, Torpedo Squadron Six from the *Enterprise* appeared on the scene. Like Waldron's doomed squadron, it, too, had no fighters to protect it. Lieutenant Commander Eugene E. Lindsey led his fourteen TBFs against the *Akagi*, Nagumo's flagship. Ten of Lindsey's planes were quickly shot down, including his; the survivors dropped their torpedoes without making a hit.

Two minutes later, at 1000, Torpedo Squadron Three from the *Yorktown* made its attack. Thirteen Devastators made their run on the *Akagi* and then shifted to the *Hiryu*. They had six fighters with them, but the fighters were quickly smothered by the defending Zeros. Unimpressed by the slaughter, Lieutenant Commander Lance E. Massey led his TBFs closer and closer. Again the planes began to hit the water. Five of them succeeded in dropping their torpedoes, but once again all missed. Two planes of the squadron returned to their carrier.

Commander Mitsuo Fuchida, who had led the attack on Pearl Harbor but was unable to fly at Midway because of an emergency appendectomy, observed the action from the flagship *Akagi*.

Most of the credit for this success [in destroying the at-tacking torpedo planes, he wrote] belonged to the brilliant interception of our fighters, whose swift and daring action was watched closely from the flagship. No less impressive was the dauntless courage shown by the American fliers,

* Ensign Gay, after a day in the water, inflated his life raft when night came on. The next day a Catalina rescued him. See *Life* magazine, August 31, 1942.

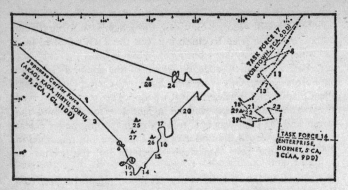

THE BATTLE OF MIDWAY, JUNE 4, 1942

1.	0430	Japanese launch attack on Midway.
2.	0430	*Yorktown* launches search: "Proceed southwesterly and attack enemy carriers."
3.	0545	Japanese carriers sighted by PBY from Midway.
4.	0630	*Yorktown* launches 6 fighters, recovers 10 dive bombers and 6 fighters.
5.	0702 to 0806	*Enterprise* and *Hornet* launch 20 fighters, 67 dive bombers, and 29 torpedo bombers.
6.	0710 to 0730	Torpedo bombers from Midway attack Japanese carrier force.
7.	0710	*Tone* search plane sights Task Force 16.
8.	0755	Dive bombers from Midway attack Japanese carrier force.
9.	0810 to 0839	B-17s and dive bombers from Midway attack Japanese carrier force.
10.	0837	Japanese begin recovering Midway strike.
11.	0838	*Yorktown* launches 17 dive bombers and 12 torpedo bombers.
12.	0905	Nagumo signals: "Proceed northward after recovering planes. We plan to contact and destroy enemy task force."
13.	0906	*Yorktown* launches 12 fighters.
14.	0928	*Hornet* torpedo bombers attack Japanese carrier force.
15.	1000	*Enterprise* and *Yorktown* torpedo bombers attack Japanese carrier force.
16.	1025 to 1030	*Kaga, Akagi,* and *Soryu* knocked out by *Enterprise* and *Hornet* dive bombers.
17.	1100	*Hiryu* launches dive bombers.
18.	1205	*Yorktown* attacked by *Hiryu* dive bombers. Three hits.
19.	1210	*Enterprise* and *Hornet* recover planes.
20.	1331	*Hiryu* launches torpedo planes.
21.	1442	*Yorktown* hit by two torpedoes.
22.	1500	*Yorktown* abandoned.
23.	1530	*Enterprise* launches 24 dive bombers.
24.	1700	*Hiryu* knocked out by *Enterprise* dive bombers.
25.	1920	*Soryu* sinks.
26.	1925	*Kaga* sinks.
27.	0500, 5 June,	*Akagi* scuttled.
28.	0510, 5 June,	*Hiryu* scuttled.
29.	0600, 7 June,	*Yorktown* sinks.

who carried out the attack despite heavy losses. Shipboard spectators of this thrilling drama watched spellbound, blissfully unaware that the worst was yet to come.

Out of forty-two torpedo planes, only a handful had managed to launch their torpedoes, and not a hit had been made on the Japanese force. Thirty-six of the TBFs had been shot down. It was a tragic, useless slaughter.

It was tragic, but it was by no means useless. Unwittingly, perhaps guided by Providence, the sacrifice of the torpedo planes opened a fatal hole in the Japanese defenses.

Lieutenant Commander Clarence McClusky, in command of the *Enterprise* air group, had sent his fighters to cover the flight of Torpedo Squadron Six. In the error they had attached themselves to the *Hornet*'s group and so had gone toward Midway instead of toward the Japanese fleet. A few had never located either group and by chance found themselves over the Japanese carriers at the crucial moment. After helplessly observing the slaughter of the torpedo planes. Lieutenant James S. Gray of the *Enterprise* reported by radio the presence of the Japanese carrier force. His report was the first one that either Spruance or Fletcher had heard indicating that the enemy had been definitely located.

McClusky, leading two squadrons of *Enterprise* dive bombers, heard Gray's message and the order from the flagship, "Attack! Attack!" Reaching for his mike button, he replied, "Wilco as soon as I find the bastards!"

In a few moments he found them. In a few moments more, the course of the war was changed.

The Japanese formation had been badly scattered by its wild maneuvers in dodging the torpedo-plane attacks. Low on ammunition, many of the Zero fighters requested permission to land on their carriers for replenishment, and the carriers were maneuvering to take them aboard. Other Zeros were sweeping out to the limits of the horizon, low on the water, to try to intercept any further torpedo-plane attacks. The carriers, in addition to rearming their fighters, were preparing to launch an all-out attack against the American carriers. Everyone's attention seemed to be directed to the ships or to the waters around them, even that of the lookouts. The peaceful sky above was ignored.

Flying at nineteen thousand feet, McClusky's attack force of

211

two squadrons, totaling thirty-seven planes, saw three carriers fairly close together and another, the *Hiryu*, some distance to the north. McClusky decided to take the two carriers to the south and west and ordered Lieutenant Wilmer E. Gallaher to follow him in an attack on the one to the south (*Kaga*), while Lieutenant Richard H. Best was to lead his squadron against the westerly one (*Akagi*).

Only three minutes after the last of the torpedo planes had been beaten off, McClusky pushed his stick over. Up and up crept the airspeed indicators. The Japanese carriers were turning into the wind to launch their own strike.

"Helldivers!" screamed a Japanese lookout.

Startled men turned their eyes toward the skies. From everywhere, it seemed, black planes were screaming down on them, growing larger every second. A few guns opened up, but it was too late. Nagumo had been caught with his planes down.

Three bombs smashed into the flight deck of the *Akagi*. Planes being fueled and planes spotted for takeoff exploded and burned, hurling flaming debris everywhere. A huge hole appeared in the flight deck, just aft of the midships elevator. A bomb plunged through to the hangar deck and detonated stored torpedoes.

Admiral Nagumo refused to believe that his flagship was doomed. Captain Taijiro Aoki, knowing better, urged him to leave. "Admiral, I will take care of the ship. Please, we all implore you, shift your flag to *Nagara* [a light cruiser] and resume command of the force." When Nagumo still refused, his staff dragged him by force to a rope leading from the flag bridge to the main deck. Sorrowfully Nagumo climbed down and boarded a destroyer, which took him and his staff over to the *Nagara*.

The *Kaga* fared no better than the flagship. Four bombs hit her almost at the same instant that the *Akagi* received her death blows. One bomb hit near the bridge, killing most of the officers there, including the commanding officer, Captain Jisaku Okada. The ship was soon burning furiously and drifted to a stop in the gentle swells. For six hours, the senior surviving officer, Commander Takahisa Amagai, fought to save the ship. At 1410 he observed three torpedo wakes streaking toward the helpless ship. Two of the torpedoes missed, and the third failed to explode. They had been fired by the American submarine *Nautilus*, which had been in the uncomfortable position of having the battle take place in the center of her patrol grounds. Looking for an opportunity, the *Nautilus* had found one in the plight of the hapless *Kaga*.*

A strange thing happened as a result of the *Nautilus*'s attack. The one torpedo that hit broke in two, and the warhead sank. Several Japanese sailors clung to the floating aftersection, and it served as a highly unexpected life raft, something its designers could not have had in mind.

Both the *Akagi* and the *Kaga* were *hors de combat*. But the Japanese troubles were not over. Lieutenant Commander Maxwell F. Leslie's Dive Bombing Squadron Three had left the *Yorktown* more than an hour later than the dive bombers from the *Enterprise*, but had flown a more direct route and, by sheer chance, had arrived over the Japanese carrier formation at the same moment as McCluskey's two squadrons. Without any coordination with the *Enterprise* planes, Leslie picked out the *Soryu* and pushed his plane over in its dive.

Aboard the *Soryu*, deck crews were readying planes for takeoff. The sight of the blazing *Kaga* distracted their attention, and when they looked up it was to see Leslie's dive bombers hurtling down on their own ship.

Three bombs hit in rapid succession, and the *Soryu* was quickly a hell of flame and smoke. The ship lost all power, and all her fire mains were cut. Within twenty minutes, her captain realized that the situation was hopeless and ordered, "Abandon ship." As the men went over the side, Captain Ryusaku Yanagimoto stood on the bridge watching them and refused to leave. A chief petty officer, a former wrestling champion, was sent to bring him off, by force if necessary. But the obvious

* The *Nautilus* reported that she had hit and sunk a *Soryu*-class carrier, and this version has been accepted in most accounts of the battle. But the *Soryu* survivors report there was no attack on that carrier by a submarine at any time, and she was too far from the *Nautilus*'s position to have been the victim. The *Nautilus* reported that she was promptly depth-charged, and only the destroyers guarding the crippled *Kaga* made any depth-charge attacks that afternoon. The *Kaga* and *Soryu* appeared almost identical, except that the former was twenty-five feet longer. It would not have been difficult to confuse them in the necessarily hurried glimpses through a periscope.

will power and determination of the Captain to go down with his ship stopped the chief, and he sorrowfully returned to his companions.

The *Soryu* sank at 1913 that evening, her Captain still on the bridge, singing the Japanese national anthem. She was followed twelve minutes later by the *Kaga*, which had also lost her fight for life. About the same time, Captain Aoki ordered abandonment of the stricken *Akagi* and requested permission of Admiral Nagumo to have one of the destroyers put the flagship to rest at the bottom of the ocean. Unexpectedly, Admiral Yamamoto intervened by radio from his flagship *Yamato*, ordering that the sinking be delayed.

Yamamoto's main body, four hundred and fifty miles behind Nagumo's carrier force, was still in the fog on the early morning of June 4, and the Admiral feared that the carriers might be hampered in launching their planes. However, the fog burned off as morning wore on, and everything seemed auspicious for the great attack. Reports of the attacks on Midway reached flag plot on the *Yamato*, and everything they heard was encouraging. Even the discovery of the American carrier force did not long disturb the equanimity of the assembled staff.

Silence fell over the battle. No messages were received for nearly two hours. Then a message came in from Rear Admiral Abe aboard the *Tone*. Admiral Yamamoto groaned aloud as he read it;

FIRES RAGING ABOARD KAGA, SORYU, AND AKAGI RESULTING FROM ATTACKS BY ENEMY CARRIER AND LAND-BASED PLANES. WE PLAN HAVE HIRYU ENGAGE ENEMY CARRIERS. WE ARE TEMPORARILY WITHDRAWING TO THE NORTH TO ASSEMBLE OUR FORCES.

There was only one thing to be done, and Yamamoto did it. He planned to assemble all his forces, both from the Aleutians and from around Midway, and try to overwhelm the Americans by sheer weight of numbers. It was a counsel of desperation, and he was desperate. Although the fog had closed in again, he ordered a speed of 20 knots. Through the thickening weather, unguided by radar, the Japanese ships raced, their officers of the deck unable to see their own bows. A collision would sink both ships in a flash. But there were no collisions.

The *Hiryu* was still undamaged. Except for a few ships needed to assist the three burning carriers, the fleet re-formed around her. On her flag bridge, Rear Admiral Tamon Yamaguchi, Commander Carrier Division Two, was determined to hit back at the enemy. Miraculously, the *Hiryu* was not attacked then, and Yamaguchi was able to get his strike off. At 1040, eighteen dive bombers and six Zeros took to the air and headed northwest. Lieutenant Michio Kobayashi, leading the attack, spotted several groups of American dive bombers returning to their carriers, and he shadowed at a safe distance.

As the Japanese neared the American carrier force, the *Yorktown*'s radar picked them up and coached the CAP to an intercept. In a hotly contested dogfight, all but eight of the Japanese planes were shot down. Two more were splashed by ships' gunfire, but the rest attacked the *Yorktown*. At 1220, three hits were made, all of them serious, but none vitally wounding the ship. One hit the stack and ruptured the uptakes so that fires were snuffed out in five of the ship's six boilers. The *Yorktown* gradually drifted to a stop. Another hit knocked out the radios and radars, so unable to maintain command, Admiral Fletcher shifted his flag to the cruiser *Astoria*.

Damage-control parties worked so effectively that in a little over an hour the *Yorktown* had four boilers back on the line, was making 20 knots, and was preparing to launch fighters.

Spruance, nearly thirty miles away, heard of the attack and dispatched two cruisers and two destroyers to augment the *Yorktown*'s screen. Scarcely had they arrived when the radar on one of the cruisers picked up another wave of Japanese planes. These were the last planes Yamaguchi had remaining, ten torpedo planes and six fighters. They had left at 1245 on the two-hour flight to the American carrier force.

The *Yorktown* managed to get eight fighters into the air to join the four already circling the task force. But these planes from the *Yorktown* had only about twenty-three gallons of gasoline apiece—scarcely a combat ration. They joined their companions and all strove valiantly to intercept. Half of the Japanese fighters and half of the torpedo planes were shot down. The ships fired into the water ahead of the torpedo planes, sending up huge geysers that could smash a plane if it hit them. Four of the torpedo planes managed to get their torpedoes off. The *Yorktown* dodged two of them, but two more slammed into her port side. Her rudder was jammed, power connections were broken, and the ship listed rapidly to port, coming to rest twenty minutes later twenty-six degrees over. The time was 1442.

Less than twenty minutes later, fearing that his ship would capsize, Captain Elliott Buckmaster ordered the *Yorktown* abandoned. Men entered the water in good order and kept up their spirits by high jinks, laughing, singing, and joking until they were rescued.

A flight of ten scout bombers from the *Yorktown* was returning to its carrier after a fruitless search, when suddenly, they spotted something below. It was the *Hiryu*, accompanied by two battleships, three cruisers, and four destroyers, heading north, about a hundred and ten miles from the crippled *Yorktown*.

Fletcher was in no position to do anything about this latest sighting, but Spruance was. The *Enterprise* launched twenty-four dive bombers, ten of them belonging to the *Yorktown*, and the *Hornet* sent sixteen more, half an hour later. By 1530 the launch was completed and the planes sped directly to their targets. These pilots were veterans by now, all having participated in the morning attack on the three disabled Japanese carriers. The *Enterprise* planes arrived over the *Hiryu* about 1700. The lone carrier had only a handful of planes aboard, having stripped herself for the second attack on the *Yorktown*; the ones remaining had come in after the last attack had been launched.

As the *Enterprise* planes dived on the *Hiryu*, Lieutenant Gallaher, whose squadron had disposed of the *Kaga* that morning, saw his first bombs miss as the *Hiryu* swerved under full right rudder. Her violent maneuvering did her no good. Four bombs hit, smashing an elevator and knocking out all communications and facilities in the island, the brains of the ship. Minutes later the *Hornet* planes arrived and, seeing the *Hiryu* disabled, turned their attention to the other ships. They obtained several near-misses on the battleship *Haruna,* on the *Tone* and the *Chikuma,* but got no hits.

The *Hiryu* was done for. Nothing could be done to save her, and the captain ordered the survivors to leave her. Admiral Yamaguchi refused to leave, and he and the Captain were last seen standing on the bridge, waving to their erstwhile shipmates. At 0510, June 5, the destroyers *Kazagumo* and *Yugumo* fired torpedoes into the cripple. She settled lower and lower in the water, and the destroyers withdrew, confident that they had done their job. Later in the morning she was reported to be still afloat, but search planes could not find her. She was never heard from again.

Not since fifteen British ships of the line under Admiral Sir John Jervis and Commodore Horatio Nelson defeated twenty-four Spanish ships off Cape St. Vincent on February 14, 1797, had such a complete and dramatic reversal of fortune taken place at sea. The Japanese had lost all four of their big carriers; two-thirds of the carriers that had begun the war with the attack on Pearl Harbor were on the bottom. The Midway operation was stopped cold.

It was a time for reassessing the situation. Could the Japanese do nothing to retrieve the operation? Was there anything more the American forces could do?

Aboard the *Yamato,* staff officers suggested one plan after the other to gain something from the battle. Now Yamamoto's folly in scattering his forces so widely became painfully apparent. It was impossible to get them together in time to do any good. Optimistic reports from Nagumo's force declared that at least two of the American carriers were damaged, so that American air superiority would largely be nullified. Yamamoto finally decided to pin every hope on a night surface attack with all the big ships he could scrape together from his scattered forces. Night would nullify American air strength, and the Americans had no ship larger than a cruiser present. When the news of the crippling of the *Hiryu* arrived, Yamamoto did not cancel the order; instead he sent out a strangely optimistic signal to all his forces, saying in part: (1) The enemy fleet has been practically destroyed and is retiring eastward. (2) Combined Fleet units in the vicinity are preparing to pursue the remnants of the enemy force and, at the same time, to occupy Midway.

217

In view of its complete detachment from reality, this message can be most charitably viewed as a morale builder.

Later, as the chance hourly seemed less and less of forcing an engagement with a fleet they could not find, Admiral Yamamoto decided to call off the whole operation.

"But how can we apologize to His Majesty," asked one officer; "for this defeat?"

"Leave that to me," replied Yamamoto. "I am the only one who must apologize to His Majesty."

Sorrowfully, the Chief of Staff sent out the word to scuttle the tortured *Akagi* and to cancel the Midway operation. There remained nothing to do but to extricate the forces as quickly as possible.

Vice Admiral Takeo Kurita was speeding through the night toward Midway in his flagship *Kumano*. With him were three other heavy cruisers, *Suzuya, Mikuma,* and *Mogami,* and two destroyers. His mission was to bombard Midway at dawn on June 5. Kurita was only ninety miles from Midway when he received the order to cancel the attack. Obediently the ships swung around and headed northwest. Shortly after they had settled down on their new course, lookouts on the *Kumano*'s bridge spotted the American submarine *Tambor* lying on the surface. Kurita immediately ordered an emergency forty-five-degree turn to port, but the *Mogami*, last ship in column, failed to get the word. Her speed of 28 knots unchecked, she plowed into the port quarter of the *Mikuma* next ahead. Damage to the *Mikuma* was not severe, but the *Mogami* lost all of her bow forward of number one turret. Leaving the two damaged cruisers behind with the two destroyers for company, Kurita sped on to his scheduled rendezvous with Admiral Yamamoto.

When the *Yorktown* was abandoned, effective command of the American forces passed to Admiral Spruance. Shortly after 1300, June 4, after Fletcher had arrived on the *Astoria,* Spruance reported to him: "TF 16 air groups are now striking the carrier which your search planes reported. . . . Have you any instructions for me?"

"None," replied Fletcher. "Will conform to your movements."

It must have been a sore blow to Fletcher to turn command over to his subordinate, but it was a sound decision. Spruance still had two effective carriers and a well-trained carrier flag staff.* He could judge the situation in a way that was denied Fletcher.

The obvious temptation was to pursue the Japanese to the westward in hopes of mopping up the entire force. It was a temptation. Spruance wisely rejected. Even though the Japanese Navy had lost all its big carriers, Spruance could not know this, and if he moved after them, he might run into air attack and certainly into superior surface forces. Although the scorpion's sting had been extracted, there still remained the powerful jaws. And Spruance did not propose to sail blindly into them.

> I did not feel justified [he wrote] in risking a night encounter with possibly superior enemy forces, but on the other hand I did not want to be too far away from Midway the next morning. I wished to have a position from which either to follow up retreating enemy forces or to break up a landing attack on Midway.

At dusk, therefore, Spruance headed eastward and steamed away from the Japanese for five hours. When midnight came, he reversed course so that he would be back in the area at daylight. How sound his decision was can be seen when the tracks of the Japanese and American forces are compared. If Spruance had plunged west in hot pursuit, he would have run into a powerful Japanese surface concentration shortly after midnight. That the Japanese battleships, cruisers, and destroyers could have polished off his carriers and their escorts is a foregone conclusion. By his prudence Spruance preserved the fleet that would soon make America's first tentative steps toward the offensive in the Pacific.

The next day, June 5, was anticlimax. All Japanese forces were retiring from the scene. Midway-based pilots were in an angry mood, for the Japanese submarine *I-168* had kept them awake by shelling the atoll. As soon as they could, search Catalinas went out to look for her. It would have been better for the Americans if the planes could have found the submarine, for we shall hear of her again. They could not locate her, but stumbled on the crippled *Mogami-Mikuma* group

---

* He had Halsey's experienced staff complete.

making its painful way northwest at 12 knots.

Twelve B-17 Flying Fortresses already in the air were told to attack the cruisers, but they failed to find them. A flight of six SBDs and six obsolete SB2U Vindicators were the only other planes available on the island, and they took off shortly after 0600. At 0745, they spotted a trail of oil on the water and followed it to the two cruisers. Such a mass of antiaircraft fire arose that the planes were able to do no better than six near-misses. Captain Richard E. Fleming, USMC, his plane fatally hit, managed to crash it into the *Mikuma,* but it hit a turret and did little damage. The two cripples held their course undisturbed for the rest of the day. On June 6, their luck ran out.

Enterprise search planes discovered them early that morning, and three attack waves were sent after them from the two carriers. The *Mogami,* apparently favored by the fates, survived several bomb hits and eventually reached Truk for a patch job before returning to the home islands for complete repairs. It was over a year before she was able to fight again.

The *Mikuma* received the brunt of the attack. When her stored torpedoes detonated, the two destroyers with her took off survivors and left her to the mercy of the wind and sea. She sank that night. Another score was paid by this attack, for it had been the *Mikuma* and *Mogami* that sunk the *Perth* and *Houston* after the Battle of the Java Sea.

Throughout the afternoon of June 4 and all through the night, the abandoned *Yorktown* had continued to float in mute protest of her desertion. During the night she had been guarded by the destroyer *Hughes*, but the guard was not assigned to help her—merely to ensure that she did not fall into the hands of the enemy.

The next morning, the *Hughes* lookouts observed machine-gun splashes in the water around the carrier. She sent over a boarding party, who discovered two seriously injured men left for dead when the ship was abandoned. Also, several coding machines had not been destroyed. The skipper of the *Hughes* informed Fletcher and Nimitz that in his opinion the *Yorktown* could be saved. A small minesweeper, the *Vireo,* which had been near French Frigate Shoal, arrived on the scene and attempted to take the carrier in tow. All day long she struggled, barely able to make steerageway. The *Hughes* and the destroyer *Gwin* stood by to lend assistance, joined later by the *Monaghan*. Finally a salvage party arrived in the destroyer *Hammann*. The destroyer went alongside and secured herself with lines, while she passed over pumping hose and electrical power lines. Captain Buckmaster led the work, extinguishing the one remaining fire, pumping out water, jettisoning topside weight, and generally making encouraging progress. The *Yorktown* could still be saved.

The Japanese submarine *I-168*, prowling around after her shelling of Midway, received orders from Yamamoto to go get the carrier his scout planes had reported. She closed to the reported position, but nothing was there but open sea.

Work continued on the *Yorktown*. Slowly the list came off. Things were looking better and better. The day wore on into night. The destroyers snuffled around listening for submarines, watching for planes or ships. June 6 dawned clear and fair, and the morning brought the *Yorktown* nearer to safety.

At 1331, Lieutenant Commander Yahachi Tanabe raised the periscope of *I-168*. He had spent the last twenty-four hours in searching, and now his efforts were rewarded. Seven destroyers appeared in the periscope, and in the center of them was the crippled *Yorktown*. Closing to nineteen hundred yards, *I-168* fired a spread of four torpedoes. One struck the *Hammann*, still alongside the carrier. The hapless destroyer broke in two and sank almost immediately, taking eighty-five of her crew with her. Another torpedo missed, but two struck the *Yorktown*'s starboard side.

The destroyers swarmed in like an angry pack of wolves. Depth charge after depth charge shook the submarine; over sixty near-misses were counted. At length, one pattern blasted her to the surface. The triumphant destroyers rushed in for the kill, and the *I-168* took to the depths again, heedless of her injuries. After midnight, battery power and air running out, the submarine was forced to surface. She came up to fight to the last, but only open water greeted her. The destroyers had called off the attack only a few minutes earlier.

Captain Buckmaster still hoped to save the *Yorktown*, but her wounds were too severe. She listed more and more, and sounds of breaking plating and machinery could be heard below. The *Vireo* cut the towline, and the salvage party transferred to a destroyer. At 0600, while the escorting destroyers half-masted colors and the crews, heads uncovered, came to attention, the *Yorktown* rolled over and sank in twelve thousand feet of water.

All that remained of the battle was the mopping up. Spruance, who had been following the retreating Japanese to the westward, decided on the evening of June 6 that he was getting too close to Japanese air strength on Wake. His destroyers were running low on fuel, and his air crews were worn out after three days of continuous fighting.

Nimitz had some apprehension that the Aleutian phase of the battle might now develop into a storm, so he began to redispose his forces, including the *Saratoga*, which had arrived in Pearl Harbor on June 6, to take care of that threat. It soon became evident, however, that nothing was brewing up there, and all forces returned to port.

The Battle of Midway was the first real Japanese defeat at sea since the sixteenth century. The Imperial Navy had lost four front-line carriers, a heavy cruiser, and over three hundred aircraft. The Japanese loss of thirty-five hundred men included over a hundred of their most experienced carrier pilots, and this shortage could never be made up throughout the war. As opposed to these losses, the United States had lost the *Yorktown*, the *Hammann*, and about a hundred and fifty aircraft. Three hundred and seven Americans died in the battle, but their sacrifice was not in vain. For this was Japan's last offensive. Henceforward, the Japanese were to respond to American challenges.

The flood tide of Empire had passed its peak.

CHAPTER EIGHT

June-July: "Second Front Now!"

> *"He will maintain his argument as well*
> *as any military man in the world."*
> Shakespeare, Henry V

The Boeing Clipper circled low over Washington past the Washington Monument, and landed smoothly on the Potomac River a little after seven o'clock on the evening of June 18, 1942. Out stepped Britain's Prime Minister, Sir Alan Brooke,

Chief of the Imperial General Staff, Sir Hastings Ismay, Churchill's Chief of Staff, and several of the Prime Minister's personal attendants. They had been in the air twenty-six and a half hours, but were rested and well fed, since the plane was equipped with berths and a well-stocked larder. Churchill's insistence on eating in accordance with his "tummy time" rather than "sun time" assured all passengers of frequent breakfasts, dinners, or luncheons. As the Prime Minister demanded food every four hours, all washed down with champagne and brandy, it became, as Brooke later wrote, "a little trying on the constitution."

Since Churchill's last visit in December, the whole complexion of the war had changed. Most of the Far East had been lost. Rommel's drive threatened Suez and the entire Middle East. And it appeared that Germany's second-year offensive against Russia might soon knock her out of the war.

New decisions had to be made.

While Brooke and his aides went to discussions with the American Joint Chiefs of Staff, Churchill flew up to Hyde Park, where President Roosevelt was taking a brief vacation. Roosevelt met his distinguished visitor at the New Hackensack Airport, and they immediately embarked on a series of conferences. Churchill was dressed in a pale-blue "zip suit," as he called it, a full-length set of coveralls. He loved these garments, wearing them on all possible and impossible occasions. He even wore one that evening for dinner, though his host, the President, was wearing a white dinner jacket. It is recorded that the Prime Minister did have the grace to apologize.

Churchill's sudden trip to the United States was but one of a series of V.I.P. crossings of the Atlantic as the Western Allies tried to work out some common strategy for the war. At the Arcadia Conference the two fundamental decisions reached were that the war against Germany would have primary attention and that each theater of war would have a supreme commander whose appointment would be determined on national, political, and military grounds.

Various possible operations had been considered during the Arcadia Conference—plans to hit at France and Germany by air, plans to land on the continent of Europe in the coming months, perhaps as early as 1942, a plan, code-named Gymnast, to land in French Morocco. But nothing final had been settled.

In April, the U.S. Army Chief of Staff, General Marshall, and Harry Hopkins as the personal representative of President Roosevelt had arrived in London, bearing with them the American ideas for joint action with the British. The War Plans Division of the Army had worked for months on these proposals, and they had been approved by the President, who, nonetheless, had some misgivings.

Hopkins and his party had flown the Atlantic in a chartered Pan American Boeing Clipper, and consequently had a comparatively easy journey, with a weekend stopover at Bermuda. Hopkins had suffered considerable hardship in his previous trip via Army bomber, and in his precarious state of health, it was no trivial matter for him. This time, however, he arrived comparatively fresh on the morning of Wednesday, April 8. They met with Mr. Churchill at 10 Downing Street that afternoon.

Mr. Roosevelt, reflecting the feeling of most of the American public, was anxious for American troops to come to grips with the Germans somewhere, sometime, during 1942. To this end, the proposals Hopkins and Marshall presented to the British envisioned a landing in the Cherbourg area in the fall of 1942, to be followed by a direct cross-Channel invasion in the spring of the following year. Meanwhile, American troops would be sent in increasing numbers to Britain for training. In conferences lasting several days, these ideas were presented, discussed, revised, and given the careful scrutiny of the British Chiefs of Staff. Many other aspects of the war came into consideration as well, but the fundamental purpose of the conference was British agreement to the American proposals.

Fundamental to American thinking in proposing these operations was the belief that Russia must be sustained in the war at all costs. It was a known fact that in 1942 Russia was engaging more German troops than all the other twenty-five of the United Nations put together. And no serious military man on either the British or American side was willing to risk his reputation on an absolute prediction that the Germans would not defeat Russia in the coming summer campaigns. Both the President and the Prime Minister, as well as all members of the Combined Chiefs of Staff, well remembered the Russian collapse and surrender to Germany in 1917. The Soviets were unquestionably a tougher nut than the Czarist troops had been; the question was, *how* tough?

The American proposal for Sledgehammer, the landing in the Cherbourg area in the fall of 1942, was originally presented as an emergency operation, a kind of sacrifice landing to be made in the event of a Russian collapse. Since not many American troops would be ready by that time, Sledgehammer would have to be largely a British operation, and the British looked upon it with jaundiced eyes. They thought that even Roundup, the main invasion in the spring of 1943, was somewhat dubious of fulfillment. However, all sides agreed that the buildup of American forces in Britain would be a good thing. This phase of the American plan, known as Operation Bolero, was therefore implemented and continued throughout the year.

Before Hopkins and Marshall left London, they had obtained "agreement in principle" with the American proposals, with the single proviso that sufficient strength must be maintained in the East to keep the Germans and Japanese from joining up in India or elsewhere.

The phrase "agreement in principle" was to cause much misunderstanding between the British and American leaders for the next few months. To the British the words seemed to mean, "We will examine these proposals very closely, for they represent something we ought to do if we can. We will let you know if we think it is possible." To the Americans the words seemed to mean, "We have agreed what we are going to do; now let's work out how to do it."

Hopkins's and Marshall's report to Roosevelt on their return suggested that the British acceptance of the American proposals was somewhat less than enthusiastic. Roosevelt, learning that Soviet Foreign Minister Vyacheslav Molotov was expecting to visit London soon, suggested that he come to Washington first, so that the American plans could be presented to him before he saw the British. Churchill balked at the idea, preferring to present the British views first, before Roosevelt's enthusiasm committed the Allies to imprudent action. The ostensible purpose of Molotov's visit to London was the text of certain agreements between the Soviet Union and the United Kingdom, but, of course, he was primarily interested in the prospects of a second front in 1942.

In the Russian view, Britain and America were doing little, allowing Russia to bear the principal weight of the German

225

attacks. The United States and the United Kingdom could contribute nothing but supplies in direct support of the Russian armies. There were only three routes by which supplies might reach the Soviets, and they were all fraught with difficulty or danger. The first was across the Pacific to Vladivostok. Since Russia was not at war with Japan, and the Japanese had no desire to offend the Soviets, the Japanese allowed neutral and Russian ships to go to Vladivostok with no interference. However, once there, goods had to be transported 5,787 miles to Moscow. Each bullet sent in that manner had to come halfway around the world before it could be fired at the Germans.

The second possible route was through the Persian Gulf to Basra and over the Iranian railroad. However, the railway was mostly single-tracked, the port of Basra was completely inadequate, and a ship could make only two round trips a year between either Britian or the United States and Basra. Even at that, at the end of the war, many cargoes were still piled up awaiting transshipment.

The best known route, the most fruitful, and the one most fraught with danger was via North Russia, either to Archangel or to Murmansk. This involved taking ships north of Norway, where they were threatened by German surface forces, U-boats, and the Luftwaffe based on Norwegian airfields. Each convoy movement involved a major naval operation, and at that, losses were almost insupportable. For example, during April, May, and June of 1942, eighty-four ships had been sent out to Russia, bearing 522,000 tons of cargo. Only forty-four arrived, with 300,000 tons. Some had been diverted to Scotland; the rest had been sunk or had foundered. Nor was this the worst. The sinkings increased. The Russians accused the British of "stealing" their lend-lease goods and of "timidity" in pushing the cargoes through.

It was against such a background of feeling that Molotov made his visits to London and Washington.

Molotov received scant comfort in London. He was in a suspicious frame of mind to begin with and put little faith in his British hosts, even when it came to protecting his personal safety.

His room [wrote Churchill] had been thoroughly searched by his police officers, every cupboard and piece of furniture and the walls and floors being meticulously examined by practised eyes. The bed was the object of particular attention: the mattresses were all prodded in case of infernal machines, and the sheets and blankets were rearranged by the Russians so as to leave an opening in the middle of the bed out of which the ocupant could spring at a moment's notice, instead of being tucked in. At night a revolver was laid out beside his dressing gown and his dispatch case.

Although agreement was easily reached over the treaties, the ostensible purpose of Molotov's visit, the British refused to make any categorical statements on the prospect of a second front. Molotov demanded a landing by Britain and the United States sufficiently large to force the Germans to withdraw at least forty divisions from the Russian front. The landing had to be in Europe, and it had to be in 1942. Since the Germans already had some fifty divisions in France, it would be a tall order to make them pull out forty more.*

To soften their refusal to commit themselves, the British suggested that Mr. Molotov stop in again at London after he had held consultations with President Roosevelt, and with this sop, Molotov had perforce to be content.

Churchill's fertile brain, meanwhile, had come up with a new alternative. While Molotov was winging his way across the Atlantic, the Prime Minister telegraphed Roosevelt what the Americans felt was an ominous message. It said in part:

We are working hard with your officers, and all preparations are proceeding ceaselessly on the largest scale. Dickie [Mountbatten, British Commander of Combined Operations, i.e., Commandos] *will explain to you the difficulties of 1942 when he arrives. I have also told the staffs to study a landing in the north of Norway, the occupation of which seems necessary to ensure the flow of our supplies next year to Russia.* I have told Molotov we would have something ready for him *about this* to discuss on his return here. We did not go deeply into it in any way. *Personally I set great importance upon it if a good plan can be made. . . .*

We must never let "Gymnast" [landing in French

* A German division contained about 12,000 men.

227

North Africa] *pass from our minds. All other preparations would help, if need be, towards that.* [Italics supplied.]

Although Roosevelt personally favored the idea of a landing in French North Africa, he had accepted the Army plan for Sledgehammer-Roundup, and was willing to go along with it. To the members of the Joint Chiefs of Staff, however, this message implied that Britain was putting the accepted plan for direct assault on Germany on the back burner and turning to diversionary operations that would uselessly expend Anglo-American lives and treasure. In particular, the American Joint Chiefs disliked Churchill's pet scheme for the Norway operation. Churchill was always fascinated by the idea of landing in the far north and working gradually down the Norwegian mountain ranges. To the Joint Chiefs the plan, Operation Jupiter, seemed the wildest of eccentric operations, the wildest folly.

They need not have worried about Jupiter, since Sir Alan Brooke, Chief of the Imperial General Staff, felt precisely the same way—it was one of his few points of agreement with the Americans—and the plan died a-borning, in spite of all the eloquence Churchill produced in its favor.

The prospects of a revival of Gymnast, however, seemed far more dangerous to Marshall and the others. Here was a diversionary idea that would open up a new front on a different continent from where the main decision lay. Worse, an operation in North Africa in 1942 would inevitably make Roundup impossible for 1943, an unacceptable idea to the American Joint Chiefs.

Molotov arrived in Washington May 29, the day after Churchill's telegram, and went immediately to the White House for a conference with Roosevelt and Hopkins. Since no military advisers were present, the conference was largely given over to gettting acquainted and to diplomatic matters. It was not until the next day that the second-front problem was faced directly.

On the morning of May 30, General Marshall and Admiral King joined Roosevelt and Hopkins to meet with Molotov. Here they quickly came to the crux of the matter. If, said Molotov, the Western Allies could land enough strength to draw off forty German divisions, then the Soviets could win on the eastern front, and the war would be decided in the year 1942. If not, then the Soviets would do their best, but would not be responsible for any consequences. If, he continued, the Soviets were unable to withstand an all-out German push, then Britain and the United States would be faced with a much stronger enemy than at present, and the Soviet Army would not be there to help them.

Marshall countered that the obvious requirement was not the diversion of German infantry but diversion of the Luftwaffe from the Soviet front. It was his hope to be able to engage and defeat the German air arm, which, he admitted, could be brought into action only by an infantry landing.

Certainly, from these conversations, Molotov believed that the United States was committed to a landing in Europe in 1942. Although no absolute promise was made, Molotov considered he had obtained his goal. In the final conference he had asked the direct question. "What answer shall I take back to London and Moscow on the general question that has been raised? What is the President's answer with respect to the second front?"

Roosevelt's answer was that American planners were in conference with the British and that "we expect to establish a second front." Again, this was no firm commitment, but Molotov believed it was. His belief was strengthened by the words of the communiqué released to the press after the conferences were over: "In the course of the conversations full understanding was reached with regard to the urgent tasks of creating a Second Front in Europe in 1942."

This communiqué was not actually released until after Molotov had returned to London, and Churchill as well as Roosevelt had approved it. More cautious than the Americans, the British presented Molotov with an *aide-mémoire*:

We are making preparations for a landing on the Continent in August or September, 1942. . . . Clearly however it would not further either the Russian cause or that of the Allies as a whole if, for the sake of action at any price, we embarked on some operation which ended in disaster and gave the enemy an opportunity for glorification at our discomfiture. It is impossible to say in advance whether the situation will be such as to make this operation feasible when the time comes. *We can therefore give no promise in the matter*, but provided that it appears sound and sensible we shall not hesitate to put our plans into effect.

Since the *aide-mémoire*, by its very nature, could not be made public, the Russian people interpreted the published words of the communiqué as a promise of a second front in 1942. So, too, the Soviet leaders chose to believe.

After Molotov's departure from London on his return to Russia, Churchill and the British Chiefs of Staff spent the next few weeks in studying their commitment to the second front and the implications of it in terms of men and materials. The more they thought about it, the more impossible the American plan seemed. The "emergency measure," Sledgehammer, seemed to them absolutely suicidal; a maximum of five divisions, only two of them American, could possibly be landed and supported in the Cherbourg area during 1942. The great bottlenecks were the state of training of the American soldiers and the shortage of transatlantic shipping. In the British view it takes two years to make a soldier; the Americans were trying to do it in nine months or so. The Battle of the Atlantic was at its height; sinkings by submarines had risen from 327,000 tons in January to over 700,000 tons in June. The hundred and forty-four ships lost to U-boats in June meant the loss not only of the cargoes the ships were carrying, but also of the cargoes they might have carried in future voyages. Sinkings were still outrunning building of new ships at the rate of two and a half to one.

The British Chiefs of Staff felt no confidence whatever in the ability of a lodgment of a mere five divisions to hold its beachhead in the face of the fifty-odd German divisions in France. The War Cabinet agreed and made an absolute decision that the British would not be a party to a landing attempt unless it could be launched with enough strength to enable it to remain in France. There would not be another Dunkirk.

This decision made Sledgehammer impossible and raised grave doubts about the feasibility of Roundup as early as the spring of 1943. For the British believed it would be impossible to build enough strength in Britain by means of the Bolero buildup by that time. As a result of this decision, Churchill decided there was nothing for it but to have another meeting with Roosevelt and sell him on either Gymnast or Jupiter.

One of the reasons for Churchill's desire to confer with Roosevelt at this time was to reach an agreement over exchange of information on a project both nations were working on—very secret, and very dubious of success. Its code name was Tube Alloys. It is now known as the atomic bomb.

Scarcely had Churchill and Roosevelt returned from their weekend at Hyde Park and begun their first conference with members of the Combined Chiefs of Staff when a secretary entered the room with a telegram for the President. Mr. Roosevelt read it silently and passed it to Churchill without comment. It was the news of the fall of Tobruk. Sir Hastings Ismay, Secretary to the War Cabinet and Churchill's personal Chief of Staff, has recorded the incident. "This was a hideous and totally unexpected shock, and for the first time in my life, I saw the Prime Minister wince. . . . For a moment or two no one spoke. The silence was broken by President Roosevelt. In six monosyllables he epitomized his sympathy with Churchill, his determination to do his utmost to sustain him, and his recognition that we were all in the same boat. 'What can we do to help?' "

Churchill asked that more tanks be sent to Auchinleck, and General Marshall complied at once, even though this meant that they had to be taken from American army units that had received them only a few days earlier.

As a result of the fall of Tobruk, Churchill faced a vote of censure in the House of Commons. Because of the situation in the Western Desert and the challenge to his authority, Churchill was urgently needed at home. Therefore, the primary question of the meeting, the one the British had crossed the Atlantic to settle, was scarcely touched on. Before he left, Churchill handed a note to Roosevelt, putting the issue squarely:

. . . We hold strongly to the view that there should be no substantial landing in France this year unless we are going to stay.

. . . No responsible British military authority has so far been able to make a plan for September, 1942, which had any chance of success unless the Germans become utterly demoralized, of which there is no likelihood. Have the American Staffs a plan? At what points would they strike? What landing-craft and shipping are available? Who is the officer prepared to command the enterprise?

. . . But in case no plan can be made in which any responsible authority has good confidence, and consequently no engagement on a substantial scale in France is possible in September, 1942, what else are we going to do? Can we afford to stand idle in the Atlantic theatre during the whole of 1942? Ought we not to be preparing within the general structure of "Bolero" some other operation by which we may gain positions of advantage, and also directly or indirectly to take some of the weight off Russia? It is in this setting and on this background that the French Northwest Africa operation should be studied.

Like King Charles's head, Gymnast kept turning up in Churchill's correspondence. It was beginning to get on Marshall's nerves.

At 11 P.M., Churchill's Boeing Clipper took off again from Baltimore to return the Prime Minister to face his accusers in Parliament. After an uneventful trip home. Churchill allowed the debate in the House of Commons to run its course. Following a ringing defense of his position, he called for a vote. The censure motion was defeated 475 to 25, but even the twenty-five votes against him hurt Churchill keenly.

Allowing Churchill barely time to recover from the Parliamentary crisis, Roosevelt pushed for a showdown on plans for 1942. Time was drawing on, and if anything was to be done, plans had to be made—and right speedily. The challenge to Churchill's leadership had robbed the two men of their chance to thrash things out together, and as Roosevelt felt he could not leave the United States at that time, he decided to send Hopkins, Marshall, and King to London with full powers to reach a decision. The three men left Washington on July 16, bearing a long, detailed set of instructions to guide them. The key paragraphs were:

5. In regard to 1942, you will carefully investigate the possibility of executing SLEDGEHAMMER. Such an operation would definitely sustain Russia this year. It might be the turning point which would save Russia this year. SLEDGEHAMMER is of such grave importance that every reason calls for accomplishment of it. You should strongly urge immediate all-out preparations for it, that it be pushed with the utmost vigor, and that it be executed whether or not Russian collapse becomes imminent. In the event Russian collapse becomes probable SLEDGEHAMMER becomes

not merely advisable but imperative. The principal objective of SLEDGEHAMMER is the positive diversion of German Air Forces from the Russian Front.

6. Only if you are completely convinced that SLEDGE-HAMMER is impossible of execution with reasonable chances of serving its intended purpose, inform me.

7. If SLEDGEHAMMER is finally and definitely out of the picture. I want you to consider the world situation as it exists at that time, and determine upon another place for U.S. troops to fight in 1942.

This was one trip Hopkins did not want to make. Normally he loved the pomp and ceremony of mysterious flights, meetings with high officials, and all the aura of V.I.P. treatment. But this time, he wanted to stay home and get married. He had recently become engaged to Mrs. Louise Macy, a widow from New York. The President had promised to act as best man. Thus it was with considerable reluctance that Hopkins boarded the plane.

Arriving safely in Prestwick, Scotland, on July 18, they found the weather was too bad for them to continue by air and boarded the special train Churchill had sent up to meet them. Churchill demanded that the train stop at Chequers, the Prime Minister's country estate, but since Marshall and King were anxious to get to London to begin discussions with the American military authorities immediately, the train rolled on into London.

No sooner were they installed in the fourth floor of Claridge's Hotel than the phone rang. It was a furious Churchill. Hopkins eventually placated him, reporting to Roosevelt, "The Prime Minister threw the British Constitution at me with some vehemence. As you know, it is an unwritten document, so no serious damage was done. Winston is his old self and full of battle."

Hopkins decided that he had better go back to Chequers to mollify the Prime Minister, so he left Marshall and King to discussions with General Dwight D. Eisenhower, who had come to London a few weeks before to take charge of the "Bolero" buildup.

When Monday rolled around and formal meetings took

place with the British, the familiar deadlock seemed inevitable. But there was a subtle change. Whether the Americans were discouraged at the implications in Roosevelt's letter of instructions, or whether they felt that the British were absolutely adamant, they gradually allowed Sledgehammer to pass from the consideration. At one point in the discussions, Hopkins scribbled a note, probably to Marshall, "I feel damn depressed."

Sledgehammer having finally been killed, Roosevelt cabled his instructions to proceed with Gymnast in an enlarged concept, the targets to be Casablanca on the Atlantic coast of French Morocco, and Oran and Algiers in Algeria. Both the British and the Americans hoped that the Anglo-American forces would be able to land with no opposition from the Frenchmen in those North African colonies.

These hopes were doomed to disappointment.

Once agreed on the operations for the year, the British pressed to postpone the final decision until September 15, but Roosevelt would have none of this. He cabled that the landings for Gymnast should take place no later than October 30. Perhaps wearied of dissension, the British gave in, and the planning proceeded, "full speed ahead," as Roosevelt cabled Churchill.

Since the invasion of North Africa was to be primarily an American operation, an American commander in chief was necessary. On July 26, Marshall informed Eisenhower he had been selected to lead the first Allied offensive against the Germans. At the same time, for security reasons, the code name of the operation was changed to Torch, selected personally by Churchill, no doubt for its symbolic implications.

The long, sometimes acrimonious, debate over strategy finally settled, there was nothing for the American party but to return to Washington—King and Marshall to their desks, and Hopkins to his bride-to-be.

The wedding took place in the White House on July 30, with the President as best man. They honeymooned on a farm in Connecticut. The rumormongers and the unfriendly press, meanwhile, had produced a totally unfounded story that they had spent their wedding trip in luxury on a government-owned yacht at the taxpayers' expense. Large sections of the business community and many of the public hated Hopkins and his influence in American politics and would go to any length to discredit him. In the case of his honeymoon, however, there

234

were no grounds. Hopkins seems to have been the one best able to bring the British and American high officials together, and for this he deserved better of his countrymen. But his reputation from New Deal days clung to him, and to some minds, he was perhaps even worse than "That Man in the White House."

* * * * *

Coast Guard Seaman Second Class John C. Cullen was walking his "beach pounder's beat" near Amagansett, Long Island, in the midnight fog of June 13, 1942. It was pushing on toward one o'clock in the morning, and it was a dark and dismal time to be abroad; with the chill air cutting through his jacket, Cullen had to move rapidly to keep warm. His flashlight beam was quickly swallowed up by the fog.

All at once the beam caught the figure of a man.

"Who are you?" challenged Cullen.

"We're fishermen from Southampton and ran ashore here," was the reply.

Satisfied, Cullen invited the man and his companions to accompany him back to the Coast Guard Station at Amagansett, half a mile away.

The man demurred. Cullen became more insistent. Then the conversation took a peculiar turn.

"How old are you?" asked the stranger.

"Twenty-one."

"Do you have a father?"

"Yes."

"Do you have a mother?"

"Yes," in a bewildered tone.

"Well, I wouldn't want to have to kill you."

There was a pause as Cullen wondered what to do.

The stranger broke the pause. "Forget about this," he said, "and I'll give you some money and you can have a good time." He offered two fifty-dollar bills. Cullen refused. "Here's three hundred dollars," continued the stranger, pushing the money into Cullen's hand. "My name is George John Davis," he continued. "What's yours?"

"Frank Collins," replied Cullen. Then he hurried and ran off into the fog to report the strange proceedings to his superiors.

"George John Davis's" real name was George J. Dasch.

With three companions he had been landed moments before on the Long Island coast in a rubber raft from the German submarine *U-202*. Four days later, at Ponte Verda Beach, near Jacksonville, Florida, four other men were landed from *U-584*. Eight men, in all, had come to sabotage America's war production.

As a result of the prompt FBI roundup of enemy aliens after the Pearl Harbor attack, the Nazi government had no reliable agents able to move freely about the country to commit acts of sabotage. The eight men selected to be landed from U-boats had all lived many years in the United States. The twenty-two-year-old Herbert Haupt was an American citizen by virtue of his father's naturalization. All the others were German citizens, although Dasch himself had completed all requirements for naturalization except for the final swearing-in ceremony. Two of the saboteurs were very early members of the Nazi party, and several during their previous stays in the United States had been members of the German-American Bund.

After their respective landings, the two groups of men split up and went to various parts of the country. They had orders to commit no acts of sabotage for some time while they became established in their respective communities. Each was equipped with $4,000 in American money; in addition, the two leaders, Dasch and Kerling, each had $70,000. Also, each man had $450 in spending money for his immediate needs.

Congratulating themselves on their fortunate escape from the Coast Guardsman, Dasch and his three companions caught the Long Island Railroad 6:57 train to Jamaica, where they split into two groups, arranged to meet that afternoon in New York, and bought clothes before catching another train to Manhattan. Here Dasch and his companion, Ernst Peter Burger, checked into the Governor Clinton Hotel and went to an Automat to meet their co-conspirators.

Coast Guardsman Cullen ran all the way back to the Amagansett Coast Guard Station. He reported the strange incident to the chief in charge, who phoned for help and then armed the four men he had available and raced with them to the spot where Cullen had encountered Dasch.

As they were searching for evidence, they heard sounds of a motor starting and, looking out, were able to see the shape of a submarine. Cullen soon discovered a package of German cigarettes.

As Coast Guard intelligence officers arrived, Cullen and Chief Warren Barnes returned to the Amagansett Station and counted the bribe money. Dasch had short-changed Cullen; instead of three hundred dollars, there was only the sum of two hundred and sixty. The money was put away for safekeeping and as possible evidence.

The search of the beach continued and soon disclosed buried duffel bags containing German uniforms and boxes with explosives. By noon the FBI was on the job. There was no doubt that a party of saboteurs had been landed. It was up to the FBI to find them.

In New York, Dasch was growing hourly more nervous. His imagination saw suspicion in the eye of every policeman he passed. His companions seemed unreliable, ready to panic. He decided to turn himself in to the FBI.

Being the sort of man he was, he could not do this simply. He had delusions of grandeur; he saw himself talking to a spellbound J. Edgar Hoover, leading a party of FBI agents to the other seven, and being feted, honored, and celebrated in the press and in the mind of America. He went about his disclosure in the worst possible way; his every move, once he had called attention to himself by a mysterious call to the New York office of the FBI, and an equally baffling trip to the Washington headquarters, seemed self-serving, rather than the act of the dedicated anti-Nazi he claimed to be.

With Dasch's assistance or without it, the seven invaders were soon caught. The FBI had a line on some of them even before Dasch revealed himself. To Dasch's fury, he found himself indicted with the rest on charges of attempted sabotage and spying.

President Roosevelt convened a special military tribunal to try the eight men. The appointed defense counsel challenged the competency of the tribunal to try enemy aliens, and the Supreme Court met in extraordinary session to consider the challenge. It was rejected.

The trial took place in extreme secrecy. It lasted twenty-seven days, while the prosecution piled up damning evidence against each defendant. Press coverage was barred, even though the news of the capture of the saboteurs had been released after the capture of the last of them. Most of the American people had already made up their minds; it was a case of "verdict first, evidence afterwards." The only question, most people felt, was whether the men should be shot or hanged.

Life magazine presented the story of the capture under the headline "THE EIGHT NAZI SABOTEURS SHOULD BE PUT TO DEATH." An American Legion unit volunteered the services of its members as a firing squad. Another writer suggested taking them up to twenty thousand feet in an airplane and shoving them out with cheesecloth parachutes "to flop around with the rest of the buzzards."

In the tribunal it was much more complicated than that. Each man was represented by counsel; each man had the right of cross-examination; but there was no jury. Instead, a court of seven generals was named to hear the evidence, reach the verdict, and impose sentences. An important proviso was included in the tribunal's commission. Instead of requiring the tribunal to observe strict rules of evidence as would be the case in a civil court or in a court-martial, it was permitted to consider evidence which, in the mind of the president of the tribunal had "probative value to a reasonable man."

There would be no appeal from the court's decision. As convening authority, President Roosevelt would review the findings and approve or mitigate the sentences.

The defense took the line that no acts of sabotage had been committed and that at least one of the men had given himself up voluntarily. The prosecution's view was that merely entering the country in time of war with intent to commit sabotage was enough to warrant the death sentence. The tribunal agreed. All eight men were condemned to death, although the sentences were not made public at that time, for the papers had to go to Hyde Park for the President's approval.

After Roosevelt had been over the "veritable bale" of papers submitted to him, he approved the verdict of the tribunal, but because Dasch had been of assistance in finding the others and because Burger had turned himself in shortly before he would have been captured anyway, the President mitigated their sentences. Dasch was sentenced to thirty years at hard labor and Burger to life imprisonment. The rest were to be electrocuted.

At noon on Saturday, August 8, the first of the six condemned men entered the execution chamber of the District of Columbia Jail. Outside, a practice air raid was in progress. The order in which the men died has never been revealed, but by 1:20 that afternoon it was all over. At three o'clock, the jail door opened and six blanket-covered forms were brought out on stretchers, to be taken to Walter Reed Hospital for autopsy. Later they were buried in Blue Plains, the Potter's Field for the District of Columbia, apart from the other graves.*

"Roosevelt's blood purge continues," screamed the German radio broadcasts. British and American people were not impressed. They were still remembering one of Hitler's "blood purges" in a little town of Czechoslovakia.

On the morning of May 29, 1942, Deputy Chief of the Gestapo Reinhard Heydrich was riding in his Mercedes sports car near Prague. Two Czech partisans hurled a bomb at the car, shattering "Hangman" Heydrich's spine. Among the most-hated men in Germany, Heydrich in his sadism outdid most. But in revenge for his death, the Germans almost outdid Heydrich.

Deciding arbitrarily that the assassins had come from the little village of Lidice, the Germans moved in late on the night of June 9. They ordered all inhabitants to assemble in the square, taking their money and valuables with them. A woman and a child who attempted to escape were promptly shot. The remaining women and children were taken to the school for the rest of the night, while the men were incarcerated in stables, barns, and cellars.

Beginning at dawn the next day, the men were brought out in batches of ten into a garden and shot there. All day long the slaughter went on, until all hundred and seventy-two of the adult males had been killed. Seven women were taken to Prague and shot. The rest, a hundred and ninety-five, were taken to Ravensbrück Concentration Camp. Forty-two died of maltreatment, seven went to the gas chamber, and three disappeared without a trace. Four of the women, about to give birth to children, were taken to a maternity home, delivered of their babies, and then sent to Ravensbrück. Before they left, they saw their newborn children murdered.

As for the children, ninety in all, they were taken to a con-

* In April 1948, President Truman commuted the sentences of Dasch and Burger, and they were deported to Germany.

centration camp. Seven who passed examination by Nazi "racial experts" were taken to Germany to be brought up by foster parents. Later, others were sent in the same fashion, and some to Poland for *Sonderbehandlung*, a euphemism for the gas chamber.

The population disposed of, the Germans buried the dead in a common grave and then plundered and burned the houses to wipe out the village completely. The next day the newspaper *Der Neue Tag* announced triumphantly: "Since the inhabitants of this village have, in the most uncompromising manner, opposed the published laws through their activity and support in the murder of Heydrich, the male adults have been shot, the women sent to a concentration camp and the children placed in suitable educational institutions. The buildings have been razed to the ground and the name of the place has been erased from the records."

Alas for the power of human vanity. News of the massacre had no sooner reached the free world than Lidice rose again. Steel Park Gardens, a small town near Peoria, Illinois, announced it had changed its name to Lidice. San Geronimo, Mexico, also became Lidice. The name Lidice, instead of becoming a symbol of terror, became a symbol of defiance, a symbol of outrage at German *Schrecklichkeit*.

* * * * *

"Where shall we spend our vacation this summer?" With the kids out of school, and the traditional holiday times coming up, many a husband and wife asked each other that question. But now there was no easy answer. Gasoline rationing in the Eastern states and the promise of no new tires throughout the country inhibited most people who would have loaded up the old family car and driven off to somewhere else. Air travel had not yet become popular, and the few planes available for civilians were subject to cancellation for military use. Buses and trains were impossible. Hosts of people jammed the stations, hoping to get on, but servicemen had to go, and there were few seats or berths left for civilians. Every day, every hour, trains and buses pulled out leaving disappointed travelers behind. New and stricter travel regulations became effective on June 15. Luxuries disappeared.

Beach resorts on both coasts offered little. On the Atlantic side, much of the sand had been ruined by oil from sunken ships. If you took a walk along the shore, you had a reasonable chance of stumbling over the decomposing corpse of a drowned sailor. On the Pacific side, beaches bristled with barbed wire to discourage fancied invaders. Dude ranches, which had advertised the "wide open spaces" now found those same spaces kept their patrons from reaching them. Up and down and across the land, Americans had become almost immobilized.

The best thing to do was stay home and spend your vacation on the golf course or in the swimming pool. But, just a minute. Swimming pools came under the ban on nonessential new construction, and the ones operating were jammed. And how do you get to the golf course? On June 9, the Office of Defense Transportation ordered inter-city bus companies to cut out express routes and to stop sending special buses to golf courses, race tracks, special excursions, and amusement places in general. You could walk. It was hard on the shoes and on unaccustomed muscles, but at least muscles and shoes were not rationed. Not yet, at any rate. Shoes soon would be.

Grumbling over his hard lot, John Q. Citizen tended to stay at home. He worked in his Victory Garden, or puttered around the house, getting in his wife's way and irritating the kids, who didn't know what to do with themselves. He even read a book. Libraries noted a fifteen percent rise in borrowings. *The Robe* by Lloyd Douglas, the story of a young Roman tribune who carried out the execution of Christ, topped the bestseller lists in the late summer. John Steinbeck's *The Moon Is Down* handled the story of the German occupation of Norway in a somewhat gingerly manner. Louis Bromfield dealt with espionage in Paris in *Until the Day Break.* Historical fiction included Carl Carmer's *Young Ames* and Branch Cabell's *The First Gentleman of America.* Ideally suited to light summer reading was John Jennings's *Gentleman Ranker,* a story of the American Revolution. Hesketh Pearson brought out his *G.B.F.,* a biography written with the assistance of the subject, the cantankerous Irish playwright. Philip Guedella capitalized on the moment with *Churchill,* a sprightly and well-written book. Samuel Eliot Morison's *Admiral of the Ocean Sea* depicted the life of Columbus from a mariner's point of view.

Current events inspired many books during the year.

241

Perhaps the most important was Joseph E. Davies's *Mission to Moscow,* an account of his ambassadorship to the Soviet Union, which revealed Mr. Davies's complete belief in the honesty and sincerity of Stalin and the Russian officials he dealt with. Elliot Paul's *The Last Time I Saw Paris* was a nostalgic picture of Paris life just before the war. It gave rise to a hit song of the same title.

See Here, Private Hargrove by Marion Hargrove and *Private Breger,* a book of cartoons by Dave Breger, illustrated the unending war between the military and the civilian mind, the story of the downtrodden civilian-soldier worm from the worm's point of view.

Dealing with military problems from a more serious approach were W. F. Kernan's *Defense Will Not Win the War* and Alexander de Seversky's *Victory Through Air Power.* Perhaps the best of these was Hanson W. Baldwin's *Strategy for Victory.* All these writers were, of course, handicapped by not knowing the full details of the situation, but their works were widely read and widely quoted. Even children's literature was affected by the war. An example: Helen O. Watson's *Top Kick, United States Army Horse.*

If you got tired of the hammock and the book, there were always the movies. The war dominated new releases, with semi-documentaries like *Wake Island* and *The Navy Comes Through.* Light musicals included *Footlight Serenade, Springtime in the Rockies, Ship Ahoy, Panama Hattie, Louisiana Purchase. King's Row* and *The Magnificent Ambersons* appeared as serious fare. Biography was popular, with *Gentleman Jim, The Moon and Sixpence, Yankee Doodle Dandy,* starring James Cagney as George M. Cohan, and the tear-jerker *The Pride of the Yankees,* with Gary Cooper as Iron Man Lou Gehrig.

The privations of the stay-at-home vacationers seemed the more bearable because an unwarranted optimism swept the country with the news of the victory at Midway. Predictions were freely made that the war could not last another six months, and thoughtless officials did little to discourage the rumors. For example, when Shut Out beat Alsab in the fashionable Belmont Stakes, Admiral Adolphus Andrews made a little speech promising the U.S. Navy would shut out the Japanese just as Shut Out had shut out Alsab. It was an innocent remark, but susceptible of misinterpretation. The incorrigible optimism of the people was sometimes fostered by the politicians, who could not bring themselves to tell hard facts to the public. After all, there was an election coming up in November.

In spite of rumors to the contrary, most people were well aware the war was going on, and they were anxious for Washington to straighten out the confusion. The rubber mess was getting worse, and by June it had become so entangled with gasoline rationing that no one could tell where the real shortage lay. Even the President hedged in discussing the rubber shortage, and it took nimble footwork on the part of Donald Nelson and Leon Henderson not to contradict the boss in public.

To conserve fuel oil, homeowners were asked to convert to coal if at all practical. On June 1, lawn mower production was stopped for the duration, as was that of pocketknives, manicure sets, and carving implements. Silk stockings had long since disappeared, and even rayon was called to the service. Nylon had been on the market for only a few months before it was diverted from the stocking counter into parachute material. In a few months a pair of nylon stockings was commanding as much as twelve dollars on the black market, and there were many stories of girls selling their virtue for a pair or two of the precious items. Zippers were converted from metal to plastic, often highly unreliable. They could be depended on to jam at the wrong moment. So temperamental were they that striptease dancers refused to use them on their breakaway costumes. They went back to old-fashioned snap fasteners to be sure they could complete their acts. The show must go on!

* * * * *

"I want to talk to you about rubber—about rubber and the war—about rubber and the American people."

President Roosevelt was addressing the nation in a "Fireside Chat." He was less than frank, perhaps because he himself was not ready to accept the implications of all of his own statistics. Although his tone was encouraging, his figures were not. He began by saying that ninety-two percent of the nation's normal rubber supplies had been cut off by the war. (Even the remaining eight percent had to come through U-boat-infested

243

waters, so to assume that all of it would arrive was perhaps a trifle optimistic.) He spoke glowingly of the "huge stockpile" and the "great new synthetic-rubber industry." The total available for 1942, assuming no losses from U-boat sinkings, was 1,241,000 tons.* Of this, 813,000 tons would be required for the military, Lend-Lease, and other essential commitments, leaving only 428,000 tons at the beginning of 1943. Since the nation's twenty-seven million cars annually used up about seven million tons of crude rubber, it was not difficult to project that unless drastic measures were taken, soon there would be no cars on the roads. The obvious answer was nationwide gasoline rationing to save tires, but Washington was not yet ready to accept that solution. They believed the public would not stand for it. There was another solution, announced Roosevelt cheerfully. In the rivers and lakes, in junkyards and in basements, hanging from trees as children's swings and from boat sides as fenders were millions of old tires. These could be reclaimed and put to good use. From June 15 to 30, the country would concentrate on a vast scrap-rubber drive. Take your old tires, worn-out hot-water bottles, rubber door-mats, and what-have-you to your neighborhood gasoline station. The dealer will pay you a cent a pound (which the government will refund him), and we will collect enough rubber "to build the planes to bomb Tokyo and Berlin—enough rubber to build the tanks to crush the enemy wherever we may find him—enough rubber to win the war."

The country was perhaps a little suspicious of collection drives. The previous summer, before war came to the United States, housewives had been exhorted to relieve the aluminum shortage by contributing their cooking utensils in a nationwide drive. They had responded loyally, even though department stores kept right on selling new aluminum pots and pans. The kitchenware lay undisturbed in huge piles until after Pearl Harbor, while experts tried to figure out what to do with it, since scrap aluminum is not readily convertible. Eventually, most of it was ground up as powder to use in incendiary bombs. This fiasco had caused considerable disillusionment. Subsequent drives to save tin cans so the tin could be reclaimed had come to nothing, since the tin lining could not be

* Including 54,000 tons of synthetic produced and used by the Russians.

economically removed. The best this did was prepare the public for canned goods with a different sort of lining. Newspapers had been collected with such success, particularly by the Boy Scouts, that the War Production Board had to beg them to call it off. Pulp mills were bursting. A *New Yorker* cartoon by Barlow depicted the situation of Scouting in 1942. It showed an older Scout pulling a children's wagon loaded with a bundle of old newspapers and explaining to a younger companion: ". . . and then sometimes we'd go on long hikes in the woods and then we'd sit around and tie all kinds of knots and sometimes we'd rub two sticks together and start a fire and . . ."

After the collection period had been extended to ninety days, the results were some 450,000 tons of scrap rubber, considerably less than the millions of tons the Administration had hoped for. Since the results of the drive were not announced in the same blaze of publicity that had marked its launching, everyone thought it was a great success. Publicity was wonderful.

As summer came on, the Roosevelt Administration became increasingly conscious of what is now called its "image." So many contradictory stories were coming out of news on both the military and the Washington fronts that it was possible to believe anything or nothing. Archibald MacLeish's Office of Facts and Figures might be contradicted by Lowell Mellett's Office of Government Reports. Robert Horton's Office of Emergency Management was often at odds with Wild Bill Donovan's Office of the Coordinator of Information. The Army and the Navy were sometimes out of step with all of these agencies and with each other.

With a stroke of the pen Roosevelt abolished all four of those offices and gave their functions to veteran newscaster Elmer Davis as head of the newly created Office of War Information. Because of his long experience as a reporter for *The New York Times* and radio commentator for CBS, Davis had the respect of Washington's press corps. It is remarkable that when the war ended, Davis still had this respect, even though O.W.I. had practically none at all.

The trouble was that Davis and the O.W.I. had been given impossible tasks. First, they were supposed to present a single voice of Washington, where the voices were loud, clangorous, and at odds. Davis was far too intelligent and too honest a man

245

to permit O.W.I. to be turned into a propaganda bureau for the Government, but the Administration desperately wished to avoid public bickering in the press; it wished to give the appearance of unity and competence, when often there was none. All offices were directed to submit their stories to O.W.I. for distribution, but this did not stop disgruntled officials from leaking other sides or parts of a story to a selected reporter.

The other chief difficulty concerned military security. No one, Davis or any newspaperman, wanted to publish information that would be of aid to the enemy. But both the Army and the Navy often classified matters in order to avoid embarrassment to officials, or simply because some of the officers felt that what went on in the Army and the Navy was none of the public's business. Their motto was that of William H. Vanderbilt: "The public be damned!"

At a press conference in mid-June a reporter asked Secretary of War Henry L. Stimson whether Davis would supervise Army and Navy communiqués.

"Is Mr. Davis," asked Stimson bitingly, "an educated military officer?"

The answer was, of course, no. But neither, it might be added, was Mr. Stimson.

Determined to find out the exact status of his agency *vis-à-vis* the Army and Navy, Davis sent one of his chief assistants to cover the trial of the eight Nazi saboteurs. There was no intention of revealing military secrets; the reporter would sit in the courtroom and would clear his story each day with the president of the tribunal, Major General Frank R. McCoy. At least, that was the proposal.

Davis's representative had no chance to explain it to General McCoy. After he had waited for an hour to see the General, an aide brought him a note: "The General does not wish to see the gentleman. The gentleman need not wait."

Furiously Davis took his case to the White House, but Roosevelt backed up the Army. The only concession was that the Army and the Navy would turn their communiqués over to O.W.I. for release; how much or how little was in them remained the perquisite of the services. Davis would have resigned, except that he realized that his successor might be more amenable to Army ways than he was. In his position he could carry on the fight, however hopeless, for honest coverage of the war.

As comment on this state of affairs, *The Detroit News* ran a cartoon by Burt Thompson purporting to illustrate the "Evolution of Communications" in six phases.

Phase 1. A runner bearing a tablet.
Phase 2. The Pony Express.
Phase 3. The railroad.
Phase 4. Air mail.
Phase 5. Radio broadcasting.
Phase 6. A turtle labeled "Official War News" with a sheet of paper in its mouth.

The service attitude of Father-knows-best was more suited to the small professional corps the Army and the Navy had been. But now that they were becoming "citizens' services," the attitude was less justifiable. Draft boards were finding it increasingly difficult to come up with the required numbers of men. Pay was raised to $50 a month for a private, and family allowances were set up, so that his wife would receive $22 a month of his pay and $28 more from the Government. The hope was to encourage volunteers among the men classified 3-A, deferred for family reasons. At the end of June, men of eighteen and nineteen were registered for the draft, although they could not be called until they reached twenty, and a little later the 1-B men, those with minor physical defects, became liable to induction for limited military service.

The Women's Army Auxiliary Corps was by this time well launched under the leadership of Colonel Oveta Culp Hobby. It was irreverently referred to as Mrs. Hobby's Waacs Works. The girls sometimes called themselves "Hobby-horses." At this time legislation prohibited women of any of the armed forces from serving outside the United States. The only exceptions were nurses attached to hospital units and hospital ships.

To amuse the men in the service and to inform them as well, the Army sponsored a magazine to replace the *Stars and Stripes* of World War I. The new magazine, *Yank*, written and edited mainly by enlisted men, printed cartoons, stories, pin-ups, and features calculated to appeal to the ordinary soldier. The magazine is credited with coining the expression "G.I." as a term of reference to the citizen in uniform. An early issue contained an article called "Learn to Fight Dirty." Sample instruction: to take care of an enemy sentry, "jump on his back, reach both arms around his neck and shove a foot against the back of his knee. The impact is guaranteed to double him up like a jackknife and if you twist at the same time you'll sever his spinal cord." The most famous feature to appear in *Yank* was the regular cartoon by young Bill Mauldin, featuring the two dogfaces Willie and Joe. To most G.I.s these two tired, dirty, unshaven soldiers epitomized the war.

Servicemen were beginning to return from areas of action, bringing with them stories of harrowing experiences. Even the first dead were returned for burial. The first to be laid to rest in his hometown cemetery was Marine Private Otto J. Weiner, Jr., of South St. Louis. Admiral Hart had returned from the Java debacle, and Admiral Halsey nursed his dermatitis in Richmond, Virginia. A member of the House of Representatives came back from a spell of active duty with the Navy to recover from a bout of pneumonia. The President invited his young friend, Lieutenant Commander Lyndon Baines Johnson, to breakfast and to hear about his experiences in the Pacific. Commented Johnson, "There is one thing they are not short on out there, and that is courage and guts and fighting spirit. They've got plenty of that."

It was Johnson's last experience of active duty. Under a new order, the President ruled that members of Congress would stay in Washington unless he decided they were needed on active service. That order tied not only Johnson of Texas but also Representatives Francis E. Walter of Pennsylvania and Warren G. Magnuson of Washington to their desks on Capitol Hill.

* * * * *

The day dawned cloudy but with good visibility on the Fourth of July. Or rather, it did not dawn, for there had been no night for the men aboard the ships of PQ-17, a convoy bound for North Russia.* The smooth sea and the five hun-

---

* Convoy designations were a kind of shorthand, adopted not so much for security reasons as for convenience. Convoys on a given route kept the same letter designation, but were numbered serially. ON represented outbound North Atlantic convoys from the United Kingdom to Canada, and later New York. The reverse route was HX. The letter S could be added to designate a slow convoy. PQ convoys ran from the United Kingdom to North Russia, while those in the other direction were designated QP. PQ-17 was the seventeenth convoy run over that route.

dred-foot cloud ceiling brought cold comfort to seamen intent on bringing their cargoes through, but it must have gladdened the hearts of Luftwaffe pilots based in northern Norway. It was just the weather they wanted. They could remain above the clouds until the last moment and then dive on their victims. The fireworks of this Fourth of July will never be forgotten by any who lived through them.

North Russian convoys were expensive. Small and infrequent by North Atlantic standards, they came to represent a symbol of aid to the Russians that had, for political reasons, to be kept going. They had begun in August 1941 under British escort and responsibility. Only two of a hundred and ten ships had been lost on this route up until March 1942. Then, as the sun began to rise above the horizon for longer than a few moments at a time, the Nazis moved Luftwaffe squadrons to Norwegian airfields in the far north. Losses began to mount with PQ-13 when five ships were lost out of nineteen. It was not only Nazi air power that perturbed the men who had to make this journey and the men who had to send them out. Hitler's "intuition" had perceived that the British would make a landing in Norway, and he had moved the remaining big ships of the German navy to Norwegian waters. The most formidable of these was the *Tirpitz*, 35,000 tons of deadly naval might. Her presence meant that the British would have to send capital ships along with the PQ convoys.

PQ-14 in April lost one ship, but sixteen turned back because of heavy ice. In early May, PQ-15 lost four out of twenty-five.

President Roosevelt had sent several American ships to Scapa Flow to relieve British ones for the Madagascar operation. The American battleship *Washington* was therefore available to help the *King George V* in providing distant cover for PQ-16. This convoy sailed from Iceland on May 21 and quickly ran into difficulties. It lost seven ships, all to air attack, but its steady convoy discipline and the spirited defense of the close escort prevented further harm.

In view of the increasing difficulty of the North Russian convoys, the Admiralty had for some time recommended that they be abandoned until winter with its protective darkness again would make them feasible. But the need to assist Russia loomed so large in the minds of both Churchill and Roosevelt that all other considerations had to take a second place. The convoys would go on whatever cost.

Vice Admiral Otto Schniewind, German northern fleet commander, was determined to block the next convoy. In addition to Luftwaffe elements and U-boats, he had available the pocket battleships *Scheer* and *Lützow* with six destroyers at Narvik and the battleship *Tirpitz* and the heavy cruiser *Hipper* at Trondheim, with four destroyers. On word that PQ-17 had been discovered, Schniewind planned to sail with the Trondheim ships to join those from Narvik and fall on the hapless merchantmen, completely obliterating them. He code-named this operation Rösselsprung (Knight's Move).

British Intelligence was well aware that the Germans would oppose PQ-17 with powerful surface ships, and it caused much disquietude in the Admiralty. Because of the danger of U-boat attacks, which in previous convoys had sunk the cruisers *Trinidad* and *Edinburgh*, the Naval Staff determined that no combatant ship larger than a destroyer would go east of twenty-five degrees east (that is, east of North Cape). This decision meant that the convoy would have no adequate surface protection for the last eight hundred miles or so of its journey. "The strategic situation," wrote the Commander in Chief, Home Fleet, Admiral Sir John Tovey, "was wholly favourable to the enemy."

British misgivings might have been allayed had the Admiralty known of the special orders sent by Hitler to Admiral Schniewind to avoid all risks. On "no account [was he] to allow the enemy to score a success against the main body of the fleet."

But the Admiralty did not know of these orders, though it might have been guessed from previous behavior of German naval elements when challenged by the British. And not knowing, they had to act as if the greatest danger was the fact. It is against this fact that the Admiralty's otherwise incredible actions in connection with PQ-17 must be judged.

Convoy PQ-17, consisting of thirty-three merchant ships, three rescue ships, and a fleet oiler, sailed from Iceland on June 27. Twenty-two of the merchant ships were American. The unusually large escort of six destroyers, two antiaircraft ships, and eleven smaller antisubmarine escorts was supplemented by two submarines, which were supposed to ambush any German surface ships attempting to close the convoy. (It might be added that this idea was completely unsuccessful; indeed it never worked during the entire war.)

Two combatant groups also put to sea to support the convoy. A cruiser task force under British Rear Admiral L. H. K. Hamilton in H.M.S. *London* had, in addition to the flagship, three American cruisers, two American destroyers, and seven British destroyers and corvettes.

Admiral Tovey himself in H.M.S. *Duke of York* commanded the covering force, which included the American battleship *Washington*, the British aircraft carrier *Victorious*, the heavy cruiser *Cumberland*, the light cruisers *Nigeria* and *Manchester*, two American and at least nine British destroyers and corvettes. In all, the combatant ships outnumbered the convoy. But, unfortunately, when they were needed most, the combatant ships were not there.

Because the polar ice pack had retreated, the convoy was routed unusually far north, to put as much distance as possible between it and the German air bases in Norway. For four days all went smoothly. Then, on July 1, a German reconnaissance plane snooped the convoy, reporting its presence to Admiral Schniewind. The German forces were soon on the move, and by July 3, the *Tirpitz, Hipper,* and *Scheer* had rendezvoused in Altenfjord near North Cape and were poised for action.*

U-boats attacked on July 2, but were driven off by the close escort under Commander John E. Broome, RN. That afternoon the convoy passed the westbound Q-13, returning from Murmansk. Two air attacks developed on July 3, but again no ship was hit. Admiral Hamilton's Support Force moved into sight, but as it remained to the northward of PQ-17, its value in antiaircraft protection is dubious.

The convoy steamed steadily on. The watches changed routinely, and the daylight continued, even though fog mercifully closed in, affording some protection to the plodding ships. Suddenly at 0300, "through a hole in the fog," a Heinkel 115 appeared and launched a torpedo that hit the American Liberty Ship *Christopher Newport* amidships. All power lost, she drifted to a stop and was abandoned and sunk by one of the escorts.

The day wore on, and it was nearing time for the combatant ships to turn back. Admiral Hamilton, taking advantage of the

* The *Lützow* and three destroyers ran aground in Narvik harbor and took no further part in the operation.

discretionary clauses of his orders, elected to stay with the convoy as long as possible. He decided to stay until 2200 that evening.

It was as well that he did, for a heavy air attack developed about 1915, sinking two ships and badly damaging a third, which had to leave the convoy but eventually reached port. The rest of the planes were beaten off by heavy, accurate gunfire. As long as the convoy was intact, its massed gunfire was enough to give the German airmen a formidable nut to crack.

In London, Admiralty misgivings were mounting. Because of low visibility, naval reconnaissance had lost track of the German heavy ships, and fears grew that they were all at sea about to fall on the merchantmen and the puny close escorts of the convoy. Even Admiral Hamilton's cruiser Support Force would be in deadly danger from the *Tirpitz* and her consorts. Admiral Tovey's heavy battleship-carrier Covering Force was too far west, shepherding QP-13, to be of any use to the threatened PQ-17, which, in any event, had reached waters where the British were unwilling to hazard their large warships. A decision had to be taken, and at once. If they kept the convoy together, it could be easily overwhelmed by the Nazi surface force. If they dispersed it, the surface force would have great difficulty in finding and sinking more than a few; on the other hand, the dispersed ships would be easy victims of air or

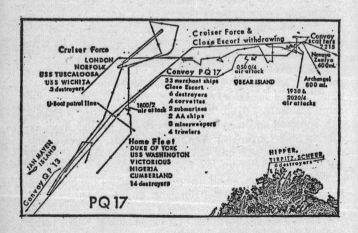

252

submarine attack. A decision had to be made, and they made it.

It was the wrong one.

Shortly after 1900, Admiral Hamilton received a message from the Admiralty: MOST IMMEDIATE. CRUISER FORCE WITHDRAW WESTWARD AT HIGH SPEED. A few minutes later, a second order arrived: IMMEDIATE. OWING TO THREAT OF SURFACE SHIPS, CONVOY IS TO DISPERSE AND PROCEED TO RUSSIAN PORTS. Then came one more: MOST IMMEDIATE. CONVOY IS TO SCATTER.

When Admiral Hamilton read these messages together, he could draw only one conclusion: that at any moment the masts of German surface forces would be looming up over the horizon. He concluded that the Admirality had information he did not have, so he lost no time preparing for action. The "Most Immediate" prefix to the messages was used only in times of highest emergency, so action had to be swift.

Commodore Broome rightly felt that if the convoy was to scatter, his escorting ships could be of little use to them, but they might be invaluable to Hamilton in the coming surface action, so he most reluctantly took his destroyers to join the cruiser Support Force.

These orders are probably the most flagrant example of the danger of high command interfering with the decisions of the commander on the scene. The First Sea Lord, Admiral Sir Dudley Pound, and his staff did not and could not know the situation in the convoy, since it was, of course, observing radio silence. They should have passed on the information they had, leaving the ultimate decision to the man who knew all the circumstances. But they did not, and catastrophe ensued.

The irony of the situation was that there was no danger from German surface forces. The *Tirpitz* and her consorts sailed on July 5 from Altenfjord, but confused by conflicting reports from Luftwaffe pilots, they returned to port a few hours later. The only remaining danger was from U-boats and air attack, and this the convoy, even without the Support and Covering Forces, could have handled without prohibitive losses.

The Luftwaffe fell on the hapless, unprotected merchant ships without mercy. Ship after ship was pounded to death. Crews struggled in the icy water and some mercifully found oblivion in a few minutes from the numbing cold. Others burned to death from the blazing oil on the water. More fortunate ones found refuge in lifeboats, faced with a two-hundred-mile trip to land. One crew in lifeboats refused rescue from another ship, preferring to take their chances in their open boats. It was a good decision, for their would-be rescuer was sunk the next day.

A few ships made it to safety. Some took refuge in the ice and then went on to Novaya Zemlya, where they formed a rump convoy of five ships and set out again for Russian ports. Three of them reached port. Seven more from another rump convoy came in a few days later. Three more ships made it independently. In all, only eleven merchantmen and two rescue ships out of the thirty-seven that had left Iceland got through. Only three had been lost while the convoy was intact, and only two from the rump convoys. Two had returned to Iceland. Seventeen ships had been lost after the convoy dispersed and while the single ships had no protection except for their own inadequate antiaircraft guns. The losses of PQ-17 were not insupportable; the losses when it ceased to be a convoy were.

As a result of this somewhat inglorious operation, Admiral King became increasingly hostile to further joint operations with the Royal Navy. It was not long after that the *Washington*, the *Wasp*, and the American cruisers turned their bows toward the Pacific. They would be needed there.

CHAPTER NINE

Guadalcanal: The Hellhole of Victory

Regions of sorrow, doleful shades, where peace
And rest can never dwell.
Milton, Paradise Lost

Out of the darkness, out of the tropical night, came the ships. Nodding and bobbing in the gentle swell, they hissed the waves aside as they bore their cargoes of men and guns, rifles and ammunition, bulldozers and K-rations, bandages and blood plasma, hopes and fears. With them they bore an invisible passenger who was awaiting his fulfillment—death. He was to be surfeited before the Solomon Islands could become a backwash of the war.

On they came, twenty-three of them, escorted by six heavy cruisers, two light cruisers, fifteen wolfhounds of the sea, ships of all work, sleek and powerful destroyers, and five minesweepers. On board the transports and combatant ships alike, men waited anxiously for dawn. For some it would be the last they would ever see. Many others had a few more hours or days to live. Men and ships would die over a piece of land few Americans had heard of before that seventh day of August 1942. The world has since remembered it—Guadalcanal.

A Marine grave on Guadalcanal bears an epitaph that tells the story:

> And when he goes to Heaven
> To Saint Peter he will tell:
> Another Marine reporting, Sir;
> I've served my time in Hell!

When Don Alvaro Mendaña discovered the Solomon Islands in 1560, he believed he had rediscovered King Solomon's fabled Ophir and named the islands for that most famous of King David's sons. Here, he was sure, would be found vast stores of gold. He was nearly the last man to have anything favorable to say about those carrion slabs of volcanic rock that trail in a southeasterly direction for six hundred miles from Rabaul. After Mendaña's departure, the islands lay well forgotten for some two hundred years until they were rediscovered by the French explorer Bougainville. He and subsequent visitors saw no gold; they recognized these islands for what they were—pestilential hellholes, inhabited by headhunting Melanesians who hated interlopers even more than they hated each other. Each island contained several tribes, and each tribe had its own language. Over the years the natives had been largely undisturbed except by missionaries and copra traders. The center of this activity was the tiny island of Tulagi, sheltered in a bight of Florida Island, across from Guadalcanal.

War changes the value of many things and of many places. A rocky, barren knoll scorned by generations of farmers may become a position costing the lives of thousands of men. The Second World War wrought its changes of values, but none more strange than that which placed the Solomon Islands so high on the scale of worth. Major efforts of both the United States and Japan would center on them for nearly a year and a half. Over a dozen sea battles and as many land battles raged over territory the world had been willing to forget for nearly four hundred years.

The Catalina droned on across the Coral Sea. Routine search was the order of the day. All around the aircraft, from horizon to horizon, nothing was visible except the glint of sun off the dancing waves. The gunners sat relaxed, drinking coffee and shooting the breeze, ready to man their weapons if necessary. The plane rocked gently as "George," the automatic pilot, made slight corrections to hold course and altitude.

The navigator passed a slip of paper to the pilot: "Landfall on San Cristobal in five minutes." Almost on schedule, the mountainous island at the southeast end of the Solomon chain rose above the horizon. The pilot spoke into the intercom.

"Man your guns."

It was no part of the plane's mission to fight, but it was as well to be prepared. The Japanese, after all, had a seaplane base at Tulagi, and they liked to shoot down unwary reconnaissance planes. Soon San Cristobal was passing under the starboard wing of the plane. Ahead loomed the next large island—Guadalcanal. Just across the Sound lay Tulagi, where they could expect trouble.

Altering course to fly the length of the island, the plane commenced its run, the gunners watching the sky, the pilot attending to the progress of the big "Cat," while the co-pilot and navigator scanned the steaming forest and jungle below them.

Suddenly the co-pilot nudged the pilot and pointed. The Japanese were clearing an oblong strip near the northern coast of Guadalcanal. It could only be an airstrip.

Now the patrol was by no means routine. Rear Admiral John Sidney McCain in his headquarters at Noumea vitally needed this information. He commanded all Allied aircraft in the South Pacific area, and a Japanese airfield on Guadalcanal would drastically affect his problem.

Checking to make sure that the camera was working, the pilot made a run over the just-begun airfield and then banked away to pass Tulagi hurriedly. No change there. Now, let's head for the barn!

On his arrival at base, the pilot hastily reported to the operations officer, filled with the importance of what he had seen. He knew it would cause a flurry of excitement.

Not in his wildest dreams could the pilot have known the importance that would be attached to his sighting report. Admiral McCain was interested—so interested that he passed the word on to Vice Admiral Robert L. Ghormley, Commander South Pacific forces, who passed it on to his boss, Admiral Nimitz, at San Francisco for a conference with Admiral Ernest J. King, Chief of Naval Operations and Commander in Chief of the U.S. Fleet. As a member of the Joint Chiefs of Staff, King had, only three days earlier, on July 2, 1942, put his name to a directive for the course of the Pacific war. Now this directive would have to be modified.

As early as March 5, 1942, King had summarized his plans for the Pacific to the President:

Hold Hawaii
Support Australasia
Drive northwestward from New Hebrides.

While the British seemed to hold the view that the war in the Pacific could be left in a state of suspended animation until the Allies were ready to turn and deal with it, King in a memorandum to General Marshall on June 25 flatly predicted that the Japanese would neither stand still nor allow the Allies to do so. If nothing was done in the Pacific, the Japanese would keep coming, would certainly push the Americans back to their own doorstep and would quite possibly seize Australia.

King had a strong ally in his support of the need for seizing the initiative in the Pacific. General Douglas MacArthur from his base in Australia had repeatedly urged the offensive. Immediately after the Battle of Midway, he had offered to capture Rabaul, provided he have under his command a division trained in amphibious warfare and a naval task force with at least two carriers. This view was rejected by the Joint Chiefs of Staff on several grounds, but largely on the ground that Rabaul would be too tough a nut to crack and too difficult to hold, if taken.

As a counterproposal, King reverted to his third point in his

257

memorandum of March—drive northwestward from New Hebrides. At a meeting of the Joint Chiefs on June 25, he proposed that the First Marine Division, en route to Australia to join MacArthur's command, form the spearhead for an advance in the Solomon Islands, specifically to recapture Tulagi. Marshall concurred, but wanted the operation to be under MacArthur's command. King violently disagreed. It must be commanded by the Navy, since the troops available were Marines and their transportation and protection must be furnished by naval ships. Firmly he insisted that the command and the responsibility be vested in the hands of the soft-spoken, gentle-mannered Texan, Admiral Chester W. Nimitz, Commander in Chief of the Pacific Fleet and Pacific Ocean Area.

The antithesis of the quarterdeck martinet, Admiral Nimitz nonetheless exercised unquestioned command. His quiet manner disguised an almost infinite capacity for work, and his clear grasp of his area and its reponsibilities, his judgment of risks, and his vast professional abilities enabled him to make firm, sure, correct decisions. No better man could have been found to bear the responsibility for the huge Pacific Ocean area he commanded.

Few people have a grasp of the vast distances involved in the war against Japan. If we overlay a map of the United States on one of the Pacific Ocean with New York City at Pearl Harbor, Guadalcanal is some twenty-four hundred miles south of Los Angeles. Tokyo falls a thousand miles northwest of Seattle. In actual air-line distance, it is approximately four hundred miles farther from Honolulu to Sydney, Australia, than it is from Honolulu to New York.

On July 2, the Joint Chiefs of Staff issued a directive for the first American offensive of the war. Its ultimate objective was to regain control of New Britain, New Ireland, and New Guinea. The operation was to be accomplished in three phases, the first two of them to be run simultaneously.

1. The seizure and occupation of the Santa Cruz Islands and Tulagi, under the command of Nimitz, with a target date of August 1, 1942.

2. The seizure and occupation of Lae, Salamaua, and the northeast coast of New Guinea, to be under the command of MacArthur.

3. The seizure and occupation of Rabaul and adjacent

258

positions in the New Guinea-New Ireland area, to be under the overall command of MacArthur.

Since MacArthur's Southwest Pacific area as originally drawn had included the Solomons group, it became necessary to move the boundary in order to bring the lower Solomons under Nimitz. Accordingly the eastern limit of MacArthur's command was set at longitude 159° East, a few miles west of Guadalcanal.

On receipt of the Joint Chiefs' plan, Admiral Nimitz flew to San Francisco to confer with Admiral King. The latter made it very clear to CINCPAC that little could be spared in the Pacific for the operations that were then on the books or might have to be undertaken in the future. First call on the resources of the Allies—men, ships, aircraft, supplies, ammunition, gasoline, fuel oil—was to go to Operation Torch, the invasion of French Northwest Africa at Casablanca, Oran, and Algiers planned for early November. The Pacific was to be the orphan child. The saturnine Admiral King was the only fairy godmother for Pacific operations—as weird a bit of miscasting as has ever been set by capricious fate. And in this case the Cinderellas—Pacific operations—were not told to be home by midnight. They were to go and stay.

While King and Nimitz debated their problems, the message from the plane that had scouted Guadalcanal reached them. In a flash, both admirals realized their plans had to be changed. The Japanese could not be allowed to establish an operational airfield on Guadalcanal. If they did, the precarious American positions on Noumea, Efate, and Espiritu Santo might well become untenable, and ships bound for Australia from the United States would have to add hundreds of miles to their voyages in order to stay out of range of Japanese air that could easily be established on those islands.

Fortunately for the American position, the First Marine Division was en route to New Zealand and had already been alerted to take part in the Tulagi operation. Since the Japanese had to be stopped in their building of an airfield in Guadalcanal, the decision was hell on earth.

On July 10, Nimitz sent Admiral Ghormley, Commander South Pacific (COMSOPAC), his operation order for the seizure of Guadalcanal and Tulagi, assigning him the First Marine Division and all the ships he could scrape together. Both Ghormley and MacArthur felt the operation was premature, but Marshall, King, and Nimitz agreed that it had to be done at that point and at that time. Since Ghormley was subordinate to Nimitz, and since MacArthur's only concern in the operation was to furnish supplemental air searches, they perforce had to accept the decision.

The date was July 10. The landing was scheduled for August 1. Only three weeks remained for detailed planning, for training, and for movement of forces to the area of operations. It was impossible. The invasion was postponed until August 7, 1942, six additional days being all King and Nimitz felt could be wrung from the inexorable passing of the days and hours toward the moment when the airfield on Guadalcanal could begin to send its planes and the destruction they carried to the American toeholds in the South Pacific.

Although Admiral Ghormley was in nominal command of the operation, he could exercise tactical control neither from his headquarters at Auckland nor from his secondary one at Noumea. Accordingly, the Officer in Tactical Command (OTC in Navyese) was Vice Admiral Frank Jack Fletcher, USN, the victor of the battles of the Coral Sea and Midway. Fletcher flew his flag on the carrier *Saratoga*, and so was with the Air Support Force, which comprised in addition to the *Saratoga*, two other carriers, *Wasp* and *Enterprise*, the battleship *North Carolina*, five heavy cruisers, one light cruiser, sixteen destroyers, and five oilers.* This force was commanded by Rear Admiral Leigh Noyes, but Fletcher in the first action off Guadalcanal seemed to conceive his role as Carrier Group Commander rather than overall commander. At least his orders showed excessive concern for the carriers and insufficient concern for the troops and their supporting ships. Fletcher's actions made Admiral Noyes little more than a passenger on his flagship.

In command of the Amphibious Force was Rear Admiral Richmond Kelly Turner, USN. As a captain he had taken the *Astoria* to Japan bearing the ashes of the Japanese Ambassador to the United States. The Japanese had made much of

---

* Other combatant ships were: Heavy cruisers *Minneapolis, New Orleans, Portland, Salt Lake City, San Francisco;* light cruiser *Atlanta;* destroyers *Aaron Ward, Balch, Benham, Dale, Farenholt, Farragut, Grayson, Gwin, Laffey, Lang, MacDonough, Maury, Phelps, Stack, Sterrett,* and *Worden;* oilers *Platte, Cimarron, Kaskaskia, Sabine,* and *Kanawha.*

this gracious gesture. Subsequent gestures of the dynamic, gray-haired, ferocious-browed Kelly Turner the Japanese felt considerably less gracious.

Turner's Amphibious Force was divided into two parts: one designated for Tulagi, and one for Guadalcanal. After delivering their charges of transports to the beaches, certain of the combatant ships would band together to form a defense force under the leadership of Rear Admiral V. A. C. Crutchley of the Royal Navy. Turner flew his flag in the transport *McCawley*, known throughout our South Pacific as the "Wacky Mac." Crutchley's flagship was H.M.A.S. *Australia*. Fifteen transports and cargo-transports were selected to bear their troops to Guadalcanal while four transports and four destroyer-transports would deliver their cargoes to the smaller target of Tulagi.*

Before this force could sail, much work had to be done in the brief remaining hours. When planners began to seek specific answers to specific questions they found a blank wall of ignorance. Charts of the area were hopelessly out of date. Planters from the area remembered little of military worth. Where were the channels? Where were the shoals? What was the beach gradient off the proposed landing sites? To answer some of these questions, Lieutenant Colonel Frank B. Goettge, intelligence officer for the First Marine Division, organized a photo-mapping reconnaissance flight from Australia. The flight was successfully made and the results were rushed to

---

* These ships were: Heavy cruisers H.M.A.S. *Australia* (F), H.M.A.S. *Canberra, Chicago, Vincennes, Quincy, Astoria;* light cruisers H.M.A.S. *Hobart, San Juan;* destroyers *Selfridge, Patterson, Ralph Talbot, Mugford, Jarvis, Blue, Helm, Henley, Bagley, Hull, Dewey, Ellet, Wilson, Monssen, Buchanan;* minesweepers *Hopkins, Trevor, Zane, Southard, Hovey;* transports *McCawley* (FF), *Fuller, American Legion, Barnett, George F. Elliott, Hunter, Liggett, Crescent City, President Hayes, President Adams;* cargo-transports *Bellatrix, Libra, Alchiba, Fomalhaut, Betelgeuse, Alhena;* for Guadalcanal. For Tulagi, transports *Neville, Zeilin, Heywood, President Jackson;* destroyer-transports *Calhoun, Gregory, Little, McKean.* Rear Admiral John Sidney McCain was to provide air searches from various bases in the South Pacific, supplemented by searches from MacArthur's forces in the Southwest Pacific area. Submarines *S-38, S-39, S-41, S-43, S-44* and *S-46* supported the operation by patrols in the general region. (All ships U.S. Navy unless otherwise designated.)

processing plants. Then they disappeared into a maze of red tape; finished maps were packed into boxes that disappeared into a vast pile of boxes. They were next heard of in 1948, six years after the need of them had passed.

A few meager, often inaccurate, bits of intelligence concerning the target area were accumulated. They had to do. Each reliable piece of information would aid immeasurably; each unreliable bit would cost lives; no one could tell which was which.

In view of the many uncertainties enshrouding the operations, Admiral Ghormley called a conference on July 26 of all commanders at a rendezvous four hundred miles south of Fiji, far out of sight of land in order to hide the presence of the ships from prying eyes. Unable to come himself, Ghormley sent his Chief of Staff, Rear Admiral Daniel Callaghan, to represent him. The principal leaders of the expedition were there to welcome him: McCain, Fletcher, Turner, and the quiet, unassuming commander of the First Marine Division, Major General Archie A. Vandegrift, USMC. Archie Vandergrift was a "Marine's Marine," a reincarnated Stonewall Jackson in his care for his men, a Grant in tactical brilliance, and entirely himself in his pride and determination as a United States Marine. As he sat in the flag wardroom on the *Saratoga*, waiting for the conference to begin, Vandegrift's mind was busy on the million and one details of the forthcoming operation.

Presently Admiral Fletcher called the meeting to order. As OTC and senior officer present, he dominated the meeting. Passing out the few copies of his operation orders (There were not enough copies to go around, so Admiral Callaghan had none to take back to his boss, Admiral Ghormley), he made a startling announcement.

"Gentlemen," he stated flatly, "in view of the risks of exposure to land-based air, I cannot keep the carriers in the area for more than forty-eight hours after the landing."

Both Turner and Vandegrift protested vehemently and violently. It would take at least four days to unload the transports and cargo ships, four days to give the Marines the necessities of life, food, bullets, gasoline, and other vital—literally vital—equipment. If Fletcher withdrew his carriers, the only force with sufficient strength to counter certain Japanese reaction, Turner would have to withdraw his ships as well, cruisers, destroyers, minesweepers, transports and cargo ships—the whole works. Left behind at the mercy of what the Japanese would be sure to throw at them would be Vandegrift's Marines with less strength than he needed for the job at hand and the certainty that enemy reinforcements would greatly increase the proportions of the job.

To these protests, Fletcher turned a deaf ear. Of all the flag officers present in that room, he was the only one who had seen combat in the present war. Perhaps more firmly than anyone present, he had an understanding of the value of carriers in the war against Japan. He had commanded American carrier forces in the Battle of the Coral Sea, and, although he had turned back the Japanese assault on Port Moresby, he had lost the huge *Lexington*, sister ship of the very ship he was now riding. He had commanded American forces in the Battle of Midway, and although he had inflicted overwhelming defeat on the Japanese, he had lost the carrier *Yorktown*.

He was absolutely right in his belief that the United States could not afford to lose any more carriers at that time. Yet he recognized as well as anyone else the implications of his decision, and especially what it must mean to General Vandegrift and his Marines. In his judgment, no other decision was possible. It was no easy thing for him to face lifelong friends with so unpalatable an announcement.

Admiral Callaghan summed up the views when he said it appeared to him that Fletcher had a different view of his mission from that held by Turner and Vandegrift. Fletcher, he said, conceived of his job as a hit-and-run raid to soften up the obstacles ashore; the other two felt it was to give protection throughout the unloading phase, at least. While this was highly desirable, Fletcher felt that the risks to the carriers outweighed the risk to the troops.

Fletcher offered to modify his plans if ordered to do so by Admiral Ghormley. This concession was really no concession at all, for one of the most sacrosanct and generally valid axioms of warfare is that the commander on the scene knows the conditions far better than his senior hundreds of thousands of miles away can possibly know them. Far more military disaster has resulted from untimely interference by high command than from on-the-spot blundering by the local commander. If Ghormley had issued such an order, it would have implied lack of confidence in Fletcher. He would have had to order

Fletcher's relief along with the change in orders.

Thus the order stood.

While the leaders conferred, the whitehats and Marines rehearsed the landing at Koro Island in the Fijis. They did gain useful experience in putting the landing craft in the water and in forming up in waves, but could not land because of a coral reef and the need to conserve the boats for the real thing. As it was, several were put out of action, so that men had to work feverishly to repair them in time.

"Our dress rehearsal stunk," said one Marine officer. "Everything went wrong."

General Vandegrift put it more succinctly.

"It was," he pronounced, "a complete bust."

A bad rehearsal makes a good performance. So runs an old adage of the theater. Burdened as he was by the knowledge that he and his men would soon be on their own on a hostile, unknown island, exposed to almost unimpeded Japanese counterattack, General Vandegrift had to find what comfort he could from the saying. There was little else of comfort. Yet he faced the future with the same quiet confidence he faced life. He was a Marine, and he knew that the Marines' primary job was to fight. He knew his men would not let him and their country down.

The night was ideal. A light haze shrouded the waning moon, making detection difficult, but not interfering in the least with the officers of the deck as they quietly ordered slight course and speed changes to preserve their stations in the formation. Fletcher's carriers steamed in the Coral Sea south of Guadalcanal, waiting for dawn to send their Wildcat fighters and Dauntless and Avenger bombers in to assist the Marines. On the hangar decks mechanics made final adjustments to engines, checked aircraft controls, calibrated instruments. Others filled the gas tanks and the machine-gun magazines. Bombs were tenderly loaded into the bomb bays. In the galleys, cooks and bakers were preparing early breakfasts for all hands. Thousands of eggs, hundreds of gallons of coffee, scores of loaves of bread were prepared. In quiet corners rigged as chapels, chaplains conducted services.

On the transports many of these scenes were duplicated. Boat engineers checked their engines; coxswains looked over their craft; boatswain's mates inspected the falls and davits. In the troop compartments some men snored loudly, but many lay staring into the darkness. Were they afraid, these sleepless men? Certainly. All normal men are afraid when they go into combat, especially for the first time, or even the hundredth, for familiarity does not breed contempt. But most of the fears were not of wounds or death. Will I live up to it? they thought. Will I behave as the Corps expects, as my buddies expect, as I myself expect me to behave? Not a few of these men rose early to do as others on other ships were doing; making their way along darkened spaces and passageways, they found the makeshift chapels, these men who might soon meet their Maker.

During the midwatch in the small hours of D-day, August 7, 1942, the ships were steaming along in formation on course 040°, almost northeast. Ahead and on each flank, destroyers snuffled the ocean, invisible feelers probing underwater for lurking Japanese submarines. Lookouts peered into the misty night.

The minutes passed by. A lookout spoke.

"Land broad on the starboard bow, sir."

"Very well," replied the Officer of the Desk, glancing round to see that the Captain had heard. To be sure, he repeated the report.

"Very well," acknowledged the Captain. "Go to General Quarters."

"Aye, aye, sir," acknowledged the OOD. He nodded to the boatswain's mate of the watch. The petty officer stepped to the announcing system and threw the switches over. A long, trilling wail emerged from the bosun's pipe he set to his lips.

"General Quarters. General Quarters. All hands man your battle stations!"

The ship sprang to life as men raced to their stations. Then, prepared to fight, she fell quiet again. Throughout the force, the scene was repeated.

On the flagship, Turner's *McCawley*, time passed by. At 0240 a message was relayed to flag plot.

"Cape Esperance bears 090, sir, distant thirteen miles."

On receipt of this report, in response to signals, the ships bound for Guadalcanal, Transport Group X-ray, changed course to the right to pass south of Savo Island which loomed up ahead, a grim sentinel guarding the entrance to Savo Sound—soon to be renamed Ironbottom Sound. Transport Group Yoke, destination Tulagi, held course a bit longer until

265

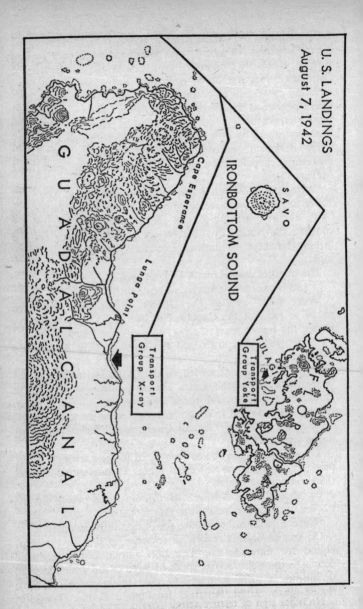

U. S. LANDINGS
August 7, 1942

IRONBOTTOM SOUND

SAVO

GUADALCANAL

Cape Esperance

Lunga Point

Transport Group X-ray

TULAGI

FLO

Transport Group Yoke

it was directly north of Savo Island, then turned southeast to head for the transport area off Tulagi.

So far there was no sign of the Japanese. Could it be that the operation had attained surprise?

As the ships crept closer to the beaches, there was still no reaction. The transport areas were about four to five miles from the designated beaches. On Tulagi the selected landing area, Beach Blue, was on the western end of the southern shore. Beach Red on Guadalcanal lay with its western end four miles east of Lunga Point at the mouth of the Tenaru River and just over three miles from the vital airfield.

At 0613, with surprise complete, the cruiser *Quincy* shattered the silence with a crashing broadside, joined in immediately by the *Vincennes, Astoria,* and four destroyers throwing their shells against the defenders on Guadalcanal. Two minutes later the cruiser *San Juan* and destroyers *Monssen* and *Buchanan* presented Tulagi with a similar treatment. The travel-poster aspect of the tropical islands just before dawn swiftly disintegrated as ugly shell bursts knocked down trees and dislodged the wet sand and tossed the tangled undergrowth into yet more impenetrable tangles.

No answer, no sign of life appeared on the beaches. Was this an elaborate trap?

By 0645 the transports were in place in the designated transport areas. Carrier planes buzzed overhead, now and then buzzing down on the beaches like angry hornets, spurting bullets from their machine guns. The key order was issued.

"Land the landing force!"

At Admiral Turner's request, General Vandegrift set the time for H-hour on Guadalcanal at 0910. Expecting, on the basis of intelligence reports, to find 5000 troops on the island, the planners had designated the larger force for Guadalcanal and the smaller one for the far smaller target of Tulagi.

As the transports were gliding to their stations, a Japanese auxiliary schooner loaded with gasoline set sail from Tulagi for Guadalcanal. The destroyer *Selfridge* and several carrier planes pounced upon the hapless schooner, sending her quickly to the bottom; her cargo blazing fiercely on the surface of the water briefly marked her grave. A single misguided Japanese plane flew over the formation, but was quickly shot out of the sky by an American fighter.

No other sign of enemy activity could be seen.

Aboard the transports, Marines assembled at their debarkation stations. Hesitation and self-doubting were things of the past. Davits swung out the 36-foot Higgins boats and 36-foot LCPRs* and boatswain's mates supervised lowering them into the water. Ships' cargo booms made light of the 45- and 56-foot LCMs,** boats capable of handling a small tank or carrying fifteen tons of cargo. Soon the personnel boats were playing follow the leader in several circles of the quarters of the transports. As called, they came alongside.

Other seamen rigged the debarkation nets, huge nets, made of heavy manila line, that would serve as ladders by which the Marines would enter the boats. It was a breathtaking climb down the nets, a rifle slung over your shoulder, a pack on your back, and heavy "boondocks" or combat shoes on your feet. As the ship rolled gently you would be swung out over the water and then slammed into the side with a bone-shaking thud. You gritted your teeth and kept going. Finally you were in the boat.

As the boats were loaded, they moved off to their prescribed positions in their proper waves near the line of departure, some 4000 yards from the nearest transports and 5000 yards from the beach.

At 0913 the first wave grounded off Beach Red on Guadalcanal, and springing out into the shallow water, the Marines, landing in a formation two battalions wide, made their way up the beach, ready for anything. Now was the moment when the Japanese would hit back.

On they went, their rifles ready, their nerves tense, eyes on the menacing jungle ahead.

Nothing.

There was no opposition.

Unbelieving, the Marines pressed on. It was too good to be true.

But it was true. The Japanese had retreated into the jungle.

All that day unloading continued, and by nightfall 11,000 troops were on Guadalcanal, while the beach was piled high with supplies.

On Tulagi things were not going quite so smoothly. H-hour had been set for 0800, more than an hour earlier than on

* Landing Craft, Personnel, Ramped.
* * Landing Craft, Medium.

Guadalcanal. The ship-shore movement proceeded much as it was to do across the sound. But the situation was more complicated, and there were fewer forces to handle it. Instead of fifteen transports, there were four. Tulagi is tucked into a bay of the larger Florida Island, and Japanese defenders on the point of land at Haleta on Florida could have presented a nasty situation with enfilading fire on Beach Blue on Tulagi. To prevent this situation, a company of Marines under Captain Edgar J. Crane landed at 0740 near Haleta, unopposed as it happened, although reconnaissance had spotted Japanese troops there two weeks earlier.

Tulagi itself is about two miles long and half a mile wide, lying in a northwesterly, southeasterly direction. It is heavily wooded. It is hilly, with the highest point rising 350 feet above the beach level. Most of the development of the copra traders lay in the southeast part of the island, and the Japanese had taken these over and developed them into a seaplane base, adding antiaircraft guns and other military equipment.

In view of these defenses and also the presence of cliffs dominating all possible landing beaches in this part of the island, Marine planners had decided to locate Beach Blue on the southern coast of Tulagi, about half a mile from the northwestern end.

The selected beach was less than ideal. A note on a map used in the planning characterizes Beach Blue as, "bordered with coral reefs. Due to uncertain tides, landing not practical except amphibian tanks or rubber boats."

In spite of this grim warning, the planning officers selected this area as the best available. So it was that in the early morning hours of August 7, Marines embarked in the boats and landing craft of their four transports and four destroyer-transports. There they bobbed about in the gentle swells of Savo Sound.

It was while they were loading the boats that the Guadalcanal-Tulagi operation—Operation Watchtower in the planners' jargon—suffered its first casualty. One of the Marines was killed by accidental discharge of a rifle while he was still aboard the destroyer-transport *Little*.

His death was but the first entry on a long list destined to be inscribed before an end could be made of the Solomons campaign.

The laconic note on the planning chart proved to be far

more reliable than most of the information available about the Solomons Islands. The landing craft running in toward the beach, loaded with fiercely intense, combat-ready men, pushed on. Then came a series of grinding crunches. The landing craft had run aground on the treacherous coral. Some managed to get as close as thirty yards from the beach, but others were stuck well over a hundred yards out.

There was nothing for it. Over the sides sprang the Marines, rifles held high over their heads to keep them out of the water. Some sank to their waists, and others to their shoulders, as they waded in toward the beach.

Now was the time for the Japanese to open up against these half-submerged Marines who could offer no real defense. Officers, gunners, and lookouts on the supporting ships, the light cruiser *San Juan* and the destroyers *Buchanan* and *Monssen*, watched the wooded slopes behind the landing beach intently, ready to smash to bits any enemy position that attempted to interfere with the landing.

Fortunately for the Marines, the Japanese had thought as little of Beach Blue as a possible landing site as the author of the note on the Marine planning chart. Beach Blue was undefended. The Marines of the first wave reached shore without the loss of a man. So did the second wave, coming in a few minutes later.

Immediately on landing, the first two waves penetrated across the island, forming a line facing toward the southeast. Meanwhile a battalion under Lieutenant Colonel Harold E. Rosecrans had landed and swept to the northwest, encountering no resistance.

The troops advancing to the southeast, the First Raider Battalion, under the command of Colonel Merritt A. Edson, began to meet opposition and suffer casualties as they reached the cleared areas of the former British Government stations and the copra plantations. Japanese resistance was centered in a ravine that could not be cleared out until the next day.

The islets Tanambogo and Gavutu, lying east of Tulagi, offered much more stubborn resistance than Tulagi itself. The Japanese defenders were alert, and the first attack on Tanambogo that evening was beaten off with severe losses. Gavutu was somewhat easier, and once the island was secured, adequate forces were sent to Tanambogo, which was overrun on August 8.

270

No reliable figures on Japanese casualties on Tulagi, Tanambogo, and Gavutu are possible. Marine intelligence officers estimated that there had been about 1500 Japanese, about equally divided between the three islands. Perhaps seventy escaped to Florida, where they spent the brief remainder of their lives as fugitives from Marine patrols and headhunting natives. Twenty-three Japanese were taken prisoner. All the rest perished.

Marine casualties were 144 killed or missing and 194 wounded. The Japanese death rate was approximately ten times that of the Marines.

On Guadalcanal, advancing troops continued to find no enemy. By dusk two regiments, the First Marines and Fifth Marines, had advanced about a mile, hacking their way through the jungle. There they took positions for the night, preparing to assault and overrun the airfield the next morning.

At 0930, on August 8, the First Battalion of the First Marines advanced on the airfield. They reached it at 1600 that afternoon, their advance slowed by the jungle and not by the Japanese. At the same time, the First Battalion, Fifth Marines, was advancing across the Ilu River to Kukum village, which had been the Japanese headquarters.

Both at Kukum and at the airfield, the Marines found large quantities of Japanese rifles, ammunition, gasoline, oil, trucks, a few machine and antiaircraft guns, as well as quantities of food and beer and sake. There was even some electrical equipment—radios and two radar sets. At the airfield, soon to be named Henderson Field in honor of Marine Major Lofton Henderson, a pilot killed in the Battle of Midway, there was an immense amount of equipment, and the runway had been completed for a length of 3600 feet.

The most important task of the Marines was now to consolidate their defenses into a perimeter to withstand the inevitable Japanese counterattack. The enemy might have left the target area, but they had not left the island. Meanwhile, the order of the day was to establish as strong a defense as possible and get as many supplies unloaded as they could before the transports had to leave. That the Japanese would strike back was certain. The question was where, when, how?

While the Marine pickets watched the forbidding jungle and cursed the stinging, biting tropical insects, their eyes intent for

271

any suspicious movements, the Japanese were setting forces in motion for their counterblows.

When they came, they hit by air and by sea. Just a few hours away lay the worst defeat ever suffered by the United States Navy in battle.

CHAPTER TEN

The Battle of Savo Island

> The death-fires danced at night.
> Coleridge, "The Rime of the
> Ancient Mariner."

On Tulagi a Japanese radio operator sat hunched over his key, tapping out the letters of the Kana Code. Around his shack American shells were falling. Grimly he kept on. The time was 0800 on the morning of August 7, 1942. As the operator straightened up, his message complete, a shell smashed into his shack, wiping the transmitting station and the operator out of existence.

Six hundred miles to the northwest at Rabaul, another Japanese radioman passed the message on to his superior, and it soon reached the hands of Vice Admiral Gunichi Mikawa. "Enemy force overwhelming," he read. "We will defend our posts to the death, praying for eternal victory."

Grim-faced, Admiral Mikawa considered what more he could do. Since 0630, when the first warning of American attack had reached him, he had ordered long-range search planes to the vicinity of Guadalcanal to find the enemy. He had but one idea—attack.

When he received the last message from Tulagi, he sent for the commander of his fighter squadron, Commander Tadashi Nakajima, and ordered him to attack. The stunned Nakajima looked at the distance—six hundred miles. There was nothing to spare, literally nothing. Unless they could refuel at the unfinished airstrip in Buka in the northern Solomons, they would have no time over the target and little chance of getting back.

Off they went, eighteen Zeros, flown by the most experienced pilots. Scarcely had they got off when Rabaul was raided by B-17s from General MacArthur's Southwest Pacific command, but they struck the airfield, not the harbor, so Admiral Mikawa could spare them but a passing glance. His responsibility was the major attack at Tulagi and Guadalcanal, not the minor one at Rabaul.

As commander of the newly activated Eighth Fleet, or Outer Seas Force, he had ready at hand a powerful force of cruisers and destroyers, but no aircraft carriers. Nor could he issue orders to the Army forces present, for the Army jealously guarded its prerogatives as the senior service. Their strategy committed them to drive across the Owen Stanley Mountains to Port Moresby on the southern coast of New Guinea. No mere American diversion on Guadalcanal could turn the Army from its chosen track.

Yet Guadalcanal must be reinforced. Bit by bit he scraped together 410 men from his own command, equipped them with rifles and a few machine guns, and loaded them on the transport *Meiyo Maru*. By midnight the transport, inadequately escorted by the cargo carrier *Soya* and the minelayer *Tsugaru*, was steaming by Cape St. George on the southern tip of New Ireland when she encountered two torpedoes from the United States submarine *S-38*. Shuddering to a stop, the *Meiyo Maru* sank, with a loss of 342 officers and men.

The reinforcement of Guadalcanal would have to be postponed.

These minor efforts occupied but a fraction of Admiral Mikawa's time. He must smash the landing if he could. He proposed a daring plan and sent it to Tokyo for approval. Back came the answer: "Carry out attack as planned."

Knowing nothing of the American plans, Mikawa intended to take all the fighting ships he could find and boldly smash through the American forces guarding the landing, sink the transports, and use his big guns to cut to pieces the Marines who were even then moving toward the airstrip, the future Henderson Field. Against the unknown numbers of American ships he could pit but five heavy cruisers, two light cruisers, and a single destroyer.

To do even this, he had to assemble his forces. That very morning, three of his heavies had left Kavieng for Manus, headed the wrong way. Two others were en route to him at Rabaul. With him at the moment he had only the two light cruisers and the destroyer.

In anticipation of the command, the three heavy cruisers changed course. By early afternoon the entire force had reached the vicinity of Rabaul.

Admiral Mikawa now faced a personal decision. As a major fleet commander, he should remain where he could exercise command, where he could both receive and send radio messages. At Rabaul he had the facilities. If he went to sea, his command voice could be stilled, for all his ships would observe strict radio silence.

There was really no dilemma. Nearly all his available force was going into action on a desperate, perhaps suicidal, mission. The code of the warrior required that he lead his men. His duty as he saw it and his desire coinciding, Admiral Mikawa embarked in the heavy cruiser *Chokai*, which promptly broke his red-and-white-striped personal flag. Ordering his other cruisers to form a column behind him, he took departure from Cape St. George and headed to pass to the east of the Solomons chain for the first leg of his mission.

Looking around his flagship, Admiral Mikawa could note with satisfaction her high degree of readiness. Ten years old, the *Chokai* boasted a well-trained and dedicated crew. Without fail they would employ her ten 8-inch guns with deadly accuracy, while her six 4.7-inch guns stood ready to drive off any impertinent aircraft. Torpedomen stood at her eight 24-inch torpedo tubes, ready to shoot off the most deadly torpedoes in any navy in the world. When the first eight fish were gone, they had sixteen more ready to load in the tubes.

The thrust of the deck reminded Mikawa that the *Chokai*'s engineers had all the speed he could desire. They could drive her turbines to send her through the water at over 35 knots, more than he would use, since he would be limited to 33 knots, all that could be coaxed out of the *Tenryu*.

The four sister ships of Cruiser Division Six steamed behind the flagship. Three of them, the *Aoba, Kinugasa,* and *Furutaka,* had been completed in 1926, and the fourth, the *Kako,* was a year older. They displaced 7100 tons instead of the 9880 of the flagship and carried six 8-inch guns apiece. Their decks bore eight torpedo tubes, each of which could be reloaded once.

Astern of the *Kako* steamed Mikawa's two light cruisers, first the venerable *Tenryu,* in service since 1918. As armament she bore four 5.5-inch guns and a single 3-incher, but the old

274

lady had plenty of sting in her six torpedo tubes. The slightly younger *Yubari* followed with four tubes; she had the smallest torpedo load of any ship in the formation, but her six 5.5s made her formidable. Last of all came Mikawa's single destroyer, *Kamikaze*, the only antisubmarine vessel in the formation. She had only four 4.7-inch guns, but her torpedoes could be deadly.

Seven ships knifing through the water—indeed a small force to throw at the Allied naval strength off Guadalcanal. How many there might be, Mikawa had no idea. His chief concern was the American carrier force—unlocated and unassailable. His only chance, Mikawa realized, was to attack by night, hit hard and fast, and be out of reach of aerial counterattack by dawn.

A night action it would be. With his staff navigator, the Admiral pored over his charts, calculating speeds and distances. He could be off Savo Island in the early morning hours of Sunday, August 9. [Japanese forces kept Tokyo time during the Solomons operations, while U.S. forces kept local time (-11). Thus, Japanese accounts show times two hours earlier than American ones. In this book local time (-11) is used.] This would give him a mere two hours to destroy the Allied forces and be off up the passage between the Solomons, a passage later known to the Americans as the Slot.

Mikawa saw another obvious advantage to his plans for a night action. The Japanese Navy had trained gruelingly in after-dark operations for years. No risk had been too great, no demand on the crew too severe. For three months at a time during the peacetime years, the Japanese fleet had held highly secret exercises in the storm-racked waters of the North Pacific. Ships had collided; sailors had worked until they had dropped in their places, only to be kicked back to their stations by their petty officers. If a man fell overboard, he was gone. The ships could not and would not stop to pick him up.

From this dedication, this brutality, this ruthlessness, came efficiency. Inefficient officers and men were mercilessly weeded out. Tactics were perfected. The Japanese optical industry had given the Navy superior binoculars, while their torpedo experts had produced a torpedo whose performance put every other torpedo in the world to shame. The standard steam-propelled American torpedo was 21 inches in diameter, and it carried 780 pounds of explosive. At high speed—45 knots—it could travel 6000 yards; at low speed—26.5 knots—15,000 yards. In contrast, the Japanese oxygen-propelled torpedo had a 24-inch diameter, carried a thousand-pound charge, and could travel 22,000 yards at high speed of 49 knots, or 40,000 yards at the low speed of 36 knots. Known to American sailors as the "Long Lance," this torpedo was the most-feared Japanese weapon until the advent of the suicide or kamikaze tactics.*

In contrast, American fleet exercises had customarily taken place in the waters of the Caribbean, or west of Panama, or off Pearl Harbor, when good weather could be expected. Emphasis on safety, comfort, morale, and economy had hampered training. The Japanese had been ruthlessly severe. The Americans had been too lax. There can be no question as to which ships were more efficient in the battle that was only hours away.

For reasons of deception and safety, Mikawa planned to cut across the northern end of Buka at the head of the Solomons chain, pass east of Bougainville, and then cut in between that island and Choiseul to enter the Slot. From there he would head straight for Savo, leave the island to port, brush past any defenses, smash the amphibious shipping on the Guadalcanal side of Savo (Ironbottom) Sound. He would then cross over to Tulagi, repeat the process, and pass north of Savo back up the Slot.

Such in brief was his battle plan. He realized that his only chance of success lay in surprise. The chance seemed slim. He would have to steam several of the daylight hours of August 8 through the restricted waters of the Slot where the Americans would be sure to have search planes to spot him. Yet it was his only chance. Through the night his ships sped on.

Although he did not know it, he had already been spotted and reported. The submarine S-38, which would later foil his effort to reinforce Guadalcanal by sinking the *Meiyo Maru*, had been so close to their track as they passed Cape St. George that she had been unable to get her torpedoes ready

---

* The Japanese word *kamikaze* means "Divine Wind" and was first applied to the typhoons that destroyed the invasion fleets of Kublai Khan in 1273 and 1279. Japanese destroyers were often named for winds, and it is mere coincidence that the only Japanese destroyer in this action bore the same name later applied to the Japanese suicide Special Attack Corps.

before the Japanese warships were past. Pitching and rolling in the wash from the Japanese cruisers, S-38 surfaced and sent a contact report: TWO DESTROYERS AND THREE LARGER SHIPS OF UNKNOWN TYPE HEADING ONE FOUR ZERO TRUE AT HIGH SPEED EIGHT MILES WEST OF CAPE ST. GEORGE.

At first light, while he was still to the east of Bougainville, Mikawa ordered the heavy cruisers to launch their scout planes and send them to reconnoiter the waters off Guadalcanal. Four planes went off, one each from the *Chokai*, *Aoba*, *Kinugasa*, and *Kako*, while engine defects caused the *Furutaka*'s plane to abort the mission. With the cheers of their shipmates ringing in their ears, the pilots set out on their search patterns.

While he waited, Admiral Mikawa broke up his formation, scattering his ships over the sea, so that if he was spotted, the Allies might be deceived with respect to his force and his intentions.

His ruse worked. About 1020 a Lockheed Hudson bomber of the Royal Australian Air Force circled Mikawa's ships for a few minutes and then drove off on its patrol. To deceive the pilot, Mikawa briefly reversed course so that he would seem to be heading back for Rabaul. A few minutes later, after recovering his search planes, Mikawa was distressed to sight another Hudson low on the water. Irritated, the Japanese admiral ordered his ships to fire on it, and it went on its way.

Certain now that he had lost all hope of surprise, Admiral Mikawa doggedly resumed his course for Bougainville Strait.

But the fates seemed to be on the side of the Japanese that day. The sighting reports made by the pilots of the two planes did not give him away. If anything, they confused the Allied commanders, causing them to make a false estimate. We will learn later the incredible story of these sighting reports.

The *Aoba*'s search plane had not come back with the others, having flown farther, over Guadalcanal itself. Unlike the pilots of the other planes, this airman had something to report. Savo Sound, he said, held a battleship, six cruisers, nineteen destroyers, and eighteen transports. Since his planes the previous day had reported sinking two cruisers, a destroyer, and six transports, Mikawa was, not unnaturally, upset. If his attack reports had been accurate, there should not have been such a powerful force in Savo Sound. He was also concerned that his searches had discovered no carriers, although he knew they must be in the area because of the number of reports of carrier planes he had received.

One small silver lining was apparent. The enemy force was divided between Guadalcanal and Tulagi. With luck he would be able to destroy them piecemeal, before they could combine against him.

Admiral Mikawa was not one to turn back. The attack would go on. Air strikes from Rabaul might weaken the Allied force. With no apparent concern, Mikawa waited for results to reach him. Later in the afternoon he sent the *Aoba*'s plane off again to bring the latest word from Savo Sound.

The plane never returned.

At 1620 Mikawa signaled his battle plan to all ships. He formed his forces with two divisions, the two light cruisers and the destroyers, as an advance guard to engage any pickets, with the heavy cruisers as a main body. If no opposition was encountered, the light ships would fall in at the tail of the column and join the rush in. Passing south of Savo, the Japanese force would engage first on the Guadalcanal side, then cross to Tulagi as previously planned. All ships would stream white sleeves on each side of the bridge as recognition signals.

As the ships steamed through the dazzling blue waters of the Slot, lookouts carefully scanned the skies and the surrounding sea. Admiral Mikawa could not rid himself of anxiety over the American carrier force. The next few hours before sunset would be the most dangerous time. His ships would be easy targets against a determined, powerful torpedo- and dive-bomber attack. The Army Eleventh Air Base Headquarters at Rabaul had its own notions of its role. It was futile even to request air cover for his force.

The danger would be even greater, Mikawa believed, on the return passage, but if he had by that time succeeded in his mission and knocked out the enemy landing on Guadalcanal, the loss of his entire force and his own life with it would hardly matter. The important thing was to get there.

Suddenly a lookout reported a ship's mast ahead to starboard. Were they to be detected at this late hour? As the ships went to battle stations and guns trained on the stranger, anxiety mounted. It was all dissipated in a few moments when the stranger was identified as the seaplane tender *Akitsushima*.

Near sunset, when floating debris would not reveal his

course to scouting aircraft, Admiral Mikawa ordered all combustible material not needed for fighting to be jettisoned. Over the side went depth charges, loose gear about the decks, and excess fuel for the cruiser scout planes.

Soon thereafter Mikawa sent a signal with an obvious Nelson touch to his little fleet: IN THE FINEST TRADITION OF THE IMPERIAL NAVY WE SHALL ENGAGE THE ENEMY IN NIGHT BATTLE. EVERY MAN IS EXPECTED TO DO HIS UTMOST.

As the Japanese drew nearer to Guadalcanal, they were able to pick up the high-frequency radio transmissions of the Allied fleet. Such calls as "Red 6 to Red Base" and "Green 2 to Green Base" could only mean the presence of carriers. But where were they?

Darkness fell. The Japanese were cheered when they received reports that an air attack by the Army had set on fire two heavy and two light cruisers and a transport. The odds were becoming more even.

The ships had now resumed their single-column battle formation, and at 2313 Mikawa launched his cruiser float planes to reconnoiter Savo Sound and to drop flares on the disengaged side as the Japanese cruisers went into action. These brilliant magnesium lights would silhouette the Allied ships, providing perfect points of aim for the Japanese gunners and torpedomen. Watching the planes disappear into the darkness, Admiral Mikawa proudly thought of the young pilots who manned them. They knew their ships could not pause to pick them up. When they had finished their jobs, they would not have enough gasoline to get back to Rabaul. Perhaps they could reach Buka. Probably not. At midnight all ships went to battle stations. Speeding along at 26 knots, their phosphorescent wakes creaming out behind them, the Japanese ships were poised and deadly. Forty minutes later, the Admiral and his staff could discern the loom of land on the port bow. It was Savo Island. Almost there.

Scarcely had the island been identified when the starboard lookout shouted, "Ship approaching, thirty degrees starboard!" "Prepare for action," ordered Admiral Mikawa quietly. "Left rudder. Slow to 22 knots."

The phosphorescence of the wakes subsided a trifle as the Japanese ships turned away from the contact. If possible, Admiral Mikawa wished to avoid premature disclosure. But if the ship, now identified as a destroyer, should give any indication she had seen them, Japanese guns were ready to blow her out of the water.

Slowly the destroyer* closed the range. Then, incredibly, she reversed course to starboard and proceeded unconcernedly on her way.

At that instant the port lookout reported, "Ship sighted, twenty degrees to port!"

"Right rudder," ordered Mikawa. "Steer course 150 degrees."

The second destroyer** had her stern to the Japanese force and was slowly drawing away. She disappeared into the darkness, giving no sign of alarm.

Ordering the destroyer to keep an eye on the two American destroyers, Mikawa pushed on with his seven cruisers, stepping the speed up to 30 knots.

At about 0130, with Savo Island abeam to port, a lookout reported a cruiser seven degrees on the port bow. To the experienced eyes of Captain Toshikazu Ohmae, Mikawa's Chief of Staff, it could only be another destroyer.

False alarm.

Seconds seemed to drag. Then, at 0136: "Three cruisers, nine degrees starboard, moving right!"

At that moment one of the cruiser planes dropped a flare. Boldly silhouetted were three cruisers moving northwesterly, serenely, placidly.

"All ships attack!" ordered Admiral Mikawa quietly.

A minute later a salvo of torpedoes leaped from the tubes of the *Chokai*, slapped into the water, and raced, silent and deadly, toward their unsuspecting victims.

At that moment Allied defenses were at their lowest point since the *Quincy* had opened the attack some forty-three hours earlier. Crews were worn out from incessant labor, intermittent air attacks, and long hours at their battle stations.

For nearly two days there had been no rest for anyone, afloat or ashore. While the combatant ships provided gunfire support or stood guard for the landings, transports and cargo

---

* She was the U.S.S. *Blue* assigned to patrol the entrance between Savo and Cape Esperance on Guadalcanal.

** The U.S.S. *Ralph Talbot*, patrolling the passage north of Savo as far as Florida Island.

ships worked feverishly to unload troops and the things they would need for fighting and for bare existence.

Equipment and supplies of all kinds began to pile up on the beaches. Boat crews drove swiftly ashore, hurriedly unloaded their cargoes, and returned to their mother ships for another load.

Soon the beach began to be crowded. Then it was jammed. In the planning no one had given enough thought to the problem of dealing with the supplies once they had been set on the edge of the shore. The troops detailed for the job had been swept into the defense perimeter that General Vandegrift was establishing. The Navy men thought it was the Marines' job to handle the cargoes, while the Marines felt, quite naturally, that their duty was to fight. After all, they were Marines, not stevedores.

At length, the Navy supplied fifteen men from each cargo ship as a beach party, but even their best efforts were not enough. At one time a hundred boats were beached and unloading, while fifty more waited offshore for a strip of beach large enough for them to come ashore. During the first night, unloading had to be suspended for three precious hours while men worked until they vomited, then worked some more to clear away the mounds of supplies.

Mountainous though these supplies seemed, the demands were even greater. Some eleven thousand men had been landed on Guadalcanal and six thousand more on Tulagi. Four days would be the least required to unload the goods the ships had brought. If there were delays, it would take longer. And there were delays. Each time an air attack came, the transports and cargo ships had to stop unloading, raise their anchors, and join in an antiaircraft formation. Otherwise they would be sitting ducks.

Japanese air attacks were not long in coming. Although the fighters Admiral Mikawa had sent were ineffective, planes from the 25th Air Flotilla, also based at Simpson Harbour in Rabaul, attacked twice on August 7, hitting the destroyer *Mugford*. The vessel suffered only slight damage, but the bomb explosion cost the lives of twenty-two men.

Planes from Admiral Fletcher's carriers parried the worst of the air attacks, both on that day and the next. F4F Wildcats, the Navy's best carrier fighters, swarmed over the approaching enemy planes. They seemed uncanny in their accuracy in being in the right place at the right time. This advantage was the result of skilled fighter director officers in the *Chicago*. Detecting the enemy attack on the air search radar, the fighter directors could order planes to meet the oncoming Japanese under conditions of advantage. To be sure, through an error in coding, the first group of *Enterprise* fighters was sent off directly opposite to the enemy, but subsequent groups made good contacts. By the time the day was over, the Japanese had lost sixteen aircraft to the Americans' twelve. But the transports had been saved.

The night of August 7/8 passed peacefully enough. Men ashore worked on the chaotic supply system. Marines held their defense perimeter, while groups of ships guarded the three entrances into Savo Sound. The only disturbances of the night were the screams of jungle birds or an occasional rattle of shots as trigger-happy Marines saw Japanese troops in passing shadows. A more ominous sound was disregarded by all—the monotonous slap-slap of the men ashore trying to smash the pesky *Anopheles maculipennis,* the malaria-bearing mosquito.

Saturday, August 8, saw resumption of the activities of the day before. While heavy fighting continued across the sound on Tulagi and the small islands, on Guadalcanal the Marines would not encounter enemy resistance until that night.

About noon, Japanese aircraft attacked again. As they roared in low on the water, the cruisers opened up on them with all guns, main battery as well as antiaircraft. Observers counted twenty-six of these torpedo planes; only three got through, and they were so shaken by the intense fire that they could accomplish little. Only the hapless destroyer *Jarvis* experienced a hit; she was severely damaged.

A few minutes later a group of dive bombers attacked, falling victims to both carrier planes and ships' gunfire. One Japanese pilot, realizing his plane was fatally hit, aimed his burning wreckage toward the nearest ship, crashing into the bridge. This was the transport *George F. Elliott*. Soon the ship was a blazing wreck from stem to stern, a drifting, abandoned hulk. So, a menace to all ships present, she had to be finished off. The destroyer *Hull* fired four torpedoes into her at close range, but the *Elliott* refused to sink. On she drifted, by now out of the danger area. Since night was falling, they left her to be dealt with on the morrow. Throughout the night she blazed, a beacon to the Japanese, a Viking's funeral, perhaps, hours ahead of time.

With darkness coming on, the ships took up the night stations they had guarded the night before. Admiral Turner, in his flagship *McCawley*, off Lunga Point on Guadalcanal, considered the events of the day and his plans for the next. Various intelligence reports of Japanese activity had reached him. The heavy air attacks that day had presaged heavier assaults in the near future. What the Allied forces had experienced so far was but a reflex reaction of competent commanders striking back with what they had. When the Japanese got organized . . .

His reflections were interrupted about 1830 by the arrival of a messenger from the flag coding room. He bore a dispatch sent by Admiral Fletcher at 1807, after the day's flight operations had been completed.

With amazement and dismay, Turner read the dispatch:

FIGHTER PLANE STRENGTH REDUCED FROM NINETY-NINE TO SEVENTY-EIGHT IN VIEW OF THE LARGE NUMBER OF ENEMY TORPEDO PLANES AND BOMBERS IN THIS AREA I RECOMMEND THE IMMEDIATE WITHDRAWAL OF MY CARRIERS X REQUEST TANKERS SENT FORWARD IMMEDIATELY AS FUEL RUNNING LOW.

The message was not even addressed to Turner, the man who would be in the position of a man riding a tiger if the carriers pulled out. Surely Fletcher could have done him the courtesy of telling him first. Instead it was to Admiral Ghormley, a thousand miles away, at Noumea, who had no means of knowing the situation. Since Fletcher was in command of the entire operation, not merely the carrier force, he presumably had considered all the implications of his early withdrawal. Ghormley could only agree.

Fletcher had not considered all the implications. The phrase "my carriers" in the message gives him away. Fletcher's two previous actions at Coral Sea and Midway had been in the role of carrier commander, and he still thought of them first. Both the *Lexington* at the Coral Sea and the *Yorktown* at Midway had been sunk as a result of aircraft torpedo attacks, and Fletcher had an inordinate fear of torpedo planes off Guadalcanal.

Although his force had not even been sighted by the Japanese, he felt it was high time to get out.

There are two types of military commanders: those who see opportunities, and those who see difficulties. Fletcher was inclined to be the latter.

Nor was fuel the real problem. All the heavies had enough for at least nine days' operations on board, and although the destroyers averaged only fifty percent full, they could fill up from the heavy ships. From the fuel logs of all ships present,* it is apparent that Fletcher's carrier force could have operated at least another three days in the area and could have reached Noumea without refueling.

Fletcher, in retrospect, seems unjustified in leaving Turner "bare arse," as that exasperated commander put it. Yet, in one way he was right. The United States could not afford to lose any more carriers. As we review the situation today, it seems that he would not have lost them. But he could not know that on August 8.

Not waiting for an answer, Fletcher pulled out soon after sending his dispatch. As Mikawa's force approached Savo Sound, the most powerful American force in the area was moving directly away from the battle scene.

Aboard the *McCawley*, Turner felt it imperative to discuss the situation with the senior commanders, General Vandegrift of the Marines and Admiral Crutchley, commanding the surface forces. At 2030 he sent a message to both commanders urging an immediate meeting.

When Turner's summons reached Crutchley, he had completed his dispositions for the night. Rear Admiral V. A. C. Crutchley, a British officer "of the old school" had placed his forces to cover the three possible entrances to the sound. Far to the east, in the least likely area, steamed a small force under the American Rear Admiral Norman Scott. He had the two light cruisers, U.S.S. *San Juan* and H. M. Australian Ship *Hobart*, as well as two destroyers. The *San Juan* was the only ship in the entire force with the new SG surface radar; she was stationed in the least likely avenue of approach.

To cover the two much more likely passages north and south

---

* The fuel logs of the *Wasp* were lost when she was sunk on September 15, but estimates placed her fuel supply at twelve days' steaming.

of Savo Island, Crutchley further split his forces. To the north were the cruisers *Vincennes, Astoria,* and *Quincy,* escorted by the destroyers *Helm* and *Wilson.* This group had no flag officer present and was under the tactical command of Captain Frederick L. Riefkohl, skipper of the *Vincennes.* These ships patrolled in column, every half hour turning ninety degrees to the right.

The monotony of this patrol was equaled only by that of the Southern Force. Here Admiral Crutchley had his own flagship, *Australia,* followed by the Australian cruiser *Canberra* and the American *Chicago,* accompanied by the destroyers *Patterson* and *Bagley.* This force simply steamed back and forth, an hour each way, between Savo and the transport area.

As early warning pickets, Crutchley stationed the destroyer *Blue* southwest of Savo and the *Ralph Talbot* to the northwest, with instructions to patrol at right angles to the course up the Slot. At best, these two destroyers were too close in to give timely warning; at worst, they could be twenty-five miles apart, unable to spot an enemy or to contact each other or the force commander as a result of the spotty radio reception in the area.

Admiral Crutchley issued no battle plan except to say that the *Vincennes* group would operate independently, generally conforming to the movements of the *Australia* group. He belonged to the Nelson school: "No captain can do very wrong if he places his ship alongside that of an enemy." Such a directive was adequate at the Battle of Trafalgar, but it was not enough off Savo Sound in August 1942. All that Crutchley had achieved was to divide his force into three groups, incapable of mutual support, and none strong enough to stop the force approaching at twenty-two knots. If Admiral Mikawa had been permitted to station the Allied ships himself to suit his own purposes, he could scarcely have improved on Admiral Crutchley's dispositions.

When Admiral Crutchley received Turner's summons, he set out at once, taking the *Australia* with him!

He reasoned it would be easier to find the flagship at night from the deck of his cruiser than from a small boat blundering about in the darkened sound. Merely signaling Captain Howard D. Bode, USN, captain of the *Chicago,* to take over command of the Southern Force, he proceeded to the rendezvous.

Not then or later did anyone think to inform Captain Riefkohl on the *Vincennes* in the Northern Force. Yet, with Crutchley's departure, Captain Riefkohl became senior officer. Thus, all unknowing, he held the authority and the responsibility in the forthcoming action.

Although Captain Bode now commanded the Southern Force, he did not trouble to exchange station with the *Canberra*, in spite of the fact that the senior officer customarily leads in such a formation. He expected the *Australia* to return before morning and did not relish the maneuvering necessary to reverse the order of the two cruisers.* If nothing else, Captain Bode's taking the lead position would have shown that he had taken command. He did not. The *Chicago* continued to plod along in the *Canberra*'s wake.

Captain Bode went to bed in his sea cabin. It had been a hard day.

The *Chicago*'s skipper was not the only one to seek his bunk. By midnight all five of the commanding officers of the cruisers constituting the Southern and the Northern Force had retired, each where he could be reached at a moment's notice.

They were not to be granted that moment.

It was ten-thirty that night (2230 in Navyese) before the *Australia* found the *McCawley* and Admiral Crutchley, reached Admiral's quarters of the flagship. Late as he was, another forty-five minutes passed by before the spare frame of General Vandegrift appeared. He was accompanied by his operations officer, Colonel Gerald Thomas.

"Jerry and I were pretty tired," Vandegrift noted, "but these two [Turner and Crutchley] looked ready to pass out."

Admiral Turner wasted no time in getting to the point of the meeting. As the officers drank coffee, Turner showed the others Fletcher's dispatch. In view of this action, Turner said, he felt he ought to pull the Amphibious Force out the next morning. In the absence of air cover, the transports and cargo ships would be easy targets for Japanese planes.

Realizing that the ships were less than half unloaded, Turner anxiously asked General Vandegrift what he thought.

---

* The maneuvering to accomplish the exchange would have been simple. At the time for the next 180-degree turn, the two cruisers would have only had to reverse course simultaneously rather than in succession. Either maneuver has about an equal degree of danger.

"We are in fair shape on Guadalcanal," replied the General, "but I don't know about Bill Rupertson* on Tulagi. He has been fighting ever since his landing, and I doubt if he's gotten much supply ashore. I must certainly check with him first."

The conferees also discussed the possibility of other Japanese reaction to the Guadalcanal landings. No doubt about it, the Japanese were moving toward the area. The question was—with what?

Turner discussed the intelligence he had available. The report of *S-38*, the first observation of Mikawa's force, was too early and told him only that Japanese ships were in the area and moving somewhere.

To keep an eye on the approaches from the northwest, Turner told the others, he had reviewed the searches that covered the area, and, dissatisfied with the coverage afforded by General MacArthur's planes from New Guinea and by Admiral McCain's from the Espiritu-New Caledonia region, had requested a special afternoon search of the Slot by McCain's planes. He had heard nothing from this search and assumed it had been negative.

But as Captain Queeg said, "You can't assume a goddamn thing in the Navy." The special search had not been flown because of the weather, and the message reporting the fact had been held up in McCain's radio shack.

One sighting report Turner did have. It was from one of the two Hudson bombers that had sighted Mikawa's force that morning. Here was solid evidence.

But was it?

The first sighting had taken place at 1026 that morning. The Australian pilot calmly continued his patrol throughout most of the afternoon. His clear instructions were to break radio silence in the event of a major sighting, or if he could not get through on the radio, to return to base, then less than two hours away. He did neither. Patrol complete, he touched down at Milne Bay on the southeastern tip of New Guinea. There he had his tea, and then, as an afterthought, reported his contact.**

* Brigadier General William A. Rupertson, USMC, commanding in the Tulagi area.

** So far as is known, the pilot of the second Hudson never reported his sighting.

It was near sundown when the sighting report finally started on its way to the men who needed it most—Admirals Turner and Crutchley. From Milne Bay it went to Port Moresby by radio, whence it was relayed to Townsville, Australia, thence on to Lieutenant General George C. Kenny in Brisbane. Kenny sent it across the city by dispatch rider to MacArthur's headquarters. MacArthur passed it by land line to Canberra, where the U.S. Navy radio station put it on the "Bells" broadcast and also relayed it to Pearl Harbor for retransmittal to the fleet on the "Fox" broadcast.*

At 1845 Turner received the report, now eight hours and nineteen minutes old. In these days of radio, the information had traveled at an average speed of 42 miles per hour from the point of sighting only 350 miles from Turner's flagship.

By the time he received it, Turner could order no supplemental searches, for darkness was already falling. The best he could do was to discuss the "hard" intelligence with the others.

This is what the dispatch said:

THREE CRUISERS THREE DESTROYERS TWO SEA-PLANE TENDERS OR GUNBOATS COURSE ONE TWO ZERO

About the only correct things in the message were the total numbers of ships and the course, Mikawa had—remember —five heavy cruisers, two light cruisers, and one destroyer. Total: eight. The course, thirty degrees south of east, was about right.

The unfortunate thing was the phrase, "two seaplane tenders." Even though this was only a tentative identification by the pilot, Turner and Crutchley seized upon it to deduce that the Japanese were setting up a seaplane base, probably on Rekata Bay on the northwestern coast of Santa Isabel. On this assumption, they concluded the principal threat would be air

* A major problem in wartime is radio communication with ships at sea which must maintain radio silence. To ensure receipt of vital information, powerful Navy shore radio stations transmit serially numbered broadcasts to all ships. Each ship listens to one or more of these stations, copying all traffic but deciphering only messages concerning it. "Fox" was the term used for such a broadcast from Pearl Harbor and "Bells" that from Canberra.

attack the next day, not surface attack that night or later.

All the more reason to remove the fragile amphibious ships. The Marines would just have to dig in and hold on.

The conference broke up about midnight, and Admiral Crutchley offered to take General Vandegrift in his barge to the minesweeper *Southard,* which was to take the General to Tulagi. Scudding rain clouds and flashes of lightning followed by deeper black meant that it took some time to find the *Southard* and more to return Admiral Crutchley to his flagship. Since so little of the night remained, Crutchley decided not to rejoin the Southern Force, but to patrol independently west of the transport area.

Again he informed no one of his decision.

On the ships of the Southern and Northern Patrol Forces, officers and men had settled down to another night of routine steaming. After long hours at General Quarters, with all the crew at battle stations and the ship sealed up with all watertight doors closed, some of the skippers had relaxed the conditions to permit half the crew to sleep at their battle stations.

Dead-tired men dropped where they stood when the order came and slept where they dropped. Those less fortunate ones in the duty section shot the breeze in low tones in order not to disturb their shipmates.

Off Savo, outside the sound, the two pickets *Blue* and *Ralph Talbot* droned along on their lonely patrols at about twelve knots. Steer southwest for half an hour, reverse course, steam northeast half an hour, reverse course, steam— The sheer monotony must have been deadly.

It was.

Although the Japanese passed less than five miles from the *Blue* and less than seven from the *Ralph Talbot* and clearly saw both ships, neither American destroyer had the slightest inkling that any Japanese ships were closer than Rabaul. So the Japanese approached. The destroyers had turned away from the enemy, the *Ralph Talbot* moving sedately off toward Florida Island and the *Blue* imperturbably to the southwest. It is as though they were opening giant double doors to let the Japanese pass.

On the bridge of the *Canberra*, Lieutenant Commander E. J. Wright stood his watch as principal control officer with the aid of Sub-Lieutenant M. I. Gregory as officer of the watch. The ships of the Southern Force were moving slowly northwestward, occasionally discerning the loom of land from Savo amid the frequent rainsqualls. On the starboard bow trudged the destroyer *Bagley*, and on the port bow, the *Patterson*.

The time was 0143. A blinker light on the *Patterson* began to stutter a message. Simultaneously, a lookout on the *Canberra* shouted, "Alarm starboard, green twenty!"*

The *Patterson*, the only ship in a position to see and the only one with crew alert enough to take advantage of the opportunity, had spotted something—several ships—ahead.

Her skipper, Commander Frank R. Walker, USN, at once sounded the tocsin both by radio and by blinker:

WARNING—WARNING—STRANGE SHIPS ENTERING HARBOR

The warning was in vain. There was no time for the *Canberra* and *Chicago* to react before they were in action. The Northern Force was too occupied with a course change for the *Patterson*'s warning to get through. The line was busy. No one on the bridge of any of the three northern cruisers heard the *Patterson*'s alarm.

All ships had had a possible warning earlier, if they had only chosen to understand it correctly. Cruiser planes from the Japanese force had arrived over the harbor shortly before midnight. Although one of them was spotted by the *Ralph Talbot*, which promptly broadcast the sighting, the report reached very few ships. The shortwave radio, TBS, then in use could not reach as far as Turner's flagship twenty miles away. Other ships attempted to relay the warning, "Plane sighted over Savo Island heading east." Turner never got it.

Several ships sighted the Japanese cruiser planes during the next two hours and all, unfailingly, identified them as friendly.

The innocence born of a quarter-century of peace died hard. After Pearl Harbor, one could have expected the American

* The British report relative bearings with numbers from 0 to 180 preceded by the color *green* or *red* to indicate starboard or port; the colors correspond to those of the running lights. American practice is to use degrees from 0 to 360, going completely around the ship to the right, beginning at the bow.

Navy to be expecting Japanese surprises, not to assume the best when the Japanese were around.

But they did.

No one who lived through the night just ahead was ever the same as before. At last the simple trust of the Americans gave way to suspicion of anything or anyone. If, on the next night, the Angel Gabriel had flown over the area, he would have been fired upon.

Having cruised around over Savo Sound with complete impunity, the Japanese pilots were able to tell Mikawa the location and composition of the Allied forces in the area. Then, as they sighted Mikawa's ships moving in, they retired skillfully behind the ships of the Southern Force and dropped flares.

Hell seemed to break loose all at once. When the planes dropped their flares, Japanese torpedoes had been swimming for five minutes. Bathed in the unearthly light behind them, the *Canberra*'s watch officers peered ahead, just discerning the shape of a strange ship.

Suddenly the shape—or was it shapes?—ahead belched fire and steel. Instinctively flinching from the flashes ahead, the officers felt the deck hit their feet with sledge-hammer blows as torpedoes smashed into both bows.

Seconds later the shells arrived. Captain Frank E. Getting was mortally wounded. Other shells knocked out plot, so that the ship's main battery could not be fired as a unit. Her main guns stayed where they were, useless, impotent. The ship managed to get off a few shells from her 4-inch secondary battery and two torpedoes, but the result of this gallant effort was exactly nothing.

In less than five minutes, the *Canberra* was dead in the water, listing ten degrees to starboard, all power lost.

While the *Canberra* was absorbing her first blows, the destroyers *Patterson* and *Bagley* did their best to hit the enemy. Commander Walker ordered the *Patterson* to fire torpedoes, but as he spoke, the roar of his own guns drowned out his words. He did not know until much later that the torpedoes had not been fired.

Soon shells from the Japanese secondary batteries began dropping around his ship. Inevitably they began to hit. His ship was stabbed by Japanese searchlights, and in a few minutes the *Patterson* was out of action.

The *Bagley* rushed in to the attack, but when she reached

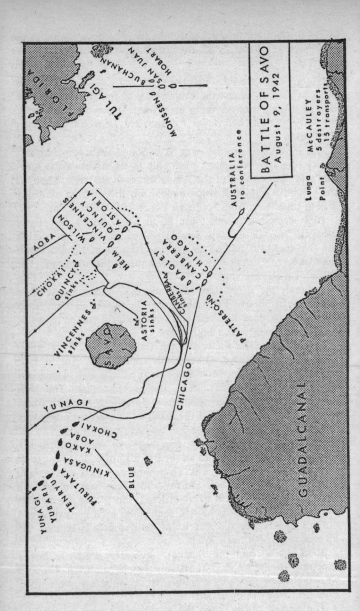

BATTLE OF SAVO
August 9, 1942

FLORIDA

TULAGI

BUCHANAN
SAN JUAN
HOBART
MONSSEN

AUSTRALIA
to conference

Lunga
Point
McCAULEY
5 destroyers
15 transports

AOBA

CHŌKAI

WILSON
VINCENNES
QUINCY
ASTORIA

HELM
BAGLEY
CANBERRA
CHICAGO

QUINCY
sinks

VINCENNES
sinks

CANBERRA
sinks

ASTORIA
sinks

PATTERSON

YUNAGI

CHŌKAI
KAKO
AOBA

CHICAGO

BLUE

KINUGASA
FURUTAKA
TENRYU
YUBARI
YUNAGI

GUADALCANAL

torpedo position, the firing primers had not been placed in the torpedoes. Cursing under his breath, Lieutenant Commander George G. Sinclair ordered, "Left full rudder!" to bring his port tubes to bear. The turn completed, he fired the torpedoes, but it was a stern chase by this time, and none of the torpedoes hit.

The Japanese disdained to reply, for they had their eyes on a better target. The *Chicago* was now in their gunsights.

In response to the noise and confusion ahead, the Officer of the Deck of the *Chicago* summoned Captain Bode, who arrived on the bridge just in time to hear lookouts report torpedo wakes approaching. Turning to starboard to avoid one set of torpedoes, the *Chicago* took a "fish" to port which blew away her bow for a distance of sixteen feet.

Trying to see the enemy, Captain Bode ordered starshells fired, but all were duds. Soon shells began to fall on the unprepared cruiser, bearing death and havoc with them. In four minutes the *Chicago* was out of action, her big guns still amidships.

Captain Bode had his hands full for the next few minutes. He was too busy; his thoughts were all for his stricken ship.

Incredibly, he sent no warning to the Northern Force.

Admiral Mikawa, delightedly watching the extraordinary success of his efforts thus far, ordered a gradual turn to port to engage the second force that his float planes had told him would be to the northeast. In the dark, his force split into two groups during the maneuver, the *Yubari, Tenryu,* and *Furutaka,* in that order, heading up close to Savo, while the *Chokai* led the *Aoba, Kako,* and *Kinugasa* farther to the east.

Mikawa was about to surround the Northern Force.

All that evening the three cruisers of the Northern Force, the *Vincennes, Quincy*, and *Astoria*, had steamed in a square five miles on a side, changing course ninety degrees to the right every half hour. On the port bow of the *Vincennes* was the destroyer *Helm,* and on the starboard, the *Wilson*.

Ever since 2030, Captain Riefkohl of the *Vincennes* had been senior officer present and officer in tactical command (OTC), but he did not know it.

In the absence of explicit warning from either Admiral Crutchley or Admiral Turner, Captain Riefkohl assumed—that word again—that the reported Japanese surface force would be no menace that night. Hearing the *Ralph Talbot's* warning of a plane and having the report of a later sighting of a plane by one of his own lookouts, he investigated and finally concluded that the plane had been a carrier plane sent from Fletcher's force to drop a message.

On this assumption, he went to bed.

When he spotted searchlights, gun flashes, and fires to the south, Lieutenant Commander Cleaveland R. Miller, Officer of the Deck of the *Vincennes*, hesitated at first, but finally decided that the Captain should be informed. Captain Riefkohl rushed to the bridge as the general alarm was raucously shattering the stillness about the decks. He was not seriously perturbed. Probably, he assumed, a small Japanese ship was trying to sneak into the harbor past the Southern Force.

Lieutenant Commander John D. Hayes, engineering officer of the *Astoria*, had been relieved as superior of the watch shortly before midnight. He turned in. The next thing he knew, the general alarm was sounding and a messenger was shining a flashlight in his eyes.

"Gee, Mr. Hayes," he said. "The shells are sure flying up there."

Commander Hayes rushed for the forward engine room, manning his battle station at main control, as other men were manning theirs throughout the ship.

A few minutes earlier, Lieutenant Commander James R. Topper, who had relieved Commander Hayes on the bridge, after seeing flares and unidentified aircraft, decided he had better inform the Captain. Scarcely had he sent off the messenger when he was flabbergasted to hear his own main battery of nine 8-inch guns crash out with a full salvo as the general alarm sounded its insistent summons.

Arriving on the bridge at that moment, Captain William G. Greenman demanded to know who had sounded the alarm and who had ordered the guns to open fire.

Topper replied that he had no idea, his words almost drowned out by the roar of a second salvo.

By this time Captain Greenman was convinced that the *Astoria* was firing on her own companions.

"Let's not get excited and act too hastily," he said. "Cease firing."

Topper agreed with his captain and passed the order, to the

disgust of Lieutenant Commander William H. Trusdell, the gunnery officer—the man who had ordered the salvos.

From his higher vantage point he had seen the flares and then the unmistakable cluttered superstructures of *Nachi*-class cruisers.

"What are you firing at? Cease firing!" came the order from the bridge.

"Japanese cruisers! Request permission to resume firing!"

Still unconvinced, Captain Greenman stared out into the blackness just in time to see shell splashes falling around the *Vincennes*. That was enough.

"Commence firing!" he roared. "Left standard rudder!"

Making a slight turn to port to clear the firing range for the *Quincy*, Captain Greenman muttered, "Own ships or not, we've got to stop them!"

Then ahead he saw an appalling sight—the *Quincy* and *Vincennes* both afire and losing way. Pulling farther left to avoid overrunning the *Quincy*, Captain Greenman felt his own ship shudder under the impact of shells. Becoming aware that the ship was slowing, although his order had been "All engines ahead full," he called the engine room to ask what speed the engineers could give him.

"None," replied Commander Hayes tersely.

Japanese shells had, by this time, knocked out all power and had scored a direct hit on Turret Number One, killing everyone inside. Turrets Two and Three continued to fire in local control for several minutes. Although they could not know it, her gunners had sent one shell of her last salvo screaming onto a forward turret of the *Chokai*.

Then the Japanese were gone. The ship that had three years earlier borne the ashes of the Japanese Ambassador to Tokyo lay blazing, listing, and helpless.

The *Quincy* had even less opportunity than the *Astoria*. She managed to get off two full salvos before Captain Samuel N. Moore decided that the ships blistering him with their searchlights might be friendly. Accordingly, he ordered recognition lights turned on. His horrified subordinates, realizing that the lights would only provide the Japanese with a point of aim, tried to get him to change his mind, but by that time it made no difference. A Japanese shell found one of the scout planes astern and set it afire. Flames spread to the aviation gasoline

295

stored there, and the *Quincy*'s stern provided the Japanese gunners with all the light they needed.

Shell after shell they pumped into the stricken ship. One of the first slammed into the bridge, killing almost everyone there and mortally wounding Captain Moore. Torpedoes tore into the engineering spaces, and the ship drifted to a stop. Unable to locate the executive officer and presuming him dead, Lieutenant Commander Harry B. Heneberger, the gunnery officer, ordered the ship to be beached.

The ship heeled more and more to port as the bow dipped farther and farther into the water. Realizing the helpless situation, Commander Heneberger ordered, "Abandon ship!"

It was just in time. As men threw floater nets and life rafts into the water, the stern began to rise. At 0235, just half an hour after action had begun in the Northern Force, the *Quincy* capsized, seemed to struggle in her death agony, as she gave a convulsive twist that lifted her stern straight up. Then, quietly, as though to reclaim her dignity, she slipped beneath the water.

She was the first of many ships to go down in Savo Sound—so many that the sound was christened Ironbottom Sound, and so the name appears on charts today.

Since the Japanese had come upon the Northern Force from astern, the *Vincennes*, first in column, was last to be engaged. Captain Riefkohl, OTC of the Northern Force and, though he knew it not, of the entire western patrol force, was summoned to the bridge when the flares dropped, illuminating the *Canberra* and *Chicago*.

When Captain Riefkohl reached his post, he and his executive officer, Commander William E. Mullan, felt underwater explosions—probably torpedoes hitting the *Canberra* —saw gun flashes, and heard firing.

"It's probably the *Australia* group engaging planes," decided Captain Riefkohl.

It was the *Australia* group engaging, but not planes. And the *Australia* was not there.

Captain Riefkohl ordered speed to be increased to 15 knots, and a few minutes later saw his three ships illuminated, each by a searchlight from a different ship. He concluded the Southern Force had strayed north of the dividing line and were now looking for suspicious ships.

"Turn those searchlights off us. We are friendly," he said into the TBS, the voice radio.

Just as a precaution, he ordered the guns trained on the nearest ship.

Shell splashes suddenly rose only five hundred yards short of the "Vinny Maru," as her crew called her. The *Kako* had them in her sights.

"Commence firing!" roared Captain Riefkohl, all doubts set to rest.

The *Vincenne*'s second salvo was her one success, for a shell tore into the port steering engine room of the *Kinugasa*. Simultaneously, the Japanese cruiser's lights went out, and the men of the *Vincennes* thought they had driven her off.

The hope was vain. The Japanese had turned off their lights because they could now see the targets and had no further need for them. Japanese gunners and torpedomen settled down to what was little more than target practice.

As Captain Riefkohl desperately tried to maneuver out of harm's way, Japanese shells made a carnage of her topside. Then torpedoes from the *Chokai* ripped her number four fireroom open to the sea. Eight minutes later, another torpedo hit in the number one fireroom, and the ship staggered to a halt.

Two new searchlights appeared from the side so far unengaged, and Captain Riefkohl, assuming they came from his own forces, took the opportunity to hoist the battle colors to replace those shot away.

Nothing could have pleased the Japanese more. Believing the *Vincennes* to be an admiral's flagship, they redoubled their efforts. After a few moments of this treatment, the gunnery officer reported that every gun on the *Vincennes* was out of action.

Action for the *Vincennes* ceased only when the Japanese passed beyond range, and her crew began the hopeless struggle to save their ship. The list steadily increased, and at about 0230, Captain Riefkohl gave the order to abandon. About twenty minutes later, the ship rolled over on her side and sank.

The two destroyers *Wilson* and *Helm* tried to do what they could, but it was not much. The *Wilson* fired a few torpedoes and lobbed 5-inch shells in the direction of the Japanese searchlight; the *Helm*, maneuvering violently, nearly collided with her sister; after this both ships lost touch with the enemy.

Aboard the Japanese flagship *Chokai*, Admiral Mikawa had reason for great satisfaction. The action thus far had been total victory. According to their calculations, five heavy cruisers and four destroyers had been sunk. If this estimate was optimistic, it was not far wide of the mark.

But what should he do now, Mikawa pondered. He had come this far to get the transport force, and was he to turn back, his task unaccomplished? Should he leave well enough alone and get out while he still could, or should he drive in to polish off the now helpless transports?

He looked around his damaged flagship. A shell from the *Quincy* had found its way into flag plot, where it had exploded, destroying his charts and plans. This was inconsequential. His force was somewhat scattered, and he believed it would take at least two and a half hours to round them up and reach the enemy anchorage. That would make it 0500, just an hour before sunrise.

At sunrise he could expect American carrier planes to be swarming around him like wasps, and there would be scant chance for any of them. In his fatalistic, Oriental way, Admiral Mikawa gave no thought to the question of his personal survival. That did not matter, but the ships must be preserved for the Emperor. The risk from the carrier planes was too great. They would return to Rabaul.

Far to the southeast, the *Saratoga, Enterprise*, and *Wasp*, the carriers that gave Admiral Mikawa so much concern, had long since been out of range. Admiral Fletcher had not waited for Admiral Ghormley's approval to begin his withdrawal. As soon as he had sent his famous message, he ordered course southeast, at 15 knots. When he reached the far end of the Solomons chain, not having received approval from Admiral Ghormley, he hesitated, then began, reluctantly, to retrace his way toward Guadalcanal.

About this time, stray radio messages from the Guadalcanal area began to dribble in, giving evidence of some sort of action. The skipper of the *Wasp*, Captain Forrest Sherman, suggested three times that his ship be sent back with a couple of destroyers to help out. The *Wasp*'s air group had had special training in night operations. The nominal carrier group commander, Admiral Noyes, refused even to forward the request to Admiral Fletcher.*

About 0330, Fletcher received Ghormley's approval of his withdrawal. He hesitated no longer. By morning all carriers were well clear of the Solomons.

Ordering all ships to assemble in column north of Savo, Admiral Mikawa headed up the Slot at 30 knots. On the way out, the Japanese again spotted the northern picket, the destroyer *Ralph Talbot*. They had let her go the first time. Not so now.

The game little ship and her aggressive captain, Lieutenant Commander Joseph W. Callahan, accepted the challenge of the multiple Goliaths. He got off a few salvos, but soon his ship was in flames and listing twenty degrees. A providential rainsquall came over and probably saved her from extinction.

Finally satisfied, the Japanese force departed.

There remained only the picking up of the pieces. From the *Australia*, Admiral Crutchley had watched the shooting, the flares, and the explosions and had been helpless to intervene. Admiral Turner, who had made up his mind to retire with his transports at first light, knew as little as his British subordinate. They could only wait for the morning and what it might bring.

When dawn came, it revealed a horrible sight in the waters of Ironbottom Sound. Great gouts of oil floated on the surface, partly hiding bits of wreckage and forms of men, some swimming, some clinging to wreckage, and some huddled in rafts, some floating lifeless, their inert forms responding only to the purposeless, ceaseless motion of the waves. In the distance could be seen the listing, burning hulks of the *Canberra* and *Astoria*.

Around and among the survivors nosed the destroyers carefully moving to pick up as many men as possible. Captain Bode in the wreck of the *Chicago* took charge of the rescue work, directing the *Patterson* to stand by the *Canberra* to assist in the fire fighting. Explosions kept the rescuer at a distance

---

* A study of the charts indicates that the *Wasp* planes would have had about 150 miles to go. If they had been launched at once, they could have caught Mikawa a few miles northeast of Savo. Or, if Fletcher had turned his entire carrier force northwest and launched a full strike up the Slot at dawn, it could have been upon the Japanese south of Santa Isabel.

for some time. The *Bagley* went alongside the *Astoria* to take off personnel and to help put down the flames.

Every so often, rescue work would have to be broken off, as destroyers were summoned to run down a fancied submarine contact. False alarms. There were no Japanese submarines within a hundred miles.

The fight to save the *Astoria* was slowly being lost. Although damage-control parties were making progress in extinguishing the flames, they could not control the flooding. The list increased to about six degrees, at which point her engineering officer, Commander Hayes, reported stability was lost, and she rolled over and sank at 1215.

The *Canberra* had already gone to her grave. Early in the morning Admiral Turner had ordered that the ship should either join him by 0630 or be sunk. Removal of the crew took longer than anticipated, but by 0700 every person still alive had been transferred to one of the destroyers. About 0800 the destroyer *Ellet* sent a torpedo into her, and the Australian cruiser took the final plunge.*

In view of the impossible situation both afloat and ashore, Admiral Turner reconsidered his intention to withdraw at dawn. Lifesaving would take many hours, and those hours could be spent in unloading more supplies for the Marines ashore. All through the morning and early afternoon, sweating men cursed and manhandled boxes, crates, containers, until they were ready to drop.

Just before 1600 the transports, cargo ships, destroyers, cruisers, mine craft—everything—pulled out for Noumea in two groups. Behind them they left four units of fire,** thirty-seven days' store of food—and the Marines.

The Marines promptly went on two meals a day.

On the morning of August 10 the American submarine *S-44* was patrolling east of New Ireland. At 0800 her skipper, Lieutenant Commander John R. "Dinty" Moore, raised the periscope for a look around. Suddenly the scope stopped its turn.

* On October 14, 1943, the U.S.S. *Canberra* was commissioned at Bethlehem Steel Shipbuilding Company, Quincy, Massachusetts, the only ship in the American Navy to be named for a foreign city.
** A unit of fire is the amount of ammunition expended in a day's combat, based on average combat conditions.

300

"Bearing—mark!"

"One-two-five," replied the assistant approach officer.

"Range—mark!"

"Nine thousand."

"Down scope!"

The periscope slid back in its well, and "Dinty" Moore announced, "Four cruisers headed right at us."

The ships were the four cruisers of Cruiser Division Six, the *Aoba*, *Kinugasa*, *Furutaka*, and *Kako*. Admiral Mikawa had sent them to Kavieng where they would be safe from Allied plane attacks, while he took the *Chokai*, the two light cruisers, and the destroyer to Rabaul with him.

The proud victors of Savo were steaming confidently along in their two groups. Mikawa arrived at Rabaul a little after 0730, and the four bound for Kavieng had only seventy miles to go.

"Dinty" Moore stalked his prey and let them come to him. Frequent, short glimpses through the periscope gave him the course and speed. The range closed. Finally, when the last ship was only seven hundred yards away, came the order:

"Fire one!"

"One's away!"

"Fire two!"

"Two's away!"

"Fire three!"

"Three's away!"

"Fire four!"

"Four's away! All torpedoes forward expended! All torpedoes running hot, straight, and normal!"

"Down scope! Take her down to a hundred and thirty feet!"

"A hundred and thirty feet, aye, aye!"

Thirty-five seconds later the torpedoes hit. The *S-44* bucked in the explosion, recovered, and made off.

The *Kako*, struck amidships, broke her keel and sank within five minutes.

The last act in the Battle of Savo was over. The first installment of revenge had been paid.

CHAPTER ELEVEN

August: The Rubber Mess

The rubber mess is growing less.
And less is more than it was before.
And more is none for anyone.
                                                Anonymous

During the summer of 1942, the politicians could tell the American people that their sons would be going into battle. The one thing they could not tell them was that they could not drive their cars. It was an election year, that season of a politician's life when unpleasant truths must be hidden or blamed on someone else.

The problem was simple. As Mr. Roosevelt said in a "Fireside Chat," ninety-two percent of the nation's rubber supply had come from Far Eastern sources, and these sources were now controlled by the Japanese. Eight percent of the normal supply was not enough to supply the military necessities, let alone provide any doormats, or any of the myriad other products in which rubber is used in a contemporary society. From rubber pants for the diaper set to cane tips for nonagenarians, conveniences and necessities disappeared. Make do with what you have, because there won't be any more.

Most importantly, this stricture applied to the tires on the family car, on the taxis, trucks, buses, motorcycles, bicycles. When they were gone, that was it, for the duration. Everyone knew this; it had been repeated in the papers, on the air, and in the magazines.

It soon became evident, however, that the American people simply would not limit their driving enough to get through the war on their present tires. In the first place, no one knew how long the war would last. America did not even begin the road back until August at Guadalcanal, and the vigorous Japanese counterattacks threatened to drive the Marines into the sea. Not until October and November would the first major offensives come off, and they would be in Africa, not Europe, against Germany, not Japan. The absolute necessity was to save the rubber on the tires of America's motor vehicles. The only way to do this was to ration driving, and the only way to ration driving was to ration gasoline.

This was where the confusion, deliberate and otherwise, entered the picture. U-boat depredations off the Atlantic coast had caused severe petroleum shortages in seventeen eastern states. Gasoline rationing had been imposed there because there was an actual shortage of all sorts of oil fuels; this rationing was not a rubber-saving expedient. It was a grim necessity.

Partial rationing of a country inevitably caused grumbling. At the boundary, wherever it might be placed, there had to be a region where a change of a few miles or a few feet spelled the difference between unlimited gasoline, as in the old days, and strict rationing. It was crazy, and people said so.

What would the people think? That was the big question. They thought the whole thing absurd in Texas and Oklahoma, in Louisiana and New Mexico, in every state where they could see oil-storage tanks brimming full, where they had the stuff running out of their ears. Now they were being told the whole country might have to submit to rationing of gasoline. There's plenty of gasoline! What's that got to do with rubber, anyway?

More heat than light was cast on the subject by such outbursts as this one by Congressman Leland M. Ford:

Here we have the spectacle of our government telling seventeen states they cannot have gasoline, giving as a specific reason the lack of transportation facilities in the way of tankers, pipe lines, and tank cars not now available. Now then, when resistance and objection is made by the seventeen states to this program, these officials say it is going to be made national.

In those districts where they have more gasoline than they know what to do with, and have no facilities to store it, cannot get priorities to build such facilities and will therefore have to resort to burning it, these people are told their gasoline consumption will have to be curtailed. The reason given to these people out there is, "It is not a gasoline shortage but a rubber shortage."

What is the whole program? Why are not our people told the plain, honest-to-God truth?

The people had been told the truth repeatedly, told it in plain, unvarnished terms by such men as Leon Henderson, Donald Nelson, and Arthur Newhall, Rubber Coordinator for WPB. But since shortages existed and, by definition, the Congressmen could not be wrong, these administrators must be. Hence began the hue and cry over "the rubber mess."

Eventually what had to be done was done, and no blood ran red in the nation's streets. No bands of armed revolutionaries descended on the gasoline refineries or on the officers who imposed rationing. The people grumbled and took it.

The critics who claimed that there was no program were simply talking through their hats. There was a program, but like everything else before Pearl Harbor, it was too little and too late. Take the oil shortages of the Eastern Seaboard first. Why spend millions of dollars to build pipelines from the Gulf States to New England when the tankers were doing the job adequately and well? No one anticipated the devastating results of the U-boat onslaught. When the tankers were lost and oil polluted the beaches at Miami, Virginia Beach, Atlantic City, Coney Island, and the rest, then—and only then—they began to think about pipelines. But now the steel needed to build pipelines was all spoken for—to build ships, tanks, trucks, rifles, guns, and what-have-you for the Army, the Navy, the Marine Corps, the Air Force, the Coast Guard, the merchant marine, the factories to make more ships, tanks, trucks, rifles, guns, and what-have-you. What came first? By mid-June, Petroleum Coordinator Harold L. Ickes (the Old Curmudgeon, as he liked to call himself) had succeeded in wresting a hundred and twenty-five thousand tons of steel from Nelson's WPB in order to build a twenty-four-inch pipeline from Longview, Texas, to Salem, Illinois, at a cost of thirty-five million dollars. There its capacity of two hundred fifty thousand barrels a day (six million, three hundred thousand gallons) could be fed into an east-west pipeline to bring fuel oil to the coast. Note; that is fuel oil, not gasoline.

What about synthetic rubber? There's the answer.

There *was* the answer. The program existed and was going ahead as fast as possible, but it, too, had got off to a late start. The reason was the same prewar mentality that had caused so much other grief.

As early as 1940 a subcommittee of the Defense Commission had made a survey of rubber and the nation's probable requirements in the event of war with Germany and in the event of war with Japan. Their report recommended that the nation immediately embark on a program for a twentyfold increase in its synthetic-rubber-producing capacity, from five thousand to a hundred thousand tons a year. This modest program would, the committee felt, give a head start until more factories could be built, if war came.

The Defense Commission accepted the report and tried to get the money to build the synthetic plants. The only place the funds would be available to them was through Mr. Jesse Jones's Reconstruction Finance Corporation. Jones, at heart a banker rather than a man of strategic vision, decided the report was far too pessimistic. He could see no point in spending money to build factories to produce something that might not be needed. He refused to approve the funds, and the factories were not built.

OPM must share some of the blame, too, for as war came closer during 1941, it made little effort to stockpile or to revive interest in synthetic rubber production. Not until after nine-tenths of the supply of natural rubber evaporated was the program put into high gear. Then it, too, had to contend with allocations, to stand in line to get the necessary materials to build the factories. Even with a crash program, the best anyone could hope for in 1942 was about two hundred thousand tons of synthetic. A stockpile existed of a little over five hundred thousand tons of natural rubber and some forty-seven thousand tons of reclaimed rubber. If this were all expended, it would come to about a tenth of the annual normal peacetime requirements.

The United States promptly made arrangements to take the entire natural rubber supplies of many Central and South American countries, but all this together would not save the situation. Until an adequate synthetic industry was built and in operation, the nation was in trouble for its war needs, and there was cold comfort for the man who needed to drive his car.

No one could tell the American people they could not drive their cars. Then, as now, the nation simply could not carry out its business without the transportation provided by the privately owned automobile. Public transport cannot carry the load, and many people live nowhere near a public transportation line. There could be no question of building more buses and streetcars to carry the people. The materials were needed for war. If a man was to do his work at the office, on the farm, in the factory, at the shipyard, at the store, he had to have his car. The problem was to restrict his use of it so his tires would last. Even the most optimistic projections of rubber supplies could give little if any cheer to the motorist.

But Mr. Roosevelt did not like to face up to the inevitable conclusion. He treated the rubber problem with insouciance. He seemed to hope it would go away. At the time he announced his plans for a nationwide rubber scrap drive, he said he thought nationwide gasoline rationing might be needed to save rubber. But he went on to say, he hoped substitutes would be found to make it unnecessary, or perhaps the scrap drive might save the day. He said he couldn't blame any man living in an area where gasoline was plentiful for wanting to drive his car as much as he liked. At the end he observed that he was completely confused by the whole rubber situation and doubted if he could write an account of it that made sense.

This was enough. The floodgates opened, and the storm descended on everyone who had anything to do with the rubber program. If Mr. Roosevelt, with his remarkable astuteness, was confused, then it followed there was mismanagement somewhere. The men in charge were responsible; the mess was their creation.

Everyone with an idea descended on Washington. Inventors brought in their favorite schemes to make rubber from anything and everything, from straw and sawdust, from grass cuttings and rhubarb, from animal fat and rayon, from alcohol and milkweed, from gin and tonic. Each panacea promised millions of tons at no cost to the war effort and happy motoring for the public. Only the stubbornness of Henderson, Nelson, Newhall, and their kind barred the Promised Land. Something had to be done.

A rebellious Congress passed and sent to the White House a bill to take rubber production away from WPB and vest it in a totally separate agency, along with authority to take whatever priorities and allocations were needed. Perhaps the WPB program had been too favorable toward butadiene based on petroleum; the Congressional committee charged that alcohol-based butadiene would increase production. This was true, Nelson confessed in the hearings, but WPB was now including that method. But the worst thing was that the bill would have

306

taken control of war production from WPB, where one authority was needed, and split it so that rubber would come ahead of ships, tanks, and guns. The result would be chaos.

These arguments did not impress the Congress, but they brought the President up short. As well as anyone else, he knew the dangers of splitting allocation authority, of the disruption of the war economy that would inevitably follow the Gillette Bill creating the rubber commission. Forced to look squarely at the problem, Roosevelt promptly vetoed the bill and appointed a commission to give him a report on the whole situation. To head this commission he selected the venerated "elder statesman" of businessmen, Bernard M. Baruch.

Baruch had become a legend in his own lifetime. As head of wartime production in the first World War, he had come to know Washington and its ways; he knew the world of finance and business inside out. He had become a Delphic oracle on all such matters and, according to legend, he transacted all business on park benches, preferably one in Lafayette Park, winter or summer, spring or fall, rain or shine, snow or blazing heat. Roosevelt, the master magician, had come up with the one man no one dared belittle. The rubber problem was as good as solved.

Baruch and his committee of distinguished men, including James B. Conant, President of Harvard, and Karl T. Compton, President of M.I.T., set to work at once, analyzing, probing, asking questions, consulting experts, and doing a great deal of hard thinking. On September 10, they issued their report.

It contained nothing any well-informed man did not know. The nation was desperately short of rubber, but by dint of expanding a bit on the existing plans for the growing synthetic rubber industry, a program of recaps from reclaimed rubber for essential driving, the wheels could be kept turning. There were two kickers to the report. First, the committee recommended the appointment of a Rubber Administrator with complete powers, although under WPB as far as allocations were concerned. This meant that the man who had really solved the rubber problem months before, Arthur Newhall, had to go, to make room for the president of the Union Pacific Railroad, William N. Jeffers. Newhall lacked the color and table-pounding drive needed to make his presence felt in

307

Washington. Jeffers had these qualities in large measure. Newhall glimpsed the Promised Land, but it was Jeffers who entered in.

The other, most widely felt, most severe blow was, as anyone could have predicted, a recommendation for nation-wide gasoline rationing. This was combined with a thirty-five-mile-per-hour speed limit throughout the country and periodic tire inspections to reveal excessive wear and possible cheating.

So proposed. So ordered. Nationwide gasoline rationing became effective December 1, 1942, and to the amazement of the cynics in Washington, the public did not rebel. Perhaps the people were ahead of their leaders. Perhaps they realized the war had to be won on the wheels of America's cars as well as on the battlefield. Rubber never became plentiful during the war, but everyone got by.

* * * * *

Ever since he had returned to London from Washington in June, Churchill had been fuming over the progress, or lack of it, in the North African desert. The fall of Tobruk had become an obsessive symbol to him. Worse, General Auchinleck refused to leap off on a premature offensive despite peremptory demands from the Prime Minister. Something was wrong, and it was up to him to stir things up. Churchill, therefore, decided to go to Cairo and get the war moving.

Also, Stalin had to be informed that there would be no second front in Europe that year. Churchill was the natural one to tell him, since he had done more than anyone else to block the second front. It would be easy to combine the trip to Moscow with the trip to Cairo, and on August the Prime Minister set out on this formidable journey. His plane flew by way of Gibraltar and then south over Spanish and French Morocco, eastward across the Sahara for hour after hour until it reached the Nile. Then it turned north until it landed safely at the Cairo airport.

All important people of the Middle East Command—except General Auchinleck—were on hand to meet the Prime Minister. So was General Brooke, the Chief of the Imperial General Staff, who had flown out a day earlier in order to stop at Malta for an inspection.

Churchill was in a mood for no nonsense. Since, it seemed

to him, nothing was being done in Egypt, it was pretty clear that heads were going to roll.

This trip to Cairo and Moscow reveals Churchill at his worst and at his best. As Sir Hastings Ismay once told Auchinleck, "Churchill could not be judged by ordinary standards. . . . He was indispensable and completely irreplaceable. The idea that he was rude, arrogant and self-seeking was entirely wrong. He was none of these things. . . . He was a child of nature. He venerated tradition, but ridiculed convention." He was impatient, he was demanding, he was a sore trial to all who had to work with him, and to a man they loved him. Once he had an idea or a prejudice firmly fixed in his mind, it was almost impossible to shake it loose. It is said he looked upon himself as the reincarnation of the Duke of Marlborough, the man he considered to be Britain's greatest soldier. He conceived his role as Minister of Defence to be that of supreme maker of strategy, which his Chiefs of Staff were to implement. Yet, at the same time, he expected them to be critical of his ideas and to implement only those they considered sound. Thus he could throw out a dozen or more schemes for annoying the Axis, trusting that Brooke, Pound, Tedder, and the rest would winnow out the wheat from the chaff. Never once during the entire war did he override the united professional judgment of his Chiefs of Staff. But he let them know they had been in a fight before he gave up a favorite plan. He wanted to know everything and the reasons for everything. And he wanted results. A large number of his memoranda were headed "Action this Day." Woe betide the officer who did not respond within hours or even minutes.

Ever since Rommel's drive had run out of steam in early July as a result of the First Battle of Alamein, Auchinleck had kept him off balance with a series of probing attacks. The result was to force on Rommel the stabilized warfare he most feared, since it gave all the advantages to the British; they had been trained for that kind of warfare, and the Afrika Korps had not. "Yesterday [wrote Rommel to his wife] was a particularly hard and critical day. We pulled through again. But it can't go on like this for long, otherwise the front will crack. Militarily, this is the most difficult period I've ever been through. There's help in sight, of course, but whether we will live to see it is a question. You know what an incurable optimist I am. But there are situations where everything is dark."

Auchinleck's contribution had been to save Egypt and to reduce his opponent to near-despair. His reward was to be relieved of his command.

When Churchill stepped off the airplane at Cairo airport, he had as good as made up his mind to replace Auchinleck. Not only did he have Brooke with him as his principal military adviser; he had summoned Wavell from India and Field Marshal Smuts from South Africa. Thus, with Tedder, RAF commander in the Mediterranean, Sir Henry Hardwood, Commander in Chief of the Mediterranean Fleet, and Sir Miles Lampson, the Ambassador to Egypt, Churchill had all the panoply of power his nature craved. Auchinleck, who had refused to compete in the game of personal pomp, flew to Cairo only when ordered that afternoon. Churchill gave him no hint that his days in command were numbered. Instead, they discussed the military situation, but it is doubtful that the reserved Auchinleck had much if any effect on his mercurial superior. Churchill pressed him to set a date for a big offensive against Rommel. "I could see [wrote Brooke] that he did not approve of his replies. He is again pressing for an attack before Auchinleck can possibly get ready. I find him almost impossible to argue with on this point." Dissatisfied, Churchill finally let Auchinleck leave after nearly three hours of argument.

Three days later, after an inspection trip to Auchinleck's Eighth Army headquarters, Churchill decided to split the Middle Eastern Command in two, a Near East Command to include Egypt and the canal zone, while Palestine, Persia, and Iraq would keep the name of Middle East Command. He intended to transfer Auchinleck to the latter area, not exactly an unimportant one, since the Russians were falling back before a determined German drive into the Caucasus, and there was at least the possibility that the Nazis would soon push into Persia and Iraq to the Middle Eastern oil and a possible link-up with Rommel east of Cairo.

Churchill offered the new Near East Command to Brooke, who turned it down with keen regret. He felt it was more important for him to continue as C.I.G.S., especially as he felt he was the only one who could exert some "limited amount of control" over Churchill. He may have been right.

Grumbling, Churchill accepted Brooke's refusal, although naturally the C.I.G.S. could not tell the Prime Minister his real reasons. Together they decided General Sir Harold Alexander was the right man for the job and sent instructions that he was to be detached from Eisenhower's staff in England, where he had been working on the forthcoming Torch operation.

For command of the Eighth Army, a job Auchinleck was still holding as well as the Middle East Command, Churchill pressed hard for Lieutenant General W. H. E. Gott, an experienced desert fighter who had commanded the Thirteenth Corps. Churchill was much impressed with him in the one interview they had together, but Brooke felt Gott was too tired, and Gott himself felt that a man with new ideas was necessary.

The problem became tragically academic when Gott was killed as his plane was shot down by a German fighter. A new commander for the Eighth Army had to be selected all over again.

This time the mantle fell on Montgomery. Lieutenant General Sir Bernard L. Montgomery had just been assigned to Eisenhower's headquarters to take the place of the departed Alexander, when he too was snatched away. Eisenhower felt, quite naturally, that the British were giving less than their best efforts to the planning for Torch.

All arrangements had been made, and there remained nothing but to inform Auchinleck that he was being relieved. Since Churchill little relished the task of telling him, he wrote the fallen general a note and dispatched an aide with it to the Auk's headquarters. The bearer, Colonel Sir Ian Jacobs, recorded later in his diary: "I felt as if I were just going to murder an unsuspecting friend. After offering the condolences of the Prime Minister and the C.I.G.S. on the death of General Gott, I handed the C.-in-C. the letter I had brought. He opened it and read it through two or three times in silence. He did not move a muscle and remained outwardly calm and in complete control of himself."

Auchinleck refused the offer of the Persian-Iraq Command, preferring retirement. He so informed Churchill in an interview the next day that the Prime Minister described as "bleak and impeccable."

Soon, two new brooms swept in from London, Alexander and Montgomery. Each had very distinct ideas of what needed to be done. Their arrival and their subsequent measures brought a surge in the spirits of the Desert Rats. But, without depreciating their contributions to the African war, it must be stated that they built on the foundations Auchinleck had laid and implemented his strategy.

By this time Churchill had little time or energy to spare, for the next stage of his journey lay before him. He had to go to Russia and explain to Stalin why there would be no second front in 1942. It was not a journey to his liking.

The Prime Minister's party filled three Liberator bombers when it left Cairo shortly after midnight in the early hours of August 11. After a stop at Teheran for fuel, Churchill's plane arrived in Moscow late in the afternoon of August 12. Here a Soviet deputation and an honor guard conducted him to a state villa, where the Prime Minister had time to freshen up before a meeting with Stalin at seven o'clock that evening.

"The first two hours were bleak and somber," wrote Churchill. He reminded Stalin that no promise had been given for a return to the Continent in 1942 and produced the *aide-mémoire* to prove it. As the interview progressed, Stalin became more and more frigid, exclaiming impatiently after a time that he understood the British were unwilling to take any risks, and that the Russian view was different. Troops were no good unless they were blooded, and the only way to get them blooded was to put them in combat. At length he concluded by saying that if the British were not going to launch a second front in 1942, he could not force them to do so, but he did not agree with their arguments.

Then Churchill mentioned the proposal for Torch, the landing in North Africa. He drew a picture of a crocodile and introduced the concept of the "soft underbelly" of Europe. At this, Stalin's imagination caught fire. He became intensely interested, saying, "May God prosper this undertaking."

After Stalin had shown his grasp of the strategy by summing up its advantages, the meeting ended on a harmonious note, and Churchill returned to his villa.

The next night, at eleven o'clock Churchill went again to the Kremlin for another interview with Stalin. This time he was accompanied by Brooke, whose plane had been delayed by engine trouble, and by W. Averell Harriman, the American roving Ambassador, as a representative of President Roosevelt. To the surprise of the British, the second-front argument started all over again. It was as though the previous discusson of Torch had never taken place. "When are you going to start

312

fighting?" asked Stalin. "Are you going to let us do all the work while you look on? Are you never going to start fighting? You will find it is not too bad if you once start!" He then raged on to accuse the British and Americans of bad faith in not delivering more goods via the North Russian route.

At these remarks, Churchill lost his temper and crashed his fist down on the table and told Stalin at length his ideas of what fighting was. As he waxed more eloquent, Stalin stopped him and with a broad grin said, "I do not understand what you are saying, but by God, I like your sentiment!"

The next day, August 14, was given over to rest and to a state dinner, so there was no progress made in the discussions. On the fifteenth, Churchill had a late meeting with Stalin, since he was scheduled to take off at dawn the following day. This farewell interview started out in a formal fashion, but Stalin suddenly asked the Prime Minister to come to his house for a drink. One drink led to another, and then to dinner; it was very late before Churchill was able to get away. The British party, meanwhile, was waiting at the state villa, having no dinner lest their impetuous leader break in on them before they had finished. They propped their feet up on chairs and waited, wondering what could be the result of a meeting between the unpredictable Churchill and the inscrutable Stalin.

Things had gone well, as Stalin worked himself into a hospitable mood over the liquor and a roast suckling pig, whose head he offered Churchill. When Churchill refused with a slight shudder, the Russian leader tackled it with relish. They ironed out the details of the communiqué while Stalin devoured his pig. The informal meeting seemd to do more than anything else to bring whatever understanding was possible between the two leaders.

It was not until three-thirty in the morning that the Prime Minister arrived back at the state villa for a few minutes of rest before leaving for the airfield. The planes left at five-thirty for the long flight back to Cairo.

While Churchill had been in Moscow, another Malta convoy had fought its way through. Five out of fourteen merchant ships made it, although the survivors were sunk in Malta, but not before most of their precious cargoes had been unloaded. These deliveries relieved the near-famine conditions on the island, and so strengthened the military threat that Malta became a dagger poised over Rommel's back.

On his return to Cairo, therefore, Churchill found considerable satisfaction in the way things were going. Malta was no longer imperiled, and the colorful Montgomery, who had taken over the Eighth Army, appealed to the Prime Minister's sense of dash and élan. He visited Monty in his headquarters at Burg el Arab near the sea and had a swim in the blue waters of the Mediterranean. While he was walking to the beach, Churchill saw about a thousand British troops splashing about in the water and running up and down the beaches. Each seemed clad in a pair of white swimming trunks. "Why do the War Office go to the expense of sending out white bathing drawers for the troops?" asked Churchill petulantly. "Surely this economy should be made." Of course the economy had been made; the Prime Minister was not looking upon bathing trunks.

Churchill was so taken by Monty's enthusiasm and self-confidence that he wished to stay in Egypt to observe the attack Rommel was expected to make before the end of August. But he was needed at home, so when the battle began on August 31, Churchill knew about it only from the dispatches he read in his office at 10 Downing Street.

While Churchill was on his travels, there took place an event that proved how right the British had been in insisting on no landing in Europe in 1942. This was Operation Jubilee, a large scale Combined Operations raid on the port of Dieppe. Originally scheduled for early June, the operation had been abandoned when two of the transports assigned were hit by enemy aircraft. The troops were off-loaded and the plan was suspended indefinitely. Indeed, Admiral Mountbatten, head of Combined Operations, who had originally conceived the idea, considered the whole operation canceled and turned his attention to other things.

For a variety of reasons, in spite of the possible compromise of security, the plan was revived and set for August 19. In England, as in America, cries of "Second Front Now!" were heard at gatherings in Trafalgar Square and at Hyde Park Corner. The motto appeared painted on walls, and liberal columnists and radio commentators added their voices to the chorus. None of those crying this insistent slogan had any idea of the enormous amount of preparation such a venture would require, nor of the vast number of men, vehicles, ships, landing craft, aircraft, tons of ammunition, tankloads of oil and gasoline needed even to begin it. Also none of the strident critics would be among those who would have to go up on the landing beaches swept by deadly swaths of machine-gun fire. Most of these reasons could not be made public, and the asinine chorus went on.

It was partly to still these cries and partly to test the Allied ability to land and capture a major port in the face of determined enemy defense that Operation Jubilee was reinstated. New devices and new techniques were to be tried out, and combat troops would gain useful lessons in going ashore under enemy fire. If they lived to learn them.

Because a crucial part of the test was to see whether a port could be taken and made usable for resupply of forces ashore, the planners decided to employ neither an airstrike on the city of Dieppe nor heavy bombardment from naval ships in support of the landings. Also, the Army insisted on a surprise landing. Ignoring the lessons of Gallipoli in 1915—that troops simply could not disembark from small boats in the face of heavy enemy gunfire—the planners insisted on heading directly for the town of Dieppe, making that the main thrust. The original plan had called for landings east and west, followed by pincers operations against the town itself. This was abandoned to the magic phrase "frontal assault," and although the flanking operations remained part of the plan, they were distinctly secondary.

The idea that surprise could be decisive was a favorite in Army planning, both in London and in Washington. None of the officers concerned seemed to have any idea of the destructive capability of powerful shore bombardments accompanied by air strikes from naval and air force planes. Discounting what they did not know firsthand, they insisted on surprise, which might or might not be attained. It scarcely ever was.

Because of the Army's reluctance to use heavy guns, the Navy assigned no ship larger than a destroyer to the operation. And these eight destroyers were all Hunt class, nearly the smallest on the Navy List. All were armed with 4-inch guns. Intelligence sources revealed that the defenders had 5.9-inch guns protecting the town.

The troops assigned to the mission were mostly Canadian. A large number of these had been in England for nearly a year, doing nothing, and their commander, General McNaughton, insisted that some of them be used. As a result, nearly five thousand Canadians formed the assault troops. A thousand Commandos were to land on the flanks to knock out the heavy guns, and a small number of American Rangers were assigned to accompany the Commandos for observation and training.

The Royal Air Force gave heavy air support to the operation, largely to keep the German Luftwaffe away. Thus most of the aircraft assigned were fighters, not bombers.

The raiding force sailed from Portsmouth, Newhaven, and Shoreham on the night of August 18, and by three the next morning was off Dieppe. Troops were transferred to landing and assault craft, and the Commando units headed for their assigned targets, four or five miles on either side of Dieppe. The western assaults went off smoothly, and the gun emplacements were knocked out with little loss of life.

This success was the only thing that went right about the whole operation.

The eastern group of Commandos blundered into a small German coastal convoy. The sharp action that ensued completely destroyed the surprise on which all else rested, and the raiding force bound for the eastern gun battery was dispersed. Only a handful won their way ashore, and although they tried gallantly, they were unable to silence the battery.

Meanwhile, the main assault against Dieppe itself was sent in. A murderous fire opened up, and men began to drop even before they set foot on the beach. Tanks, which were supposed to clear the way, ran into roadblocks and could do nothing to help the men who were helplessly pinned down. Some soldiers huddled at the foot of a seawall, unable to go either forward or backward. Ships attempted to assist with their guns, but their 1-inch, 2-inch, and 4-inch projectiles were not of much use. The presence of a battleship, wrote the Naval Force commander, "would probably have turned the tide in our favour."

Unable to obtain a clear picture of what was going on, the Army commander sent in his reserves, but they could do little other than add their corpses to those of their already fallen comrades.

At length the recall signal came, and the men began to try to make their way back to their boats. An eyewitness described the scene as another Dunkirk. Tanks and equipment had to be abandoned, and struggling men threatened to swamp the rescue boats. By 1220 the officer in charge of the evacuation reported that the beach was clear, and the force began to withdraw. The flagship, the destroyer *Calpe*, made a sweep toward the beach, coming under heavy fire, but finding no one who might be brought off. She, too, set the course for home. During the evacuation, the RAF performed prodigies of valor, driving off German fighters and bombers so successfully that only one destroyer was lost of the major ships present. The pilots, however, could not retrieve the situation.

All reputable accounts term Operation Jubilee a disaster. Over two-thirds of the Canadian troops were lost, and nearly a quarter of the Commandos. About twenty-two hundred of these soldiers were taken prisoner. Naval casualties were a destroyer, thirty-three landing craft, and about five hundred and fifty men. The RAF lost a hundred and ninety men, mostly from single-man fighters. A hundred and six aircraft were lost in all. In contrast, the German losses from all causes were about six hundred men and forty-eight aircraft.

In view of these grim figures, it caused General Eisenhower considerable embarrassment when an American newspaper headlined the story of the raid: "Americans Land in France." Only about forty Americans were involved. The story did nothing to improve Anglo-American relations. Fortunately, Eisenhower was able to reach an understanding with the British officials who mattered. Unscrupulous journalism is not unknown in Britain either.

American journalists had plenty else to write about. On Guadalcanal, things were going from bad to worse. At home, papers were still recalling the story of the capture and execution of the U-boat spies and the action of the United States Government in bringing a charge of treason against Mr. and Mrs. Hans Haupt and several others who had aided the eight men. Mr. and Mrs. Haupt were the parents of the youngest of the would-be saboteurs, and it was to them he had turned when he made his way into the United States.

It was a time of reaping the crop of quiet investigation of subversion. Hundreds of thousands of inquiries had been made, and thousands of persons were arrested. A few trials, such as that of Max Stephan of Detroit, made the news. It was the first trial for overt acts of treason of the war. Given a remarkably fair day in court, Stephan was convicted and sentenced to death.

A fire broke out in the Big Top of the Ringling Brothers,

Barnum and Bailey Circus during a performance at Cleveland, Ohio. It was the worst circus disaster of modern times, with several people killed and hundreds injured in the panic that followed. Several valuable circus animals had to be destroyed, and for days afterwards, police were bothered with reports—mostly imaginary—of lions in the living room, tigers on the terrace, or monkeys on the mantelpiece.

The insatiable armed forces drew ever deeper on the men and women of America. From village and farm, from city and town, from school and factory they came to put on khaki or white star to show husband or son in the service. Here and there the star was gold, for one who had given his life for his country. There would be more gold stars—many more.

In addition to Johnny the gas-station helper and Mr. Chance the insurance man, the famous went to war. President Roosevelt's four sons were all in the service. Major James Roosevelt, U.S. Marine Corps Reserve, had served at Midway. Lieutenant Colonel Elliott Roosevelt of the Army Air Forces was nearly shot down by a German plane when he was performing liaison duties with the RAF in Africa. Ensign John Roosevelt, a Supply Corps officer, worked in the Naval Supply depot at Oakland, California. His brother, Franklin, Jr., also in the Navy, was a Lieutenant (j.g.) on a destroyer performing convoy escort duties in the North Atlantic.

Clark Gable turned his back on his Hollywood career to enlist in the Army as a private. Maurice Evans, the famous Shakespearean actor, and a naturalized citizen, was a Captain in the Army. Richard Barthelmess was a Lieutenant in the Navy. Jackie Cooper, former child actor of the "Our Gang" comedies, served as a Staff Sergeant in the Air Force, and Crooner Rudy Vallee was a Chief Petty Officer in the Navy. Most of these big names in show business ended up in the Special Services, whose job it was to entertain the troops. Bob Hope, who never joined the service, did most for troop morale all over the world. His running gag was that he was classified 4-Y (for yellow)—coward. With Francis Langford, his show later performed in North Africa, in Europe, and in the Pacific.

Tiger first baseman Hank Greenberg, who had been drafted before Pearl Harbor and had risen to Sergeant, was in August promoted to Second Lieutenant. Many other professional ballplayers were in Commander Gene Tunney's physical conditioning program in the Navy.

While their men went to war, the people at home began to feel new restrictions. Coffee was cut back to sixty-five percent of last year's supply. Soon it would be rationed. The OPA followed this by announcing two meatless days a week. Every Tuesday and Friday the public was urged to abstain from meat on the tables. Restaurants featured only fish and cheese dishes on those days. This was just the beginning. OPA announced that nationwide meat rationing at the rate of two and a half pounds a week would begin the first of the year. Overall consumption of meat was going up, largely because the services fed their men more meat than they had been getting in private life. The average recruit gained nearly ten pounds his first few months in the service, but it was not fat. Hard exercise and generous rations hardened him up.

He had need of all the training and conditioning he could get. Hard campaigning lay ahead. Although actual fighting was months in the future for most of them, their brothers and friends at Guadalcanal were learning about the Japanese the hard way.

CHAPTER TWELVE

Guadalcanal Again

"Attienti ben, chè per cotali scale"
disse 'l maestro, ansando com' uom lasso,
"conviensi dipartir da tanto male."

"Hold on, for by such stairs,"
said the master, panting like a worn-out man,
"must we leave so much evil."

Dante, Inferno

Dawn on August 9 revealed the sparkling waters of Savo Sound stained with great blobs of iridescent fuel oil. Small black shapes littered the area—men, living and dead, who the night before had confidently manned their battle stations. Burning ships marred the lovely horizon. The softly lapping

319

waters at Lunga Point contrasted cruelly with the scenes of death and devastation offshore.

Over a thousand living men were in the water, clinging to wreckage, to orange crates, to life jackets, to anything that promised a few moments of support. Many were bleeding from fearful wounds. A man let go of a spar and floated face down in the water, his body undulating with the motion of the sea. Then another. Then more, by dozens and scores. Sharks appeared, attracted by the scent of blood. Screaming men were suddenly jerked beneath the surface, disappearing with awful finality.

Boats from the surviving ships, from the Marine foothold ashore set out on rescue missions. They shot the sharks and saved the men—over seven hundred of them. The ships that were still seaworthy removed survivors from the ships that had lasted the night but could live no longer. Two cruisers, the *Quincy* and *Vincennes,* had gone down during the darkness. The fight to save the *Canberra* and *Astoria* was futile. The Australian succumbed first, being put out of her misery by an American torpedo at about 0800. The *Astoria* suffered longer, finally going down about 1215, after all efforts to put out her fires had failed.

As Admiral Turner put together the picture of what had happened that night of horror, he realized that he could not keep his defenseless transports and supply ships off Guadalcanal much longer. He had no Navy left to defend them. About noon the ships began hoisting in their boats, and late in the afternoon they pulled out, accompanied by the few surviving combatant ships.

The Marines were holding the bag.*

General Vandegrift wasted no time in recriminations at the Navy's apparently callous desertion of the First Marine Division. Instead he set to work on his three gravest problems: supply, defending himself against enemy counterattacks, and completing the airfield.

* After the Marines were relieved on Guadalcanal, they had a mock medal struck in Melbourne. On the obverse was an arm with admiral's stripes dropping a hot potato into the hands of a Marine on a tropical island, with the motto FACIAT GEORGIUS [Let George do it]. On the reverse was the rear end of a cow near an electric fan and the motto: "In fond remembrance of the happy days spent from August 7th 1942 to January 1943. USMC."

Because of air attacks, the Battle of Savo, and the hurried retreat of the Navy, supply deficiencies were everywhere. The Marines had no heavy artillery to speak of. A few 75-mm. "half-tracks" and a handful of 37-mm. field pieces had been landed. In addition, the Japanese had left behind one 3-inch gun and a supply of ammunition for it. There was no radar, except Japanese, no construction equipment, and only half the supply of ammunition required for the division's small arms.

To protect his position, Vandegrift set up a perimeter defense around the airfield to guard against both counterattack and enemy infiltrations. The rest of his men were kept in reserve or set to work with the First Marine Engineer Battalion finishing and improving the airfield, now named Henderson Field in honor of a Marine dive-bomber pilot killed in the Battle of Midway. They had little to work with except handcarts, a few Japanese trucks, shovels, and their hands. Daily tropical rainstorms turned the field into a morass of sticky mud. The kunai grass, growing as tall as a man, could slash to the bone with its saw-toothed edges. It was too green to burn and had to be chopped down with bayonets or knives. In spite of all these difficulties, the first plane—an amphibian, appropriately enough—landed there on August 12, and five days later, Vandegrift reported to Ghormley that the field was ready to operate. On August 20, U.S.S. *Long Island*, an escort carrier converted from the freighter *Mormacmail*, approached San Cristobal and flew off nineteen F4F Wildcat fighters and a dozen SBD Dauntless dive bombers. In a little over an hour the planes began to land on Henderson Field.

"*Now* let the bastards come!" yelled one of the marines.

That night they came.

The American landings on Guadalcanal and Tulagi had caught the Japanese Imperial Headquarters by surprise. It was decidedly inconvenient for them, for they had recently committed themselves to a strategy of taking Port Moresby by marching overland across the tail of New Guinea. Completely underestimating the American strength on Guadacanal, perhaps because they wanted to, the Japanese High Command concluded that there were only two thousand Americans on the island. In actuality there were seventeen thousand. Lieutenant General Harukichi Hyakutake received the job of driving the Americans off Guadalcanal with the forces he had at hand,* while the main drive against Port Moresby would continue undiminished. As a result of this miscalculation and his own overconfidence, Hyakutake assigned only a thousand men to the task, under the command of Colonel Kiyono Ichiki. Landing eastward of the American position, he intended to work around to the west and roll up the American flank and rear. A small detachment of the Special Naval Landing Force was landed at Tassafaronga, to the west of the American position on Lunga Point.

Around midnight on August 18, Marine sentries heard the wash of vessels passing close inshore and the pound of motors, and rightly concluded that something was up. They were hearing Ichiki's men on their way to their landing at Taivu Point, some twenty-odd miles east of the American beachhead. Thus alerted, the Marines expected trouble and got ready to meet it.

The next day a Marine patrol ambushed a Japanese one sent out by Ichiki and killed thirty-one of the thirty-four men in it. The pockets of the dead were filled with valuable intelligence materials, charts, diaries, codes, letters, and maps showing the Marine positions south of Henderson Field.

The Marines strengthened their eastern flank with wire and trenches, put out listening posts, and sited a 37-mm. gun. Then they waited, prepared to give Ichiki a warm reception. In front of them was the Tenaru River,** which the Japanese would have to ford to make their assault.

At 0240 the Japanese attacked. Charging along a sandspit, screaming and yelling, bayonets gleaming in the flares set off by the defenders, some two hundred raced to their deaths. Officers and men fell, but that did not stop the survivors. On they came, some even into the Marines' positions, where they were met with knives, bayonets, pistol fire, machetes. Before dawn every Japanese who had made the assault was dead. Ichiki had thrown away the lives of his élite troops to no purpose.

As the battle died down, a gravely wounded native crawled into the Marine lines. This was Sergeant Major Vouza, a

* These forces had been originally designated as garrison troops for Midway. The Battle of Midway left them without a job.

** The Battle of the Tenaru River was actually fought across the Ilu River, but the confusion of names in the original reporting has caused the name to stick, and it has been officially changed to Tenaru. It is reminiscent of Bunker Hill and Breeds Hill.

retired member of the British island constabulary. With the arrival of the Japanese, he had volunteered to serve as a scout once more and was to prove his worth again and again. Before he collapsed, he revealed the position of Ichiki's camp to the east. No one who saw him expected Vouza to live, so severely had he been tortured by the Japanese, who had caught him in possession of a tiny American flag. Here is Vouza's own account of his experience:

Well, I was caughted by the Japs and one of the Japanese Naval Officer questioned me but I was refuse to answer & I was bayoneted by a long sword twice on my chest, through my throught, a cutted the side of my tongue & I was got up from the enemies & walked through the American front line & there [I found] my Officer Mr. Clemens . . . Both got the reports information by one of the Colonial of the American Marine Div. his name was Col. Buckley that I was wounded. So then boths Major Clemens & Staff Sgt. Daniel Pule they came up to the front line & took me to the American Hospital at Lunga Gaudalcanal & there they done the treatment and the wounded was healthed up, only 12 days I was in Hospital.

Vouza's information enabled Vandegrift to send out the First Battalion, First Marines,* under Lieutenant Colonel Lenard B. Cresswell to attack Ichiki's position from the south. The sweep was completely successful. Ichiki's entire force, except for a few stragglers, was wiped out, losing about nine hundred men in its own attack and in Cresswell's counterthrust. Thirty-four Marines were killed, and seventy-five wounded. Ichiki, by some fluke escaping the slaughter, retired into the jungle, reverently tore up his regimental colors, burned the scraps, and committed hara-kiri.

Score one for the Marines.

When the news of Ichiki's defeat reached Japanese headquarters at Rabaul, planners immediately decided on another scheme to throw the Americans off Guadalcanal. Still pushing the New Guinea drive for all it was worth, and more, they decided that fifteen hundred troops would be enough to drive

* The designation "First Marines" means First Regiment of the First Division, *not* the First Division as a whole.

the bothersome Marines from their toehold at Lunga Point. This relatively puny force was to be supported by all the naval strength the Japanese Combined Fleet could gather for the effort, including two big carriers and a light carrier. Meanwhile, nightly bombardments by naval ships and daily bombings by aircraft would wear the Marines down and keep them off balance for the forthcoming encounter.

The Marines were learning how miserable a place Guadalcanal can be. Nearly everyone was afflicted with dysentery. Huge mosquitoes bit painfully, and the Marines scratched and swore. Soon men were coming down with a particularly virulent form of malaria. Drenching rains turned foxholes into mud baths. Even an earthquake came along one night to rob the men of sleep. If these natural difficulties were not enough, the men had to work or fight off infiltrators until they were too dog-tired to care what they were doing or where they were. Almost nightly they endured bombardment from Japanese naval ships and by day bombing from high flying Japanese planes. The pilots from Henderson Field did their best, but there was never enough in the way of planes, or spare parts. Still, American air strength, such as it was, managed to keep the Japanese naval forces out of the area during the day. At night all that changed. The waters of Savo Sound, now being called Ironbottom Sound, belonged to the Americans by day and the Japanese by night, when the "Toyko Express" ran.

To add to the misery, the Japanese developed the practice of sending a lone plane down each night to fly over the island, keeping the Americans from the sleep they so desperately needed. There were two of these planes, which seemed to come on alternate nights. One, whose engines were out of phase, was called "Washing Machine Charlie"; the other was "Louie the Louse." Sometimes Charlie and Louie were merely snoopers; sometimes they dropped random bombs; sometimes they dropped flares, which might or might not signal the start of a bombardment from Ironbottom Sound.

Such was life on Guadalcanal. Work, patrol, take cover, repair damage, try to protect the perimeter, sleep when you can, curse the weather, the mosquitoes, the "trots," the chow, the Japanese—above all, the Japanese.

Some of the Marines added the Navy to their curse list. While they endured the miseries of the 'Canal, the Navy, so they fancied, was swinging around the hook at Noumea enjoying good food, showers, movies, and—most envied—peaceful sleep.

The Navy's turn was coming, and soon.

American naval intelligence, assisted by Australian coast-watchers and reconnaissance aircraft, picked up Japanese naval movements and reported a powerful force moving down from Truk in five groups. Spearheading the advance were the Coral Sea veterans *Shokaku* and *Zuikaku*. Another group contained two battleships and three heavy cruisers. A third group had the light carrier *Ryujo* as bait to attempt to draw any attack by American carriers. There was a transport group, and a support group was nearby to lend a hand to anyone in trouble.

To oppose this formidable Japanese fleet, Ghormley had three carriers, the *Enterprise, Saratoga,* and *Wasp* (newly arrived after her deliveries of Spitfires to Malta a few weeks earlier). A fourth carrier, the *Hornet,* was on her way out, but would not arrive in time for the forthcoming battle.

As usual for him, Fletcher, commanding the United States carriers, weakened his force on the eve of battle by sending the *Wasp* and her escorts to the south to refuel. Thus, just as in the Coral Sea, Fletcher faced the *Shokaka* and *Zuikaku* with only two carriers. Also, just as at the Coral Sea, the first strong American attack fell on the Japanese "bait" carrier, *Ryujo*. Under heavy bombing she did not last long and went down that evening, August 24.

Meanwhile the two Japanese carriers were launching an all-out attack on the Americans. As their planes raced toward Fletcher's position, everyone knew what was coming. More prudent than he had been either at the Coral Sea or at Midway, Fletcher had retained some fifty-three fighters as a combat air patrol. Fighter-director officers attempted to vector these aircraft to meet the oncoming Japanese as they were detected by radar, but the lone communications channel was so cluttered with unnecessary chitchat from the pilots that they could not get through. There was nothing to do but wait.

Suddenly at 1641 silvery shapes could be seen in the air. The Japanese planes had arrived. Antiaircraft fire filled the skies. No ship contributed more than the new battleship *North Carolina,* recently arrived in the area. Stationed 2500 yards astern of the *Enterprise* as she was, she was able to keep the Japanese pilots busy for a time. But, in the heat of the battle, the *Enterprise* poured on 30 knots, and as the *North Carolina*

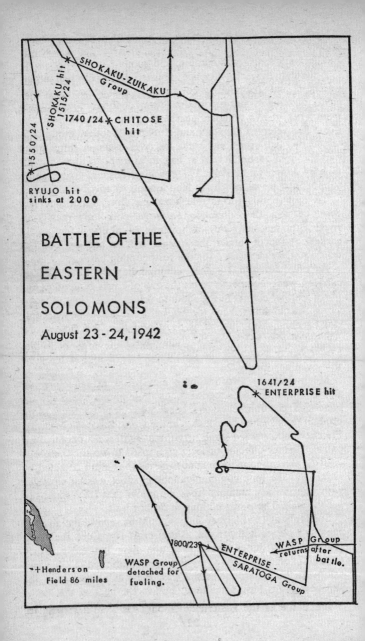

SHOKAKU-ZUIKAKU Group

SHOKAKU hit 1515/24

1550/24

1740/24 ✳ CHITOSE hit

RYUJO hit sinks at 2000

BATTLE OF THE

EASTERN

SOLOMONS

August 23 - 24, 1942

1641/24 ✳ ENTERPRISE hit

WASP Group returns after battle.

1800/23

WASP Group detached for fueling.

ENTERPRISE - SARATOGA Group

← +Henderson Field 86 miles

could do no more than 27, the distance between the ships inevitably opened. The *Enterprise* received the first bomb hit she had ever known. The bomb crashed through the after elevator, penetrated the hangar deck, and exploded inside the ship. Thirty seconds later a second bomb struck in almost the same spot. A few moments later, she took a third near the island, but this caused only minor damage.

From the other ships and to the eyes of the jubilant Japanese pilots, it looked as though the *Enterprise* was in bad trouble. Flames rose into the air, and dirty smoke rose higher. Damage-control parties worked putting out fires, shoring bulkheads, and patching the holes in the deck. Within an hour, the *Enterprise* seemed as good as ever as she turned into the wind to recover aircraft.

But just as with the *Lexington* at the Coral Sea, trouble was brewing below decks. Water from the fire fighters shorted out a steering motor, and smoke overcame the watch before they could shift to standby. The big carrier began to circle, out of control, and only nimble ship-handling by skippers of her escorts averted collisions. Finally, half an hour later, Chief Machinist William A. Smith managed to cut in the auxiliary motor and the *Enterprise*'s troubles were over for that day.

The *Saratoga*'s aircraft, meanwhile, had attacked the seaplane carrier *Chitose,* which was heavily damaged but survived to make trouble later.

This action ended the Battle of the Eastern Solomons. Fletcher, wisely concluding that he would be heavily outgunned at night, when his carriers could operate no aircraft, decided to move to the south out of reach of the enemy. Admiral Kondo pursued the American forces until midnight and then turned back so as to have his ships out of range of American air by first light.

The main battle was over, but Rear Admiral Raizo Tanaka, in command of the Transport Force, was not willing to call it quits. He pressed on to land his troups on Guadalcanal, coming under heavy air attack from planes based on Henderson Field. In spite of the loss of a transport and a destroyer, and a severe hit on his own flagship, Tanaka was pressing on until recalled by orders from Rabaul. The troops he was shepherding were to come down in succeeding nights by means of the Tokyo Express.

The Battle of the Eastern Solomons was a strange one, in

327

that a powerful Japanese fleet, far stronger than that of the Americans, had been able to accomplish none of its objectives. Caution induced by Midway had evidently guided the Japanese commanders. At the cost of damage to the *Enterprise*, the United States naval forces had turned back the Japanese while sinking a light carrier, a destroyer, and a transport, and damaging several other ships.

Rack one up for the U.S. Navy.

The next six weeks in the Guadalcanal area was a period of few headlines, but of much misery. Death stalked the unwary in the jungles and at sea. Each side was getting ready to fight again, but watching warily the actions of the other, probing, stalking, seeking to wear the enemy down.

The Tokyo Express ran almost nightly, and a few troops at a time came ashore, four hundred this time, five hundred the next. Although General Hyakutake still considered the New Guinea campaign the primary show, he kept on the buildup on Guadalcanal. Inexorably the numbers of Japanese rose, while the Marines tried to hold on, receiving few reinforcements and little in the way of supplies.

As August entered its last day, more grief came to the U.S. Navy, for the Japanese submarine *I-26* slipped a torpedo into the starboard side of the *Saratoga*. Although the ship was in no danger of sinking after prompt damage control, she had to leave the area, and it was three months before she was ready again. Before she left, she flew off her aircraft to reinforce Henderson Field. The "bell-bottom aviators" exchanged clean staterooms and wardroom meals for tents and Spam on the 'Canal, but they did yeoman service with the Marine pilots against the Japanese in the coming weeks and months.

September brought small comfort to the Marines on Guadalcanal, nor to ComSoPac, Admiral Ghormley in Noumea, nor to General MacArthur watching the advance of the Japanese toward Port Moresby. There was so much to be done and so little to do it with. Nightly the Tokyo Express brought more troops to threaten the small area near Lunga Point held by the United States forces. Nightly, Washing Machine Charlie or Louie the Louse kept the Marines awake, so they were in poor shape to defend themselves, repair the airfield, and keep the planes in the air. Sometimes Louie would drop a flare, which signaled a naval bombardment of the airfield. Sometimes he dropped the flare when no bombardment ensued.

In Washington, in Noumea, and in MacArthur's headquarters in Australia, pessimism over the Guadalcanal operation ruled the day. In fact, some officers were readying press releases to prepare the public for the abandonment of the American position in the Solomons.

At a meeting in Noumea on September 4, most of the area high command argued the situation out. MacArthur, fearing the success of the Japanese drive along the coast of New Guinea, claimed all the reinforcement troops in the area should be sent to beef up his command. Not so, argued Nimitz, Turner and Ghormley; they knew that if Guadalcanal were not reinforced, the Japanese could recapture it any time they were prepared to make a major effort. The Under Secretary of the Navy, Mr. James Forrestal, learned enough from his inspection trip to Noumea to convince him that Guadalcanal must be held. He hurried back to Washington to do all he could to help Ghormley and Vandegrift.

There were three vital needs at Guadalcanal: more troops, more supplies, more aircraft. The Joint Chiefs of Staff, except for Admiral King, were reluctant to send as much as a kiddie car to the South Pacific; they were far too much concerned with the buildup for Operation Torch, the invasion of North Africa, scheduled for November.

Under Ghormley, Admiral Turner was doing his best to send supplies up the 'Canal. It was a chancy business, and many and grievous were the losses. Toward the middle of the month, the Seventh Marine Regiment embarked from Espiritu Santo to lend a hand at Guadalcanal. This precious convoy of six troopships had to be protected at all costs, so the carriers *Hornet* and *Wasp,* the battleship *North Carolina,* seven cruisers, and eleven destroyers were assigned as a support force to supplement the local escort. Under a beautiful blue sky they sailed that fifteenth day of September, the carriers well ahead of the troopers. About 1445, as the *Wasp* was returning to base course after launching aircraft, two torpedoes from the *I-19* slammed into her. Seven minutes later, *I-15* put a torpedo into the *North Carolina.* Another fish from the same submarine blew the bow off the destroyer *O'Brien.* The bat-

329

tleship and the destroyer survived to reach port, but the carrier did not.* The flames spread out of control, and after the survivors had been removed, the *Wasp* was finished off by five torpedoes from an American destroyer.

In spite of the costly brush with the Japanese submarines, Turner pressed on with the transports, and the Seventh Marine Regiment reached Lunga Roads safely at dawn on September 18. While the troops were unloading, their escorting destroyers practiced marksmanship on enemy emplacements along the coast. The Marines enjoyed the spectacle hugely; the same cannot be said for the Japanese.

The newcomers to the 'Canal looked in dismay at their new home. There was nothing about it they liked. And, they moaned, they were too late. They had missed the big fight.

While they were in their transports, still swinging around the hook at Espiritu Santo, their mates on Guadalcanal had fought the biggest action of the campaign and had thrashed the Japanese so soundly that it would be a month before they could try again.

One of the runs of the Tokyo Express down the Slot had brought Major General Kiyotake Kawaguchi to take command of Japanese forces. He had promised Hyakutake that by the first of October the Americans on Guadalcanal would be eliminated and his superior could move his headquarters to Henderson Field. But it was not to be.

Almost as soon as he reached Guadalcanal, Kawaguchi's troubles began. With about thirty-five hundred men he established a position at Tasimboko, about twenty air-lines miles east of Lunga Point. A small Japanese detachment to the west of Lunga Point was under the command of Colonel Akinosuka Oka. Thus, the two Japanese forces were separated by about thirty miles as the crow flies, but more like sixty as the soldier had to walk in the jungle. Before either Kawaguchi or Oka could move, men had to hack trails through the worst

---

* The *North Carolina* was detached that night to proceed to Tongatabu under escort of two destroyers. She was later repaired at Pearl Harbor and returned to the Solomons in time for the battles of November. The *O'Brien* was not so well fated. Patched up in Espiritu Santo and Noumea, she set out for the West Coast of the United States, but she literally shook herself apart on the passage and foundered off Samoa on October 19. Happily another ship was nearby and rescued her crew.

of the jungle to reach the clearer spaces inland. And it was while they were so engaged that the first disaster hit the Japanese.

Vandegrift, aware of the activity on each of his flanks, had decided to do something to stir the enemy up. To Colonel Merritt Edson, USMC, he assigned a small force made up of two under-strength battalions brought over from Tulagi. Embarked in two destroyer-transports and two yard-patrol craft, the troops made a good passage to Tasimboko and landed at dawn on September 8. At this point the goddess of fortune intervened on the side of the Americans, for two transports were passing by, attending to their own affairs, but Kawaguchi decided that they were bringing still more troops and radioed Tokyo that a major landing was under way. Then, leaving his breakfast on the table and most of his supplies, he fled precipitately into the jungle with all his troops.

The delighted Marines surveyed the bonanza—food, medical supplies, ammunition, beer, and *sake,* but there was no time to pick it up and take it with them. So they set about destroying it, first putting in their pockets a few samples for their private use. A goodly quantity of Japanese beer and *sake* reached appreciative consumers in this manner.

A look at the documents discovered in this raid revealed that the Japanese force at Tasimboko was far larger than Vandegrift had thought. It was obvious that a major attack was coming. The question was: where and when?

The Marine perimeter around Henderson Field was his main defense line, but it would be folly to put all his troops evenly around it. He had to beef up likely points, and he had to maintain a reserve. After a study of the map, Colonel Edson spotted a ridge about a mile southeast of Henderson Field. From this ridge troops could command the airfield and the approaches to it. Vandegrift decided to make "Edson's Ridge" or "Bloody Ridge," as it came to be known, the focal point of his defense.

On September 12, Kawaguchi, who had chosen the ridge route to the airfield, began probing attacks against Edson's positions. He followed quickly with his main body, and heavy fighting ensued, but the Marines held. The night passed with little sleep on either side, for the Japanese kept attacking in banzai charges, with no effect except heavy losses to themselves. Vandegrift expected the main attack to come the morn-

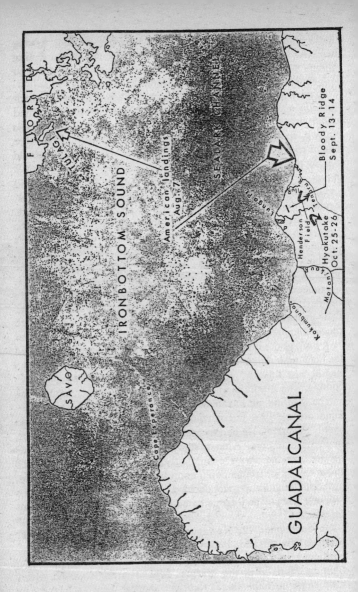

FLORIDA

TULAGI

American landings
Aug. 7

IRONBOTTOM SOUND

SEALARK CHANNEL

Bloody Ridge
Sept. 13 - 14

Lunga Pt.

Henderson Field

Hyakutake
Oct. 25-26

Matanikau

Koli Pt.

Cape Esperance

SAVO

GUADALCANAL

ing of September 13, and he was frankly worried, having wearied troops and few reserves. No attack developed during the daylight hours, although Henderson Field was subjected to heavy bombing by Japanese aircraft.

When night came, the last Japanese aircraft departed for Rabaul, and Kawaguchi's troops prepared to attack. They had no artillery, for their guns had been lost at the time of Edson's raid on Tasimboko. This fact did not deter them, for they were confident that the indomitable spirit of the samurai would carry them through to victory.

At about 2100, Louie the Louse dropped a flare, and Kawaguchi's assault jumped off. Screaming "Maline, you die!" about two battalions rushed Edson's positions on the ridge. Heavy fighting continued throughout the night, and at one point, the Japanese seemed about to overrun Vandegrift's command post. Scathing fire from rifles, artillery, mortars, machine guns and well-laced grenades coolly handled by the Marines eventually won out, and as daylight came, the Japanese assaults ceased. Flanking attacks by Colonel Oka's troops were similarly repelled. A battalion under Lieutenant Colonel Kusukichi Watanabe, part of Kawaguchi's force, had been detailed to dash in and seize the airfield under the cover of the main attack against Bloody Ridge. Instead, they had waited apparently expecting orders. But none came, and the battalion stayed where it was.

Grim-faced, Kawaguchi sent for Watanabe. "Coward!" he roared. "Commit hara-kiri!"

Some Japanese high officials wondered why Kawaguchi did not commit hara-kiri himself. His attack was a total failure, and his force was in no shape to mount another offensive for some time to come. He had left six hundred dead on the ridge and had another hundred or so killed or missing in the jungle. About five hundred were wounded. His two assault battalions were almost wiped out. Forty Marines were killed and about a hundred wounded during the assault on the ridge. The Japanese would have to try again. But it would be October before they were ready to make their next big push.

The Marine forces spent the time given to them in cleaning up the debris of Bloody Ridge and in extending their perimeter westward across the Matanikau River. On October 8, by curious coincidence both Vandegrift and Lieutenant General Masao Maruyama, who had succeeded to command on

Guadalcanal, mounted an offensive in the Matanikau River area. The U.S. attack broke through first, and when it was over, the Japanese had lost another seven hundred men killed.

The bad news did not deter General Hyakutake, who reached Guadalcanal around midnight on October 9. He had come to take over all ground forces on the island, and the drive to eject the stubborn Marines would continue. Help was on the way, for the Jaapanese Navy was sending a bombardment force down the Slot to coordinate with the Emperor's warriors in their ground assault on Henderson Field.

American intelligence had failed to anticipate the movement of Japanese naval forces toward Ironbottom Sound at this time, but Fortune intervened again on the side of the Americans, for a regiment of the Americal Division was en route to Guadalcanal and had to be protected in its passage. Three covering groups were assigned this task, one based on the carrier *Hornet*, one on the battleship *Washington*, and a cruiser force, Task Force 64, under Rear Admiral Norman Scott. Scott's instructions provided that he was to make a sweep looking for enemy forces, once the convoy of troops was safely delivered. Thus it was that Task Force 64 was in the neighborhood of Cape Esperance when the Japanese bombardment group under Rear Admiral Aritomo Goto came down from Rabaul.

On the afternoon of October 11, air reconnaissance reported two cruisers and six destroyers coming down the Slot. This was the news Admiral Scott had been waiting for, and he headed his force toward Guadalcanal at 29 knots. He planned to be off Cape Esperance to welcome the Japanese when they got there.

Norman Scott had had a distinguished career in the Navy, and he was an aggressive commander who longed to get in a good blow at the Japanese. He had had time during his command of Task Force 64 to drill his ships extensively, with special emphasis on night action. Also, he had laid out a careful battle plan that he intended to implement in the coming engagement.

Task Force 64 included two heavy and two light cruisers, Scott flying his flag in the heavy, *San Francisco*. His selection of flagship was unfortunate, for the *Helena*, one of the light cruisers, was equipped with the latest surface-search radar. The *San Francisco* carried only an undependable early version, whose emissions were susceptible of detection by equipment the Japanese were known to have. Therefore Scott had forbidden the *San Francisco* to use her radar during action.*

Scott formed his nine ships into a battle line, three destroyers forming a van division, the four cruisers coming next, the flagship leading, and two more destroyers bringing up the rear. The *Helena*, with her valuable radar, was at the tail of the cruiser line.

While waiting for contact with the enemy, Scott patrolled the opening between Cape Esperance, on the northwestern tip of Guadalcanal, and Savo Island. It was through this passage that Mikawa had brought his cruisers for the disastrous Battle of Savo Island. Scott sent his cruiser scout planes off to search, but only two of them made it. One burst into flames on takeoff, and the *Helena* failed to receive the order to launch, so Captain Gilbert C. Hoover ordered the plane jettisoned as a fire hazard in the coming action.

One of the spotting planes reported three ships near Savo Island, but Scott distrusted the report, believing the main Japanese body to be still coming down the Slot. By this time he was approaching Savo on a northeasterly course, so he ordered a countermarch to head back on the reverse course and cover the entrance once more.

His countermarch maneuver was absurdly complicated, considering the conditions. It was night; few ships had radar, and contact with the enemy was expected moment by moment. He risked having his formation in confusion at the crucial moment. In fact, the countermarch nearly cost him the battle.

When the order for the countermarch was given, the *San Francisco* swung left in a 180-degree turn. Each of the three cruisers and two destroyers astern of her followed around in succession, turning where the *San Francisco* had done. This part worked well and was simple enough. But the three van destroyers had also to turn in a separate column movement, then speed up and run past the other ships to resume their stations at the van of the formation. This movement put them on the side of the force where the enemy could be expected to ap-

---

* Scott's failure to realize the value of radar in night action was shared by most flag officers of the time. They simply had had no opportunity to see it work and had little conception of its possibilities. They preferred "seaman's eye" and "seaman's instinct."

pear. And it was just then that he did appear.

Shortly before Scott ordered the countermarch, the *Helena's* radar detected a target moving down the Slot, about fourteen miles away. It was moving toward them at about twenty knots. For some reason, the *Helena* did not report this contact for fifteen minutes, at which time Scott was in the middle of his maneuver. When she did report, she reported "five bogies." According to the jargon, "bogies" are air targets, and this caused confusion. So did doubt as to whether the reported bearing was true or relative.

While Scott and his staff were debating these puzzles, two of the three van destroyers were coming up the starboard side of the formation. But unknown to everyone, the *Duncan* had made a radar contact and had headed westward to investigate. Scott's formation was beginning to lose coherence.

About 2345, the *San Francisco's* fire-control radar picked out a radar blip at a range of five thousand yards. Since Scott was not sure where his van destroyers were, he did not know whether the contact was the enemy or one of his own lost sheep.

It was the enemy.

Admiral Goto had with him three heavy cruisers, the *Aoba*, flagship, leading the way, followed by the *Furutaka* and the *Kinugasa* in column. On either bow of the flagship was a screening destroyer. Goto was concentrated on one objective—the bombardment of Henderson Field. His guns were still trained in, and he had no radar. Like a lamb, he marched on to the slaughter.

The skipper of the *Helena* had no doubt that the ships only five thousand yards away were the enemy. His radarmen had tracked them from the first contact, and there was no question of it. He requested permission to open fire and thought he received it. Scott, however, because of the ambiguity of the voice radio language, thought he was acknowledging a message.

Without further ado, at 2346, the *Helena* fired a full salvo from her 6-inch guns, her 5-inch guns contributing their bit for good measure. The other ships followed suit almost at once, their shells screaming down on the trapped Japanese.

Inadvertently, Scott had achieved the Admiral's dream; he had capped the enemy T, so that all his guns could bear on the enemy, who could reply only with his forward guns. But the difficulty was that, like Jellicoe at the Battle of Jutland, Scott did not have a clear picture of the situation and failed to realize his tremendous advantage. In fact, convinced that his ships were firing on his own destroyers, he ordered Cease Fire only a minute after the *Helena* had opened up.

Admiral Goto, strangely enough, reached a similar conclusion, that he was being fired upon by a small reinforcement

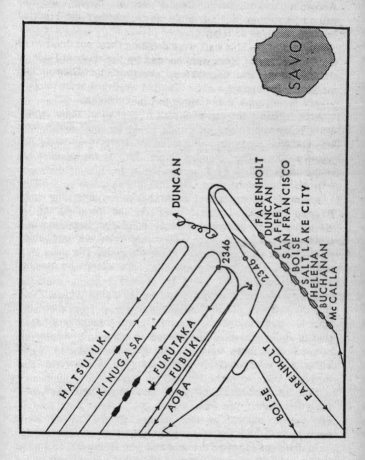

BATTLE OF CAPE ESPERANCE, OCTOBER 11-12, 1942

group carrying troops and supplies to Guadalcanal, so he, too, ordered fire suspended. It was his last order. No sooner had he given it than American shells smashed into the *Aoba*'s bridge, mortally wounding him.

The *Aoba* came right in a 180-degree turn, followed by the *Furutaka*, both ships heavily damaged from American gunfire, which had slackened but not ceased on Scott's order. An exchange of messages between Scott and his destroyers assured him that they were all right and it was really the enemy he was shooting at, so at 2351 he ordered his ships to begin shooting again.

By this time the *Kinugasa* was making her turn, but swung in the wrong direction, thereby avoiding the worst of the American shelling.

This period was a hot time for the three American destroyers, formerly the van of Scott's force. Caught between the big boys on each side, their men could see the shells arching overhead, some dropping uncomfortably near. Soon the *Farenholt* and the *Duncan* were hit, unfortunately by American as well as by Japanese shells. In spite of their uncomfortable circumstances, they blazed away with enthusiasm at the enemy as long as they could. No ships could long stand the punishment the Japanese were receiving from the American guns. The destroyer *Fubuki* blew up and sank, the victim of the guns of nearly every ship in Scott's force. The flagship *Aoba* was on fire; so was the *Furutaka*. The latter ship was mortally wounded; she made it a few miles back toward the Slot before she went down. The *Aoba* kept going, while the surviving Japanese destroyer stood by the dying cruiser. Only the *Kinugasa* was still in the fight. Recovering from their surprise, the gunners spotted the light cruiser *Boise* and began pouring shells into her. She started to blaze and would undoubtedly have been sunk had not Captain Ernest G. Small deliberately interposed his *Salt Lake City* to draw fire and allow the *Boise* to make her escape. After a few minutes of gunfire, the *Kinugasa* drew away and retired with the *Aoba* and a destroyer up the Slot.

As usual, reports of the damage to the enemy were overestimated, and the Navy Department announced to the world that four Japanese cruisers and four destroyers had been sunk, a fourfold exaggeration in both categories. Also, because of his tremendous victory, Admiral Scott became something of an oracle on tactical matters, and his formation was widely adopted, with the destroyers tied to the ends of the cruiser line, thereby depriving them of effective use of their primary weapon—torpedoes.

However, the Japanese had been stopped again, and another attempt to knock out Guadalcanal had failed.

Rejoicing over the victory of the Battle of Cape Esperance was somewhat premature. Under cover of the action, the Japanese had landed additional supplies, including some heavy field artillery. Two nights later, as this battery, which the Marines called "Pistol Pete," was churning up large holes in the runway, Vice Admiral Takeo Kurita brought the Battleships *Kongo* and *Haruna* into Ironbottom Sound and began to give Henderson Field a good working over. With shells from Pistol Pete coming in from one direction and 14-inch contributions from the two battleships arriving from another, the Marines spent a miserable night. For eighty minutes, Kurita leisurely lobbed his shells in, unopposed by anything from shore or on the water. The only American naval vessels in the area were four PT boats. Out they came in a gallant and futile charge on the battleships. By some miracle they escaped damage, but they inflicted none. Their arrival, however, induced Kurita to break off the action, for he knew not what might be behind the PT boats.

The next morning, as the dazed Marines crawled out of their foxholes, they looked upon a scene of devastation. Less than half of the ninety aircraft so laboriously assembled at Henderson Field remained operational. Almost all of the gasoline stores had been destroyed. The runway was a mass of shell holes from one end to the other. There were many dead and wounded, and Pistol Pete was still firing, inflicting more casualties and tearing up the airfield still further. Two air raids during the course of the day inflicted more damage. Henderson Field was out of commission for the time being. Fortunately for the American cause, the Seabees had constructed a fighter strip a little distance away, and this was still usable.

The next night was a repetition of the one before, but in smaller measure, for it was only cruisers, not battleships, that tossed their calling cards ashore. They fired over seven hundred rounds before going about their business elsewhere. At dawn the Marines had the agonizing experience of seeing several enemy transports lying off Tassafaronga a few miles to the west, calmly unloading troops while Japanese planes buzzed protectingly overhead.

And there wasn't a thing the Marines could do about it.

Major General Roy Geiger, the Marine air commander, told his pilots to climb into their planes and break up the landing. Someone told him there was no gasoline to be had.

"Then, by God, find some!" he roared.

Finding some odd drums that had been hidden in the fields, and siphoning gas from damaged planes, they got enough to get a few planes in the air. By noon, gasoline began to arrive from Espiritu Santo, flown in by transport aircraft.

With these measures, the desperate Americans managed to force the Japanese to beach three transports and to withdraw three more. All of them were damaged, and all troop units were more or less badly cut up.

Even a bombardment that night by two more cruisers could not dampen the spirits of the Marines, who had at last been able to get a bit of their own back.

If the spirits of the men on Guadalcanal were lifted by the action on October 15, those of the high commanders were not. Admiral Nimitz wrote, "It now appears that we are unable to control the sea in the Guadalcanal area. Thus our supply of the positions will only be done at great expense to us. The situation is not hopeless, but it is certainly critical." About the same time, Secretary Knox, who the previous December 6 had proclaimed that "the Navy is ready," stated to a reporter that he "would not make any prediction, but every man will give a good account of himself. . . . Everybody hopes that we can hold on."

* * * * *

A Navy Coronado flying boat droned its way from Suva to Noumea. On board as passengers were several naval officers, the highest ranking being Vice Admiral William F. Halsey, now recovered from his dermatitis and raring to go. While waiting to take up command of a task force built around the *Enterprise,* he had decided to make an inspection tour of the South Pacific area. His mind was busy, storing up impressions and ideas for use in his new command.

About 1400 the Coronado set down on the water of Noumea harbor, and before Halsey could reach the door of the plane, a motor whaleboat pulled alongside. Thinking it was transportation to take him to Ghormley's flagship, Halsey stepped aboard. An aide handed him an envelope containing a dispatch from Nimitz: YOU WILL TAKE COMMAND OF THE SOUTH PACIFIC FORCES IMMEDIATELY.

"Jesus Christ and General Jackson!" exclaimed Halsey. "This is the hottest potato they ever handed me!"

For some weeks Nimitz had been concerned over the state of affairs in the South Pacific. Ghormley had worked himself and his staff to the limit, but it seemed that his successes were few and his losses high. No man could have tried harder, but perhaps Ghormley was the kind of commander too prone to see difficulties where perhaps another man might see opportunities. Given the conditions existing in the South Pacific in August 1942, it is very hard to see how another commander could have done any better. Yet it is an axiom of military practice that when one commander fails to accomplish the objective, he should be relieved by another man, whose different viewpoints and ideas may bring about the desired results. So it was now. On October 15, Nimitz reached the conclusion that "the critical situation requires a more aggressive commander." The next day Admiral King agreed to Halsey's appointment as ComSoPac. With many regrets, Halsey relieved his old friend and pitched into the task at hand.

On Guadalcanal the news of Halsey's take-over was like a shot of whiskey to a nearly frozen man. "I'll never forget it," wrote one officer. "One minute we were too limp with malaria to crawl out of our foxholes; the next, we were running around shouting like kids."

It was at a grim moment that Halsey assumed command, for big things were stirring. The Japanese were moving forces for another combined air-sea-land attack against the Lunga position that would go on until General Vandegrift, his staff officers, interpreters, an American flag, and white flag advanced to surrender.

Immediately after he assumed command, Halsey sent word to Vandegrift to report to Noumea for a conference as soon as conditions on Guadalcanal permitted. Two days later, on October 20, Vandegrift reported on Halsey's flagship *Argonne*. Also present were Major General Alexander M. Patch, commander of the Army forces scheduled to relieve the First Marine Division, Major General Millard F. Harmon, senior

Army officer in the South Pacific, Lieutenant General Thomas Holcomb, Commandant of the Marine Corps, and Rear Admiral Richmond Kelly Turner.

Vandegrift and Harmon summarized conditions on Guadalcanal. It was a depressing picture of shortages, exhausted men existing on insufficient food, sleepless nights, and disease. Turner reported on the Navy's difficulties: few ships, no bases in the area, enemy submarines, and the inability to keep Japanese reinforcements from reaching the island. Halsey's face got craggier and craggier, grimmer and grimmer, as he listened. Drumming his fingers on the conference table for a moment, he turned to Vandegrift and shot a question at him.

"Are we going to evacuate or hold?"

"I can hold," replied Vandegrift carefully, "but I've got to have more active support than I've been getting."

"All right. Go on back. I promise you everything I've got."

Halsey's command of the South Pacific was not twenty-four hours old when the Japanese began their next major offensive against Guadalcanal. Japanese reinforcements had been reaching the island at the rate of about nine hundred a night. The Japanese high command had at last relegated the New Guinea campaign to second priority and were bending all efforts toward the recapture of Guadalcanal. But they still underestimated the strength of Vandegrift's forces, and they underestimated the difficulties of moving through the turgid jungles of the hated island.

October 22 was the day General Maruyama planned to hoist the flag of the Rising Sun from the flagpole at Henderson Field. He planned to send his main attack around through the jungle to strike from the south, while a diversionary assault would be made across the Matanikau River. A powerful force of the Japanese Navy operated to the north to keep the Americans from reinforcing the island and would be ready to move in once they received word Henderson Field was taken.

Halsey, meanwhile, was doing all that he could to make good on his promise to Vandegrift. A part of the operation plan had been the seizure of Ndeni Island in the Santa Cruz group. In spite of the grave situation on Guadalcanal, troops had been held back to engage in this second assault, as possession of the island would give an air base some two hundred miles closer than Espiritu Santo to Henderson Field. Turner and Ghormley insisted on keeping Ndeni on the list in spite of the violent objections of Vandegrift and of General Harmon, senior Army commander in the South Pacific. At the moment Halsey took over command, the Army 147th Infantry, less two battalions, was en route to Ndeni. Halsey's first major decision was to cancel the Ndeni operation entirely and to divert the troops to Guadalcanal. "This decision," he wrote, "brought me considerable adverse criticism, but I never had reason to regret it; Ndeni's importance soon evaporated."

Aware of the impending Japanese push for Guadalcanal, Halsey sent all the ships he could scrape together to sea to sweep around the Santa Cruz Island and then be ready to fall on the flank of Japanese sea forces heading for the Solomons.

Thus the stage was set for the October crisis.

For a week before his target date of October 22, General Maruyama attempted to soften up the Marine positions around Lunga Point. Meanwhile, he moved his forces eastward through the jungle to a point south of Bloody Ridge.

Maruyama's march through the jungle was a nightmare to the Japanese. There were no jungle trails, and they had to hack their way. The fetid heat of the day and the bone-chilling rains of the night weakened the men as they tried to drag their heavy artillery pieces through the muck, up hills, across swamps, through narrow passages where every tough jungle vine seemed to reach out to snag the equipment and rob it of its precious momentum. Bit by bit the equipment was abandoned, piece by piece the guns discarded in the slime of the jungle.

Inevitably the march fell behind schedule, and the determined Maruyama had to postpone the assault for two days.

On the western end, Major General Sumiyoshi apparently did not receive the word to delay the attack, for he hit the Marine positions on the Matanikau River on the original schedule. His attack was a complete failure, but it did serve to draw the Marines' attention from the real threat developing to the south.

According to his revised plan, Maruyama was supposed to jump off at 1700. As his troops were moving toward the line of departure, two hours previous to the planned assault, the heavens opened. Torrential tropical rains fell on attacker and defender alike. The jungle floor became mud, then a swamp. It was impossible to see more than a few yards in any direction. Units lost coherence, and when the rains ceased, it took the

343

Japanese hours to round their men up. It was not until midnight that the signal for the advance was finally given. Screaming and yelling, the Japanese soldiers advanced to their deaths. Carefully sited artillery mowed down most of them, and when dawn came, the Marines counted nearly a thousand Japanese corpses in front of their lines. The next night the stubborn Japanese tried again. The result was the same. The whole attack was a complete failure.

The land thrust had been beaten back. What of the Japanese fleet coming down from Truk?

As usual, the Japanese had divided their overwhelming powerful naval forces into several groups, affording the American forces an opportunity to hit a section on something approaching equal terms. It was the situation of Midway all over again. To annihilate the remaining American naval strength in the South Pacific, Admiral Yamamoto sent two main forces, an Advance Force consisting of two battleships, five cruisers, a light carrier, and fourteen destroyers, and a Striking Force of two large carriers, a light carrier, two battleships, five cruisers, and fifteen destroyers. In addition there were supply forces, land-based air, a submarine force, and miscellaneous destroyers and a cruiser on other supporting tasks.

What did Halsey have to throw at these juggernauts? He had two carriers. The *Enterprise* had returned, patched up from her damage in the Eastern Solomons battle. The *Hornet* was still spoiling for a fight. He had the battleships *South Dakota* and *Washington,* nine cruisers, and twenty destroyers. There was land-based air at Espiritu Santo and at Henderson Field, but in the area of the battle, the Japanese had two hundred twelve aircraft on their four carriers as opposed to a hundred sixty-nine on the two American flattops.

Knowing that surprise was the only chance for the outnumbered American forces, Halsey directed his task force commanders to sweep around the Santa Cruz Islands and attempt to attack on the enemy flank. He organized his forces into three task forces, keeping overall tactical command in his own hands. Task Force 16 had the *Enterprise* and *South Dakota* with two cruisers and eight destroyers. Task Force 17 had the *Hornet,* four cruisers, and six destroyers. Task Force 64, under Rear Admiral Willis A. Lee, built around the battleship *Washington,* operated at some distance and did not engage the enemy during the battle.

As had happened at the Battle of the Coral Sea, each of the forces lashed out at the other with air strikes, hoping to get in the first blow and to repel the aircraft thrown in by the enemy. Since the Japanese did not intend to engage until they received word that the Army had captured Henderson Field, they remained at some distance. However, at 0126 on October 25, the naval liaison officer with Maruyama's troops triumphantly radioed: "Banzai! Occupied airfield at 2300." The naval forces began to move toward Guadalcanal.

At 0623 another radio message arrived to state that the report had been premature. But it was too late to avoid contact. The Japanese had been spotted by American search planes, and battle loomed for October 26.

As dawn approached near the Santa Cruz Island, a message from Admiral Halsey chattered into the radio rooms of the American ships: "ATTACK—REPEAT—ATTACK."

The Battle of the Santa Cruz Islands depended on the skill and determination of the aviators on each side. The Japanese did better against ships, and the Americans did better against aircraft. When the smoke of battle cleared away, the carriers

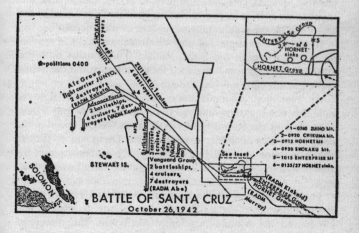

BATTLE OF SANTA CRUZ
October 26, 1942

Zuikaku and *Zuiho* were heavily damaged. However, the *Enterprise* had been badly hit again, and, worst of all, the *Hornet* was on the bottom. On the other hand, the American flyers had combined with the ships' gunners to shoot down about a hundred enemy aircraft. And the loss of their first-line pilots was beginning to hurt the Japanese. They were losing airmen faster than they could train them, and the situation grew worse as the months went by.

With word that the attack on Lunga Point had failed and that Maruyama's forces had been shattered, Yamamoto recalled his naval forces. The October crisis was over, and Guadalcanal had been saved again.

But the American Navy had not a single operational carrier in the South Pacific.

Shortly before the Battle of Santa Cruz was fought, President Roosevelt reached the conclusion that Guadalcanal and the South Pacific Command as a whole were getting the short end of the stick because preparations for the forthcoming North African landings dominated thinking in Washington. "My anxiety about the Southwest Pacific [he wrote the Joint Chiefs of Staff on October 24] is to make sure that every possible weapon gets into that area to hold Guadalcanal, and that having held it in this crisis that munitions and planes and crews are on the way to take advantage of our success."

It would take time for the reinforcements the President demanded to reach the South Pacific. To buy this time had cost the lives of many brave men. Many more would die before sufficient strength reached the area.

At Noumea, where Halsey had scarcely had time to establish headquarters ashore, the *South Dakota* and *Enterprise* rang to the hammers of repair crews. Night and day the eerie blue lights of welders could be seen. There was no time to waste, for already intelligence was picking up reports that the Japanese were about to make another, even more powerful, attack.

Taking advantage of the brief lull, Admiral Halsey flew up to Guadalcanal to get a firsthand view of the detested island. He toured the Marine positions, talked with the men, and made his presence felt by every American on the island. That night, as he was trying to sleep in Vandegrift's quarters, Washing Machine Charley flew over to pay his compliments with a few bombs, and a Japanese destroyer or two routinely shelled Henderson Field. Halsey tried to sleep through the excitement. "I called myself yellow—and worse—and told myself, 'Go to sleep, you damned coward!' but it didn't do any good; I couldn't obey orders."

The next morning he held a press conference, and one reporter asked him how he planned to win the South Pacific campaign.

"Kill Japs, kill Japs, and keep on killing Japs," answered Halsey.

Meanwhile, both sides continued their buildup for a crucial battle. As fast as he could, Halsey sent ships with supplies to Guadalcanal, and more and more aircraft arrived at Henderson Field. The Tokyo Express ran on the nights of November 2, 5, 7, 8, 9, and 10. Something was about to happen.

The Japanese were preparing to shoot the works.

The heavy reinforcements landed by the Tokyo Express were the rest of the Japanese Thirty-Eighth Division, and their instructions were to make an all-out assault on the Lunga position as soon as the last of the troops arrived in mid-November. They were embarked in ten transports and entrusted to the care of the indomitable Rear Admiral Raizo Tanaka. They were to have a rough passage to Guadalcanal.

In preparation for the offensive by the Thirty-Eighth Division, the Japanese Navy planned heavy bombardments of Henderson Field and committed two forces. The first, under Vice Admiral Hiroaki Abe, had two battleships, a light cruiser, and six destroyers. The second, under Vice Admiral Nobutake Kondo, had two heavy cruisers, as well as other forces, assigned. It was a formidable array. And what was left in Halsey's locker to oppose them?

When the word reached Halsey's headquarters at Noumea that the Japanese fleet was on the prowl, Rear Admiral Norman Scott, victor of the Battle of Cape Esperance, was approaching Guadalcanal in his flagship *Atlanta* with four destroyers in company. This little group was shepherding three cargo ships carrying the 182nd Regimental Combat Team to reinforce the Lunga position. In the early hours of November 11, Scott's group was joined by five cruisers and ten destroyers under the command of Rear Admiral Daniel J. Callaghan. Also in company was Rear Admiral Richmond K. Turner in the *McCawley*, which was doing double duty as flagship and troop transport, with three transports.

About 0530, November 12, the transports reached Lunga anchorage and began to unload troops. Knowing that a Japanese air attack might come at any moment, all hands worked feverishly to get as much ashore as possible. Their haste was justified when word came from a coast-watcher during the early afternoon that enemy bombers and fighters were on the way.

Turner immediately ordered unloading suspended and got his ships moving and into a tight formation to give maximum concentration of antiaircraft fire. Perhaps at this moment he regretted detaching a cruiser and three destroyers to join the *Enterprise* group pelting up from Noumea.

The Japanese air attack came in about an hour later. Skillful ship-handling and intense gunfire and determined help from Henderson Field pilots kept injuries to a minimum. The destroyer *Buchanan* had considerable topside damage from "friendly" antiaircraft fire, and a shot-up Japanese plane was deliberately crashed into the after control station of the *San Francisco*. The hit smashed a fire-control radar and killed or wounded some fifty men.

When the attackers departed, Turner's ships returned to the unloading area and worked on until the coming of darkness made their departure inevitable. In spite of the interruption, all the troops and about ninety percent of their supplies had been landed.

Observations from search planes during the day had revealed heavy enemy forces coming down the Slot. They would reach Ironbottom Sound that night and subject the troops to a heavy bombardment, unless they were stopped. With a heavy heart, Turner ordered Admiral Callaghan to stop them.

Rear Admiral Callaghan, who was senior to Scott, had taken over command from his classmate,* but had largely adopted Scott's concept of action as used in the Battle of Cape Esperance. Until October, he had been Admiral Ghormley's Chief of Staff, but it was said he made things so miserable for everyone around him in his anxiety to get a sea command that they finally obliged him. Now at the head of Task Group 67.4, comprising five cruisers and eight destroyers, he made some of the same mistakes Scott had made. He put all his forces in a

* Both were members of the class of 1911 at the Naval Academy.

single line, with four destroyers leading and four destroyers bringing up the rear, thereby depriving them of the freedom of action they would need for a coordinated torpedo attack. Also, he stationed his ships without regard for their radar capabilities. Except for the *O'Bannon* in the lead destroyer group, all ships with the latest radar, three cruisers and one destroyer, brought up the rear of the formation.

Perhaps it was sentiment that dictated Callaghan's choice of flagship. Up until May he had been commanding officer of the *San Francisco*. He knew her, knew her men, and trusted them. He was called (but not to his face) "Uncle Dan" by his men, and it may have been this warm personal rapport that led him to his fatal choice. For the *San Francisco* still had no effective search radar.

Having conducted Turner's transport group safely beyond Ironbottom Sound, Callaghan brought his task group back into those waters by way of Lengo Channel about 2200, steering parallel to the coast on a course of 280°. It was a clear night, with no moon, a slight easterly breeze, with occasional lightning. Few men knew what to expect, for Callaghan had not told his commanding officers what he knew, nor had he issued a battle plan.

Callaghan knew well enough what lay ahead. He knew that he was taking his ships up to face two battleships. His only chance was to surprise and cripple them before their 14-inch guns blew his cruisers out of the water. On he advanced, as the ships' bells marked the passage of time. Eight bells struck. It was now Friday, the thirteenth. Eight ships and hundreds of men would not live to see its end. Nor would Admirals Callaghan and Scott.

At 0214 the TBS* woke to life on the *San Francisco*'s bridge. "Contacts bearing three one two and three one oh, distant two seven oh double oh and three two oh double oh yards."

The *Helena*'s radar had picked up Admiral Abe's group of

* TBS was a high-frequency voice radio of short range used for communication between ships. As the only VHF radio on those ships, it had to be used for administrative, command, and maneuvering messages. Sometimes it was jammed up with routine conversation when something vital had to get through. Callaghan was trying to maneuver his ships and get tracking information through this one radio channel.

the battleships *Hiei*, flagship, and *Kirishima*, the light cruiser *Nagara*, and eleven destroyers. The battleships were in column, with the *Nagara* and destroyers forming a horseshoe screen ahead and on the flanks.

On the flag bridge, Callaghan's staff tried to plot the position and movements of the Japanese force as additional information came in from the *Helena* and *O'Bannon*. Callaghan turned north, apparently in an attempt to cross the T as Scott had done earlier, but he wasted precious minutes. He had achieved surprise, for Abe had no idea of his presence. The range closed, the two forces approaching each other at a relative speed of about forty knots.

Still no word came to open fire.

Suddenly, at 0141, seventeen minutes after the first contact, the destroyer *Cushing*, leading Callaghan's force, sighted two Japanese destroyers close ahead. His hard left swing avoided a collision, but threw Callaghan's line into confusion. The *Atlanta* had to come hard left to avoid the destroyers.

At last Callaghan picked up the TBS. But it was not to order his ships to open fire.

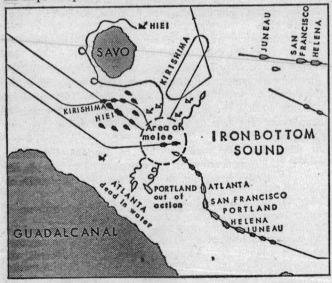

BATTLE OF GUADALCANAL: CRUISER ACTION,
NOVEMBER 13, 1942

"What are you doing?" he asked the *Atlanta*.

"Avoiding our own destroyers," replied her skipper, Captain Samuel P. Jenkins.

Confusion compounded on the flag bridge as more and more reports jammed the TBS. It was clear something was out there. But what was it? And where?

The Japanese destroyers, meanwhile, had promptly reported contact with the American forces to Admiral Abe, and Callaghan's precious surprise was lost. Yet he hung on. Four crucial minutes went by while Callaghan changed course to the northwest to head for the enemy. Then, at 0145, he ordered, "Stand by to open fire!"

Thus began one of the wildest melees in all the history of sea fighting. It is impossible to reconstruct the ships' tracks of this dreadful night. Callaghan drove his formation directly into the center of the Japanese formation, so that ships became hopelessly intermixed, and no one could distinguish friend from foe. At 0150 came the word: "Odd ships commence fire to starboard, even ships to port." Even as the words were spoken, enemy shells smashed into the *Atlanta*'s bridge, killing Admiral Scott and nearly everyone else there. Callaghan's confusing order hamstrung his offense, for some of the odd-numbered ships could see no targets to starboard and had good ones to port. Luckily, however, it soon ceased to have any meaning, and gunners fired on anything they could see.

The stricken *Atlanta* was still shuddering from the shell hit when one or two torpedoes tore into her. She sagged dead in the water, out of the fight and mortally wounded. Death and destruction rained on all ships; some, particularly the thin-skinned destroyers, sank at once; others lasted a little longer. A few survived, a pitiful few.

The destroyers *Cushing* and *Laffrey* attacked the battleship *Hiei* with torpedoes, but all missed. A single salvo from *Hiei*'s 14-inch guns sent the *Laffrey* to the bottom. Two more destroyers, *Sterett* and *O'Bannon*, attacked, but their torpedoes either missed or failed to explode. The *Sterett* was hit twice during this encounter, but probably by one of the destroyers. About the same time, the *Hiei* took shells from an American cruiser, so that her steering engine rooms and her fire-control radar were knocked out. Confused by the milling ships and by the intrepid American destroyer attacks, Admiral Abe decided to take his force back up the Slot. The bombardment was obviously impossible, and the only thing was to get out of the situation as best he could. The *Hiei* proved unmanageable, however, and she slowly drifted around Savo Island, to become a target of air attacks the next day.

In the midst of the furious fighting, Callaghan feared that Americans were firing on each other. He was quite right. He ordered, "Cease firing own ships!" There was a brief silence as the Japanese seemed to suspend fire, too. Then, somewhere, a gun roared out, and the blazing, crashing, spew of death began again. Callaghan could do no more, so he ordered to all ships: "We want the big ones. Get the big ones first."

This was his last order. A shell ripped into the *San Francisco*'s bridge, killing Admiral Callaghan and every man on the bridge except for a quartermaster, Lieutenant Commander Bruce McCandless, and Captain Cassin Young, who was mortally wounded. "The navigation bridge was a weird place indeed in the intermittent light of gunfire," wrote McCandless years later. "It had been hit several times more during my brief absence. Bodies, helmeted and life-jacketed, limbs, and gear littered the deck. The siren was moaning and water was raining down through holes in the deck above from the ruptured water-cooling system of the forward 1.1-inch 'quads.' I could not identify Captain Young in my hasty search. . . ."

McCandless conned the ship through the milling warriors, her guns still blazing whenever her gunners spotted a target. Twice she lost steering control, plunging through the formation to the danger of both sides. At length, McCandless headed over toward Guadalcanal as the enemy disappeared.

The heavy cruiser *Portland* was hit early in the fighting, and a torpedo so distorted her stern that two screws were out of action and she could not steer a straight course. She, too, set out on a wild and erratic course through the fighting, but emerged with no further harm. The *Helena* and *Juneau* escaped with minor damage. Among the rear destroyers, the *Barton* was sunk, and the *Aaron Ward* and *Monssen* shattered. Of the thirteen American ships that entered the battle, only the *Fletcher*, bringing up the rear, escaped injury.

On the Japanese side, a destroyer had gone down, another was dead in the water, and a third had been left to aid the stricken *Hiei*. Others were damaged. With the *Kirishima*, the surviving battleship, Abe had hightailed it up the Slot to be out of range the next day.

When dawn broke over Ironbottom Sound, the crippled ships faced each other, grimly ready for another no-quarter contest. The *Aaron Ward* came under fire from the *Hiei*, but was not hit and eventually reached safety. Salvos from the *Portland* finished off a Japanese destroyer. Aircraft spent most of the day working over the *Hiei*, which went down about five miles from Savo Island.

After much struggle, the *Portland* finally reached Tulagi harbor, where her shipfitters could begin to get her in some sort of shape again. But the *Atlanta, Monssen,* and *Cushing* could not be saved. When Captain Gilbert C. Hoover, now Senior Officer Present, rounded up the American ships, he could find only his own *Helena, San Francisco, Juneau,* and the destroyers *O'Bannon, Sterett,* and *Fletcher.* At 18 knots, their battle ensigns still flying, they headed down Indispensable Strait toward Espiritu Santo.

But Friday-the-thirteenth was not done with them. About 1050 that morning, the Japanese submarine *I-26* fired a spread of torpedoes, one of which hit the *Juneau* under the bridge.

The *Juneau* didn't sink [wrote McCandless]—she blew up with all the fury of an erupting volcano. There was a terrific thunderclap and a plume of white water that was blotted out by a huge brown hemisphere a thousand yards across, from within which came the sounds of more explosions. . . . When the dark cloud lifted from the water a minute or so later, we could see nothing of this fine 6000-ton cruiser or the 700 men she carried. Those who witnessed it called this terrible end of a gallant ship the most awesome spectacle of the battle.

Now Captain Hoover was faced with a terrible decision. If he stopped to rescue survivors, he exposed his entire force to further attack. On the other hand, by not stopping, he was condemning to almost certain death any men who might have lived through the blast. He felt he had no choice. The United States could not afford to lose any more ships at that moment, with the drive on Guadalcanal still unstopped. The task group continued on its way to Espiritu Santo.

Hoover passed word of the disaster to a Flying Fortress nearby and asked its pilot to inform Admiral Halsey. Unfortunately the message never got through, and of the hundred or so survivors, all but ten perished. Five brothers by the name of Sullivan were lost in the *Juneau,* which caused the Navy Department to adopt a policy of not assigning more than one member of a family to a single ship.*

Halsey relieved Captain Hoover of his command as a result of that decision, but on sober reflection concluded that he had made a mistake and requested that he be reassigned to a combat command.

The first phase of the four-day Naval Battle of Guadalcanal was over, but there was more to come. A great deal more.

Obviously Callaghan's group had shot its bolt. More strength was needed near Guadalcanal, in a hurry.

The *Enterprise* and the *South Dakota* had long since had their repair periods cut short and were at sea, repairmen still aboard them as they tore northward. The *Enterprise's* forward elevator had been repaired—they thought, but no one, not even Admiral Halsey, dared order it tested. If it should jam in the down position, the flight deck would be unusable, and it was the only American flight deck in the whole South Pacific. The immobile elevator made plane handling awkward and slow, but it was better than nothing.

With the *Enterprise* and the *South Dakota* on their dash to the north were the battleship *Washington* and four destroyers. Halsey had hoped the wind conditions would permit this force (Task Force 16) to be close enough to Guadalcanal to allow the battleships to protect Henderson Field from bombardment the next night. But the wind was southerly, so the *Enterprise* had to reverse course to conduct flight operations, and at dawn on November 14, the battleships were still with the carrier, some three hundred forty miles from Guadalcanal.

Nothing could be done to protect Guadalcanal that night.

Kincaid in the *Enterprise* sent fifteen aircraft to beef up Henderson Field, and they enthusiastically joined the Marine fliers in putting an end to the helpless *Hiei.* That evening the *Washington,* flying the flag of Rear Admiral Willis A. Lee, the *South Dakota,* and four destroyers peeled off from the *Enterprise* and headed for Ironbottom Sound. Unable to reach his destination until the next day, Lee held back so as to arrive after dark and not tip the Japanese off to the presence of two

---

* In September 1943 a brand-new *Fletcher*-class destroyer was commissioned in San Francisco—U.S.S. *The Sullivans.*

American battleships in the area.

It was unfortunate that he could not get there in time, for shortly after midnight, Admiral Mikawa sent in two heavy cruisers that pasted the American positions for some thirty-seven minutes. The damage was less than it might have been, for the next morning revealed that only seventeen aircraft had been destroyed and another thirty-two damaged. The field could still be used.

And used it was.

Heading down the Slot from Faisi in the Shortland Islands was Rear Admiral Raizo Tanaka with eleven destroyers escorting an equal number of transports carrying ten thousand troops of the Thirty-Eighth Division and about ten thousand tons of supplies. If these troops got through, the Americans on Guadalcanal would be heavily outnumbered.

Furious at the impudent bombardment of the night before, fliers from Henderson Field were out early searching to the northwest. About 0700 reports came in that two forces had been spotted, one a hundred fifty miles up the Slot, headed for Guadalcanal, and the other a hundred thirty miles away, bearing 310°, heading away. These were marvelous targets, and the pilots were burning to get at them. Twenty aircraft left Henderson Field almost at once and headed for the nearer group, which was Mikawa's retiring bombardment force. They smashed in from all sides and severely damaged a heavy cruiser and a light cruiser. Planes from the *Enterprise*, operating some two hundred miles to the south, took over and finished off the heavy cruiser *Kinugasa*. They also severely mauled the heavy cruisers *Chokai* and *Maya*, added to the discomfort of the light cruiser *Isuzu*, and made life decidedly uncomfortable for the destroyer *Michishio*. But because the American pilots had other fish to fry, Mikawa's battered force was thereafter left in peace to make its way to the Shortlands.

Tanaka's Reinforcement Group of eleven transports and eleven destroyers had been spotted early, but was not attacked until about 0830. All day long, planes from Henderson Field and from the *Enterprise*, fighting their way through antiaircraft fire and battling Japanese Zeke fighters from the carrier *Hiyo* to the northward, smashed into this group. They planted their bombs and returned to base for more. By the end of the day, seven of the transports had been sunk. But the courageous Tanaka, using his destroyers boldly, had taken off

355

as many troops as could be jammed into them and with the four remaining transports continued, incredibly, doggedly, to push on toward Guadalcanal. It was a magnificent display of will power and determination.

Stirring as the day's events had been, they were but a warm-up for the main event that night, one of four slugging contests between battleships at sea in the entire Second World War.

Vice Admiral Nobutake Kondo had gathered under his command the battleship *Kirishima,* veteran of the battle against Callaghan two nights earlier, and with two heavy and two light cruisers and nine destroyers headed toward Savo Island from the north. He intended to complete the unfinished business of knocking out Henderson Field and the American defensive position nearby.

Rear Admiral Lee, suspecting another try at bombardment that night, entered Ironbottom Sound during the evening of November 14. Ahead could be seen a glow in the sky, Tanaka's beached and burning four transports, which had completed their runs to the 'Canal. A quarter moon was still up and cast a half light on the water and on the dark shadows of the coast of Guadalcanal to port and Savo Island ahead. Neither the eye nor radar could make out anything of the enemy. Kondo had split his forces, with a sweeping group passing east of Savo Island and his main body, in two parts, to the westward. About 2316, Lee's group, having turned westward along the Guadalcanal coast, opened fire on Kondo's sweeping group and chased it off. The bulk of Savo Island masked Kondo's other two groups from radar detection. It was several minutes before Lee's destroyers picked up and engaged Kondo's advance force, screening the heavies. Two of Lee's destroyers were sunk in this skirmish and the other two put out of action. Meanwhile, at this critical moment in the battle, the *South Dakota* had an electrical power failure, which lasted for three minutes. During her blackout, she had to make an emergency maneuver to avoid one of her own destroyers, and with no radar to guide her, turned away from the *Washington* and lost contact. While her plotting officers were still confused, she came under the fire of Kondo's three heavy ships; 8-inch and 14-inch shells plowed into her superstructure, starting fires and spreading wreckage and bits of men indiscriminately about the decks. Nonetheless, she kept firing and was soon supported by the *Washington,* whose 16-inch shells

356

began rending the *Kirishima* and then the heavy cruisers *Atago* and *Takao*.

Unable to find targets, her radars inoperative, her topside a shambles, the *South Dakota* headed south out of the battle. Lee, in the *Washington*, had been unable to raise her by radio and had lost track of her on his radar plot. He could only hope she was all right. Meanwhile, he had unfinished business with the Japanese. He headed northwest to draw Kondo's ships after him, and in a matter of moments, as he continued to engage the Japanese heavies, the *Kirishima* was helpless and circling, unable either to steer or to fight.

By this time, the *Washington* had been attacked several times by destroyers, and Lee, realizing that the attack on Guadalcanal had been beaten off, decided to retire. Kondo, left to his own devices, ordered the *Kirishima* and a crippled destroyer scuttled and headed for home.

The next morning, the troops on Guadalcanal again saw broken bodies and drowned men in the waters of Ironbottom Sound. At Tassafaronga they saw the remains of Tanaka's transports, beached and burning. They had finished their runs and landed their troops. Fliers from Henderson Field and from the *Enterprise* saw to it that they would land no supplies. Japanese troops, milling aimlessly near the beached transports, were mowed down in a terrible slaughter before they could reach safety in the jungle.

So ended the Naval Battle of Guadalcanal. The Americans had accomplished almost all of their objectives, but at what a terrible cost. The final all-out Japanese push to retake the island had failed. Friday-the-thirteenth had brought disaster to an American force and had nearly brought the leaders to despair. Sunday the fifteenth ended the Japanese offensive capability near Guadalcanal. Never again would the outcome be in doubt.

Shortly after the battle, Halsey was promoted to Admiral. When he pinned on his new four-star devices, he gave his old three-star ones to a staff officer, saying, "Send one of these to Mrs. Scott and the other to Mrs. Callaghan. Tell them it was their husbands' bravery that got me my new ones."

Following the intense action of mid-November, both sides paused to regroup. The Japanese abandoned attempts to send in troops protected by massive task forces. Instead, Tanaka

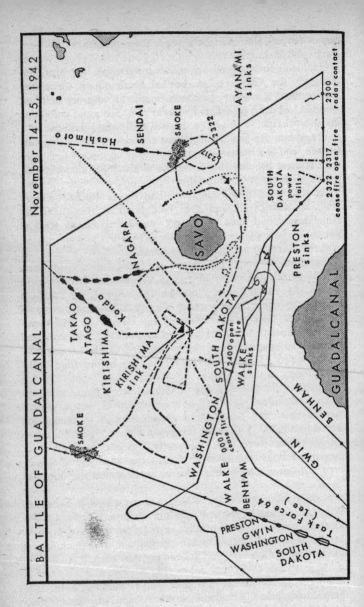

BATTLE OF GUADALCANAL   November 14-15, 1942

Hashimoto

SENDAI

SMOKE   2322
2317

AYANAMI sinks

NAGARA

SAVO

SOUTH DAKOTA
power fails

2322 2317
cease fire open fire

2300
radar contact

TAKAO
ATAGO   Kondo

KIRISHIMA

KIRISHIMA
sinks

SOUTH DAKOTA

PRESTON
sinks

GUADALCANAL

12400 open

WALKE
fire

WALKE
sinks

GWIN

BENHAM

SMOKE

WASHINGTON

WALKE
0007 cease fire

BENHAM

Task Force 64 (Lee)

PRESTON
GWIN
WASHINGTON
SOUTH DAKOTA

ran destroyers almost nightly down the Slot with a few hundred men at a time. This new version of the Tokyo Express met opposition from destroyers and PT boats at night and planes by day. Still, a trickle got through until, on December 11, Tanaka's flagship was destroyed and the valorous Admiral wounded. Then, reluctantly, the Japanese Navy decided to abandon Guadalcanal and retire to the Central Solomons.

But before this happened, they got in one more telling blow against the Americans.

Following the victory of the Naval Battle of Guadalcanal, the Marines made an effort to expand their perimeter, but got rocked back on their heels. The Japanese on the island were still full of fight and ready to take issue with any idea the Americans might have had that Guadalcanal was as good as won.

Nonetheless, the Marines were in good spirits as they sat down to eat the turkey and cranberry sauce delivered to them in time for Thanksgiving. For they had received their orders to leave the fetid island in early December and go to Australia for rest and reorganization. The men, tired, worn, racked with malaria and dysentery, still had energy enough to stuff themselves, dream of complaisant (they hoped) Sydney girls, and join in a rousing chorus of "Waltzing Matilda."

Although the Japanese Navy had long since decided Guadalcanal must be abandoned, the Army had no such notions. They therefore insisted on another push. Tanaka, meanwhile, had been doing his best to get some few supplies to the thirty thousand Japanese on the island. No longer caring to shepherd transports, he ran destroyers in with deck loads of sealed metal drums filled with medical supplies, foodstuffs, and ammunition, with enough air space left to ensure buoyancy. The cans would be shoved overboard near the island, as the destroyers hightailed it for home. Motorboats would come out from the Japanese positions and drag the drums ashore. It was an expensive and pitifully inadequate supply system.

On November 29, Tanaka set out from the Shortland Islands on just such a run. He had eight destroyers with him, six of them so crammed with supply drums the crews could scarcely move about the decks. He aimed to be off Tassafaronga on the night of November 30. He was not looking for a fight, but that is what he ran into.

About the same time as Tanaka's sortie, a cruiser-destroyer force under the command of Rear Admiral Carleton H. Wright left Espiritu Santo on a sweep into Ironbottom Sound. American intelligence had picked up word of suspicious activity in the Central Solomons. Wright was new to the area and to the ships he commanded. Only the day before he left, he had relieved Kinkaid, who had worked out a careful battle plan. Wright adopted the plan, but its execution was faulty.

About an hour before midnight on November 30, Wright's force entered Ironbottom Sound by way of Lengo Channel and moved toward the western end of Guadalcanal. He had five cruisers and six destroyers with him. Every advantage was with Wright, for Tanaka had no radar, his ships were encumbered, and he was not expecting to fight. Wright had radar, which he used, and he was looking for the enemy. At 2316, his radars picked up Tanaka's little group of eight destroyers, but he hesitated, hoping for favorable tactical situation. Precious minutes ticked by before he gave his van destroyers permission to fire their torpedoes.

At that moment the Japanese, up to that moment intent on their supply mission, spotted the Americans. Tanaka's response was swift and deadly. Japanese "Long Lance" torpedoes were quickly swimming toward the American ships, which steadily held their course. There was no precautionary zigzagging. In a few minutes, four of Wright's five cruisers had been hit. The *Northampton* sank at 0244, the last major American ship to find her grave in Ironbottom Sound. The other three damaged cruisers were out of action for almost a year. Only the *Honolulu*, by luck and skilled maneuvering, escaped damage.

The bitter lesson of Tassafaronga was that overconfidence never paid when dealing with the Japanese. It was a lesson dearly bought, but it paid off. The only satisfaction the American Navy could salvage from the battle was that they had been able to sink one of Tanaka's destroyers. It is fortunate for the Americans that Tanaka had not been in command in some of the early battles where the American margin of victory rested on practically nothing.

On December 9, General Vandegrift relinquished command on Guadalcanal to Major General Alexander M. Patch, U.S. Army. That same day the battered survivors of the First Marine Division made their way to the transports that would bear them from this hellhole which had joined Bunker Hill, Gettysburg, San Juan, and Chateau Thierry in the list of fields of valor.

To strengthen their position in the Central Solomons and to support the expected final victorious push against Guadalcanal, the Japanese had begun to construct an airstrip on Munda Point on New Georgia. Air reconnaissance had revealed its presence, and on January 5, 1943, an American cruiser force bombarded the nearly completed strip into impotence.

Although no one knew it, the Battle for Guadalcanal was won. On January 4, Premier Tojo, appalled at the attrition of men, supplies, aircraft, and ships in the battle to recapture the island, ordered that all Japanese troops must be evacuated within a month. The order was told only to the highest-level officers; the troops had to keep on fighting just as though they were going on for final victory. While General Patch pushed outwards to bring larger and larger sections of the island under control, the Japanese were executing one of the most brilliant evacuations in history. On the first night in February, they began to pull their troops out. The Americans attributed the ship movements to customary runs of the Tokyo Express. Night by night the work of taking the Japanese out went on. General Patch finally reached the former Japanese position on Cape Esperance on February 8, to find nothing but abandoned equipment and boats. Then, for the first time, he knew of the Japanese departure.

The fight was over.

"Total and complete defeat of Japanese forces on Guadalcanal effected 1625 today," radioed General Patch to Admiral Halsey. ". . . Am happy to report this kind of compliance with your orders. . . . 'Tokyo Express' no longer has terminus on Guadalcanal."

The grim scorecard for the six months of fighting on Guadalcanal reads:

Killed	Americans	Japanese
Army and Marines	1,592	23,800
Navy	2,000 (approx.)	unknown
Ships lost		
Battleships	0	2
Aircraft carriers	2	0

Ships lost	American	Japanese
Light carriers	0	1
Heavy cruisers	6	3
Light cruisers	2	1
Destroyers	14	11
Submarines	0	6
	—	—
	24	24

Hundreds of airmen on both sides were lost, and other thousands of Japanese soldiers went down with the battered transports. All this for an island nobody wanted.

Yet it was the first stepping-stone on the road back to victory in the Pacific.

After Guadalcanal, Japan had lost the war.

CHAPTER THIRTEEN

September-October: Settling Down

> "He told me, only the other day,
> that it was provided for.
> That was Mr. Micawber's expression,
> 'Provided for.'"
> Dickens, David Copperfield

Mapmakers did a roaring business in "War Atlases" and "Victory Maps" as Americans learned to cope with such names as Guadalcanal, Tulagi, Espiritu Santo, Noumea, Port Moresby, Papua. Those who had "never been good at geography" regretted their inattention in school, although it is unlikely that even the most advanced school geography course would have located a tithe of the names flooding the headlines of the papers. Soon there would be more strange names to learn, on the other side of the world, in another ocean and the names of the enemy commanders would be German, not Japanese.

In preparation for the coming offensives, American factories were by now almost on a full-time operating basis, three shifts daily being the regular thing. The rush for manpower brought factory operations into conflict with the needs of the services. Unemployment lists dropped to new lows, and manufacturers set up extensive training programs for new workers. Increasing numbers of women entered the factories, not only to do typing and clerical jobs, but to man the machines, drive the trucks and tractors, weld, rivet, and work on assembly lines. A popular song commemorated woman's new place in industry: "Rosie the Riveter."

Shop foremen soon discovered that women were better at some jobs than the men. They had more patience with dull, routine, repetitious tasks, and spoilage rates in these areas were reduced as a result. In the making of radios their fingers were better able to work in tight spots, and in aircraft factories, women could reach parts of aircraft fuselages where a man could work only with extension tools.

Industrial managers were so eager to get the services of women, once they had proved their worth, that many factories established nurseries where mothers could leave their children under supervised care while they worked at their lathes and welding machines. Former recreation areas for the workers now bristled with swings, slides, sandboxes, and other paraphernalia to exercise young muscles.

Naturally, the introduction of women into what had been an all-male world had its problems. With the feminine desire to appear well turned out on all possible occasions, many of the ladies dressed too attractively when reporting on the job. Tight sweaters not only set off a girl's figure and drew wolf whistles from the men, they sometimes caused unlucky inattention, with the result that a man might get his hand caught in a machine or lose fingers under a cutter. Wise and tactful words from the foremen usually resulted in the girls' wearing suitable work clothes that afforded protection as well as minimizing the sex appeal in the factory. Women were urged to get their hair cut short or to keep it rolled up, for more than one female employee was scalped when her hair caught in a lathe or joiner.

There were, of course, men who could not let the women alone. Naturally, most of the women knew how to handle such cases, but some Lotharios had to be warned by the foremen or even dismissed. They found curiously little sympathy from their union stewards when they complained of unfair dismissal in these circumstances. Being fired, however, was not much of a punishment, for, with factories crying for men, it was easy enough for Lupus T. Wolf, woman fondler, to get another job.

Even harder for the manager than recruiting a work force was retaining one. Scouts for rival firms were everywhere, and it sometimes happened that workers going out for lunch did not report back; they had been hired by the factory across the street. During the summer, the problem of labor piracy was rapidly getting out of hand, and contractors sometimes had difficulty in making deliveries.

In spite of these troubles, the factories hummed and turned out ever increasing amounts of material—airplanes, bullets, canteens, derricks, electrical drills, flares, gigs, hawsers, injectors, jeeps, K-rations, loading machines, manifolds, nozzles, overcoats, pumps, Quonset huts, radars, ships, tanks, uniforms, valves, windlasses, X-ray machines, yarns, zippers. The problem was to get them to the consumers, those in the cities, on the farms, in the camps, and overseas. The railroads had never worked so hard. At any hour of the night or day, long lines of cars could be seen behind puffing steam locomotives, crossing the prairies and mountains, cities and towns, bearing the wealth of America's production. Volume of freight increased thirty-three percent over the previous year, while passenger traffic was up a staggering eighty percent. Unless you knew someone who knew someone, it was practically impossible to get a Pullman berth on any long-distance train in the United States without applying several months in advance. On the chance of getting a coach seat on the transcontinental railroads, soldiers on leave, women with babies in arms, would line up hours in advance of departure time. There was never enough room for all, but under Office of Defense Transportation rules, the railroads could not add extra sections as a general practice.

Those who could get on were often leaving their loved ones behind, and passionate, tearful farewells were so common as to attract no notice. Young couples could be observed going from gate to gate in New York's Pensylvania Station, fondly embracing until the train moved out. Then they would go to where the next was scheduled and repeat the process. Quite a few trains left Pennsylvania Station every day.

Truckers carried their share of defense products, and they were the first to complain about the new nationwide thirty-five-mile-per-hour speed limit. It forced them to drive at uneconomical speeds, they complained, actually using more fuel than they would at a little higher speed. Also it threw off workdays and dispatching points. Obeying the new speed limit, a driver could not reach his normal terminal during his regular shift, so he had to be paid overtime. Truckers urged that the speed limit be upped to forty for long-distance trucking, but they received litttle encouragement and continued to urge their road monsters along at a sedate thirty-five.

As material for overseas piled up in coastal ports, the bottleneck was ships. U-boats still sank many—far too many—and the rate of building still had not caught up with the rate of sinking. As recently as 1937, there were only ten shipbuilding companies in the United States that could make ocean-going vessels of four hundred feet or more in length. By the middle of 1942, this number had risen to over sixty. Many of these yards were taken up with naval construction, but were building merchant ships as well. Prefabrication played an increasingly important part, once the Maritime Commission and War Shipping Administration agreed on simple, standardized designs for only a few types of ships. The most famous, or infamous, was the so-called Liberty Ship, of which over fourteen hundred had been ordered by mid-1942. As alike as kernels of corn, differing only in their names, these ships splashed into the water in ever increasing numbers. At the beginning of the year, the average construction time for a Liberty Ship was 241.3 days. By the middle of the year it was down to 122.5 days.

The man most famous in the shipbuilding game was Henry J. Kaiser. Before the war he had never built a ship, but in 1940, interested in the problem of emergency war shipping, he abandoned his cement company to underlings and formed the Todd-California Shipbuilding Corporation. Soon he had contracts from the British for thirty ships and completed his first, a 10,000-ton freighter, in a hundred ninety-seven days. He acquired more and more shipyards, and in June 1942 it was stated that a third of the American shipbuilding program had been awarded to him because of the rapidity with which he built ships. When the national average for completing a Liberty Ship was a hundred and fifty days, he was doing it in seventy-two. In August he built one in forty-six days, in September in twenty-nine, and in October, the *Joseph N. Teal* was launched only ten days after its keel was laid. It was delivered, complete, three days, twenty-three and a half hours later. In

November the *Robert E. Peary* was launched in four days, fifteen and a half hours. That same month, Kaiser yards delivered thirty-one, or forty-five point five percent, of all Liberties completed. Once, it is said, he had a lady visiting his office and asked if she would like to christen a ship. She said that she would, so he went to a locker and took out a bottle of champagne.

Leading the way through the noise and confusion of the shipyard, he brought his guest to an empty ways. There was nothing in it except a little bit of trash, a few puddles of water, a few Coke bottles. The lady turned to him in bewilderment. "But there's nothing there!" she exclaimed.

"Never mind," exclaimed Kaiser excitedly, examining his watch. *"Start swinging!"*

With such stories, apocryphal or true, Kaiser caught the imagination of the American public, and they were quick to spring to his defense against any criticism, fancied or real. In early September, Kaiser was accused by the Cleveland OPA of buying steel at profiteer prices to build his ships. A Government lawyer charged that Kaiser was a "scofflaw participant in illegal transactions." Most of the public felt this was pettifogging, for Kaiser was the man who got things done. Commented Columnist Raymond Clapper:

> Yes, they've got the old fellow. He was trying to build ships and doing mighty damned well at it. . . . He had to use a lot of steel. The Government would give him the contracts, but it couldn't insure him steel. . . .
>
> So old man Kaiser's people—if the Government's charge is correct—got to buying steel on the black market. . . . The OPA attorney triumphantly declared that Old Man Kaiser's outfit was now branded as a scofflaw. A scofflaw! That's just about it. Old Man Kaiser is just about as much of a criminal as all of us who used to be scofflaws drinking out of a bottle of bootleg hooch. . . .
>
> If you have to be a scofflaw to get steel out of the arsenal of bureaucracy, then that's okay with me. If that's the way Old Man Kaiser has to get his steel to build ships to carry American forces to the fighting fronts, then I hope the old man breaks every law on the books. Winning the war is more important than any regulation of any Washington bureaucrat. Give us a dozen such scofflaws around this

town and they might shorten this war and save thousands of lives. One thing is certain; they won't win this war with court orders that put our industrial Kaisers in straitjackets.

Unhappily, not all shipyards were as efficiently run as were Kaiser's. In some, mismanagement was the order of the day, and the men took full advantage of the sloppy conditions to be sloppy themselves. A reporter for the Seattle *Times* took a job in a local shipyard. He was amazed at the loafing, the lack of desire on the part of everyone to do a day's work. About ten minutes before quitting time, men would knock off and line up by the gate, waiting to rush out. Not that they had done much during their working hours, said the reporter. "Keep a wrench or something in your hand," advised a friendly welder. "Then you'll be okay."

He claimed that it was the inefficiency of management that encouraged these practices. The men wanted to work, but they had nothing to do because of poor planning. Ironically, the company had recently received the Navy "E" for efficiency.

Efficiency seemed lacking from many major-league baseball diamonds during the 1942 season, since many of the foremost players had put on another kind of uniform. As usual, the Yankees had everything their own way in the American League, ending the season nine games ahead of the Red Sox. In the National League it was quite a different story. Until September 13, the Brooklyn Dodgers had held the lead, and they seemed still a good bet to win the pennant. In August they were ten games ahead of the Cardinals. But then the St. Louis team began winning and the Bums began losing. The Cardinals won forty-three games out of their last fifty-two and on September 13 took over first place by winning a doubleheader from Brooklyn. The Bums did not give up, playing inspired ball and winning their last eight games. But it was not quite good enough, for St. Louis won twelve of their last thirteen games and ended up the winner by two full games. The Cardinals then went on to win the World Series over the highly favored Yankees, losing the first game in St. Louis, but winning the next home game and then sweeping all three of the games in Yankee Stadium. No matter which team won, servicemen had cause to cheer, for forty-nine percent of the gross receipts from the third and fourth games, an amount of

$362,926.65, went to the U.S.O., as did the entire $100,000 paid for radio rights.

FINAL STANDINGS

American League

	W	L	Percent	Games behind
New York	103	51	.669	–
Boston	93	59	.612	9
St. Louis	82	69	.543	19½
Cleveland	75	79	.487	28
Detroit	73	81	.474	30
Chicago	66	82	.446	34
Washington	62	89	.411	39½
Philadelphia	55	99	.357	48

National League

	W	L	Percent	Games behind
St. Louis	106	48	.688	–
Brooklyn	104	50	.675	2
New York	85	67	.559	18
Cincinnati	76	76	.500	29
Pittsburgh	66	81	.449	36½
Chicago	68	86	.442	38
Boston	59	89	.399	44
Philadelphia	42	109	.278	62½

World Series

Game One	*Game Two*	*Game Three*
New York 7	New York 3	St. Louis 2
St. Louis 4	St. Louis 4	New York 0

Game Four	*Game Five*
St. Louis 9	St. Louis 4
New York 6	New York 2

Joe Gordon of the Yankees was voted Most Valuable Player in the American League, and Cardinal pitcher Morton Cooper won the same honor in the National League. Ted Williams of the Red Sox had the highest batting average of either league with .356.

In spite of the excitement of the pennant race in the National Leauge, it was a sad year for baseball, for gross receipts were falling, and teams were faced with additional loss of key players in the forthcoming season. In addition, they agreed to restrict their travel schedules and to conduct their spring training closer to home. Yet baseball, with all its troubles, kept on all through the war.

As always, when the World Series rolls around, sports fans

had begun to turn to football. The college teams were hard hit by the draft, so that sixty or more colleges had given up intercollegiate football for the duration. In others, the rule to prevent freshmen from playing was relaxed in order to fill out the squads. There was an overall decline of nineteen percent in attendance at football games, in spite of the fact that training camps fielded teams composed of all-star players of the previous years. The annual Army-Navy game was played in Annapolis before twelve thousand people, instead of in Philadelphia before a hundred thousand as usual. Navy upset the heavily favored Army team, 14 to 0.

Men and women, war workers and servicemen, housewives and schoolchildren all needed to be entertained. The movies that kept coming from Hollywood continued to feature the patriotic war quickies, but there were also adventure types such as *Son of Fury, The Black Swan, Tarzan's New York Adventure,* as well as more serious fare: *The Tuttles of Tahiti,* starring Charles Laughton, *Tortilla Flat,* and *The Male Animal.* Broadway was getting ready for the new season. One of its first offerings was a farce by Howard Lindsay and Russel Crouse entitled *Strip for Action.* It dealt with a burlesque company descending on an Army camp. One of the gags featured a stripteaser trying to persuade a stuffy Army officer to let her do her act for the trooops. "Aren't the boys fighting for American womanhood?" she inquires. "Indeed they are," is the reply. "Well, then," she asks, "why can't we show them what they're fighting for?"

Popular music continued to reflect the war. In addition to "This Is the Army, Mr. Jones," "Johnny Doughboy Found a Rose in Ireland," "I Left My Heart at the Stage Door Canteen," "This Is Worth Fighting For," and "Don't Sit Under the Apple Tree with Anyone Else but Me," three war songs led all others in the hearts of servicemen and people at home: "The White Cliffs of Dover," Irving Berlin's sentimental "White Christmas," and a song inspired by a fancied remark of a chaplain at the time of the Pearl Harbor attack, "Praise the Lord and Pass the Ammunition," a song so popular that the Office of War Information asked radio stations to broadcast it no more frequently than once every four hours.

"Sleepy Lagoon," "One Dozen Roses," "Moonlight Cocktail," and the "Jersey Bounce" were examples of straight music from Tin Pan Alley. But, other than war songs, the nation hummed and skipped to a little ditty beginning, "I've got spurs that jingle, jangle, jingle . . . "

Colleges and universities faced more difficult problems than failure to field adequate football teams. The supply of male students was rapidly drying up, except for students rated 4-F by their draft boards. Increasingly, campuses echoed to marching feet, as the Army and Navy established training programs for their men there, both officer and enlisted. The Navy V-7 and the Army Specialized Training Program (ASTP) sent thousands of men through their own curricula, not those established by the trustees of the host institutions. Harvard Business School sheltered a section of the Navy Supply Corps training for reserve officers, while across the Charles, officers attended the Naval Communications School. Nearby, Army and Navy chaplains-to-be learned to minister to all faiths regardless of their own.

Criticism continued to mount of inequities in the draft law. In some districts there was a backlog of men in the unmarried under-twenty-five group. In other places married men and even fathers were hearing the summons. Pressure mounted for changes, but inequities were not at once corrected.

The pinch on civilians grew ever tighter. They were even threatened by a rider on the draft bill, a new one extending the draft minimum age from twenty to eighteen. Senator Joshua Bryan Lee of Oklahoma tacked an amendment on this much-needed bill: " . . . In the interest of the common defense it shall be unlawful within such reasonable distance of any military camp, station, fort, post, yard, base, cantonment, training or mobilization place as the Secretary of War shall determine . . . for any person, corporation, partnership, or association to sell, supply, give or have in his or its possession any alcoholic liquors, including beer, ale, or wine."

The amendment revived the old arguments between Wets and Drys dating back to Prohibition days. The Drys put on a large telegraph campaign to their Senators and Congressmen, for the actual effect of the Lee rider would have been to reimpose Prohibition on the United States. Everything was close to a military base of some kind. The Wets entered the field late, but with vigor, and since there were too many members of the United States Congress who enjoyed their own nips from time to time, and too few of the brothers' keepers, the rider dropped into oblivion. It was bad enough in the Navy, where

Josephus Daniels's General Order 99, dating from 1914, still forbade alcoholic beverages in naval ships, but at least officers and men coming in from long periods of operating at sea could still enjoy a cheering glass with buddies ashore.

Food shortages threatened, partly as a result of poor distribution over clogged railways and highways, but more importantly from loss of farm laborers to the Army and Navy. Voluntary meatless days were already in force, and it seemed that compulsory meat rationing would follow. In September it was announced that coffee rationing would begin. November 28, at the rate of one pound per person over fifteen every five weeks. This was enough to brew one cup per day per person. Immediately there appeared on the market "coffee stretchers," chickory, dried beans, and other ingenious additives to eke out the supply. The question for most people was whether it was better to have one cup of good coffee a day or more cups of vile, barely drinkable brown liquid. It was rumored that many "coffee hounds" joined the Navy for this reason; on naval ships and stations, coffee is always available, night or day. The Navy could not fight without its "Jo."

President Roosevelt had made it a habit to render one of his "Fireside Chats" to the nation on Labor Day, and on September 7 he took to the air to hurl a challenge at Congress. The danger of inflation was increasing every day, the President felt, and strong measures were needed if prices were to be kept in line. "How are we playing our part 'back home,'" asked the President, "in winning this war? The answer is that we are not doing enough."

Most of his advisers agreed that Roosevelt had the necessary powers to impose the controls, especially on farm prices, that he felt necessary. And, it being an election year, members of Congress hoped he would, so they could avoid the hard choice of voting for what needed to be done and offending voters or letting inflation get a start while, temporarily, keeping the voters happy. The curious thing is that many of the men who most loudly accused Roosevelt of acting like a dictator were the very ones who wanted him to act like one on all unpopular measures. A further irony existed in the fact that the people were ahead of Congress in their willingness to accept necessary sacrifice. Most Americans were willing to put up with any restrictions required to win the war; they only wanted the officials in Washington to take the lead. The most unpopular measure Congress could take was to show indecision, hesitation, in view of the mounting casualty lists, the growing draft calls, and the disorganized disruption of daily life. Positive leadership would be rewarded, not punished, at the polls in November.

If the vicious spiral of inflation [said the President] ever gets under way, the whole economic system will stagger. Prices and wages will go up so rapidly that the entire production program will be endangered. The cost of war, paid by taxpayers, will jump beyond all present calculations. It will mean an uncontrollable rise in prices and in wages which can result in raising the over-all cost of living as high as another twenty percent. That would mean that the purchasing power of every dollar you have in your pay envelope, or in the bank, or included in your insurance policy or your pension would be reduced to about eighty cents. . . .

Over-all stabilization of prices, salaries, wages and profits is necessary to the continued increasing production of planes and tanks and ships and guns. . . .

In the event that the Congress should fail to act, and act adequately, I shall accept the responsibility, and I will act.

. . . Today I have also advised the Congress of the importance of speeding up the passage of the tax bill. The Federal Treasury is losing millions of dollars a day because the bill has not yet been passed. Taxation is the only practical way of preventing the incomes and profits of individuals and corporations from getting too high. . . .

The Nation must have more money to run the war. People must stop spending for luxuries. Our country needs a far greater share of our incomes.

For this is a global war and it will cost this nation nearly one hundred billion dollars in 1943.

On the note of "act by October 1, or I will do it for you," Roosevelt left Congress to its dealings and deliberations and set out on a tour of the country. He wanted to see factories, shipyards, Army training camps, airfields, and naval establishments. The President was a keen observer in this kind of inspection trip and had the capability of understanding what he saw. The trip also gave him the opportunity to talk to people from every sort of life, an obvious political advantage in view of the forthcoming elections in November. While Senators and Congressmen buckled down to work on the price control measure, muttering darkly to themselves, "He really means it this time," Roosevelt was having the time of his life. Because of the obvious danger to the President during wartime journeys, the Secret Service insisted on a complete blackout on news of the Commander in Chief's movements. Although clearly seen by millions of persons during his journey, Mr. Roosevelt and his journeyings were not written up in the papers to the considerable bewilderment of the citizens. The President loved it. The press hated it. Merriman Smith, Washington reporter for the United Press, described an incident of the trip in his book *Thank You, Mr. President.*

After his daughter, Mrs. John Boettiger, had launched a ship—on the record and in full view of cameras—the President took over the meeting. There must have been twenty thousand people swarmed around a high ramp on which the President's open automobile was parked.

"You know," he said to the people over the loudspeaker system, "you know I am not supposed to be here today."

The crowd laughed and the President joined in the merriment. Damned if I saw anything to laugh about. Here was the President of the United States making an important public appearance in front of twenty thousand people, yet the newspapers and radio stations had to play like they knew nothing about it.

Although three reporters whose normal duty was to send news to thousands of outlets around the world were standing only a few feet from him, the President went on with his joke:

"You are the possessors of a secret which even the newspapers of the United States don't know," he told the shipworkers.

"I hope you will keep the secret because I am under military and naval orders, and like the ship that we have just seen go overboard, my motions and movements are supposed to be secret."

By the time Mr. Roosevelt returned to Washington on October 1, the Congress had acted, giving him the price control measure he demanded. Prices and wages were stabilized at the level of September 15, except for fruits and vegetables, which are so seasonal as to be impossible to control. Rent ceilings were extended to the entire country. Also, salaries over $5,000 per year were frozen except in the case of real promotions. Insofar as was possible, the limit of $25,000 per year was to be imposed on salaries, after payment of taxes, insurance obligations, and a vaguely defined set of "fixed obligations."

To administer this new program, Roosevelt asked his old friend James F. Byrnes to step down from his post of Associate Justice of the Supreme Court and become Director of Economic Stabilization. Byrnes's acceptance of the position relieved the President of a lot of administrative worry, but it cut into some of the functions formerly exercised by Harry Hopkins. "Shortly after Jimmy Byrnes moved in," said Hopkins, "I went to talk to him about something and he told me, 'There's just one suggestion I want to make to you, Harry, and that is to keep the hell out of my business.' He smiled very pleasantly when he said it, but by God he meant it and I'm going to keep the hell out." In view of Hopkins's character, it seems unlikely that he was able to keep this resolve.

In a few days the Congress completed its action on a new tax law for the country, most of it to be effective with the new year. But, as of November 1, Americans would be paying a new five-percent "Victory Tax" on their incomes, and several new or increased excise taxes also started on that day. The tax on liquor went up from four dollars a gallon to six, on transportation fares from five percent to ten, on telephones to twenty percent for businesses and ten percent for homes, on cameras to a whopping twenty-five percent. As of December 1, a three-percent charge on freight rates would be collected, except on coal, which was taxed at four dollars a ton. Income taxes were to take a sharp jump in the new year, and the law required quarterly payments in advance on March 15, June 15, September 15, and January 15. Corporate taxes also went up sharply, with a new excess-profits tax of ninety percent above a $5,000 exemption. A limitation was imposed that no corporation could be taxed at more than eighty percent of its net income. Individual tax rates are shown in the table on page 376.

Mr. Roosevelt was not the only well-known traveler that September. His rival for the Presidency in 1940, Mr. Wendell L. Willkie, was off on a trip around the world. In early August,

Mr. Willkie had lunched at the White House in a gathering honoring Queen Wilhelmina of the Netherlands. After the affair was over, Willkie asked for a few moments of Mr. Roosevelt's time and proposed that he make a good-will tour to Russia and China. Roosevelt approved the idea immediately and placed a four-engine Consolidated transport plane, the C-87, at Willkie's disposal for the trip. Although he was provided with his transportation, Willkie paid all his own personal expenses and was in no sense an official representative of the Government of the United States.

On August 26, his plane, christened the *Gulliver*, took off from Mitchel Field on Long Island on the first leg of its long trip. Accompanying Willkie were Joseph Barnes, once Foreign Editor of the *New York Herald Tribune*, who spoke Russian, and Gardner (Mike) Cowles, Jr., whose family owned *Look* magazine. Both were now working in the Office of War Information, and the trip with Willkie could legitimately be considered a part of their duties.

Leaving New York, the *Gulliver* flew to Puerto Rico, then down to Belem and Natal in Brazil. Thence it crossed the South Atlantic to Accra in the British Gold Coast, on to the mysterious walled city of Kano in Nigeria. Then on across the desert wastes to Khartoum in the Anglo-Egyptian Sudan, where British General Gordon had met his death at the hands of the fanatical followers of Mohammed Ahmed, self-proclaimed Mahdi, or Guide, in the Holy War against the Infidels. Thence he flew to Cairo for a visit with British Army and Navy officials, on to Lydda in Palestine. Next stop was Baghdad, then Teheran. The *Gulliver* entered Russia, stopping at Kuibishev before reaching Moscow and conferences with Stalin. Then back to Kuibishev and on across the steppes to Tashkent, entering China at Tihwa in the westernmost province of Sinkiang, to Lanchou in Mongolia, south to Chengtu and Chungking, for talks with Chiang Kai-shek. After leaving Chungking, the plane proceeded back into Russia to Chita and the capital of the Siberian Republic, Yakutsk. The next stop on the long haul was Fairbanks, Alaska, and finally back home through Edmonton, Alberta, in Canada. The journey ended at Minneapolis, and had lasted forty-nine days. Willkie lost fifteen pounds on the trip and was gray with exhaustion as he stepped down from the *Gulliver* for the last time.

As a good-will mission, Willkie's trip was an enormous success, and it demonstrated vividly a measure of Allied superiority that an unarmed plane could circumnavigate the earth in spite of the war. No Axis aircraft could hope to come close to equaling this feat; the Germans, Italians, and Japanese simply did not control enough of the world to provide the necessary fueling stops.

Willkie's journey also brought some embarrassment to Mr. Roosevelt, for after his conference with Stalin, Willkie rebuked the Allies for not having already opened a second front. Willkie had not been informed of the Allied strategic decisions already taken; he knew nothing of the forthcoming landings in North Africa, nor did his companions. Stalin, of course, already knew, having been informed by Churchill a few weeks earlier. It was utterly inconceivable to the Russian dictator that Roosevelt had not briefed his emissary, but since Mr. Willkie appeared to know nothing about North Africa, his host did not enlighten him.

Another source of embarrassment to the President was Mr. Willkie's statement made from Chungking about American failure to support China adequately. In a press conference on October, Roosevelt made slighting remarks on "typewriter strategists" and delivered a few sentences in mocking imitation of Willkie's pronunciation habits, including the well-known "Amur-r-ican people." Willkie concluded his trip, therefore, utterly furious at Mr. Roosevelt.

The President apparently regretted his tendency to mock his former opponent, for he genuinely respected Willkie, far more than he did Dewey or any other Republican of national stature. He once rebuked Hopkins for slurring remarks about Willkie, saying, "Don't ever say anything like that around here again. Don't even *think* it. You of all people ought to know that we might not have had Lend-Lease or Selective Service or a lot of other things if it hadn't been for Wendell Willkie. He was a godsend to this country when we needed him most."

Willkie responded to Roosevelt's criticism of his statements with the remark that he had been instructed by the President to do certain things. Otherwise he was on his own. "When I speak for myself," he snorted, "I am Wendell Willkie, and I say what I damned please."

In his own mind, the most important result of his journey was his concept of "One World." It had come upon him graudally, as he talked with people as he looked down on the long stretches of land through the window of his speeding airplane. On his return to the United States he set forth his vision in a book published the following spring, entitled simply *One World*.

> Freedom [he wrote] is . . . indivisible. . . . If we want to enjoy it, and fight for it, we must be prepared to extend it to everyone, whether they are rich or poor, whether they agree with us or not, no matter what their race or the color of their skin. . . . When I say that peace must be planned on a world basis, I mean quite literally that it must embrace the earth. Continents and oceans are plainly only parts of a whole, seen, as I have seen them, from the air. . . . And it is inescapable that there can be no peace for any part of the world unless the foundations of peace are made secure throughout all parts of the world. . . . When I say that in order to have peace this world must be free, I am only reporting that a great process has started which no man—certainly not Hitler—can stop. Men and women all over the world are on the march, physically, intellectually, and spiritually.

The accomplishment of Willkie's vision is not yet, and his book is largely forgotten, but the dream lives on in the hearts of men.

* * * * *

While Wendell Willkie was winging his way around the world, men were slogging their way through some of the worst terrain on the face of the earth. "If the High Command [wrote one of General MacArthur's officers] had been conducting war games and had searched for the ultimate nightmare country, Papua must have been the inevitable selection. There was something cynically malignant about the weather and the geography."

On the eastern end of New Guinea, the long Papuan peninsula forms the tail of the bird which the island resembles. On its southern coast, the harbor of Port Moresby forms an ideal natural anchorage capable of supporting the great forward base it was to become. The capture of Port Moresby had been the chief objective in the Japanese operation that led to the

Battle of the Coral Sea. It was here that General MacArthur transferred his headquarters to take command of a six-month campaign that led to some of the nastiest fighting in the entire war.

Following their defeat in the Battle of the Coral Sea, the Japanese changed their strategy to the capture of Port Moresby by an overland advance from the north coast of Papua to take their objective from the rear. In their way lay the Owen Stanley Mountains, which changed the simple hundred-mile hike into a nightmare of the labors of Sisyphus. The route chosen by Major General Tomitaro Horii led through the Kokoda Trail, used with little difficulty by the New Guinea natives, but, as it proved, impassable to the Japanese soldiers laden with guns and artillery shells and dragging field guns after them. Up to a level of about 6500 feet, the trail was bordered with jungle forest, above that, up to 13,000 feet, with a spongy moss that caused the troops to slip back two feet for every three advanced. For six long weeks they kept on, enduring incredible hardship, until on September 17 their advance elements reached Ioribaiwa, only thirty-two miles by train from Port Moresby. Here they stopped, blocked where they were by Australian troops under the command of Lieutenant General Sir Thomas Blamey. A little over a week later, the Australians began to roll the Japanese thrust back.

Another simultaneous Japanese attempt had been to land forces by sea in Milne Bay, a split in the tail of Papua. This was repulsed by air attack and by Australians who were fighting mad after they had discovered bodies of some of their comrades tied to trees and bayonetted to death. The troops were further infuriated by a sign tacked above the head of an occasional body: "It took him a long time to die."

As on Guadalcanal, Australian troops learned to let the Japanese charge into their fixed defenses rather than blunder through the jungle looking for them. Unable to penetrate the stubborn Australian defense, the Japanese evacuated Milne Bay in September, leaving some seven hundred dead out of two thousand on the island. During the evacuation the Japanese shot many of their own wounded rather than take them aboard the transports.

The two drives stopped, MacArthur began his own advance against the Japanese positions. The objectives were the tiny villages of Buna, Gona, and Sanananda, of no value to the

Allies in themselves, but vital because they commanded the Dobodura Plain, which could be developed into a major air base.

This six-month Papuan campaign, largely forgotten, took five divisions of men and a great deal of toil to accomplish. Yet there was little in the way of formal battles, either naval or land. The Air Force under Major General George C. Kenney did yeoman service in bringing supplies and in attacking Japanese strong-points in the dense growth. Heavy casualties were suffered by both sides, but the Australians and Americans had the advantage of native assistance in evacuating the wounded. A history of good treatment of the "fuzzy-wuzzys" paid off, and many an Allied soldier of the machine age owed his life to black stretcher-bearers who lived in the Stone Age.

Gona fell to the Australians on December 9, Buna to the Americans on January 2, 1943, and Sanananda to the Australians on January 18. Four days later, organized opposition ended in Papua.

The dearly won victories in Papua and on Guadalcanal set the Allied forces clearly on the road to Japan. MacArthur's South West Pacific Forces would continue up the coast of New Guinea, while Halsey's South Pacific command would begin a ten-month-long drive up the Solomons chain. Both drives were aimed at Rabaul and to the breaking of the Japanese bastions in the Bismarck Archipelago. This "Little Dual Drive" was the first real Allied offensive.* It took nearly all the next year to accomplish its objectives.

* * * * *

Sergeant Ivan Khvastantsev peered through his field glasses. "How many do you see?" he called to his observer.

"Five or six, all close together."

* The "Big Dual Drive" was begun in November 1943. While MacArthur continued his vital strategy of leapfrog landings along New Guinea and the islands near New Guinea, forces under Nimitz began a push through the Central Pacific. American landings at Tarawa and Makin in November 1943 were the first steps in this new campaign. Central Pacific forces moved from the Gilberts to the Marshalls, the Marianas, the Carolines. The two drives merged with the landings on Leyte, in October 1944. Rabaul was bypassed.

"Right. Keep out of sight," instructed the Sergeant.

With fourteen men, Sergeant Khvastantsev was guarding a road leading to Stalingrad, where German armored forces were advancing. His instructions: Destroy as many enemy tanks as you can. Don't retreat until you run out of ammunition.

The German tanks drew closer, raising large clouds of dust.

"The leader is only three hundred yards off," called the observer.

Closer and closer they came. Then—

"Fire!" shouted Khvastantsev.

American-made Lend-Lease bazookas spewed their rockets, and three tanks were knocked out, never to fight again. The other two came on, guns blazing, heading straight for Khvastantsev and his men. The Russian squad held fire until their leader spoke again. Then the other two tanks were blazing wrecks.

The Panzer Korps stopped. Its way was blocked by the wrecks of their own tanks. Khvastantsev's men were holding up an entire corps.

Another five tanks attacked. Four of them were knocked out, and the fifth scurried for shelter. Then eight tried it. Before they were driven off, leaving four smashed to bits, six of the Russians were dead and another three so seriously injured they could do nothing further. The next attack killed three more men and put a bazooka out of action. Khvastantsev was wounded, but fired the remaining bazooka by himself. Then his arm was hit, and he could no longer shoot.

Realizing the opposition was broken, the Germans came on. Khvastantsev pulled out a grenade, got the pin out with his teeth, and ran toward the Germans. Deliberately throwing himself under a tank, he released the firing lever. The explosion blew him to bits, but in his death he claimed yet one more German tank. Not a man of the detachment survived the German onslaught, but his radio operator managed to get off the story of his leader's sacrifice before he was finished off.

This little episode, which held the Germans up for only a couple of hours, was typical of the Russian defense of their country and especially of the city of Stalingrad. In that city the German Sixth Army would find its grave, and on the stubborn rock of Stalingraders' stubborn resistance foundered Hitler's hopes of a victory in Russia.

Stalingrad lies about five hundred seventy-five air miles

southeast of Moscow. It is a very strange city, lying along the west bank of the Volga River, extending some thirty-five miles along the river, but only about two and a half miles to the west. This ribbon-like city had not extended across the river to the east, since the Volga is at that point about half a mile wide. Seven ravines divide the bluff on which the city is located, separating it into districts. In the center was the famous Dzerzhinsky Tractor Factory, which had produced seventy thousand tractors a year and was now turning out tanks for the Red Army.

Such then was the bastion of Stalingrad. Its half million inhabitants were proud of its industry, the Tractor Factory and the hundred and twenty-five other factories, its three technical colleges, its schools, hospitals, theaters, and museums. All this would be destroyed, but Stalingrad would not yield.

Hitler's drive into Russia during the summer of 1942 suffered from shortages of all sorts. In contrast to the 1941 campaign, it was beset by indecision as well. The original drive had been for the Caucasus, but in July, Hitler's military genius intervened, and he sent the Eleventh Army from Sevastopol all the way to the other end of the front to help out in the siege of Leningrad! The drive in the south, into the Caucasus, stalled for lack of supplies and because Hitler scattered his forces here and there across south-central Russia. The Sixth Army before Stalingrad was held up for ten days because it had no gasoline. He pulled the Fourth Panzer Army away from Stalingrad and then ordered part of it back. This transfer stalled the drive that was progressing into the Caucasus, and as the advance continued, the Russian resistance stiffened. In late August the German momentum, such as it was, died, and for some reason Hitler failed to use the Black Sea as a supply route, even though the Russian naval forces there had been largely eliminated by Luftwaffe attacks.

At this time, the German drive from the south, from the Kerch Strait, began to get moving. Novorossiisk fell on September 6, but Hitler, growing ever more impatient with his generals, who, according to him, had a "complete incapacity for grasping essentials," relieved Halder, his Army Chief of Staff, and also List, commander of Army Group A, who commanded the entire Caucasus operation. To replace List, Hitler chose—himself.

Hitler was now head of the German State, Commander in Chief of the Armed Forces, Commander in Chief of the Army, and, by this latest move, commander of Army Group A.

Pooh-Bah would have been jealous.

The battle for the Caucasus promptly became a stalemate. When the capture of Stalingrad would have been comparatively easy, Hitler moved strength away. Now, when its capture was to prove impossible, Hitler became obsessed with the city. It had to be captured.

Bit by bit the Russians fell back before the Sixth Army; bit by bit the Germans advanced. The Luftwaffe flew thousands of sorties and dropped thousands of bombs on the city. But it still held. Laying waste as they advanced, the Germans drew ever closer to the city. Its defenders never gave up hope and never quit in their efforts to stop the Germans.

Everyone turned out to help dig an antitank ditch in front of the city. Schoolchildren and grandparents, men and boys, girls and women dug as though their lives depended on it, as they did. When one tired, another grabbed the pick or shovel and worked in his place. The main ditch they built was fifteen feet wide, twelve feet deep, and twenty-five *miles* long. This meant the moving of approximately twenty-four million cubic feet of earth and stone, all with hand tools. And the work was done in two weeks.

Hundreds of other lesser defenses were built. The streets, some of them like those of Moscow, fair and wide, were barricaded, with trenches, pits, and tank traps set up to stop the enemy. These barriers were manned by General Chuikov's understrength Sixty-Second Army and by the fighting spirit of the men and women of Stalingrad. To their backs was the Volga River. It formed both a barrier and an escape route. Women and children were sent to the other side, traveling on decrepit ferries under attack from the Luftwaffe. Russian naval gunboats afforded what protection they could and brought supplies to the men of the Sixty-Second. For them, the regulars wearing the uniform of the Red Army, and the volunteers wearing merely an armband, there was no escape. They could stop the Germans before they reached the river or throw themselves into it.

Each building of the city became a battlefield. Each step forward the Sixth Army made cost them more and seemed to win less. At first the defense was street by street; then it was block by block; then house by house. In the basements and in the sewers, the Russians lay low and then struck the German invaders from behind. It was a war of no quarter and of little hope—on either side.

By November 1, the Russians had fallen back into four pockets in the city, each isolated from the others. But even then, the defenders would not yield. For there was hope. A Russians counteroffensive was coming. Stalingrad would yet be saved.

At a British airfield in the south of England, the control tower operators began giving landing instructions. One by one, twelve American B-17s, the four-engine bomber called the Flying Fortress, bumped down and rolled along the runway, turning off finally onto a hardstand near the hangars. Ambulances, their motors running, waited nearby. Personnel cars came up to the planes as the ten-man crews got out, grinning and slapping each other on the back. These planes had just returned from the first all-American raid on enemy targets in the European theater. This raid was the beginning of the operational life of the Eighth Air Force.

The attack had been a small one, against railroad marshaling yards in Rouen, France. Twelve planes had attacked, and twelve planes had returned. Some of the bombs had even hit the target. And the raid had been made in broad daylight. It was an auspicious beginning.

The British had been carrying on the air war against Germany for three years, but they were cooperative and helpful to their new companions in the air. The Royal Air Force, divided into three sections, had borne the brunt; now they had help.

As everyone knows, the Royal Air Force Fighter Command had won the Battle of Britain in 1940. It's primary job was defense of the British Isles, but it could and did help out the other two commands by providing fighter escort as needed. Coastal Command had as its job the support of the Royal Navy, hunting down German U-boats and protecting merchant shipping, providing long-range over-water reconnaissance, and occasionally delivering attacks on German naval ships. The third major unit of the Royal Air Force, Bomber Command, was the only one available for offensive air action against the continent of Europe.

Early raids in 1940 and 1941 by Bomber Command were

puny in comparison to what was to come, and the losses were heavy. In 1940, Bomber Command dropped only 16,000 tons of bombs, less than the average of a single month three years later. In 1941 the tonnage tripled, but did little real damage to German industry. Part of the reason for this relative ineffectiveness was that losses in 1940 caused the British to adopt the idea of night bombing to make it more difficult for German defenses to oppose them. Concurrent with night bombing was the idea of area bombardment, by which the bombardiers would attempt to smother an area with explosives rather than aim for a specific point. This practice inevitably took more bombs than the American idea of precision bombing, and it caused many more casualties among civilians who had the ill fortune to live near RAF targets.

In February 1942, Air Marshal Arthur T. Harris took over as head of Bomber Command and began to reap some of the fruits of the Allied building programs. Despite having to divert aircraft to the Mediterranean and having to take on naval tasks to assist Coastal Command, he managed to increase the effectiveness of the bombing raids on German installations. His best weapon was the British-built Lancaster, a four-engine bomber, that could carry a heavier bombload than any other plane used in Europe throughout the war. American-built Flying Fortresses, B-17s, and Liberators, B-24s, also began to make their appearance, and on the night of May 30/31, Harris staged a thousand-plane raid on Cologne. In ninety minutes, 1400 tons of bombs were dropped, doing more damage than all air raids to date had done. Only thirty-six aircraft were lost. Allied morale soared, and the attack made headlines throughout Britain, America, and all the free world. The success of the raid paved the way for the enormous expansion of the air offensive against Germany. "My own opinion," said Harris, "is that we should never have had a real bomber offensive if it had not been for the thousand-bomber attack on Cologne, an irrefutable demonstration of the power of what was to all intents and purposes a new and untried weapon."

The success of the Cologne raid was repeated two nights later at Essen, and after a pause of a month, Bremen had its turn. Strategic bombing had proved itself.

Roosevelt's eagerness to have American men in the fight against Germany as soon as possible led to the early establishment of the Eighth Air Force, the American equivalent of Bomber Command. For months the Eighth Air Force was little more than an administrative staff and a hope. The British set aside airfields for staging areas and for training, and in May and June the first important contingents of American aircraft began to arrive by ship. Soon ferry pilots were flying Liberators and Flying Fortresses across the Atlantic, as the British and Canadians had been doing for some time. The route was from Presque Isle, Maine, to Goose Bay, Labrador, then to Bluie West 1 (Narsarssuak, Greenland) or Bluie West 8 (Sandre Stromfjord, Greenland), on to Reykjavik, Iceland, and then to Prestwick, Scotland. Later Ferry Command found it possible to fit planes to make it from Gander, Newfoundland, to Prestwick nonstop.

On May 8, Lieutenant General Carl Spaatz was appointed commander, Eighth Air Force, and soon afterward given the additional responsibilities of theater air commander.

The first mission flown by the Eighth Air Force took place for symbolic reasons on Independence Day, July 4, 1942. It was a short mission, in which six American crews flying in borrowed British aircraft, and accompanied by a like number of British, made a daylight raid against airfields in Holland.

Bomber Command and the Eighth Air Force were soon at loggerheads over the question of day or night bombing. The argument went to the highest command levels, with some British officers arguing that the Americans should be content with furnishing the planes and allowing the British with their wider experience to conduct the raids, at night, of course. The Americans, with the then-secret Norden bombsight, placed great reliance on daylight precision bombing. It was an act of faith, for this method of attack had never been tried in war. "Unless [wrote Eisenhower] accurate daylight bombing was feasible, I believed, large-scale invasion of the Continent would be exceedingly risky. Therefore, I maintained that even if we could carry on precision bombing only to the extreme range of our fighters, we must continue to develop the United States forces on that basis, so as to have available the great force that would be needed to carry out the preparatory work in the areas selected for invasion."

Since neither side would yield, the result was that both methods were used. By day the Eighth Air Force sent its missions to the Continent, and at night RAF Bomber Command carried out its part of the round-the-clock offensive. This was the pattern followed throughout the rest of the war, once the Combined Chiefs of Staff approved a strategic plan and established target priorities during the Casablanca Conference in January 1943. For the Eighth Air Force, the year 1942 was a year of getting ready. It flew only fifty missions that year, only five over Germany itself, and dropped only 2000 tons of bombs. In 1943 a single raid would carry many times this weight of bombs.

* * * * *

U.S.S. *Seadragon* was on patrol deep in the South Pacific. Seaman First Class Dean Rector was spending his nineteenth birthday deep inside enemy-held positions. It was not a happy occasion for him. It was not fear of the enemy. His stomach hurt.

The next day, Rector's stomach ache was no better. It was much worse. During the morning he collapsed on the deck. Pharmacist's Mate First Class Wheeler B. Lipes took a look at him and then with a grave face sought out the captain.

"It's appendicitis," he said. "It may be peritonitis. He'll have to be operated on at once."

The nearest Allied doctor was over a thousand miles away in Australia, and it would take many days to get there. In Lipes's opinion Rector would be dead before they could possibly reach the nearest friendly port with medical facilities. The *Seadragon*'s skipper, Lieutenant Commander W. E. Ferrall, accepted his judgment.

"Can you do it?" he asked Lipes.

"Yes, sir," replied the Pharmacist's Mate. "It's his only chance."

Lipes had assisted at one or two appendectomies, but now he was on his own. He hastened to sickbay to check into his equipment. Since the Bureau of Medicine and Surgery had never contemplated major abdominal surgery on a submarine, Lipes found his medical kit was sadly wanting in necessities. There was but one scalpel, and it had no handle. Hemostats for clamping blood vessels there were in plenty, but there were no retractors to hold the incision open. There was no ether cone. There was only a limited supply of ether.

With typical ingenuity, the submarine's crew set to work to remedy the deficiencies. A tea strainer with a gauze pad would

387

serve as an ether cone. A Machinist's Mate contrived a handle for the scalpel. Electricians rigged a big floodlight over the mess table in the wardroom, which would be the operating theater. The galley furnished Monel metal spoons that were bent into a U shape to perform a second tour of duty as retractors. Alcohol from one of the torpedoes was pressed into service as an antiseptic.

Finally everything was as ready as it ever would be. Captain Ferrall ordered the *Seadragon* submerged and held steady at a depth of a hundred and fifty feet. Lipes assembled his operating team—the Captain, three other officers, and himself—in the tiny wardroom. Rector was carried in and laid carefully on the table.

Lipes roused him gently and said, "Look, Dean, I never did anything like this before. You don't have much chance to pull through, anyhow. What do you say?"

"I know just how it is, Doc," whispered Rector.

Wearing reversed pajama coats tied behind them, the team got ready. The officer acting as anesthetist, on Lipe's signal, placed the tea strainer over Rector's mouth and nose and began to drip the ether onto the gauze.

"They're putting him under now!" Word was passed by word of mouth from one end of the submarine to the other.

Lipes gently painted Rector's abdomen with alcohol. Smoothing his rubber gloves, Lipes placed his little finger on Rector's umbilicus and his thumb on the point of the right hipbone. His index finger touched the swollen abdomen. This marked his point of incision. With a bold stroke, Lipes cut through skin and fat. There followed a brisk time with hemostats. Deeper and deeper Lipes went, Captain Ferral keeping a count of instruments and sponges as they went into the wound.

"Hold her steady," someone muttered to the man on the bow planes. "They've just opened him up."

Once the peritoneum was cut, Lipes began to probe with his gloved fingers in Rector's abdomen for the diseased appendix. It took him twenty minutes to find it.

The patient began to stir on the table.

"Give him more ether."

There wasn't much left, but Rector got more. He subsided. Now the appendix was out, and Lipes began the long process of closing. Suture after suture went in; sponge after

388

sponge, retractor after retractor, hemostat after hemostat came out. Captain Ferrall pointed to his check-off list. One retractor was missing. Lipes's fingers went back inside and emerged with the last of the bent spoons.

The end was in sight. Applying the final sutures, Lipes began bandaging. Just as he completed his task, the last can of ether went dry. But it was not needed any more. Thirty minutes later, Rector opened his eyes.

"I'm still in there pitching," he said.

In less than two weeks, Rector was back on watch, fully recovered.

* * * * *

On the other side of the world, Allied officers were hard at work in London, driven by the inexorable clock to tremendous efforts. Time. There was never enough of it, for the end of the possible weather to carry out the North Africa landings was fast approaching.

General Eisenhower's biggest task was to unite the men working for him into a team. It was not easy, for Briton had to work with American, Army with Navy, Navy with Air Force, Air Force with Army, and all with each other. In his headquarters in Norfolk House in St. James's Square, men had to work together if the invasion was to come off. "In the early days," wrote Eisenhower, "officers of the two nationalities were apt to conduct their business in the attitude of a bulldog meeting a tomcat, but as time went on their own discoveries of mutual respect and friendship developed a team that in its unity of purpose, devotion to duty, and absence of friction could not have been excelled if all its members had come from the same nation and the same service."

Some American officers tended to be arrogant in dealing with their British counterparts, taking the attitude that they had come to help old, blundering Britain out of a hole. The British, going into their third year of war, felt that perhaps they had learned a few lessons and naturally resented the American attitude. On the other hand, some British officers had contempt for American inexperience and refused to deal in even a civil manner with the "upstart Yanks." Officers of either service who held these attitudes did not last long with Eisenhower. On one occasion, an American in a heated argument referred to his adversary as a "British son of a bitch." When Eisenhower learned of the incident, he could find nothing to choose between the positions taken by the two officers, but he ordered the American relieved and sent home. The British officer pleaded for the American's forgiveness. "We've all learned, sir," he said to Eisenhower, "that the phrase he used is an American colloquialism which should not be taken too seriously."

"Yes," agreed Eisenhower, "but he called you a *British* son of a bitch! For that he goes home."

As deputy commander for Torch, Major General Mark Wayne Clark, USA, had mixed feelings about his assignment. He had recently been appointed to command of the II Corps based in England and hated to give up a combat command. The thought of long hours of desk work was not to his liking, but he pitched in with a will and made himself indispensable, particularly in the early weeks when he was serving as Chief of Staff as well as Deputy Commander. Although he could not know it at the time, this "desk job" would bring Clark one of the strangest adventures that ever befell a military officer.

In addition to finding the troops, supplies, and ships for transport, Eisenhower's staff had to deal with more delicate problems, amid considerable uncertainty. In the first place, the directive of the Combined Chiefs of Staff set a target date of October 1942 for Torch. Even later in the war, when experience had speeded up planning methods, three months from order to execution would have been considered too fast. Although this date could not be met, the pressure of time never let up for the staff officers. Secondly, the directive had only specified that the landing take place in Northwest Africa to assist in eliminating Rommel's forces in Libya and Egypt. Exact locations of targets had to be selected by the planners and approved by both governments. Because of their political significance and their harbor facilities, Oran and Algiers in French Morocco were essential. A third attack was possible and much time was devoted to whether it should be Bône, east of Algiers, or Casablanca, outside the Mediterranean but at the end of a rickety rail line leading to Rabat, Fez, and on to Algiers and Tunis. The British were generally in favor of the operations against Bône, since it would afford the quickest victory in Tunisia and would also bring fastest relief to the Eighth

Army in Egypt. Most Americans, however, distrusted the Bône landing as too exposed and insisted on at least one operation outside the Mediterranean. Their reasons were simple; if Franco, the Spanish dictator, should enter the war on the Axis side, the base at Gibraltar would become untenable. Hostile Spanish forces on both sides of the Strait would prevent Allied movement in or out of the Mediterranean, and the landing forces inside would be trapped.

As it happened, Franco was too cautious to enter the war, so the situation did not arise. However, Cassablanca rather than Bône was chosen as the third landing area, despite obvious hazards from the surf and its distance from the key areas of Tunisia and Libya in central North Africa. To the disappointment of President Roosevelt, who nevertheless accepted it without a murmur, the date selected for the landing was Sunday, November 8, 1942. It would have been of vast assistance to the Democratic Party to have the operation take place before election day, November 3, but Roosevelt was first of all the President of the United States, and he did not allow such a consideration any weight in the strategic planning.

For Torch to have any chance of success, it required cooperation, or at least the lack of active opposition, from the French military forces at Oran, Algiers, and Casablanca. Because the British had antagonized large segments of the French by their attacks at Oran, Dakar, and Syria in the wake of the French surrender in 1940, both Churchill and Roosevelt agreed the operation would have as American a character as possible. Americans would have the primary responsibility at Casablanca and Oran, and American troops would form the landing parties. There simply were not enough Americans ready to take on Algiers, as well, so this objective had to be largely a British operation. At one time there was considerable thought given to putting the British soldiers allocated to Algiers in American uniforms, but nothing came of that scheme.

While the British had broken diplomatic relations with France at the time of the French surrender, the United States had recognized the Vichy Government of Unoccupied France and had sent Admiral William D. Leahy there as ambassador. His reports had been invaluable during the period before the United States entered the war and for a few months afterwards. But by April 1942, Leahy felt his usefulness there was ended, and he returned to Washington, leaving the embassy in the hands of a *chargé d'affaires*. On his arrival in Washington, Leahy was appointed Roosevelt's personal representative on the Joint Chiefs of Staff and became in effect the chairman.

By the terms of the French surrender, the northern and western parts of France were occupied by the Germans, while a section in the southern part, roughly two-fifths of the country, was left under French control, its government headed by the aging Premier Pétain. Pétain was strongly influenced by his principal subordinates, Pierre Laval and Admiral Jean François Darlan. Soon after the surrender, Laval had attempted to organize Vichy France as a dictatorship and to throw its weight behind Germany. He was an active Axis sympathizer, a sincere believer in the totalitarian form of government. In this case, he went too far and was replaced as the number two man in the government by Admiral Darlan. In assuming these new duties, Darlan continued to hold his post as Commander in Chief of the French armed forces. At the time of the French surrender he was already head of the French Navy.

Darlan was an opportunist who believed that it was essential that France be on the winning side in the war. During the long months of 1940 and 1941, this seemed to be Germany, and the accounts of his collaboration with the Nazis are well documented. He appears to have had doubts of the ultimate German victory after the United States entered the war, for his zeal toward the German cause begins to slacken during 1942. In April he was replaced as Deputy Premier by the ubiquitous Laval, an event which led to Leahy's return to the United States.

These men, the figurehead Marshal Pétain, the would-be Nazi Laval, and the slippery Darlan, constituted the principal personalities of the legally constituted French Government. But in the eyes of the public on both sides of the Atlantic, the French nation was represented by the Free French under the leadership of the baffling, enigmatic, proud, irritating, demanding Charles de Gaulle.

The Americans and British landing in North Africa would not be going into enemy-held territory. They would be landing in areas owned by a nation legally neutral in the conflict, one which still had tenuous diplomatic ties with the United States.

There were no Germans in any of the three target areas. Unless the Allied troops could appear to come as liberators, it would be a clear case of naked aggression.

The Allies had to deal with some French official who could appear as a liberator, could welcome the Allied troops, and not impede their operations. Who? Pétain? Impossible. Pétain was too much dominated by Laval. Some advisers stated he was pro-Nazi himself. Laval? Obviously imposssible. Darlan? Perhaps, if he could be won over. He had made guarded overtures to an American State Department representative in North Africa, Mr. Robert Murphy. On learning of these, Churchill said, "If I could meet Darlan, much as I hate him, I would cheerfully crawl on my hands and knees for a mile if by doing so I could get him to bring that fleet of his into the circle of Allied forces."

That left de Gaulle. The Free French leader would, without question, have embraced the undertaking eagerly. It was just what he was looking for. The fact that he was, in the event, left out hurt him bitterly and caused him to have an undying enmity toward both Roosevelt and Churchill. His dislike of Churchill was tinged with respect, but he never got over his distaste for the American president.

A more fundamental reason than dislike kept de Gaulle from participation in the North African landings. De Gaulle had left France during her final hours of resistance and had proclaimed that the Vichy Government had no legal authority. The only true government of France, he said, was the Free French establishment in exile. If de Gaulle was right in this, then all French soldiers and sailors who remained at their posts and accepted orders from Vichy were either traitors or poltroons—a concept no Frenchman could accept. His participation in the ill-conceived, ill-starred expedition against Dakar in September 1940 brought him further discredit in the regular French military forces. Therefore, if de Gaulle were to be a part of the North African operation, there would be no way to deal with the Vichy French officers actually in charge of the defenses at Casablanca, Oran, and Algiers. If bloody fighting between the Americans and British on the one hand and the French on the other was to be avoided, these officials had to be persuaded to submit or at best offer only token resistance.

A year earlier the job of winning cooperation from French officials in North Africa would have been comparatively simple, for then General Maxime Weygand was head of all military forces in North Africa. He was, in spite of his role in bringing about the French surrender in 1940, strongly anti-German and would have welcomed any liberators, just so that they came in sufficient strength. But he had been relieved at the insistence of the Germans in 1941, and his command had been divided in four. Thus the chance of peaceful French cooperation was much lessened.

While these deliberations were progressing in Eisenhower's headquarters. Mr. Robert Murphy appeared in London. He had recently been in Washington, where President Roosevelt had briefed him on the Torch objectives and had directed him to report to Eisenhower to place his intimate knowledge of the French North African scene at Ike's disposal.

For security reasons, Marshall directed Murphy to proceed to London in an Army bomber under the ficticious name of Lieutenant Colonel MacGowan and to wear a lieutenant colonel's uniform. "Nobody ever pays any attention to a lieutenant colonel," observed Marshall. When Murphy landed at Prestwick, he was astonished to hear someone say, "Why, Bob! What are you doing here?" Before the pseudo-colonel could reply, the friend was hustled off to confinement, whence he did not emerge until after the landing.

Murphy briefed Eisenhower's staff on political, social, and economic conditions in Africa, later expressing amazement at how little military officers knew of political and diplomatic affairs. He was later to show that his ignorance of military affairs was even more abysmal.

The man, Murphy said, needed to lead the French was General Henri Honoré Giraud, a man who had escaped from a German prisoner-of-war camp by his own efforts and so owed nothing to the Germans. Also, he had not taken the personal oath of loyalty to Marshal Pétain demanded of all officers on active duty; therefore he was a free agent as far as Vichy was concerned. He was the man, and it was on him that the Allies pinned their hopes.

On Sunday, October 18, General Clark was summoned to Eisenhower's office at 20 Grosvenor Square. A cable from Murphy seemed to promise a golden opportunity. Murphy had been in close touch with General Charles-Emmanuel Mast, French commander in Algiers, and had arranged a secret meeting between Mast and some high officer to discuss plans for a possible Allied operation in French North Africa. Mast demanded that the American delegation should travel by submarine to a point west of Algiers on the night of October 21/22.

As Deputy Commander, Clark was the ideal one to go. He knew all details intimately, but in case anything happened to him, the operation would not be imperiled by loss of a key Commander.* Clark took with him four officers, including Brigadier General Lyman L. Lemnitzer [later Chairman of the Joint Chiefs of Staff] and Captain Jerauld Wright of the Navy [later Commander in Chief NATO Naval Forces.]

The party arranged to travel to the rendezvous by plane and submarine. The "cloak-and-dagger boys," as they called themselves, left from Polebrook airfield in southern England in two B-17s, Lemnitzer in one and Clark in the other, so that if one were lost, the other could carry on. Before takeoff, General Clark replaced his stars with the silver leaves of a lieutenant colonel—it seems everyone was getting into the lieutenant colonel act—and sought to conceal his lanky frame and the angular face that had caused Churchill to nickname him "the Eagle."

Clark confessed that the flight down was filled with vexatious thoughts—fear of being late at the rendezvous, fear of a trap or a trick. The plane, the *Red Gremlin*, piloted by Major Paul W. Tibbets, Jr., the man who later as colonel dropped the atomic bomb on Hiroshima, droned on.

Spitfires from Gibraltar roared up to meet the planes, and then came the problem of getting safely down. No plane as large as a B-17 had ever landed at Gibraltar airstrip. Fortunately all went well, and both planes pulled up and the passengers prepared to disembark. The British stopped them, explaining that the Spanish always watched activity on the airstrip and might recognize them. Clark and the others had to wait until a closed, curtained car pulled up to the aircraft to take them to the Governor's house.

After spending the night with Governor Mason MacFarlane, Clark's party embarked the next morning in the British Submarine P-219 (H.M.S. *Seraph*). "I had never been aboard a submarine before," wrote Clark. "I soon realized that

---

* He had been relieved of additional duties as Chief of Staff by Brigadier General Walter Bedell Smith.

395

they were not made for a six-foot-two man. All the time I was in the P-219 I had to bend over and watch my head. The officers' quarters, which the submarine crew had hospitably given up their passengers, was only a cubbyhole alongside the middle catwalk. When I went to the 'head' I had literally to crawl on all fours."

The submarine failed to reach the rendezvous in time for the October 21 meeting, and there was considerable doubt on whether General Mast had received word to be ready the following night.

Nerves grew tense as the evening of October 22 wore on. From the conning tower of the *Seraph* binoculars swept the shore, and a little after midnight it appeared—a white light in a house near Cherchell, some fifty miles west of Algiers.

The party went ashore in small collapsible boats called falbots, Clark weighted down by a money belt containing over two thousand dollars in gold. The trip to the beach went without incident, and when they stepped ashore, Murphy was waiting for them. He led them to a typical French colonial villa owned by a M. Tessier, who was risking his life in the common cause.

General Mast was waiting. He welcomed Clark's party and asked how he could be of use. The chief difficulty in the meeting was to keep Mast from guessing that the North African operation had passed anything but preliminary planning stages. Certainly Mast did not expect any action for several months. Actually, the landing was only seventeen days off.

These discussions consumed the morning, and General Mast had to leave at lunchtime to attend to his duties in Algiers, but members of his staff remained to give a full briefing on the defenses of Algiers.

Meanwhile the wind was rising, and Clark wanted to reembark his party that night and get the precious information back to London. He was brooding over the problem when the phone rang.

M. Tessier answered and shouted that the police were coming. The servants, curious at being turned out of the house, had informed the police that the house had been vacated and they suspected smugglers were making use of it. They were tempted by the rewards offered for the recovery of smuggled goods. They had no inkling of the real purpose of their dismissal from the house.

But Clark and his party had no way of knowing this, and it would have made no difference if they had. Whether they were to be considered as smugglers or as American agents, they could not afford to be caught. The Frenchmen melted into the horizon, while M. Tessier put the Americans in the wine cellar. As Clark and the others waited in the pitch black of the wine cellar, Murphy and Tessier entertained the police, explaining that they were having a party, that there were women upstairs, and surely the French police would not want to embarrass them.

"Mais, non! Pas de tout, monsieur!"

Nonetheless, the police were suspicious and did not leave for half an hour.

By this time, Tessier was frantic to be rid of his guests. But the surf prevented all attempts to embark in the boats. Clark tried it, stripping down to his underwear for the attempt. The boat capsized, and Clark's trousers containing the gold went to the bottom. The loss bothered him not at all at the time, but it caused him considerable ribbing later.

About dusk the police returned, but the Americans had evacuated the house. They hid out on the beach as hour after hour passed. Finally, about 0400 they tried again to launch the boats, and this time they were successful. Everyone was soaked, and their precious papers were wet, but they reached the *Seraph* at last.

As they headed back, they were met by a seaplane that took them from the confining spaces of the submarine and swiftly delivered them to Gibraltar. From there Clark sent Eisenhower an "Eyes Only" message, summarizing the events of the trip. In part it said: "Anticipate that the bulk of the French Army and Air Forces will offer little resistance whether Giraud assumes leadership in North Africa or not. . . . Also promised to furnish submarine to bring Giraud from France to North Africa. French insist this submarine must be American. Initial resistance by French Navy and coast defenses indicated by naval information, which also indicates that this resistance will fall off rapidly as our forces land."

Clark went on to describe how the conference was interrupted by the police visit. "While the Frenchmen flew in all directions, our party hid in empty repeat empty wine cellar. . . ."

Ike kept his counsel on the main parts of the message, but

the bit about the "empty repeat empty wine cellar" was too good to keep. Clark never heard the end of it.

Arriving safely back in London, Clark kept himself busy for the next few days. Among other things, the promised submarine had to be sent to bring Giraud away from France. The French had specified that the submarine be American, but this was an impossible condition, for no American submarine was within a thousand miles. After much discussion they decided to send the faithful *Seraph* on the mission, but to appear to comply with the conditions, they sent Captain Wright, scarcely recovered from the Cherchell trip, to act as commanding officer of the *Seraph*. Since Wright was not a submarine officer, Lieutenant Jewell remained in actual command, but went along with the game when Giraud came aboard. To add the finishing touches, the British crew dressed in American uniforms. It is perhaps fortunate that Giraud's English was less than perfect. Otherwise he could hardly have missed the accents of Bow Bells in the voices of the crew.*

The trip went off without incident, and Giraud was safely landed at Gibraltar, where he met Eisenhower, Clark, and the staff who had flown from England. At the first meeting, Giraud rocked them to their foundations.

"General Giraud has arrived," he said. "General Giraud is ready to assume command of the operation."

Eisenhower could scarcely believe his ears. Yet Giraud was deadly serious. The honor of France, he declared, demanded nothing less. The day before the troops were to land, a general who knew nothing of the plans, not a man of whose nationality was in the assault force, was ready to assume overall command.

It was magnificent. It was Quixotic.

It was impossible.

---

* The story of H.M.S. *Seraph* is amusingly told in *The Ship with Two Captains,* by Jerauld Wright, New York, 1960.
The *Seraph* was involved in yet another secret mission, for she was the submarine that deposited the body of the mythical "Major Martin" in the waters off Spain. A briefcase attached to the body contained papers calculated to deceive the Germans about the forthcoming landing in Sicily in 1943. It was one of the great counter-intelligence feats of the war. See Montagu Ewan, *The Man Who Never Was,* London, 1955.

CHAPTER FOURTEEN

"The End of the Beginning": El Alamein-Stalingrad

> Now entertain conjecture of a time
> When creeping murmur and the poring dark
> Fills the wide vessel of the universe.
> From camp to camp, through the foul womb of night,
> The hum of either army stilly sounds,
> That the fix'd sentinels almost receive
> The secret whispers of each other's watch.
> Fire answers fire, and through their paly flames.
> Each battle sees the other's umber'd face.
> Shakespeare, Henry V

The new broom that swept into Egypt in August was embodied in the new commander of the British Eighth Army, General Bernard L. Montgomery. Nothing had been done right before; now all would be well.

No commander in the Second World War did so much to create a personal image as Monty. Even the publicity section of General MacArthur pales in comparison with that of the new Eighth Army commander. He deliberately set about dramatizing himself, partly as a counter to the almost magical awe Rommel inspired among soldiers on both sides. But Monty genuinely loved the trappings of fame. He was determined to become the best-known British general, and he succeeded.

He was not a commanding figure, to look at him. When he talked with Auchinleck, his eyes were about at the level of the other's battle ribbons. His thin, waspish face, with its pointed nose, carried nothing of the empire-building Englishman. Almost puritanical in his outlook—he neither drank any form of alcoholic beverage nor did he smoke, and had lurking distrust of those who did—Montgomery came to Egypt determined that nothing would stand in the way of his establishing himself as a latter-day Napoleon and Clausewitz rolled into one. The Prime Minister played right into Monty's hands by fostering the legend that before the change all had been muddle and blunder in the Middle East, in order to justify Auchinleck's

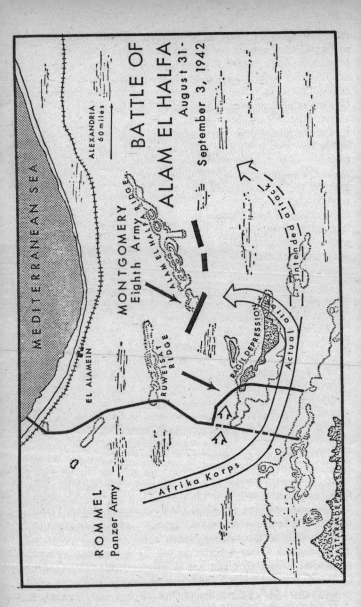

relief. Montgomery could do no wrong in Churchill's eyes, just so he produced something of a positive nature. He bluntly informed the importunate Prime Minister that he could mount no offensive before the end of October! One of the primary considerations in relieving Auchinleck was that he refused to take the road to the west before the middle of September.

But Montgomery got the ear of Mr. Churchill when the Prime Minister was in Egypt after the Moscow meeting with Stalin. Few men could charm the British war leader, but in this case Mr. Churchill desperately wanted assurance that he had made the right move. Montgomery gave up his own sleeping quarters to Churchill, plied him with brandy and cigars, and served wine in the mess; normally he would not allow it anywhere near him. He told him in detail how he expected to win the forthcoming battle when Rommel attacked in a few weeks. Never mind that it was the same plan the Auk had set forth. It was now Monty's, just as the Eighth Army was now Monty's.

Drawn up as it was near the town of El Alamein, the Eighth Army was in the strongest defensive position to be found in Egypt, with its right flank on the Mediterranean Sea and its left on the Qattara Depression. To find another spot as strong, you would have to travel fifteen hundred miles to the west to the Mareth position in Tunisia. Rommel would reach there in February of 1943. But now, at the end of August, the Desert Fox was making his final bid to realize his dream—to dine, as Napoleon had done, in the shadows of the pyramids.

About midnight on August 30, Rommel tried the maneuver that had served him so well in the past, a hook through the weak southern end of the British line, led by his panzers, while the rest of his force made diversionary attacks in the north. But this was not the Rommel of old; he was a sick man, so ill that his physician and Chief of Staff sent a message to the German High Command: "Field Marshal Rommel suffering from chronic stomach and intestinal catarrh, nasal diphtheria and considerable circulation trouble. He is not in a fit condition to command the forthcoming offensive." OKW [*Oberkommando der Wehrmacht*, Hitler's high command headquarters] refused to appoint anyone else, and just before the battle opened, the doctor was able to report: [Rommel's] "condition so far improved that he can command the battle under constant medical attention. Nevertheless, essential to have a replacement on the spot."

But Rommel was not worried about his health. His real worry was over fuel for his tanks, trucks, and motorized guns. It was essential, he had reported, that they have 6000 tons on hand. It had not arrived, even though General Cavallero, his Italian nominal superior, had told him, "You can start your battle, Field Marshal. The fuel is already on the way."

It was still not there when Rommel jumped off on the night of August 30. He had 1800 tons of the precious gasoline, and Kesselring, commanding the Luftwaffe in the Mediterranean, promised to fly in 500 tons a day.

Rommel hoped to drive his panzers as far as Gabala by dawn, but the British defensive minefield proved unexpectedly difficult to cross, and the high rate of fuel consumption during penetration caused Rommel to turn north before he was ready. By dawn he had not cleared the minefield, and he considered calling off the attack, but decided to try for a shorter gain than he had first planned.

RAF planes began buzzing around his position like hornets, taking a heavy toll of his tanks. As he advanced toward the Alam el Halfa Ridge, he ran into Montgomery's concentrated armor, well dug in and well supplied with ammunition. Monty refused to "loose" his tanks into pursuit, where they might be outmaneuvered and trapped. Instead, he had built a fort with them, and this fort laid down a withering fire. "The nonstop attacks [wrote Rommel] of the British bomber formations continued the whole day through. The British artillery was also very active and fired vast quantities of ammunition—about ten shells were answering every one of ours."

For three days—three days of slaughter—the Afrika Korps tried to break through. It was no use. Tank after tank was smashed. Sometimes a hatch would open and the crew would leap out, their clothes blazing. They would jump down, run a few paces, screaming horribly, then collapse in the sand, writhe a little, then lie still forever.

At length Rommel decided to call it off. He retired to safer ground. During the retreat, Montgomery had a beautiful opportunity to cut across his rear, but he refused to stir. He was not ready, and he would wait. Rommel wondered why he had escaped so lightly. "The impression," he wrote, "we gained of the new British commander, General Montgomery, was that of a very cautious man, who was not prepared to take any sort of risk."

Once the Battle of Alam el Halfa was out of the way, Montgomery set about retraining his soldiers. Previously, many units had to go into the front lines without adequate preparations for desert fighting, a necessity of the rapid course of the desert war. Now, with the date for his own offensive over six weeks away, Montgomery could devote time to this urgent need. And in this, he was entirely right, particularly in view of the kind of battle he planned. He was not going to try to beat Rommel at his own game. The reputation for dash and élan Monty gained in the desert is one of the great myths of the war. The battle Montgomery planned was more reminiscent of the hard-slugging trench warfare of World War I than it was of the war of movement that had prevailed in the desert up to then.

Montgomery proposed to surprise Rommel by placing his main drive in the north rather than the south. Every attack on both sides thus far had been a sweep around the south, followed by a swing to the north and the sea, to pin enemy troops in a pocket. As Montgomery saw it, the coast road offered him the best chance of a quick advance, once he had broken through Rommel's lines.

In order to deceive the Germans, Montgomery had allowed Rommel's troops to keep part of the gains they had won at Alam el Halfa so that they might have an uninterrupted view of the southern flank of the Eighth Army. In this region he built elaborate dummy supply dumps, pipelines, and pumping stations, all constructed of empty gasoline cans, bits and pieces of broken equipment, guarded by dummy figures dressed in cast-off items of uniform.

The ruse was a good one, and it deserved to work. But Rommel anticipated the form and direction of the British attack. The nature of the terrain made a breakthrough imperative, and all that the German commander could do was to wait to see where it came and mount a counterattack to stop its impetus. In preparation for the battle he could only try to make his position as strong as possible. The Italians held the central and southern parts of the line, while he massed his panzer divisions in reserve in the rear. The German infantry held the northern positions.

To protect his lines, Rommel ordered an extensive minefield

403

laid from the Qattara Depression to the sea. Over half a million mines were used in this operation, from light antipersonnel to antitank mines. The field was about forty miles long, and in places it was five miles across.

Montgomery knew perfectly well that the Germans would depend heavily on mine defenses, and much of the training of his troops was given over to their clearance. It was a ticklish job, but it never lacked for volunteers. It could never be done perfectly; the remarkable thing was that it could be done at all.

As always, Rommel was desperately short of supplies of all kinds for the battle. Many of the mines were constructed from captured British artillery shells. Especially he lacked gasoline. There was little hope for improvement, for aircraft based on Malta and British submarines in the Mediterranean were taking too heavy a toll of Axis shipping. "The longer things went on," noted Rommel, "the more obvious it became that, despite all the efforts of the Army, the supply situation could no longer be improved. It was now too late."

On September 2, leaving his deputy, General Stumme, to prepare for the battle, a very ill Rommel flew back to Germany to enter a hospital for treatment. He was allowed a month of this badly needed rest before the storm broke.

Montgomery planned his battle in three phases. He intended to reverse the usual pattern and attack with his infantry, the armor moving behind in support, instead of the other way around. The first phase he called "the break-in," as his forces penetrated the minefields. Then would follow "the dogfight," in which his infantry, supported by his tanks, engaged the main forces of the enemy through the hole that had been punched in the German defense. These two phases together he expected to take a week at least. The last phase was "the break-out" in which he hoped to develop operations "so as to destroy Rommel's forces." This last phase was never quite successful, as the wily Rommel refused to allow himself to be pinned for extinction but led his opposite number a merry chase across the desert for fifteen hundred miles and then on to Tunis to link up with reinforcements there.

Montgomery's preparations continued. He had to break his troops in on the new Sherman tanks, recently arrived as a result of Roosevelt's impulsive gesture on the fall of Tobruk in June.* The tanks had gone in one ship, and the engines in

* See p. 231.

another. The latter vessel had been sunk, but replacements were quickly sent, and by October Montgomery had them, the only real answer to the German Mark IV Specials, mounting 75-mm. guns.

Before the battle broke, Montgomery had become a familiar figure to almost everyone. He had long since discarded the "brass hat" customarily worn by British generals in favor of an Australian slouch hat with every bit of unit insignia he could pin on its side. He soon exchanged the Australian model for a black beret similarly bedecked. He adopted these odd bits of headgear to make himself better known to the men. They were also, he said, very comfortable. He went from unit to unit, encouraging, correcting, admonishing, but, most of all, allowing the troops to see him. He wanted everyone to be familiar with the general plan of the battle, explaining it himself to unit commanders, down to the level of lieutenant colonel. On a regular schedule these officers passed the word down, until two days before the battle, it had, in simplified form, reached the privates in the ranks. At that moment, all leave was canceled. The brothels and bars of Cairo and Alexandria were only memories now for the men of the Eighth Army. They would not be back.

Friday, October 23, was a day like any other in the desert. That night there would be a full moon, and General Stumme's staff noted that it would be a good time for Montgomery to make his advance. But nothing happened during the day. Montgomery held a press conference that morning, spent the afternoon at his headquarters, and after dinner read a book and turned in early. Rommel was in a hospital at Semmerling, south of Vienna. General Stumme was at his headquarters, chatting with his officers. In their bivouacks, men on both sides lay waiting—and wondering. A group of German riflemen struck up the haunting melody of "Lili Marlene," the favorite song of the Afrika Korps. A few Tommies clustered around a radio listening to "The White Cliffs of Dover" on the B.B.C.

The minutes ticked by, and men of the Eighth Army and of the Desert Air Force glanced often at their watches. Soon men were moving quietly to their guns and to the planes. The bombers were ready to take off at the given moment, ready to drop their flares to light the way for the infantry, ready to drop their bombs on gun emplacements and troop masses, to

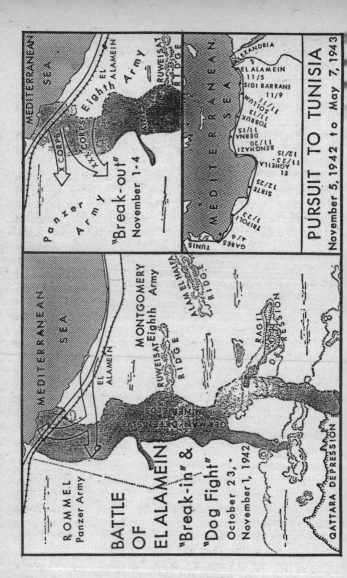

BATTLE OF EL ALAMEIN
"Break-in" & "Dog Fight"
October 23, - November 1, 1942

MEDITERRANEAN SEA

EL ALAMEIN

ROMMEL Panzer Army

MONTGOMERY Eighth Army

RUWEISAT RIDGE

ALAM EL HALFA RIDGE

GERMAN DEFENSIVE

XXX CORPS

RAGIL DEPRESSION

QATTARA DEPRESSION

"Break-out" November 1-4

MEDITERRANEAN SEA

EL ALAMEIN

Eighth Army

X CORPS

XXXX

Panzer Army

RUWEISAT RIDGE

PURSUIT TO TUNISIA
November 5, 1942 to May 7, 1943

MEDITERRANEAN SEA

ALEXANDRIA
EL ALAMEIN 11/5
SIDI BARRANI 11/9
SOLLUM 11/11
TOBRUK 11/13
DERNA 11/15
BENGHAZI 11/20
EL AGHEILA 11/23
SIRTE 12/25
TRIPOLI 1/23
GABES 4/6
TUNIS

406

darken the night for the Germans with smoke clouds.

General Stumme released a radio report to Hitler's OKW headquarters:

"Enemy situation unchanged."

At 2140 the peaceful desert night was shattered as never before in the war. Nearly a thousand British guns crashed out in response to Monty's order to fire as one battery. In a German division headquarters the concussion knocked a bottle off the table. "Monty's offensive has started," said General Lungershausen.

The bombardment that had just begun would be the most massive seen by a British army since 1918. Only the action on the Russian front exceeded it. The guns were to fire continuously for five and a half hours, except for brief, staggered pauses to cool off. Part of the fire was directed against Rommel's troops, but more at the minefields, which the Germans called "the Devil's Gardens."

At 2200 the guns shifted their targets toward the rear of the German positions, and the infantry began a cautious advance through the Devil's Gardens. Specially trained teams of mine-disposal experts led the way, cautiously feeling the ground ahead of them with mine detectors. As they advanced, they left trails of white tape to mark the cleared lanes. On either side of each unit's path of advance, tracers from 40-mm. guns kept the men to their assigned paths. In the Fifty-First British Division, attacking in the center of the thrust, kilted pipers skirled their weird, stirring music, bringing memories of the Highlands to the "Jocks." The insistent drone of "The Road to the Isles" led some to wonder whether that was, indeed, their road, for the "Isles" in the song are the celestial isles of the blessed.

The attacking force at El Alamein was truly an Empire force. From north to south of the line were the Ninth Australian Division, the Fifty-First British Division, the First South African Division, and the Fourth Indian Division. These made up General Leese's Thirtieth Corps. Behind him as a *force de chasse* was General Lumsden's Tenth Armored Corps, including the British First and Tenth Armored Divisions. Extending the line to the south, from Ruweisat Ridge on, was a Greek brigade, the British Fiftieth Division, the British Forty-Fourth Division, and a Free French brigade. In reserve was the British Seventh Armored Division. All these units south of Ruweisat Ridge comprised General Horrocks's Thirteenth Corps.

When dawn arrived on October 24, the infantry had advanced some distance in the north, at one point reaching two and a half miles, but the armor had not made the advances Montgomery had hoped for. Then followed the "dogfight" phase—a week of bitter fighting—the object to destroy Rommel's infantry. It was a cruel time, with no quarter, no escape for the committed troops.

In the German headquarters, General Stumme felt that his duty demanded he go toward the front to see for himself, just as Rommel had been wont to do. Accordingly he set off with his driver and his intelligence officer, Colonel Büchting. He drove toward the hottest part of the action. British machine guns opened up on him, and Colonel Büchting was shot through the head. Stumme, who had jumped out onto the road, managed to get a grip on the car as the driver tried to pull out of the line of fire. Apparently he fell dead of a heart attack, and the driver never noticed his absence. It was not for several days that the Germans learned his fate. In the meantime, General Ritter von Thoma assumed command.

From Hitler's headquarters came the inquiry: Was the action merely a reconnaissance in force, or a full-scale attack? The Operations Officer, General Westphal, replied: "Undoubtedly the long-expected full-scale offensive. Rommel's return essential."

In his hospital room that afternoon, Rommel received a telephone call from Field Marshal Keitel, the head of OKW. Keitel told him that the attack had begun and Stumme was missing, and inquired whether Rommel was well enough to return to Africa to take over the command. Rommel agreed, but was told to wait a few hours to see whether his return was absolutely necessary. Hitler himself called twice, ordering him back with much regret. "I took off next morning. I knew there were no more laurels to be earned in Africa, for I had been told in the reports I had received from my officers that supplies had fallen short of my minimum demands. But just how bad the supply situation really was I had yet to learn."

Just about dusk on October 25, after a stop in Rome, Rommel reached his headquarters. General von Thoma reported to him on the situation. Stumme had felt obliged to decline to reply with artillery to the British bombardment because of the shortage of artillery shells. Thus, in Rommel's opinion, the British had been able to advance farther than they should.

Even though he was exhausted from the trip, Rommel got only a few hours of sleep that night, so busy was he in trying to respond to the British attacks. On awakening early the next morning he learned that in some places the British had fired five hundred rounds of ammunition for every one the Germans could send back.

Given Montgomery's material resources and his own shortages, there was little Rommel could do to retrieve the battle. His only hope was to make it as expensive as possible for the British, in order to weaken future operations against him. In overall strength, Montgomery was at least twice as powerful as his adversary. The British started the battle with about eleven hundred tanks; Rommel had five hundred fifty-eight. Rommel had to husband his, but even so, his losses were enormous. British tank losses were even greater, but there were more in reserve, and more where those came from. Rommel received only a pitiful handful during the course of the action.*

On October 29, Montgomery revised his battle plan. His original idea had been to break out with the Australians along the coast road to the north, but the German 164th Light Infantry was holding too well, so he shifted the axis to the Kid-

* Here are shown the shattering losses of German and Italian tanks during the battle. The numbers are the tanks remaining fit for use. Repairs account for the increases on October 29 and 30.

October 24	558
October 25	445
October 26	404
October 27	368
October 28	299
October 29	320
October 30	338
October 31	325
November 1	319
November 2	187
November 3	144
November 4	12

ney Hill area, a little to the south, opposite the Fifty-First British, the New Zealanders, and the South Africans. He had further learned that the German Ninetieth Infantry Division had moved in to back up the defenders of the coast road and hoped it would be easier going in the new area.

The Aussies, however, were able to cut around the German 164th and reach the sea, only to find that most of their quarry had escaped entrapment.

The new drive in the Kidney Hill region worked well at first, and Montgomery hoped for a swift advance. The New Zealanders made a strong penetration, but on the morning of November 3 ran into one of Rommel's skillfully placed tank traps and suffered seventy-five percent casualties. Yet Rommel knew the end was approaching, for his supplies were nearly exhausted. In the German-held sectors of the line there were only thirty-five tanks in operating condition. He was ready to acknowledge defeat and thought only of getting his Army out and back to a position where he could regroup and resupply. That position was fifteen hundred miles away.

In spite of military necessity, Rommel feared he would not be allowed to do what had to be done. "It is sometimes [he wrote] a misfortune to enjoy a certain military reputation. One knows one's own limits, but other people expect miracles and set down a defeat to deliberate cussedness. . . . The Army's strength was so exhausted after its ten days of battle that it was not now capable of offering an effective opposition to the enemy's break-through attempt, which we expected to come next day."

The War Diary for the OKW for November 3 contains the following entry: "On the evening of November 2, General Field Marshal Rommel reported by telegraph that the German-Italian Panzer Army can no longer hold its present position because of the heavy attacks of the vastly superior British Eighth Army. He intends therefore to withdraw the Italian infantry divisions during the coming night and send them back to the Fuka position. The fastest divisions will cover this retreat and then also withdraw to Fuka."

Hitler, however, on reading this report, reacted as might be expected. In his view, no foot of ground should ever be yielded. Rommel was thinking of saving his Army. Hitler was thinking of positions on a map.

The retreat had already begun on November 3. Rommel entered headquarters, and Westphal handed him a telegram.

"An order from the Führer," he said bluntly.

Rommel looked at him, but Westphal kept silent. The Field Marshal dropped his eyes to the message. "It is with trusting confidence in your leadership and the courage of the German-Italian troops under your command that the German people and I are following the heroic struggle in Egypt. In the situation in which you find yourself there can be no other thought but to stand fast, yield not a yard of ground and throw every gun and every man into the battle. . . . Your enemy, despite his superiority, must also be at the end of his strength. It would not be the first time in history that a strong will has triumphed over the bigger battalions. As to your troops, you can show them no other road than that to victory or death. Adolph Hitler."

Rommel had already suspected that he might receive such an order, and had already dispatched an aide, Captain Ingmar Berndt, to talk to Hitler directly. But in the face of a direct order, and unless Berndt succeeded in changing the Führer's mind, he had no choice but to obey. He ordered the retreat stopped.

The Führer's order cost many lives, for Montgomery's caution in following up his breakthrough had given Rommel time to have extricated his entire force back to the Fuka position, some sixty miles to the west. But the opportunity had to be thrown away. Filled with despair, General von Thoma, head of the Afrika Corps, left headquarters to seek his death in battle. While death was not hard to find at El Alamein, it eluded him. He was taken prisoner by the British.

By November 4, it was clear that Hitler's order could not be reasonably carried out, and at 1530 Rommel ordered the retreat resumed. A few hours later another telegram arrived from Hitler. It gave Rommel a free hand to act as he thought best. Berndt's mission had been successful.

By now it was a case of retreating to the west in as good order as possible. For three months the pursuit went on, Montgomery never being able to pin Rommel's forces to the sea. Fuka was only a starting point. On November 11, British forces crossed the border into Libya; two days later Tobruk fell. Then Derna, Benghazi, and Agedabia. At El Agheila, the starting point for every German drive into Egypt, Rommel paused briefly. He hoped to hold there, but on December 13,

Montgomery turned his flank and forced him back to Sirte, which the British captured on Christmas Day.

The rate of advance grew slower as Montgomery got farther and farther from his supplies, but it continued inexorably. Tripoli fell on January 23, and in early February, Rommel joined with the Tunisian army under von Arnim sent to oppose the Anglo-American operations from the west.

The victory at El Alamein and the rapid pursuit of Rommel made Montgomery's name known the world over. He became known as a daring commander with glamor that endeared him to newspaper men. But what does Rommel say about the man who defeated him? It is instructive. "The principles of British command had on the whole not altered; method and rigid adherence to system were still the main feature of their tactics. . . . They actually undertook no operations [i.e., maneuvering] but relied simply and solely on the effect of their artillery and air force. Their command was as slow as ever in reacting. . . . Their command continued to show its customary caution and lack of resolute decision."

* * * * *

While Montgomery pursued the beaten Axis forces across the Libyan desert, another German army was reaching its limits. On November 12, elements of the Sixth Army under General von Paulus reached a few points on the banks of the Volga River inside Stalingrad. They got no farther. On the same day, German intelligence gloomily predicted that a massive Russian offensive in the Stalingrad area could be expected at any time.

And coming it was. The heroic stand of the defenders of Stalingrad had inspired the people from o e e d of the country to the other. They knew by now that the invaders of their motherland had to be driven out, that no other solution existed—there was no living with the Germans, for the Germans would not allow them to live. At first, not a few of the Russians had welcomed the German forces as liberators from Bolshevism. But not for long. Hitler's policy was: We are the masters; the Slavs are to work for us; insofar as we don't need them, they may die.

The S.S. followed behind the troops and put Hitler's ideas to work. *Einsatzgruppen* [Special Action Groups] were established to dispose of those—especially the Jews—for whom the Reich had no use. A scene that took place on October 5, 1942, at Dubno in the Ukraine was described by a German construction contractor at the Nuremberg tribunal:

My foreman and I went directly to the pits. I heard rifle shots in quick succession from behind one of the earth mounds. The people who had got off the trucks—men, women and children of all ages—had to undress upon the order of an S.S. man, who carried a riding or dog whip. They had to put down their clothes in fixed places, sorted according to shoes, top clothing and underclothing. I saw a heap of shoes of about 800 to 1,000 pairs, great piles of underlinen and clothing.

Without screaming or weeping these people undressed, stood around in family groups, kissed each other, said farewells and waited for a sign from another S.S. man, who stood near the pit, also with a whip in his hand. During the fifteen minutes that I stood near the pit I heard no complaint or plea for mercy. . . .

An old woman with snow-white hair was holding a one-year-old child in her arms and singing to it and tickling it. The child was cooing with delight. The parents were looking on with tears in their eyes. The father was holding the hand of a boy about 10 years old and speaking to him softly; the boy was fighting his tears. The father pointed to the sky, stroked his head and seemed to explain something to him.

At this moment the S.S. man at the pit shouted something to his comrade. The latter counted off about twenty persons and instructed them to go behind the earth mound. . . . I well remember a girl, slim and with black hair, who, as she passed close to me, pointed to herself and said: "Twenty-three years old."

I walked around the mound and found myself confronted by a tremendous grave. People were closely wedged together and lying on top of each other so that only their heads were visible. Nearly all had blood running over their shoulders, from their heads. Some of the people were still moving. Some were lifting their arms and turning their heads to show that they were still alive. The pit was already two-thirds full. I estimated that it contained about a thousand people. I looked for the man who did the shooting. He was

413

an S.S. man, who sat at the edge of the narrow end of the pit, his feet dangling into the pit. He had a tommy gun on his knees and was smoking a cigarette.

The people, completely naked, went down some steps and clambered over the heads of the people lying there to the place to which the S.S. man directed them. They lay down in front of the dead or wounded people; some caressed those who were still alive and spoke to them in a low voice. Then I heard a series of shots. I looked into the pit and saw that the bodies were twitching or the heads lying already motionless on top of the bodies that lay beneath them. Blood was running from their necks.

The next batch was approaching already. They went down into the pit, lined themselves up against the previous victims and were shot.

I saw about thirty naked people lying near the pit. Some of them were still alive. . . . Later the Jews still alive were ordered to throw the corpses into the pit. Then they themselves had to lie down in this to be shot in the neck. . . . I swear before God that this is the absolute truth.

Non-Jewish Russians received the same treatment, or worse. But it is pointless to recount further horrors. Let it suffice that they happened, and let them account for the merciless actions that took place when the Russian drive toward Berlin began on November 19, 1942.

By November the Soviets had assembled five "Fronts" in the Ukraine-Trans-Caucasus area.* From the north they were:

* The Russians used the term "Front" the way most nations use the term "Army Group." For those unfamiliar with military terminology, the following table is offered.

Unit	Composition	Commander
Squad	8–12 men	Sergeant
Platoon	2 or more squads	Lieutenant
Company	2 or more platoons	Captain
Battalion	2 or more companies	Lieutenant Colonel
Regiment	2 or more battalions	Colonel
Brigade	2 or more regiments	Brigadier General
Division	2 or more brigades	Major General
Corps	2 or more divisions	Lieutenant General
Army	2 or more corps	General
Army Group	2 or more armies	General or Field Marshal

The Voronezh Front, the Southwest Front, the Don Front, the Stalingrad Front, and the Trans-Caucasus Front. Three German Army Groups opposed this force: Army Group B opposite the Voronezh and Southwest Fronts, Army Group Don [established November 26] opposite the Don and Stalingrad Fronts, and Army Group A opposite the southern part of the Stalingrad Front and the Trans-Caucasus Front. The Germans were heavily outnumbered, and had their supply problems as well.

Hitler's OKW staff should have foreseen and provided for the coming Russian offensive. The only thing they could have done was to plan a strategic retreat, falling back to a much shorter defensive line, which they could hope to hold during the winter. But this solution found no favor with the Führer. He believed he had saved the German forces from disaster the previous winter by his "stand and die" order. Besides, a strategic retreat would have meant giving up Stalingrad. By this time Stalingrad had taken on a symbolic meaning for Hitler, and he would as soon have thought of abandoning Paris. "If we give it up now, we'll have to take it all over again," he kept repeating.

The direction of the Russian attack quickly became evident. The Don Front under General Rokossovski crossed the Don River and pushed south toward Kalach, while the Stalingrad Front under Yeremenko drove northeast toward the same objective. By November 23, their troops had met, and the German Sixth Army under General von Paulus was trapped in and around Stalingrad. It was the most expertly planned and executed Russian operation thus far during the war.

On November 22, just before the trap closed, General Paulus requested permission to evacuate Stalingrad and fight his way out. There was no chance that Hitler would agree; he had said before and he would say again that Stalingrad was German; it could not be yielded. Reichsmarshal Herman Goering, head of the Luftwaffe, head of Germany's economic structure, airily promised to supply the beleaguered Sixth Army by airlift. So far as can be determined, he made no effort to check on the capacity of the Luftwaffe to carry out this assignment, and he seems to have done little to implement his promise. But, as ever, he captivated Hitler, who took the word for the deed, the promise for the action, and the fate of the Sixth Army became certain. The *minimum* requirements of the Sixth Army were 550 tons of supplies a day. A load of 300 tons was flown in on December 5. That was the all-time high; the average was closer to a hundred tons.

On November 20, Hitler appointed Field Marshal Erich von Manstein to command the newly formed Army Group Don. Its mission was to relieve Stalingrad. Manstein was one of the most brilliant officers on the German side. His had been the conception for the Ardennes penetration in 1940 that had trapped the British and French at Dunkirk. He had won the siege of Sevastopol and was, in the fall of 1942, in command of the operations against Leningrad. Now the miracle man was expected to perform once again, to accomplish the impossible at Stalingrad.

It was not until November 26 that Manstein was able to take over Army Group Don. As he saw it, there was no hope for "fortress Stalingrad." At any cost, the Sixth Army had to break out of the trap, or it would cease to exist.

Technically the Sixth Army was under his command, but in view of the Führer's order to fight to the last man, to hold the city in spite of everything, Manstein had no real control over General Paulus. Hitler had seen to that, for he had assigned Paulus a General Staff liason officer, who was in reality the Führer's spy. This man had his own communications section for direct reports to Hitler. If Paulus had ever shown signs of independence, Hitler would have known within the hour, and the Sixth Army would have had a new commander.

Manstein's problem was to relieve the Sixth Army without endangering the whole German southern wing. Army Group A was perilously exposed in the Caucasus. A Russian thrust toward Rostov could have trapped three or four armies, and Manstein could not do a thing about it so long as Stalingrad came first in Hitler's mind. Fortunately for the Germans, the Russian drive, when it came, was not directed at Rostov, but was a massive assault all along the front held by Army Group A.

As Army Group A fell back in good order. Manstein on December 12 sent the Fourth Panzer Army to the northeast to try to link up with the Sixth Army pushing south from Stalingrad. Hitler had given permission for Paulus to try to meet Manstein's forces, but he insisted that the Sixth Army simultaneously hold in the north and west without retreat. This idiotic order naturally meant that Paulus's attempt would be too weak. Manstein's and Paulus's drives stalled some thirty miles apart. On his own responsibility, Manstein then ordered Paulus to try to break out, using all his forces, and letting Stalingrad go. Paulus, however, equivocated, pointing to Hitler's orders, and while he hesitated, the chance was lost forever.

At that moment, disaster threatened once again in the southeast. The Russian drive was pressing hard on Army Group A in the Caucasus region and threatened Manstein's position. Unless Kleist, the Field Marshal commanding Army Group A, could extricate his forces, two army groups would be trapped in a new and vastly greater Stalingrad. On December 28, Hitler, in one of his few sound decisions where the Russian front was concerned, gave permission for Army Group A to withdraw.

At this point, and at this point only, Stalingrad became meaningful to the Germans. As long as it could hold out, it tied down the Russian forces needed to cut off Army Group A. And hold out Paulus did, in spite of all reason, in spite of lack of support, lack of supplies, lack of hope.

Manstein, meanwhile, fighting against vastly superior forces, held Rostov as a route of escape for Kleist's Army Group A. In the Voronezh region to the north, the Soviets were pushing the Germans hard. On January 14, Hitler transferred Kleist's First Panzer Army to Manstein, and it made its way into Rostov. The Seventeenth Army, all that remained of Army Group A, took up a defensive position around Novorossiisk, with one flank on the Sea of Azov and the other on the Black Sea, a position they were able to hold for some months. In early February, Manstein abandoned the Rostov position to form a new defense line.

In the Stalingrad area, where the Russians in the city still held out, the entrapped Germans were approaching the end of their tether. On January 9, the Russians sent officers under a flag of truce to demand the surrender of the Sixth Army. On Hitler's orders, Paulus refused. Probably the offer was made, not for humanitarian reasons, but to release Russian troops to turn against the German forces endangered in the Caucasus. Paulus and his men continued to fight on.

It was hopeless.

On January 24, the front broke into three small pockets.

417

About the same time, Hitler promoted Paulus to Field Marshal. "No German Field Marshal has ever surrendered," he said.

On January 31, the new Field Marshal and his staff surrendered.

On February 1, the rest of the Sixth Army survivors gave in.

Approximately ninety-one thousand members of the Sixth Army entered Russian captivity. Thirty thousand wounded had been evacuated by air. The rest, a hundred and fifty thousand, had been killed or were missing.

Most of the ninety-one thousand captives wished they had joined their comrades in death. In unheated boxcars they crossed the frozen Russian steppes to prison camps in Siberia. They died, and they were killed. Only five thousand ever saw the Fatherland again.

Hitler was outraged when he learned of Paulus's surrender. He should, Hitler stormed, have committed suicide. "What cowardice to be afraid of that! Ha! Better be buried alive! And in a situation where he knows well enough that his death would set the example for behavior in the pocket next door. . . . When one's nerves break down there is nothing to do but say 'I can't go on' and shoot oneself. In fact you could say that the man ought to shoot himself. Just as in the old days commanders who saw that all was lost used to fall on their swords. That goes without saying. Even Varus told his slave: 'Now kill me!' . . . There will be no more field marshals in this war. . . . One had to assume that there would be a heroic ending."

The final irony came much later. With the name Stalingrad a symbol of Russian resistance and of Russian victory, the Soviet Government, as a part of its campaign to discredit their wartime leader, renamed it Volgograd. But its old name still is heard, even in Russia today, and its story remains a proud page in Russian history.

CHAPTER FIFTEEN

The Torch Over Africa

We carry within us the wonders we seek without us:
There is all Africa and her prodigies in us.
                    Thomas Browne, Religio Medici

The time was 0130 aboard U.S.S. *Augusta*. Major General George S. Patton, Jr., rolled out of his bunk and made his way to the flag bridge. He was boiling mad, for no less a person than the Commander in Chief, the President of the United States, had compromised the secrecy of his venture. Patton was leading American forces scheduled to go ashore in French Morocco, near Casablanca. There was no chance of surprise now.

The moment had arrived. At Oran and Algiers, British and American troops were swarming onto the beaches, protected by the guns of ships of the Royal Navy. November 8, 1942, had arrived. But, in the words of Caesar's soothsayer, not gone.

As the troops landed, due at Oran and Algiers at 0130, the B.B.C. broadcast recordings of Roosevelt's well-known voice, but in an unfamiliar tongue . . . *"Mes amis . . . mes amis. . . "* The American President called upon all loyal Frenchmen in North Africa to rally to the Allied cause.

But the landings scheduled for the Casablanca area would not take place for another hour and a half, according to the plan, and two and a half hours in actuality. If the French were going to fight, they would have a hundred and fifty minutes to make their preparations.

"O, do but think you stand upon the rivage and behold a city on the inconstant billows dancing; for so appears this fleet majestical." From England and from the United States, ships from two continents had crossed the trackless ocean to land upon a third. Never before had such an enterprise been dreamed of; never before had such an enterprise been undertaken. Operation Torch represented the absolute limit of resources that Britain and the United States could throw into

the battle without abandoning all support to Alexander and Montgomery, Nimitz and MacArthur.

Nearly four hundred and fifty ships took part in these assaults, from battleships to fleet tugs. Many more would be needed to supply the men once landed. Was this vast armada to come bearing ministers of peace or angry lords of war? No one knew.

From the earliest conception of the plan of invading French North Africa, both President Roosevelt and Prime Minister Churchill had desired above all else to avoid fighting with the French. In theory, the Allied troops would be coming as liberators from the Nazi yoke. Yet the Nazis did not occupy Algeria and French Morocco. French officials ran the civil government; French officers manned the guns and ships defending the coasts and harbors. All these men were accountable to the fictionally sovereign Vichy Government of Unoccupied France, and all had sworn personal oaths of fealty to the aging Marshal Pétain, who, in a way incomprehensible to the Anglo-Saxon mind, symbolized France.

When the Allies landed in North Africa, they would not be in the position of occupying a conquered country—at least that was the hope. But if the French did not rally to the Allied cause—what then?

It had been in an effort to avoid such problems that General Clark and Mr. Robert Murphy had met with General Mast at Cherchell. The same reason had brought General Giraud to his meeting at Gibraltar with General Eisenhower, where he had demanded that he be given absolute command of the operation even then taking place. Long into the night Eisenhower and Clark argued with the adamant Frenchman. Eisenhower told Giraud his role was to be French commander in North Africa, under the Allied Expeditionary Force Commander. Giraud refused. The "honor of France" demanded that a Frenchman be the leader.

Finally, long after the troops had begun to land, a weary Eisenhower sent his difficult visitor to bed and turned to the urgent tasks which had piled up during the colloquy. The next morning found General Giraud in a more reasonable frame of mind. He agreed to undertake the role laid out for him. Eisenhower could turn his mind to the operations in progress.

There was little that he as Supreme Commander could do at the moment. His great work of planning had largely been done in London; now he could only wait for trusted subordinates to carry out the plans, ready to intervene if it became necessary.

While Eisenhower's staff had labored so long and well in London, the generals and admirals, British and American, whose actions would put the plan into deeds, worked to prepare their men, their ships, their vehicles, and their weapons for the great task ahead. The United States Army had not made a major, opposed amphibious landing in nearly a century; the last two the British had tried, at Gallipoli in 1915 and at Dieppe in 1942, had been disasters. There was no habit of victory, no experienced know-how. There was too little time and too little knowledge of the target areas. All the myriad details of planning, gathering intelligence, training, selecting ships, building landing craft, and diplomatic liaison had to go on together.

Because British attacks on the French Fleet at Oran, and British attempts—successful or unsuccessful—against Dakar, Syria, and Madagascar had caused many Frenchmen to think of the British and the devil as synonymous, Operation Torch was to bear as American a form as possible. The operations in the Casablanca area were entirely American, while those at Oran and Algiers were both British and American. In fact, some consideration was given to placing British soldiers in American uniforms as a deception measure. The American landings near Casablanca on the Atlantic coast of French Morocco were covered by units of the United States Navy, but all those inside the Mediterranean were protected by the Royal Navy.

The feverish activity of late summer and fall of 1942 bore what fruit it could. Units of troops were loaded on transports and taken to Solomon Island in Chesapeake Bay, where they practiced debarkation into boats. But the smooth waters of the Bay would bear no resemblance to the experiences the soldiers would encounter off the shores of Africa, with ocean swell tossing the landing boats to the peril of every soldier trying to board. The U.S. Navy had expanded so fast that there were not enough experienced men to go around. On most ships, over half the men had never been to sea before, and few had been in any kind of naval engagement. The watches were manned by landlubbers whose saving grace was the desire to do a good job.

And they performed magnificently, ably led by their skip-

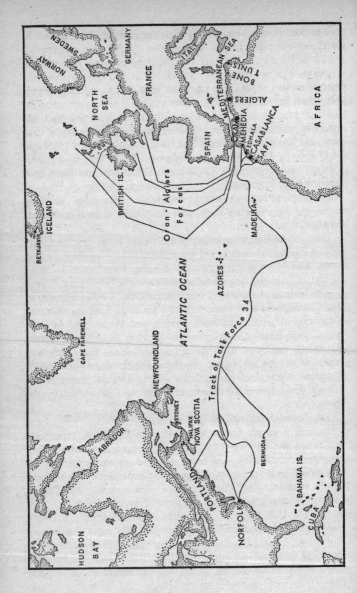

PRELIMINARIES TO OPERATION TORCH, NOV. 8, 1942

422

pers and their admirals. When the American ships designated for the Casablanca area attack, known as the Western Naval Attack Force or Task Force 34, left their ports to rendezvous at sea, they were faced with a job that would stagger a fully experienced navy. They had to convoy some thirty-five thousand troops safely through waters known to be swarming with U-boats, and land them four thousand miles away in the dark of night on an unknown shore. The one man who had to bear this enormous burden was Rear Admiral H. Kent Hewitt, USN, in the *Augusta*. The officers and men in the hundred and two ships making up Task Force 34 could help him, but they could not lift one iota of the responsibility he bore.

The track of Task Force 34 looked like that of a questing dog as the force swung in broad zigzags to avoid known and reported U-boat positions. The force filled a space of ocean roughly twenty by thirty miles, but Hewitt maneuvered it as he might have done a single ship.

On every bridge, officers of the deck intently checked course and speed, maintaining station on the guide. Occasionally one would knock off or add a few turns to adjust his ship's position in the formation. Lookouts swept the sea with their binoculars, and the invisible beams of the questing radars searched farther than the eye could see. Destroyers prowled importantly ahead and on the flanks of the formation, their sonars snuffling beneath the waters searching, searching for the U-boats that might send their deadly torpedoes into the sides of the ships or might even send equally deadly warnings to the German High Command.

Every ship held drills, drills, and more drills. Every man jack of their crews and every G.I. in the troopships rehearsed what he would be called on to do when the day came.

For several days the weather was fine for an autumn crossing. Then on November 4, when Task Force 34 was some three hundred miles west-southwest of Madeira, the seas began to make up, driven by a strong northwest wind. Prospects for a landing on the eighth seemed very grim indeed. One of the minelayers had to drop out of formation because of heavy rolling, and a battleship seemed to be in danger of losing her boats and her forward antiaircraft guns. If conditions did not moderate, there would be no hope whatever of a landing as planned. On only a dozen days a year on the average are surf conditions in French Morocco suitable for an amphibious landing; the odds were thirty to one against completion of the mission as planned.

For the next two days the storm continued, and from both Washington and London came dreary predictions of surf conditions on D-day. If a landing was impossible on the Atlantic coast of French Morocco, then Admiral Hewitt had orders to take his force through the Strait of Gibraltar and land on the narrow strip of French Morocco between Spanish Morocco and Algeria. Then Patton's forces would have to fight their way nearly four hundred miles back to take Casablanca from the rear, with no adequate ports to supply such a march by the Army.

The task-force meteorologist, Lieutenant Commander Richard C. Steere, had more cheering news. He reported that the storm was moving too fast to build up high waves off Morocco on the Atlantic side and predicted good landing conditions in the three target areas. At midnight on November 6/7, Admiral Hewitt made his decision. He chose the bolder course and decided to go through with the original plan. In twenty-eight hours, troops of the Western Task Force were scheduled to hit the beaches.

No landing was planned for Casablanca itself, for two reasons. First, no one wanted to subject the city to the damage that would inevitably follow an opposed amphibious landing. Then, too, the French had their strongest shore defenses there in the powerful El Hank battery and fort and the guns of the immobilized French battleship *Jean Bart*.* The nearest beach to Casablanca selected for a landing was Fedhala, twenty miles to the north of the city. Another fifty miles northward along the coast in Mehedia, where another landing would take place to seize the important airfield at Port Lyautey. The third landing was scheduled at Safi, a hundred and thirty-five miles to the southwest of Casablanca.

Early on the morning of November 7, Task Force 34 began to split up. The Southern Attack Group, commanded by Rear Admiral Lyal A. Davidson, sheered out to starboard and

---

* The *Jean Bart* had escaped from France just before the French surrender in June 1940. She was incomplete at the time and was damaged by British motor-torpedo-boat attacks in July, 1940. Her main propulsion machinery had been put out of commission, but she had four 15-inch guns in her forward turret that could—and did—oppose the Americans on the morning of November 8.

headed for Safi. In midafternoon, the Northern Attack Group, under Rear Admiral Monroe Kelly, turned off for Mehedia, while the main force, the Center Attack Group, under Captain Robert R. M. Emmet, held its course for Fedhala and Casablanca. Admiral Hewitt's flagship, *Augusta*, remained with the Casablanca group.

Originally the Northern Attack Group had been scheduled to land at Rabat, nearly sixty miles from Casablanca, instead of Mehedia, but the planners found too many objections to the plan. Rabat, the capital of Morocco, was a "holy city," and Patton, especially, feared stirring up the Arabs in a *jihad* or holy war. Aviators particularly desired the airstrip at Port Lyautey, although there was the Salé airport at Rabat. But the most important consideration was that the approaches to the harbor are so shallow that the landing boats were in grave danger of grounding well out from the water's edge. This would have meant that if the French opposed the landing, the troops would have to wade ashore under fire, completely unable to protect themselves.

Yet hindsight shows that Rabat would have been a better selection, for the French probably would not have offered any resistance at the capital. The local military commander of the Casablanca area, General Emile Béthouart, had everything arranged for landing at Rabat, which he had been informed would be the target. Like General Mast at Algiers, he had committed himself to support the Allied landings in the belief that they would be the first step in the liberation of France from the German overlords.

Béthouart had been told very little. The insistence on secrecy on the part of the planners had crippled the efforts of Murphy's resistance groups and proved fatal to many of the French plans for cooperation. The danger of a leak to the French defenders seemed to outweigh all else, but since on the Moroccan coast the French resisted with everything they had, it is difficult to see how much more they could have done if they had known more about the forthcoming landings. On the other hand, the French officials who did rally to the Allied cause would not have been working so much in the dark, and many lives might have been saved.

Unfortunately for the Allies, General Béthouart was a subordinate commander in Morocco. His immediate superior was the five-star Resident General of Morocco, Auguste

425

Noguès, and the overall responsibility for the defense of the area was vested in the French Navy, commanded in the area by Vice Admiral F. C. Michelier. Both of these men were determined to resist any attack by anyone of whatever side "for the honor of France."

The attitude of the French commanders, both those who joined the Allies and those who opposed them, is a difficult one for British and American minds to grasp. Because of a long experience of instability in top echelons of the French Government, a state of affairs dating from the Revolution, French officials tended to cling to established authority. The surrender of France in 1940 had undermined their national confidence, and most of them looked on the aging Marshal Pétain as the symbol of their national existence. To many, Pétain *was* France. The fact that the Marshal was much under the influence of the notorious Pierre Laval mattered not a whit. What the Marshal told them to do, they would do, with no questions asked. Except for a few men, headed by Laval, no one desired a Nazi victory; they were not pro-German—they were pro-French. Since the Marshal spoke in the voice of the only surviving French Government, they would oppose all comers, be they devils from Hell or saints from Heaven.

The handful of men who threw in their lot with the Allies were no turncoats, no traitors, though they were counted so by the men of Vichy. They were loyal Frenchmen who had come to realize that the only hope for France's survival as an independent, sovereign state lay in an Allied victory. Their duty it was to do all in their power to end the Nazi rule and to restore France to something approaching her former glories.

General Béthouart was such a man. He had been overjoyed with the knowledge that an American force was headed for Casablanca, and he had faith in American assurances that French rights would be protected. He had made all the preparations he could make without knowing the exact date of the American landing.

He was working at his desk on the evening of November 7, when a man laid a paper on his desk. He picked it up and read: "*Débarquement à 0200 demain.*" Béthouart ordered the residence of General Noguès surrounded and the telephone lines cut. Unfortunately, there was a secret line the conspirators did not know about, and Noguès alerted Michelier at

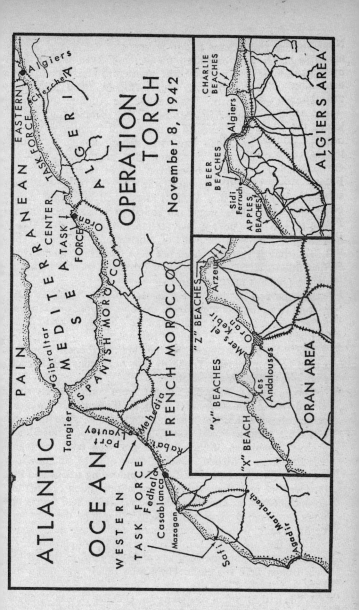

OPERATION TORCH
November 8, 1942

ATLANTIC OCEAN

MEDITERRANEAN SEA

SPAIN

Gibraltar

Tangier

SPANISH MOROCCO

FRENCH MOROCCO

ALGERIA

Algiers

Cherchel

Oran

EASTERN TASK FORCE

CENTER TASK FORCE

A TASK FORCE

WESTERN TASK FORCE

Port Lyautey

Mehedia

Rabat

Fedhala

Casablanca

Mazagan

Safi

Marrakech

Agadir

ALGIERS AREA

CHARLIE BEACHES

Algiers

BEER BEACHES

Sidi Ferruch

APPLES BEACHES

ORAN AREA

"Z" BEACHES

Arzeu

Oran

Mers el Kebir

"Y" BEACHES

Les Andalouses

"X" BEACH

427

Casablanca and ordered him to resist.

Casablanca was organized for defense, even though Michelier doubted the tale as it was reported to him. Upon being confronted with Béthouart's story, Noguès asked Michelier whether it could be true. No, replied the Admiral. No large armada was approaching Morocco. His searches out for a hundred miles had revealed nothing. Still Noguès was in a quandary. If the Allied force was strong enough, he could yield to *force majeure*, a solution that might have been to his liking, for it would have freed him of responsibility for any action. The ultimate threat the Germans still held over France was to occupy Vichy France, and all senior commanders knew Hitler would not hesitate to do so if he thought the French were in any way collaborating with the Allies. This fear paralyzed the wills of Noguès and Michelier. The tragic irony is that they need not have concerned themselves, for Hitler decided to occupy all of France as soon as he heard of the landings in North Africa.

For the rest of the night, Noguès worried. Then, as first reports from the landing beaches came in, he interpreted them as no more than a Commando raid. He gave the order to resist to the limit and arrested General Béthouart.

The decision was made. The landings in French Morocco would be no pushover. Tragically, the Americans and French were already killing one another.

The landings at Mehedia and Safi were comparatively simple. In the north, General Lucian K. Truscott, Jr., was to come ashore with some nine thousand troops, seize the city and the airfield at Port Lyautey, and then support operations against Casablanca, if the city had not been taken by then. The first wave at Mehedia touched down at 0515, an hour and a quarter later because of difficulties in loading troops and the inexperience of the coxswains. Principal opposition came from an ancient fortress known as the Kasba, which held up operations for some days. Admiral Kelly's flagship, the old battleship *Texas,* with her 14-inch guns, could have made short work of the fort, but General Truscott would not permit her to open up, distracting the accuracy of naval gunfire. He felt his own troops were too close. The Kasba finally was taken the hard way, by troops.

While early fighting was going on, Colonel Damas T. Craw of Truscott's staff believed that he could talk the French authorities into surrendering the airfield at Port Lyautey. Accompanied by the French-speaking Major Pierpont M. Hamilton, he piled into a jeep, rigged a flag of truce, the Stars and Stripes, and the French *tricouleur,* and set off. Nearing his goal, the Colonel was instantly killed by fire from a machine-gun post, and Major Hamilton was taken prisoner and conducted to Port Lyautey, where he worked on the French officer who came to interrogate him. He was not able to persuade his interrogator of the wisdom of surrender.

The escort carrier *Sangamon* flew sorties in support of the troops ashore, but any hope that her planes could operate from Port Lyautey was vain for two days. The airfield had to be captured first.

A river called the Wadi Sebou winds down past Port Lyautey and empties into the sea after making a U-turn and a wide sweep to the southwest. On its southern bank, near the mouth, stands the Kasba; a net stretched across the river right under the guns of the fortress. A raider party had been loaded in an old, cut-down, four-piper destroyer of 1917 vintage, U.S.S. *Dallas.* Her job was to proceed up the Wadi Sebou past the Kasba and land her troops to seize the airfield.

On the morning of November 8, a net-cutting party worked on the river barrier, and then the *Dallas* rammed, but the net held. It was not until two days later that the attempt came off. Further work on the net weakened it, and during the early morning hours of November 10, a group of men succeeded in cutting the wire, even though every one of them was wounded by machine-gun fire. At 0400 the *Dallas* started, a Free French pilot (who had lived all his life in the area) at the helm. By some miracle the guns of the Kasba missed the ship, and she made her way upstream, her 3-inch guns responding to fire as she went. The navigation was so tricky that in going around a bend she was cutting her way through the mud. She made it to her destination just as Army troops were moving in from the other side of the airfield, and it was not long before the Port Lyautey facility was operating American aircraft. The Kasba fell soon afterwards, and on orders from Algiers, resistance at Mehedia ceased during the early morning hours of November 11.

At the other end of the Western Task Force objectives, the attack on Safi went off well, in spite of initial French resistance. The principal French defense came from the Batterie Railleuse north of the harbor. This battery was in position to enfilade the landing beaches, but it was soon knocked out by the 6-inch guns of Admiral Davidson's flagship, the light cruiser *Philadelphia*, and the battleship *New York*. Carrier planes from the *Santee* had great difficulty in operating, partly because of the inexperience of their pilots, but they were scarcely needed, as it turned out.

The assault was spearheaded by a dash into the harbor by two old four-piper destroyers, *Bernadou* and *Cole*. They landed soldiers in the heart of the town just as the regular assault forces were hitting the beaches. By nightfall the troops had a large perimeter around the village, and the only danger was from a distance, especially from Marrakech. This counterattack did not develop any serious danger, and it ceased entirely on November 11.

Principal opposition to the American assault developed in the center, at Fedhala. Here it was that the most powerful forces were allocated—nineteen thousand troops, twenty-eight combatant ships, and fifteen transports and cargo carriers. The force was supposed to be in position about midnight and begin unloading troops into the assault boats. H-hour was set for 0400, November 8, allowing four hours for the troops to get into the boats, form their assault waves, and reach shore.

It did not work out quite that way.

The first line of transports reached its assigned position approximately on schedule and began putting boats in the water. The rest of the ships had trouble in finding their stations and so were late in contributing their boats to the boat pool.

Now it was that the lack of rehearsal and the unrealistic training took their toll. The Army was particularly anxious to have a large force ashore before dawn, which was due about 0600. Attainment of surprise was paramount in the planning, but it cost dear in terms of confusion and in loss of life. When the troops came up on the decks of the transports to man their debarkation stations, they were faced with a task that was not for the faint-hearted. Burdened with sixty-pound packs, they had to climb over the rail, descend cargo nettings serving as makeshift ladders, and find a tiny boat bobbing dangerously in the ground swell of the Atlantic. All this, be it noted, in pitch darkness. Sergeants cajoled, coaxed, urged, cursed, booted, and heaved the men over the rails and down the nets. Setting one foot cautiously below the next, scrabbling for the support of the elusive hemp, the soldiers made their laborious way, twenty, thirty, even forty feet, before they felt themselves seized by helpful Navy men and guided into the doubtful shelter of a dancing LCM. Some men slipped and fell. Their screams were cut as by a knife when they hit the water, for their packs dragged them down. A pitiful few of those who fell were saved. The rest of these unfortunates had safely crossed the Atlantic only to drown a few miles from their destination.

As each of the landing craft was loaded, it went to a holding area where it began to circle until the others of its wave joined up. Then the entire wave would head for the line of departure, some four thousand yards from the target beach.

Because of delays in transports finding their stations, in the lowering of boats, in loading them, and on finding other boats to make up the waves, H-hour had to be postponed until 0445. For the troops already loaded, this gave an additional forty-five minutes for seasickness to wreak its worst. Soon most of the troops would far rather have landed under fire than endure another minute of the awful bobbing, pitching, seemingly endless circling.

Finally, at last, at long last, they started in.

The first landing actually took place at 0500. Destroyers anchored at the line of departure, and scout boats, which had preceded the assault waves to set up lights on the shore, guided the boats to their assigned beaches. There were many mistakes, some costly, but in the main the landings came off better than could be expected. Inexperience on the part of the coxswains caused many of the loading boats to be swamped and needlessly lost. There would not have been enough boats to bring it off, if the French had seriously opposed the landings on the beach. That they did not justified the Army's insistence on surprise.

For the French were about to resist.

The landings in the Casablanca area were scheduled to begin after those inside the Mediterranean, and the broadcast by President Roosevelt that so infuriated General Patton took place at the time of the Algiers and Oran landings. Yet it seems that in Casablanca scarcely anyone heard the American President, and the communications of the French were in such a sad state the Casablanca authorities did not hear of the other landings until after sunrise. By that time, they were already engaged in action against the Americans, although they did not yet know whom they were opposing.

The principal French defenses at Fedhala were the Batterie du Port with three 4-inch guns (100-mm.), backed up by two 75-mm. guns on the cape nearby. On the opposite side of the landing area toward the northeast was the Sherki Peninsula with the stronger Batterie Pont Blondin, mounting four 5.5-inch guns (138.6-mm.).

Sporadic firing was observed a little after the troops had landed, but only from rifles and machine guns. Hope rose when two searchlights came on, their beams pointed straight up into the sky. This was the prearranged signal that there would be no resistance. But the beams quickly dropped, and soon they were seen picking out landing boats. American machine guns quickly extinguished them, and there was another lull.

As dawn came over the hills of Africa, the guns from the two batteries began to fire on the scout boats and the guiding destroyers. The skipper of one of them signaled by voice radio to Admiral Hewitt: "Firing from Fedhala and Sherki. Batter up!"

"Batter up" was the code phrase to indicate that resistance had been met. A few minutes later Captain Emmet, Officer in Tactical Command (OTC) of the Center Group, responded, "Play ball!"—that is, attack with force as necessary.

It did not take the cruiser *Brooklyn* and the destroyers long to knock out the batteries, especially after the heavy cruiser *Augusta* added her 8-inch guns and silenced Batterie Pont Blondin. Ashore, about two hundred French Senegalese troops surrendered, and by noon about forty percent of the American troops were ashore, ready to begin their advance toward Casablanca.

For this advance to be possible, the troops needed supplies, and confusion was the order of the day. It was Guadalcanal all over again. The Navy men, taking their boats into difficult waters, holding them there under heavier conditions of surf than they had ever known, believed that it was the Army's job to deal with the supplies once landed. The Army men believed their job was to fight. They offered practically no help at all in unloading or in dealing with the cases, boxes, and cans, once they were ashore. It took the combined efforts of resourceful officers in both services to make the men turn to and get the chaos ashore somewhat eased. They might have worked even faster had they known how close disaster would come to them.

At Casablanca, Admiral Michelier was reading a telegram he had just received from Marshal Pétain in Vichy. The Marshal had been roused from bed to learn of the attacks on the French possessions in North Africa and to receive a letter from President Roosevelt brought over from the American Embassy. This message had been prepared some time earlier and had been edited by Mr. Churchill, who objected to the first draft as "much too kind." The letter announced the landings and begged for French cooperation.

Pétain read the letter but seemed uninclined to do anything. He sat, almost as in a stupor, while the others debated what should be done. Then Laval arrived, having just returned from a quick trip to Germany to see Hitler. The trip had been fruitless, but Laval's arrival back in Vichy stiffened the Marshal. He consented to send a cold letter in response to the American President.

It was with shock and sadness that I learned tonight of the aggression of your troops against North Africa. I have read your message. You cite pretexts which are completely unjustified. You ascribe to your enemies intentions which have never been translated into action. . . .

I have always declared that we will defend our Empire if it is attacked. You must know that we shall defend ourselves against any aggressor, whoever he may be. You must know that I will keep my word! In our misfortunes, I preserved our Empire by asking for an armistice. It is you, acting in the name of a country bound to us by so many memories and so many ties, who have taken so cruel an initiative. France and her honor are at stake. We have been attacked; we will defend ourselves. That is the order I have given.

When Michelier read these words, he agreed with the order he had received from Noguès. He commanded his ships to get under way and his guns to fire.

By 0700 eighteen SBD dive bombers from the carrier *Ranger** were over Casablanca, while fighters were over the nearby Les Cazes airfield. French aircraft took to the air

---

* The *Ranger*, too small and slow for Pacific operations, was the only American "fleet" carrier in the task force.

and were soon in a dogfight with the Americans. The dive bombers, meanwhile, were busy dodging antiaircraft fire from the shore batteries and from the guns of the *Jean Bart*. Word was quickly flashed to Rear Admiral Robert C. Giffen, commanding the Covering Group: "Batter up!"

This word did not immediately reach the Admiral, but there was no need. Two submarines were spotted coming out of the harbor, and other pilots reported they were being fired upon. About the same moment, bluejackets on the battleship *Massachusetts* were startled as 8-inch-shell splashes rose all round them. The El Hank battery had made a straddle with their first salvo. It was good shooting—far too good for comfort.

Admiral Giffen wasted no time in ordering "Play ball!" The *Massachusetts* opened up on the *Jean Bart*, as shells from the immobilized French battleship began falling near at hand. Nine times the *Massachusetts*'s 16-inch guns roared out, belching forth their shells, nine to a salvo, each weighing over a ton. The range was between twelve and seventeen miles, and the French battleship reeled from the blows. Five times armor-piercing shells slammed into her, putting her out of action and jamming her one operational turret so that it could not be fired. It took America's newest battleship just sixteen minutes to do the job.

The cruisers, at the same time, were shooting at the El Hank battery and continued until frantic word came over the radio: "For Christ's sake quit firing—you are killing our own troops." Also : "This is from Army—you are killing townspeople, no opposition ashore." Actually cruiser shells were not causing this damage; it was a French battery firing on troops near the beach.

Taken up by the action against the *Jean Bart* and El Hank, the American Covering Group was almost sucked out of position, for Admiral Michelier had something else up his sleeve. At 0815 a very gallant group of French ships began to leave the harbor, the destroyer leaders *Milan* and *Albatros,* mounting five 5.5-inch guns, and the destroyers *L'Alcyon, Brestois, Boulonnais, Fougueux,* and *Frondeur*. Their mission was to sneak up along the coast and disrupt the landing at Fedhala.

Scout planes spotted the French ships, but the Covering Group was so far to the southeast, it became an anxious moment for Admiral Giffen, for it is only twelve miles by sea from Casablanca to Fedhala, and the big ships had a long way to go. Happily for the Americans, the cruisers *Augusta* and *Brooklyn* were near at hand, and with the assistance of two destroyers, opened up when the French ships were only four miles from the transports. The French answered with a will, but decided to break off the action and retire to Casablanca. Because of having to dodge American shells, the French were unable to make it into port, and about 1000 the *matelots'* hearts were gladdened by sight of their magnificent light cruiser *Primauguet* coming out to their assistance. Her captain had wanted to join the destroyers in their sortie, but it took longer for the cruiser to raise steam. Now here she was, a David when confronted with American firepower, but still more powerful than her consorts.

When she joined, the battle became furious. Skillfully using smoke screens, the nimble French ships were almost impossible to hit. Their guns were well served, and the French still did not know the nationality of those they were engaging. Whoever it was, they determined to make their attackers pay for attacking their territory.

By this time the *Massachusetts*, the heavy cruiser *Tuscaloosa*, and the *Wichita* came within range. The *Tuscaloosa* blew the *Fougueux* out of the water. The *Massachusetts* sank the *Boulonais*, while shells from most of the ships present heavily damaged the *Primauguet*, *Milan*, and *Brestois*. All three cripples managed to make it into port. The *Albatros*, *Frondeur*, and *L'Alcyon* tried to deliver torpedo attacks on the American cruisers, but were driven off, the *Frondeur* so badly shattered that she had to retire to Casablanca.* The *Albatros* was soon dead in the water, and immediately afterwards action was broken off.

While the American ships were engaging the French destroyers, they had to do some nimble dodging of torpedoes fired from hitherto unsuspected French submarines. Eight of then came out and made quick attacks, losing four of their number. One escaped to Cadiz, where she was scuttled by her crew, another went to Dakar, and one returned to port. One disappeared.

Only *L'Alcyon* was undamaged of the French ships that had sortied so bravely that morning. In the afternoon the French

---

* The *Frondeur* and the *Brestois* were both later sunk at their anchorages by aircraft.

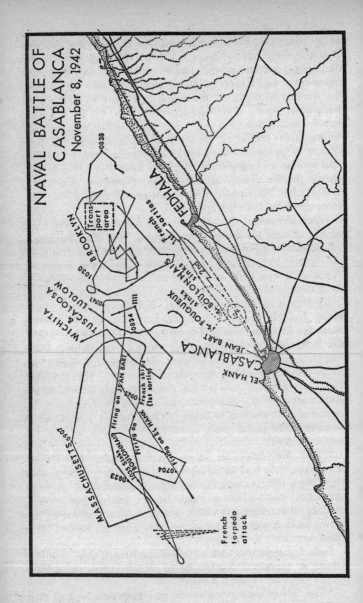

NAVAL BATTLE OF CASABLANCA
November 8, 1942

FEDHALA

Transport area

BROOKLYN 1030

0838

French 1st sorties

2nd

BOULONNAIS sinks

la FOUGUEUX sinks

WICHITA
TUSCALOOSA
LUDLOW

0741

0834

1111

JEAN BART

CASABLANCA

EL HANK

MASSACHUSETTS 0907

Firing on JEAN BART

French ships (1st sortie)

0945

BOSTON Firing on EL HANK

0823

0704

French torpedo attack

tried again, with no better success, although they almost managed to pull the *Tuscaloosa* and *Wichita* into a trap near the El Hank battery. But Michelier had no navy left. Only the *Jean Bart* and El Hank remained to him as useful weapons. The crewmen of the *Jean Bart,* working feverishly, had managed to restore her turret by that afternoon, so she was ready to fight again.

During the actions of November 8, the French Navy lost nearly five hundred killed and almost a thousand wounded. Did this slaughter have to be? Could it have been averted, saving both American and French lives to fight against the Axis?

In Algiers dedicated men, both French and American, were working to answer these questions, to stop the senseless slaughter already begun, and to prevent it from spreading.

While the Western Naval Task Force was making its way for the Moroccan beaches, two task forces under the escort of the Royal Navy had passed the Strait of Gibraltar and were heading for their respective beaches at Algiers and Oran. On the evening of November 5, these two task forces approached the Pillars of Hercules, passing through during the night hours. Men on the ships could see the lights of the Spanish shore to port and those of Tangier to starboard. The darkened shape of the Rock could be seen across the bay from Algeciras, and the shapes of the Atlas Mountains of Spanish Morocco cut the southern horizon. No more historic waters than those of the Mediterranean exist anywhere in the world. Phoenicians, Greeks, Romans, Spaniards, Turks, Russians, Germans, Italians, and Vikings had all passed through them as the American troops were now doing. On ships not far away, the comrades-in-arms of the Americans, ordinary British Tommies, were watching too, none of them, perhaps, feeling any of the history of the scene or any of the history they were about to make. On one of the American Transports a voice struck up "Ain't I Never Gonna Have a Girl in My Arms?" On a British transport could be heard "Bell-Bottom Trousers." Down in a troop hold could be heard an American voice, "Roll 'em, Joe. You're faded."

No one thought this armada could slip through the Strait of Gibraltar unnoticed. Keen eyes on the Spanish shore counted the ships and reported their observations to Berlin and to Rome. Staff officers puzzled over these large troop and warship movements. Mussolini's son-in-law, Count Galeazzo

Ciano entered in his diary for November 7: "According to the Germans, [they, the convoys], are the provisioning of Malta or an attempt at landing in Tripolitania in order to fall upon Rommel's rear. According to our General Staff, they are for the occupation of French bases in North Africa. The Duce, too, is of this opinion; in fact, he believes that the landing will be accomplished by the Americans, who will meet almost no resistance from the French. I share the Duce's opinion; in fact, I believe that North Africa is ready to hoist the de Gaullist flag. All this is exceedingly serious for us."

The Allied ships followed a course as though they were, indeed, bound for Malta. The Germans were completely deceived and made no immediate effort to attack, believing their chance would come when the force reached the Sicilian Narrows. They never got there.

The Center Task Force was under Commodore Thomas Troubridge, RN, with the troops commanded by Major General Lloyd R. Fredendall, USA. Except for the naval ships, this force was entirely composed of Americans, for the British well remembered their attack on the naval anchorage of Oran, Mers el Kebir, on July 3, 1940. They remembered and knew that the French would, too. Guarding the transports, which carried approximately thirty-nine thousand troops, was a powerful detachment of the Royal Navy, spearheaded by the battleship *Rodney* with its 16-inch guns, the carrier *Furious*, two escort carriers, a command ship, an antiaircraft cruiser, and numerous other smaller ships. Like the Casablanca landings, this one was to be made in three places: at the Gulf of Arzeu (Zebra Beaches) east of Oran, Les Andalouses (Yorker Beaches, about ten miles west of the city), and "X" Beach at Mersa bou Zedjar, fifteen miles farther on to the west. Two former United States Coast Guard cutters, transferred to the British Navy and renamed *Hartland* and *Walney*, would attempt to penetrate directly into the harbor and land troops to seize port facilities and prevent sabotage and destruction of wharves, cranes, and other equipment needed to keep the port operating.

The landing at Arzeu was the most important one, and to it the largest forces had been allocated. In that area alone, twenty-nine thousand men, twenty-four hundred vehicles, and fourteen thousand tons of supplies were put ashore from the thirty-four troop and cargo carriers present. There was none of the opposition that developed to the west; the landings were unopposed, and it was just as well, for delays and snafus jeopardized parts of the landing operation. The two landings to the west of Oran went off very smoothly. Troops were ashore almost on schedule and began a pincers against the city of Oran, while others headed for airfields at Lourmel, Tafaraoui, and La Senia. Fighting developed on land, however, and continued until the French capitulated at noon, November 10.

Before giving in, however, they gave a warm reception to the *Hartland* and *Walney*. These two ships were scheduled to enter the harbor at H plus 2 hours, that is, at 0300, November 8. They should have gone in either earlier or later, when they could have achieved surprise or after the town had capitulated. In the latter case, of course, they would not have been needed, but they were in the plan, and used they must be. Afterwards Admiral Sir Andrew B. Cunningham, RN, naval commander of the entire North African operations, wrote: "The moment chosen could hardly have been less fortunate, since the French alarm to arms was in its first full flush of Gallic fervour and they had not yet been intimidated by bombing or bombardment."

Both ships were greeted by heavy gunfire at point-blank range. The *Walney* was sunk and the *Hartland* abandoned and grounded as a total wreck. Neither was able to accomplish its mission, and about two hundred men were killed, the rest being taken prisoner. They were well treated but kept in confinement until the arrival of American troops in the city two days later.

In Algiers a group of men were gathered in an apartment at 30 Rue Michelet on the evening of November 7. From time to time, one would leave, another arrive. They hoped for the arrival of General Giraud to take charge of the rising against the Vichy authorities in order to cooperate with the expected landing of the American troops. General Mast, American Consul Robert Murphy, and others dedicated to the cause, glanced from time to time at the clandestine radio in the room. At about nine o'clock came the word they had been waiting for. The B.B.C. announcer was giving personal messages. In the midst of the words of good cheer and ill tidings came: *"Allo Robert, Franklin arrive."*

"Robert" was Robert Murphy, heading the American undercover preparations in Algeria, and "Franklin" was Roosevelt, the name code for the troops on the way. It was time to get busy. Each of the Frenchmen went to his post, to make preparations to receive in comradeship, not in arms, their liberators from across the seas.

The time was little enough—only four hours remained before the troops would begin coming ashore. Even now approaching the harbor and the landing areas was the Eastern Task Force, commanded by British Rear Admiral Sir Harold M. Burrough. Its powerful warships were guarding troopers carrying about twenty-three thousand officers and men of the British Army and about ten thousand Americans. For the sake of appearances to the French, the men were supposed to look American and were temporarily commanded by Major General Charles W. Ryder of the United States Army. As in the landings at Casablanca and Oran, the assault at Algiers was to be made on three beach areas, Beaches Apple and Beer west of Algiers, and Charlie Beaches to the east.

Not a single ship had been hit on its passage from Britain or the United States for the Torch landings. They had come safely through the Atlantic waters and into the Mediterranean, or to the coast of Morocco without casualty to Casablanca or Oran.

Luck ran out at daybreak on November 7. U.S.S. *Thomas Stone*, a naval transport, in a position about a hundred and fifty-five miles from Algiers, took a U-boat torpedo that killed or wounded nine of the crew, disabled her propeller and rudder, and forced her to drop out of convoy. With only the British corvette *Spey* as a guardian, she lay wallowing in the waves, the men wistfully watching the rest of the ships pressing on for Algiers.

Word reached the *Stone* that a tug and two British destroyers were coming from Gibraltar to assist the stricken vessel, but that bit of news did not satisfy Major Walter M. Oakes, commander of the Battalion Landing Team embarked. He proposed that he and his men be put in the landing boats and make their way across the scores of miles of water to their assigned beaches on their own. The *Stone's* skipper approved the decision. The boats were placed in the water, about eight hundred men and officers got in, and the perilous journey began.

It was a bold enterprise, but doomed to failure. The boats were never intended for such long voyages under their own power. Overheated engines, broken fuel lines, and other vicissitudes plagued them, and one by one they had to be abandoned, their crews taking refuge in the corvette *Spey*, which had gone along to shepherd them. In spite of their determination to reach their target areas in time, the men had to be content with landing in Algiers after it was all over. Their determination paid off in morale rather than in practical results.

The *Stone* was finally brought in to port, but she was too badly damaged for repair and was finally sold for scrap.

The actual landing operations were almost a repetition of those at Oran, except for insupportable losses among the landing craft. No opposition developed on any of the beaches, and soon troops were closing in on Algiers from both sides. There was also an attempt to land forces directly in the city by means of two small ships, and while it was not as costly in lives as the attempt at Oran, it fared no better. A party of men put ashore from H.M.S. *Broke* was taken prisoner, but the ship was fatally wounded. Her exploit, together with that of H.M.S. *Malcolm*, which failed to get through, was described by the French officers who witnessed it as "magnifique."

Part of the success of the operations in the Algiers region can be ascribed to the preparations of General Mast and Robert Murphy. When they received the *"Franklin arrive"* message, they set the resistance into action. Quietly, without fuss, small groups of French patriots began taking over police and power stations, communication centers, and military headquarters from other groups of equally patriotic Frenchmen who believed their duty lay in opposition to any foreigners.

Murphy hastened to the residence of the Commander in Chief of French Ground Forces, General Alphonse Juin, in the suburb of El Biar. He roused the General from his bed and told him the landings would soon be upon them. "I wish," said Murphy, "to tell you about this in advance, because our talks over the years have convinced me that you desire above all else to see the liberation of France, which can come about only through cooperation with the United States."

Juin was shocked. He argued that he should have been consulted earlier. He was torn between his desire for liberation of his country and his desire to obey orders.

Finally he turned to Murphy. "If the matter were entirely in my hands," he said, "I would be with you. But, as you know, Darlan is in Algiers. He outranks me, and no matter what decision I might make, Darlan could immediately overrule it."

"Very well," replied Murphy. "Let us talk with Darlan."

The presence of Admiral Darlan in Algiers was one of those unforeseen circumstances that might have upset everything. His son had been stricken with polio, and the Admiral had arrived only a few days before, completely unsuspecting that any kind of operation would soon be launched in the region. As head of the French Armed Forces and heir apparent to Marshal Pétain, he could command obedience as could no other man. If he commanded the French in North Africa to fight, they would fight. If he ordered no resistance, the chances were that he would be obeyed, unless his orders were countermanded by the Marshal himself.

It quickly became apparent that General Giraud had no influence whatever in the French colonies. As a man with no official position in the military command, he could command no obedience. Only through Darlan could any hope of cooperation be realized. The alternative was complete Anglo-American military occupation of all of French North Africa, which would tie up thousands of men who could better be employed in fighting the Axis.

Darlan arrived at Juin's house within twenty minutes, and Murphy laid the situation before him. The little bantam-cock French Admiral turned purple with fury. "I have known for a long time," he shouted, "that the British are stupid, but I always believed Americans were more intelligent. Apparently you have the same genius as the British for making massive blunders."

After an hour or more of argument, Darlan declared, "I have given my oath to Pétain and preserved allegiance to the Marshal for two years. I cannot revoke that now. This premature action is not at all what we have been hoping for." Under Murphy's prodding, Darlan agreed to send a message to Vichy asking for authority to cooperate with the American* landings. They started to leave, only to find the house surrounded by a group of men from the underground, and Darlan believed the worst. Nevertheless the message was taken to the naval headquarters, but the officer there refused to send it.

For several hours, Murphy, Juin, and Darlan remained in the house, until during the early morning hours the regular

* Darlan was not informed at this stage that the landings were partially British.

French forces reestablished control. Murphy's plans had been based on a swift advance into the city, and when this did not come off, the resistance groups were dispossessed. Nevertheless, the situation was impossible from the French point of view, and Darlan authorized General Juin to ask for a local cease-fire. Although this order did not apply elsewhere, it had some effect in Oran, but none at all in Casablanca.

The next day, November 9, Generals Mark Clark and Giraud arrived in Algiers from Gibraltar. Murphy demanded that Clark put on a big parade in the city to impress the French with American strength. "Run your tanks through the main streets. Show them some force. Give them a big parade."

"Okay," retorted Clark. "If you insist, I'll have all three of our available tanks put on a show."

Murphy did not insist.

On the morning of November 10, Clark called a meeting of all the principal officers on both sides. Clark and Giraud were flanked by Juin and Commodore Roy Dick, Admiral Cunningham's Chief of Staff, with Murphy attempting to call the signals. On Clark's left sat Admiral Darlan, described by General Clark as "a little man with watery blue eyes and petulant lips. He seemed nervous and uncertain, obviously ill at ease. Again and again he pulled a handkerchief from his pocket and mopped his forehead. He shifted in his chair, and his hands fumbled with the papers on the table in front of him."

General Giraud was equally ill at ease. He and Darlan detested each other, and he was in the position of a man who had made a great sacrifice for his country, only to find that it was not wanted.

Clark turned to Murphy. "We have work to do to meet the common enemy," he stated. "Is he [Darlan] ready to sign the terms of the armistice? It will cover all French North Africa. It is essential that we stop this waste of time and blood."

Clark intended to be hard-boiled. He felt that if permitted, the French would hedge, trying to gain all they could from the situation. Also, delay gave the enemy more time to move reinforcements into the area. He had Eisenhower's backing for whatever needed to be done. "Clean up that situation today," telegraphed Eisenhower, "and write your own ticket."

Darlan replied to the challenge evasively, stating that he had sent a résumé of the American terms to Vichy and proposed to take no further action until he heard from the Marshal. This did not satisfy General Clark in any way. The Vichy Government had, twenty-four hours earlier, broken off diplomatic relations with the United States, and Clark had no faith at all that Marshal Pétain would support an African armistice. He demanded that Darlan order it, and at once. He gave him thirty minutes to do so; then he would turn to General Giraud, who might or might not be obeyed.

Darlan protested that he had to wait, that he had urged acceptance of the American proposals. Wait just a bit, he urged.

"We haven't time," retorted Clark. "All Frenchmen and all Americans have the same interests at heart, and here we are fighting among ourselves, wasting time. I know that the Admiral wants, deep down in his heart, to stop this fighting between our troops. We all want to do the same thing, and we must get an order for cessation of hostilities this morning. We have the means. We have 150,000 American and British troops in French North Africa. We have the means of equipping the French Army and making this the base from which we can go into France. How anybody can fail to join us in an operation that can mean the liberation of France is beyond my understanding."

Replied Darlan, "I am completely in accord with your point of view, but I still can't act until I hear from Pétain."

Finally the little Admiral gave in and agreed to send a cease-fire order to all French forces in North Africa. As he walked out of the meeting, he remarked to Mr. Murphy, "Could I ask a favor? Would you mind suggesting to Major General Clark that I am a five-star admiral? He should stop talking to me like a lieutenant, junior grade."

In accordance with his word, Darlan ordered all French forces in North Africa to cease fire against the Americans. He reported his action in a telegram to Vichy.

Most urgent: For the Marshal Pétain.
1. The Americans, on my refusal to order a cease-fire in North Africa, have decided to deal with General Giraud and to break all contact with you.
2. I believe that this will result in grave disorder in the country and in loss of morale, and that North Africa will be lost to us.

3. Struggle is vain, bloodshed useless, and our promises have been fulfilled.

4. Therefore I have ordered suspension of hostilities in North Africa and an attitude of complete neutrality toward all belligerents, with the proviso that I keep complete authority in your name in North Africa.

5. If you approve—and I believe that it is not possible to do better—I ask you to give the necessary orders to the French warships.

6. I ask you to confirm my order to General Noguès, that he will be sure of its authenticity, as coming from me.

When this order reached Vichy, Marshal Pétain was at first ready to approve Darlan's actions. In fact, he drafted a telegram of support and was about to order it sent when the situation changed.

Laval phoned from Munich. The Germans had summoned him there to demand use of French bases in Tunis to oppose the Anglo-American forces moving in. Laval was willing, and he did not propose to allow France to be liberated by the British and Americans. France's future lay with Germany.

Some of Laval's Vichy henchmen hurriedly phoned him, tipped him off on what Darlan had done, and told him that Pétain was about to approve a cease-fire. Don't do it, pleaded Laval to the will-less Marshal. If you do, the Germans will occupy all of France.

Pétain surrendered, as always, to the dominant will of Laval. He telegraphed all naval and military commanders in North Africa: "I gave the order to defend ourselves against the aggressor. I confirm that order."

But this time the Marshal was not quite so much in Laval's pocket as everyone thought. Simultaneously he sent a secret order to Darlan disavowing his disavowal. The actual text has been lost, but participants in the event have agreed that it said in substance: "Pay no attention to my official messages and orders sent under constraint. I am in complete accord with you."

Darlan, receiving the official rejection of his orders first, attempted to revoke the nonresistance order already given. Clark refused him all communication with his aides and in effect took him prisoner. So the situation remained for the night, while Clark, badly out of his depth in the intricacies of international and French politics, sought to bring his prima donnas to some meeting of minds. General Giraud offered to renounce the high command of all French forces that had been promised him and agreed to serve under Darlan in any capacity he could.

Laval was sadly mistaken in his belief that an alliance with Germany was possible. In the first place, practically no one in the Vichy Government would have considered such action for a moment. In the second, the Germans did not want the French as allies. They had other plans. Count Ciano learned of them from Hitler on November 9. "Hitler will listen to Laval. But whatever he says will not modify his already definite point of view; the total occupation of France, landing in Corsica, a bridgehead in Tunisia."

Ciano's diary continues, describing the meeting of Laval and Hitler the next day: "Not a word was said to Laval about the impending action—the orders to occupy France were being given while he was smoking his cigarette and conversing with various people in the next room."

France's fate had already been decided while her leaders struggled, against their own interest at times, to seek the middle ground. The middle ground no longer existed.

Marshal Pétain wisely ordered that no resistance be offered the German armies moving into unoccupied France. There were no means to oppose them; the loss of life would have been useless. In stunned silence French citizens lined the streets and watched the Germans pass by. Here and there could be heard a Frenchman humming "La Marseillaise."

The occupation of France very possibly averted civil war in North Africa. When the news arrived, all officials agreed to accept Darlan's orders, and the fighting ceased. The cease-fire took effect in Casablanca just in time to prevent a major assault that would have devastated large sections of the city. Giraud accepted Darlan as overall commander of the French establishment in North Africa, while he himself would become Commander in Chief of the Armed Forces.

Darlan agreed to order the French fleet at Toulon to sail to Algiers to join the Allies. But he hedged a little in this, perhaps to keep a trump card in reserve, perhaps hoping to permit a tiny portion of France to remain free. The Germans promised they would not occupy the city and naval base of Toulon so long as the French fleet remained loyal to Vichy. In any case, Darlan's message to the commander of the Toulon fleet, Admiral de Laborde, began with the words "I invite" rather than "I order." The French fleet stayed where it was.

On Friday, November 13, Eisenhower flew to Algiers, approved everything General Clark had done, and laid his own reputation on the line in accepting the so-called "Darlan deal." "If," he wrote, "resulting political repercussions became so serious as to call for a sacrifice, logic and tradition demanded that the man in the field should take complete responsibility for the matter, with his later relief from command becoming the symbol of correction. I might be fired, but only by making a quick decision could the essential unity of effort throughout both nations be preserved and the immediate military requirements met."

Eisenhower was not fired. His actions were approved by both President Roosevelt and Prime Minister Churchill. Their only proviso was that nothing in the American and British actions was to be construed as imposing on the French any permanent form of government. Darlan's regime was only a temporary expedient based on military necessity.

What of the recognized leader of French hopes outside of the battle zones, outside of France? What of de Gaulle?

De Gaulle knew nothing of the plans for Anglo-American operations in Africa until the last moment. He had consented then to broadcast to the French people in North Africa, even to accept Giraud's command. It was a bitter pill to swallow, for de Gaulle's name was known, as it had been for over two years, as the symbol of Free France.

But de Gaulle would not be obeyed in North Africa. Everyone who had sworn fealty to Marshal Pétain—and that was everyone who held any command of responsibility in the area—bitterly hated the tall, aloof de Gaulle. If he represented France, then they were traitors. It was as simple as that. The people might have rallied to him, but those who commanded rejected him.

In spite of all the recriminations of British and American news commentators over the Darlan deal—and they were many and loud—the fact remains that de Gaulle could not have run French North Africa in November 1942. Giraud could not have run French North Africa in November 1942. Darlan could, and did. While the respected Wendell Willkie wailed, "The United States has lost moral force . . . and by it we may lose the peace. . . . With all my soul I hate this false

447

finagling with expediency," President Roosevelt kept the matter in perspective. Recognition of Darlan's usefulness at the time implied nothing for the future government of France. To have established de Gaulle as French leader would have been to impose on the French a leader they had never chosen, a leader of the Allies' choosing. Darlan and his men represented a legal continuum of French authority. Unless the United States and Britain were to establish a military rule or to control the area through a puppet of their own selection, they had to deal through established authorities, so long as those authorities were obeyed and did nothing to frustrate the operations of war.

For it was war in North Africa—a fact likely to be forgotten by the liberal critics of the Darlan deal. The Axis had not been idle in the last few days.

The only military commander in Africa who did not obey Darlan's armistice orders was Admiral Jean Estéva, Governor General of Tunisia. While the French were firing on Americans at Casablanca, Estéva's guns stood silent as German airborne troops landed in the vicinity of Tunis. Unless the Allies could move quickly, the Germans might soon be rapping on the eastern door of Algiers.

Soon after the landing, the American General Ryder was relieved by Lieutenant General K. A. N. Anderson, of the British First Army. Leaving Algiers behind, the troops began a race for Tunisia.

At first, hopes ran high. The British entered the port city of Bône on November 12 and by November 17 were in close proximity to German troops near Tunis. By November 23, German General Walther Nehring had established a perimeter extending from Cape Serrat, thirty miles west of Bizerte, down to Gafsa, where American patrols were operating. The Luftwaffe gave valiant support, and the Allied air forces were outnumbered and outclassed. Weakness in the air combined with unseasonal rains and supply difficulties foiled Eisenhower's efforts to get Anderson the strength he needed. The attack bogged down.

On December 9, General Jürgen von Arnim took over command in the Tunisian sector, and the German force was renamed the Fifth Panzer Army. Operations remained limited for two months, but the Allied High Command had to accept the certainty of a long, hard fight before the Axis forces would be driven from North Africa.

During the second week in February, Rommel's Panzer Army, Afrika, made contact with Arnim's Fifth Panzer Army. Rommel assumed command and attacked the Allies in the Battle of Kasserine Pass. He was hampered by misguided orders from above, and the German counteroffensive ended in failure. Montgomery's Eighth Army now moved in, and following the Battle of Mareth, which came at the end of March, the Axis troops were in full retreat to Tunis and Bizerte. It was not, however, until May 13, that the last of the Axis forces in North Africa surrendered. Their stubborn defense cost many lives and delayed the Allied drive into Tunisia, but it did not set back the forthcoming invasion of Sicily. Most important, it gave the British and American soldiers, from generals to privates, valuable lessons in warfare. Never again would they be the lighthearted amateurs who had landed at Casablanca, Oran, and Algiers. Now they were professionals.

At Toulon, French sentries on the ships of the French Navy looked uneasily on their homeland—now occupied by German troops. Having faith in the German word that the Axis would make no move against ships flying the *tricouleur,* Admiral de Laborde was well content with his decision to disregard Darlan's "invitation" to sail and join the Allies. De Laborde hated the British with all the fervor of his Gallic nature, and he preferred to place his trust in his country's oppressors rather than in the followers of "perfidious Albion." The Admiral slept quietly in his room on board the battle cruiser *Strasbourg.* The time was 0430. Suddenly he was shaken from his sleep. The Germans were firing on the port.

No Frenchman will ever forget that morning of November 27. It was the moment of the nadir of their fortunes. The Germans that day occupied the last square inch of European France, and their fleet paid the terrible price of faith in Hitler's word.

For some minutes after he was awakened, de Laborde debated whether to try to take his ships to sea or to scuttle them where they lay. He finally made up his mind. Turning to a staff officer, he said, "Send the order to scuttle."

In a few moments, even as German shells were beginning to land on the ships, self-inflicted explosions began to shake the French vessels. The water was too shallow for them to sink out of sight, and their wrecked tophampers remained a mute protest to the rape of France. By the end of the day, three capital ships, eight cruisers, seventeen destroyers, sixteen torpedo boats, sixteen submarines, and seventy-odd other ships were no more. Honor had been satisfied.

Not all Frenchmen were convinced that de Laborde's action was what honor demanded. De Gaulle called it "the most pitiful and sterile suicide imaginable." Others called it stupid pride.

The time is Christmas Eve. Admiral Darlan has not yet returned from lunch—a lengthy affair, prolonged, perhaps, to render additional toasts for the season.

A young man, a student at the University of Lyons under normal conditions, and an ardent Gaullist-Royalist, Fernand Bonnier de la Chapelle by name, has sought an audience with the French Admiral. Learning that he has not yet returned, the young man sits in an anteroom, quietly waiting.

At length Admiral Darlan returns. The youth jumps up, pulls out a .22-caliber revolver and fires twice into Darlan's face. Horrified guards jump on the assassin; their treatment is not gentle. Darlan slumps to the floor and is carried off to a hospital.

Alerted by telephone, Mr. Murphy and General Clark rushed to the hospital. Darlan was still alive, but he died before he could speak again. His assassin did not long survive him. He was tried on Christmas Day by a French court and sentenced to death. The execution was carried out at once by a firing squad, so rapidly that detractors of Clark and Eisenhower have since claimed that it was a plot to hush up a major conspiracy. It has even been claimed that Eisenhower and Clark were behind the assassination, in order to relieve themselves of the embarrassment of working with Darlan. This accusation is arrant nonsense. Neither man was capable of lending his influence to such an undertaking. There is a difference between expediency and dishonor. Both Eisenhower and Clark made some bad decisions during the war, but neither man soiled his hands with murder for convenience.

450

General Giraud assumed the duties Darlan had exercised, and North Africa remained stable. While the fighting continued in Tunisia, the principal Anglo-American concerns were to support the fighting front. But west of Bône, the region was turning into a gigantic base for further operations against Germany and Italy.

The Italians would be the first to crack.

CHAPTER SIXTEEN

November-December: Ring Out the Old

> *"I'm dreaming of a White Christmas."*
> Irving Berlin

Tuesday, November 3, 19442. The American people, unaware of the tale about to unfold in French North Africa, made their way to the polling places. It was an off-year election, and campaigning had attracted little attention, being overshadowed by the war news. The bitterest fight developed during the New York Democratic Convention held in Brooklyn in August. The President and his former campaign manager, James A. Farley, parted company, and a real bitterness developed. Seizing control of the Convention, Farley urged the nomination of Attorney General John J. Bennett for Governor to run against Thomas E. Dewey, who had won the Republican nomination unopposed. Roosevelt favored Senator James M. Mead as the candidate most likely to win the support of all factions in the Democratic party. "In my opinion," wrote Roosevelt, "Bennett's nomination would cause serious defections in the normal Democratic vote this fall. Further, there is no possibility of his having the support of the great majority of the independents, nor of the American Labor Party. Both of these groups would unanimously support Senator Mead."

Roosevelt's fears were realized. The Convention nominated Bennett, and the American Labor Party refused to go along with the choice. They nominated their own candidate, Dean Alfange. In November, Dewey won by over six hundred fifty thousand votes. Alfange got four hundred thousand. The curious thing is that Charles Poletti, the Democratic candidate for Lieutenant Governor, almost beat out his rival, Thomas W.

Wallace, losing by only twenty thousand votes.

Mr. Roosevelt cast his vote as usual at Hyde Park. The trends were apparent early in the evening, and the President retired before eleven o'clock.

The results of the election were disappointing to the party in power. In the thirty-two gubernatorial contests around the nation, the Democrats managed to win only fifteen; the Republicans won sixteen, and the Progressive Party one. In the Senate, the Democrats lost eight seats, but the real shocker was in the House. Here the Democrats managed to hold on to a bare majority, electing only four more than were needed for control.

Among the missing faces in Washington when the New Year came would be veteran Independent Senator George W. Norris of Nebraska, Oklahoma's Josh Lee, and New Jersey's William H. Smathers. New faces would include Michigan Senator Homer Ferguson, Will Rogers, Jr., from California, and Clare Boothe Luce of New York, playwright, editor, and wife of *Time*'s Henry Luce. To Roosevelt's intense irritation, a Republican holdover was New York Representative Hamilton Fish, a hard-core isolationist.

The setback to the Democratic cause was more than a normal off-year reaction to the party in power. Voter frustrations expressed themselves at the ballot box. Those who felt not enough was being done to win the war joined with those who complained of the draft, of rationing, of shortages. The Democrats were paying the price for America's unreadiness to accept the fact that war would come. When it came, it simply took too long for the United States to get organized. The setback could have happened to either party.

Yet Mr. Roosevelt was partly to blame. Political genius that he was, he simply lacked an equal administrative ability. In fact, he was not a good administrator at all. He could not bear to give ultimate authority to anyone. He had always to keep something back, to see to it that someone was checking on someone else, to play off one man against another, to keep all the strings in his own sinewy hands. It was his way to make himself indispensable on all occasions and anyone else dispensable, if need be. Although this system could and did work—after a fashion—it could not work efficiently, and results were too scarce to convince large segments of the American people on November 3.

Mr. Roosevelt, on the other hand, would not permit politics to interfere in the conduct of the war. Nothing would have been easier for him as Commander in Chief than to insist that Torch take place before election day. It could not have failed to reverse the trend, perhaps would even have added to the Democratic strength in Congress. But when Eisenhower postponed the operation from November 1 to November 8 on sound military grounds, the President cheerfully accepted the decision. Militarily the President was justified. Perhaps, indirectly, he was also justified politically, for except for die-hard Roosevelt haters, the people thereafter were less likely to ascribe poltical inspiration to all his actions. Perhaps one or two might be sincere, inspired from real patriotism. Even members of the Harvard Club, many of whom looked on Roosevelt as a traitor to his class, toned down their expressions of venom.

The colleges and universities suffered increasingly from the effects of the war. The able-bodied young males were mostly gone by fall. Some of them, to be sure, reappeared, their sport coats, slacks, porkpie hats, and saddle shoes exchanged for Army khaki or Navy blue, while they pursued one of the many short programs. Then these men would vanish again. Most of those remaining had very, very high draft numbers, flat feet, leaky hearts, trick knees, punctured ear drums, faulty eyesight, or any of the myriad other ills the flesh is heir to and which bring displeasure to medical officers.

Fewer young ladies were enrolled, too. Many of them had answered the call to service and were performing duties as WAACS, WAVES, SPARS, and Marines. Others had dropped out into war work, in the factories, driving trucks, buses, and taxis, or working for the Red Cross or the U.S.O. Those who went to college to seek husbands found the pickings slim indeed in the fall of 1942.

The football season had been a near-disaster. Only the services could field first-rate teams, but they were not yet organized to any great extent. Such oddities cropped up on the schedules as Great Lakes, Lakehurst Naval Air Station, Fort Monmouth, and Fort Riley CRTC. The star player of the year was Georgia's Frank Sinkwich, Heisman Trophy winner, who led his team to a season of ten wins to only one defeat in the regular season and a 9 to 0 win over U.C.L.A. in the Rose Bowl on New Year's Day. Georgia also won the Southwestern

Conference title. The Big Ten was dominated by Ohio State, with a 9-1 record, while Pennsylvania carried off the honors in the Ivy League. Ohio State also won the Associated Press poll for national rankings, beating out Georgia by a small margin.

In traditional games, U.C.L.A. beat California 21 to 0; Michigan pasted Minnesota 49 to 6, to recapture the Little Brown Jug, and Yale defeated Harvard 7 to 3.

The Associated Press All-America Team was dominated by the Big Ten.

End	Dave Schreiner, Wisconsin
Tackle	Dick Wilding, Minnesota
Guard	Chuck Taylor, Stanford
Center	Joe Domnanovich, Alabama
Guard	Gerrard Ramsey, William and Mary
Tackle	Clyde Johnson, Kentucky
End	Bob Shaw, Ohio State
Back	Frank Sinkwich, Georgia
Back	Paul Governali, Columbia
Back	Mike Holovak, Boston College
Back	Glen Dobbs, Tulsa

The 1942 season was the last season that could be called anything like normal for the duration. The demands of war and the draft would be too great next year.

In mid-November, the President signed a new draft law authorizing the drafting of men between the ages of eighteen and twenty. Three die-hard isolationists, Senators Burton K. Wheeler of Montana, Gerald P. Nye of North Dakota, and Hiram Johnson of California, had attempted to add a rider to the bill demanding at least a year's training in the United States before any teen-age soldier could be sent overseas. Having no isolationist cause to espouse at the moment, these libertarians had to be content with charging Secretary of War Stimson with "warlike proclivities" and the desire to establish a military dictatorship. Unimpressed, the Senate passed the bill with no restrictions and sent it to the White House. Young men affected by it were to register with their draft boards between December 11 and the end of the year.

Soon there came the announcement that on and after December 5, no voluntary enlistments of any sort would be accepted from men in the 18-to-38 age bracket. Enlisted draftees older than thirty-eight would be released early in the new year, unless they requested to remain on active duty. The reason for this new regulation was simple: the Army felt it was not getting its share of the better-quality men. Those with initiative, education, good physiques, and high IQs were enlisting or seeking commissions in the Navy, Marine Corps, Coast Guard, or Army Air Forces, but not, as a rule, the Army Infantry, Artillery, or Engineers. To meet its ever-growing demand for men—the Army at this time numbered five million, and it was scheduled to grow to seven and a half million—the ground services had to take the nearly lame, the nearly halt, and the nearly blind, as well as the semiliterate and the misfits who would spend as much time in the guardhouse as in their units.

Henceforth the services would submit their demands to Selective Service headquarters, which, in turn, would establish state and regional quotas. Individual draft boards would decide who went into which service. They might or might not take into account the desires of the individual man. The Navy, Coast Guard, Marine Corps, and Air Forces would all have to accept their shares of the less desirable men. The Army would be improved by this order; the other services would suffer.*

In connection with the new regulations, President Roosevelt announced a plan to send certain highly qualified men to specialized college programs while they were in the service. Nothing much ever came of the idea, for men were needed in jobs more closely related to service needs of the moment. What it needed—or thought it needed—the service taught: from first aid and fire fighting, to electronics and map reading, to the Japanese language, in an intensive program that made the Marines' Parris Island boot camp look like a leisurely vacation.

Some colleges and universities had Army and Navy con-

---

* Because there were always more than enough volunteers for the Army Air Forces, the Navy, the Marine Corps, and the Coast Guard, they had been able to take their pick and throw the rejects into the waiting maw of the Army.

tracts for scientific research, for the devices of the laboratory were proving effective in combat. Not only were radar and sonar used most effectively, but all sorts of other devices came into service. Infrared sniper scopes enabled soldiers to spot a target in the dark. Ultrahigh-frequency radio and radar baffled the enemy and added reliability and accuracy to Allied equipment. A comparatively new discipline, operational analysis, began to come into play as mathematicians studied results of past operations and constructed tables and graphs to aid in creating search patterns for aircraft, to devise more effective antisubmarine screens for ocean convoys, to determine the number and kind of shells needed to neutralize a given target in a given area.

Most important of all in the scientific bag of tricks was, of course, work on the atomic bomb. As early as October 11, 1939, Mr. Roosevelt had been alerted to the possibility of building such a bomb. On that date he had received a letter signed by Dr. Albert Einstein, written on behalf of world-famous physicists Niels Bohr, Enrico Fermi, Leo Szilard, and others. Although the President was no physicist, he had sufficient imagination to grasp some of the implications of the letter. Unfortunately the program bogged down in the mazes of bureaucracy for a time, and it was not until later, under the auspices of Vannevar Bush's National Defense Research Committee, that it got off the ground.* Soon named the Manhattan Project for reasons of secrecy, the investigations proceeded in fits and starts for some time, teams investigating different approaches through U-238 and plutonium. The British were also working on the problem of atomic fission under the code name of "tube alloys," and it was only later that the two nations agreed to pool their efforts.

On December 2, 1942, beneath the West Stands of the University of Chicago's Stagg Field, Fermi attempted the first chain reaction in a nuclear pile. It worked. It was a controlled experiment of a nonexplosive sort, as in the power plant of a modern atomic submarine. But it pointed the way. Ahead lay the massive efforts of Oak Grove and Los Alamos.

Ahead lay also the holocausts of Hiroshima and Nagasaki.

* Later reorganized under the name, Office of Scientific Research and Development to the War Department (OSRD).

Only a tiny handful knew of the potentialities of the atomic bomb. For the rest of the Americans, the problem was day-to-day living, with work in the factories, on the farms, and in the offices. The people were settling down to wartime restrictions and inconveniences as a way of life and concentrated on keeping the production going. Much had been accomplished in a year; much remained to be done. In December 1941, the monthly rate of production of tanks had been seven hundred fifty; a year later it was five thousand. Aircraft building had doubled and more, from twenty-four hundred a month to five thousand during the same period. Shipbuilding had made the most dramatic increase, an elevenfold growth from a hundred thousand tons a month to a million, one hundred thousand, or at the rate of three ships a day.

And the ships were needed. The year 1942 had been the worst of the war in sinkings by U-boats and aircraft. If losses from all over the world are considered, if those sunk by the Japanese and Italians as well as by the Germans are considered, the Allies lost ships at the rate of five a day all during the year. In the North Atlantic and Arctic areas, one thousand twenty-seven ships were lost to U-boats alone, or almost three a day, for a total of 5,704,236 gross register tons. U-boats were accounting for sixty-nine percent of all Allied shipping losses.

Although the Allies were finally building ships faster than the Axis forces could sink them, the loss rate was far too great to be endured. For untold in these grim figures is the loss of treasure and lives, the waste of resources, the cold, the fear, the misery, the sudden, flaming death when a torpedo struck home in the bowels of a gasoline tanker or an ammuniiton ship.

Yet the ships had to keep going. Ships for the foodstuffs to feed Britain and the soldiers there and in Africa. Ships to take the sinews of war to the men who needed support. Ships to bear the munitions to the embattled Russians. Ships, ships, and more ships.

The North Atlantic convoy patterns were well established by the end of the year. The feeble convoys established by midyear off the American East Coast and in the Caribbean had developed into an elaborate interlocking convoy system, with all ships provided with escorts from Trinidad, Panama, or

Texas and Louisiana on past Florida, up the coast to the transatlantic convoy termini at Halifax and Sydney, Nova Scotia.*

While the U-boats were enjoying unprecedented success off the American coast, the North Atlantic run was comparatively unmolested. For some months, no attack developed there, and supplies reached Britain as never before.

But it was too good to last. In July and August the U-boats hit again in mid-Atlantic, this time employing to the full the wolf-pack tactics Dönitz had worked on so long.

A typical North Atlantic convoy of the period consisted of thirty-five to forty-five merchant ships steaming in eight to nine columns in a box formation. Ahead and on the flanks the escort prowled about, probing with the long, invisible fingers of radar and sonar for lurking U-boats. Four principal convoys were established on this route: Fast convoys from Halifax (later New York) steamed at about nine knots and were designated HX. Slow convoys (six and a half knots) sailed from Sydney or New York, and were called SC. The reverse runs were ON, from the United Kingdom to Canada or the United States, and the slow ONS along the same route.

Before sailing, the masters of the merchant ships, the convoy commodore (and vice commodore and rear commodore, if assigned), the commanding officers of the escorts, and the escort commander attended a convoy conference where routes, signals, convoy formations, emergency procedures, stragglers' routes, and the thousand other necessities for a safe passage were discussed. Then, usually during the dark of night, the convoy would sail.

At sea a convoy can be a beautiful thing. The merchant ships are in their stations, each rolling and pitching out of phase with its companions, but somehow unified in their movements like a graceful team. The busy escorts listen, watch, and patrol back and forth looking for any interloper.

Suddenly the peace and harmony is destroyed. A crunching thud of an explosion . . . a ship sags out of position. Smoke begins to pour from her wounded side. Escorts wheel and spring on the unseen enemy, while the merchant ships turn ponderously to a new course designed to put the U-boat astern. Muffled explosions raise towering columns of water

* Later transferred to New York.

as an escort drops depth charges on a contact. Nothing happens, usually; it takes more than a single attack to flush a U-boat. Sometimes the attackers' efforts are rewarded by an oil slick, bits of wreckage, even a few bodies. On other occasions, the U-boat will rise to the surface like an ungainly whale, coming up to wage a last desperate fight for life.

When a convoy left New York, it was under protection of a light escort as far as a position south of Greenland. Here at the Western Ocean Meeting Point (Westomp, which changed for each convoy) an ocean escort took over as far as the latitude of Iceland at Eastomp. There the ocean escort peeled off to go to Londonderry for refueling, while a British escort group picked the convoy up to take it to United Kingdom ports.

The first real attack on one of the ocean convoys in the last half of 1942 took place against ON-115, a westbound convoy, during July and August. The convoy ran into a small wolfpack and suffered the loss of four ships. It was only the beginning. In August every merchant convoy on the transatlantic run was attacked, with the loss of a hundred and two ships, for over five hundred thousand tons. September and October were a little better, but not much, but November was the grimmest month of the war, with a hundred and six ships sunk in the Atlantic for a total of 636,907 tons. SC-107 lost fifteen ships between November 1 and 4. The toll might have been even worse during the month, had it not been for the North African landings, which caused the Germans to divert their U-boats south to break up reinforcements to that area.

The U-boats were not concentrating solely on the North Atlantic. There were also good pickings in the area of the Atlantic narrows between the bulge of Africa and Brazil. Refueled by "milch-cow" submarines off the Azores, the attack U-boats were able to hit at the rich trade plying between South America and Africa as well as at convoys from Britain to Capetown. The activity in this area led to one of the most disturbing incidents of the war.

On September 12, 1942, the troopship *Laconia*, a large liner of 19,965 tons, was torpedoed by *U-156* under the command of Kapitänleutnant [Senior Lieutenant] Werner Hartenstein. It was a fair day, and the ship sank slowly, so that Hartenstein was able to learn that there was a large detachment of Italian prisoners of war on board. In fact, the ship carried 2,732 passengers and crew, eighteen hundred of them Italians captured in North Africa. There were also several women and children, mostly families of British civil servants from the colonies.

Hartenstein immediately recognized that there would be huge loss of life, not only from drowning and exposure, but also from the sharks and barracuda that infest those waters, so he set about such rescue work as lay in his power.

Before she sank, the *Laconia* broadcast the emergency "SSS" signal,* and Hartenstein supplemented it with plain-language appeals in English for help from any ships in the neighborhood. He also requested instructions from Germany. Admiral Dönitz ordered *U-506* and *U-507* to assist in the rescue operations. Hartenstein took on board two hundred sixty survivors, transferring half of them later to *U-506*. *U-507* picked up another hundred and fifty-seven, and the three U-boats took lifeboats in tow. Hartenstein's boat flew a large Red Cross flag to indicate the mission of mercy the three U-boats were conducting.

French authorities at Dakar had been requested to assist, so they had sent the cruiser *Gloire* and two smaller ships to the rescue, toward the area. But before they could reach the scene, an unpleasant event took place. A four-motor American Liberator bomber flying out of a newly established base in Ascension Island spotted and circled the submarines and their tows. After a time it flew away, but returned half an hour later and dropped five bombs on *U-156*, in spite of the Red Cross flag, in spite of radio messages and Aldis-light signals that there were English on board. None of the submarines could dive, for the prisoners could not all be accommodated below. Many of them were exposed on the decks. Hartenstein refused to open fire on the Liberator, which made off after its attack.

U-156 had suffered damage and so had to break off rescue operations, putting the survivors back into the water near the lifeboats. Dönitz authorized the other two submarines to carry on with the life-saving operations, but with stern admonitions to break off in the event another attack developed. On September 17, a British seaplane attacked, but did no damage, and

---

* During the war the conventional "SOS" signal was replaced by three emergency signals designed to identify the type of attacker. "SSS" meant attack by submarine, "AAA" an attack by aircraft, and "RRR" an attack by a surface raider.

the next day, the two U-boats made a rendezvous with the *Gloire* and two French sloops and transferred the survivors. Approximately twelve hundred persons were rescued in this manner, but it was no thanks to the American Air Force. Much later the American officer who ordered the attack revealed that he considered the safety of two other ships in the area more important than the rescue work being performed by Hartenstein and his fellows. The U-boats had to be destroyed lest they attack these vessels. Just how they were to attack while they were towing lifeboats, the officer did not explain.

The unfortunate result of the *Laconia* affair was that Dönitz issued an order on September 20 that henceforth no efforts were to be made to rescue survivors of sunken ships. It was this order that brought Dönitz to trial for his life at the Nuremberg tribunal after the war.

American submarines in the Pacific were not observing laws of mercy in the war they were waging against the Japanese. Submarine warfare is a cruel, dirty business, whether waged by friend or by foe. It was an urgent necessity on both sides during World War II, and any notions of the chivalry of war had to be shelved, if the submarine was to survive.

At sea a submarine is no man's friend. Both sides had a tendency to consider any submarine contact as enemy, to attack first and investigate later, if at all. Not unnaturally, the submarines tended to operate in areas where no friendly forces were likely to be encountered. This was no particular problem for the Germans in the Atlantic, but it became increasingly difficult for the Americans in the Pacific as the year wore on.

From the first, American submarines were plagued by faulty torpedoes. Attack after attack failed, as perfectly aimed tin fish missed or exploded prematurely or failed to go off at all when they did hit. The Navy's Bureau of Ordnance was reluctant to believe anything could be wrong with their newest-model magnetic torpedo, developed in great secrecy before the war. The Bureau blamed the submarine skippers, and repeated failures shook the confidence of the submarine officers and men. By mid-year, extensive tests had shown that the torpedoes ran some ten feet deeper than set, so they passed under targets without exploding. It was another year before the reluctant Bureau would admit the results of other tests that revealed other faults in the torpedo: the magnetic exploder was unreliable; the contact, back-up exploder was too weak and likely to jam under force of a solid hit; and the torpedo ran up and down erratically in a kind of vertical zigzag, so it was sheer luck if it did hit a target. With such weapons, the American submarines had to hold the line in the Pacific as best they could while the Allied forces were being driven back. Although American sinkings amounted to less than a tenth of what the Germans were accomplishing in the Atlantic, with the sinking of a hundred and forty ships for a total of 593,165 gross register tons, the Japanese were unable to replace losses as well, and before the war was over, the attrition of the Japanese merchant marine had brought the nation close to collapse.

After the disastrous North Russian convoy PQ-17, the British were reluctant to run another, but political pressures from the Russians were too great, and in early September, PQ-18 was sent, routed as far north as the Arctic ice would ever permit. The convoy was harried almost constantly by U-boats and aircraft, losing thirteen out of the forty ships on the way.

The North Russian convoys were too expensive. There would be no more until the dark months when the sun never rose in those latitudes.

In December, the Admiralty decided to send another convoy through, but on the request of Admiral Sir John Tovey, Commander in Chief of the Home Fleet, it was split into two parts. Also, the designations were changed for reasons of security; the Admiralty was sure the Germans knew the PQ-QP designations by this time.* Thus, on December 15 convoy JW-51A sailed from Loch Ewe. It was not spotted and arrived safely and without a loss at Murmansk on Christmas Day.

With the second half of the convoy, JW-51B, which sailed a week after the first, it was quite a different story. The convoy consisted of fourteen ships, with a close escort of six destroyers and five smaller vessels under the command of Captain R. St. Vincent Sherbrooke. Two British crusiers, *Sheffield* and *Jamaica,* under the command of Rear Admiral R. L. Burnett, which had escorted JW-51A, sailed from Kola Inlet near Mur-

---

* The Admiralty was right. The Germans knew the designations, but they were fooled by the change in designation. In the German records convoy JW-51A appears as PQ-19 and JW-51B as PQ-20.

mansk to meet the convoy at the crucial moments of the passage.

All went well for the first six days on the convoy's passage. Then it ran into one of the furious gales the Arctic Ocean can provide to humble the men who go down to the sea in ships. The wind rose steadily hour by hour, and it was on the port beam, causing the heavily laden cargo ships to roll wickedly. Huge crates lashed to the decks threatened to break loose, and the top-heavy ships groaned under the strain.

Up and down. Up and down. Roll, pitch, heave. Minute by minute the creaking ships fought on. Crewmen wearing four or five sweaters and two pairs of trousers under their foul-weather clothing were so chilled that they often had to be assisted below after a four-hour watch topside.

Another danger showed itself—ice. As tons of water smashed aboard the ships and passed off into the sea, some remaining behind, to form first a thin coating and then a thick covering of ice on the decks, the gun mounts, the rigging. A cable normally as big around as a man's finger grew in size until it was as large as his thigh. All this additional weight topside—tons and tons of it—threatened the stability of the ships. Unless they could rid themselves of the ice, they might roll themselves under. Yet it would be death to any men sent out to try to clear away the ice. On the decks they would have no shelter at all from the icy blasts, from the numbing spray that could strip the skin from a man's face in a matter of seconds. At their watch stations, men had at least some shelter, some place of refuge. There was none on the open decks. There was nothing to hold on to, and a man would be swept overboard before he had taken more than a few steps. He could live at most a minute or two in the icy water.

It was even worse on the escorts. One of the men from the *Orwell* wrote: "When we hit the bad weather we found out what being in a destroyer really meant. There was the noise of the ship shuddering and creaking as she ploughed through the heavy seas. She would shake on the top of a huge wave and then plunge like a stone dropped over a cliff, hitting the bottom of the trough with a crash. Then she would struggle on to the next wave and repeat the performance, seemingly trying to outdo each effort for noise and violence. . . . After four hours on the upper deck, with freezing winds, snow showers and heavy seas breaking on board, men would come down below and almost cry with agony when the warmth of the mess brought circulation back to their frozen limbs. Often their clothing was soaking wet, with little chance of getting it dry before going on watch again."

For over forty-eight hours the gale continued, the polar winds numbing thought and action. Fatigue became a real thing, almost separate from a man's being. It was *there,* just as the wind and sea were there. You had to live with it.

When the seas at length abated, Sherbrooke looked around for his charges. Five merchant ships and two of the escorts were missing. Although another of the escort was detached to look for the missing vessels, she never found them. Four of the lost charges rejoined on their own, and so did one of the escorts. The other two vessels made their way safely to Kola Inlet.

The worst was over. Or so they thought.

Nature had thrown her worst against the convoy. Now it was the turn of the enemy.

Although the Germans had failed to spot the first section of the convoy, they soon realized that it had reached Murmansk and set about making plans for the total obliteration of the next convoy, which they believed would not be far behind.

On Wednesday, December 30, as the convoy was making 6 knots to allow the stragglers to catch up, a German U-boat passed nearby and heard the sound of the propellers; its commander promptly sent word to Dönitz, who informed the *Seekriegsleitung* in Berlin.

With Hitler's personal approval, the order went out: *Hipper* and *Lützow,* accompanied by destroyers, to sail and attack convoy.

Each of the six German destroyers sent out was superior to any of the British ones; as for the heavy ships, there was no comparison. Both the *Sheffield* and the *Jamaica* were light cruisers, mounting twelve 6-inch guns as their main battery. In contrast, the *Hipper* had eight 8-inch guns, whose projectiles were almost double the weight of those the British could shoot. But even the *Hipper* was weak compared to her consort *Lützow,* one of Germany's two surviving pocket battleships. Mounting six 11-inch guns, plus powerful secondary batteries almost as powerful as the main armament of the British cruisers, she could far outrange them and shoot them to pieces at will.

464

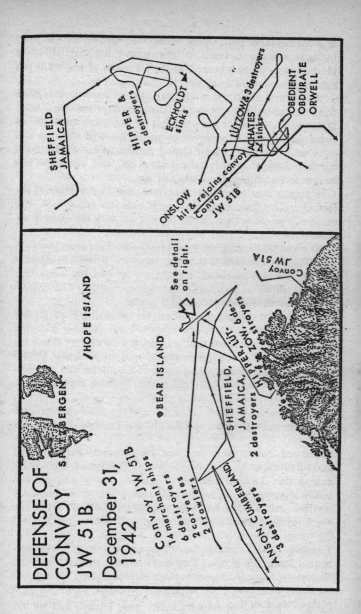

DEFENSE OF CONVOY JW 51B
December 31, 1942

SVALBERGEN
HOPE ISLAND
BEAR ISLAND

Convoy JW 51B
14 merchant ships
6 destroyers
2 corvettes
2 trawlers

See detail on right.

Convoy JW 51A

SHEFFIELD, JAMAICA, LÜTZOW, HIPPER, 6 destroyers
2 destroyers

ANSON, CUMBERLAND, 3 destroyers

SHEFFIELD
JAMAICA

HIPPER & 3 destroyers

ECKHOLDT sinks

LÜTZOW & 3 destroyers

OBEDIENT
OBDURATE
ORWELL

ACHATES sinks

ONSLOW hit & rejoins convoy

Convoy JW 51B

What hope for the British? What hope for convoy JW-51B?

There was the darkness, which meant the British would be hard to spot. There was the British experience at sea, while the Germans were stale from months of swinging around the hook at Altenfjord in northern Norway. Then, there was Hitler's "no risk policy." He could not bear the idea of losing a ship. Standing orders were for elements of the German Navy to avoid action with superior or equal forces. This warning was repeated to German Vice Admiral Kummetz just as the ships sailed. He was to destroy the convoy if he could, but above all, he was to be cautious and lose no ships.

Kummetz's battle plan was a good one. In the *Hipper,* accompanied by three destroyers, he planned to attack from the north side of the convoy, while the *Lützow* with the other three destroyers would cut off escape to the south.

At about 0820, on New Year's Eve, one of the escort spotted two German destroyers, but took them for Russian reinforcements. Ten minutes later, a destroyer spotted the same two German ships and was sent to investigate. Captain Sherbrooke signaled to all ships to prepare for battle.

By 0930 or shortly thereafter, the little force of British destroyers, minesweepers, and corvettes was engaged in trying to keep the *Hipper* from getting in among the convoy. Time after time, the *Hipper* tried to attack, only to be driven off by the plucky little destroyers. Captain Sherbrooke was severely wounded early in the battle, but refused to leave the bridge until he was forcibly led below. His second in command was sickened as he looked at his captain. Sherbrooke's left cheekbone was smashed, and his eye was hanging down on his face.

Still the action went on. The minesweeper *Bramble* was sunk, and then the destroyer *Achates.* The British replied by sinking the German destroyer *Eckholdt.* But it was not the gallant destroyers that brought this off. For over an hour the *Sheffield* and *Jamaica* had been coming on hard, and a few salvos from the former reduced the German destroyer to a flaming wreck.

Shortly after sinking the *Eckholdt,* the British cruisers, shifted fire to the *Hipper.* Two shells hit, and although they did no serious damage, it was enough for Kummetz. He ordered all forces to break off the action and withdraw.

And what of the *Lützow?* How had she fared while the

British Davids were fighting the northern Goliath?

She had accomplished practically nothing. Almost blind, knowing nothing of the movements to the north, she bided her time. About 1140, she spotted a target and opened up with her big guns, but succeeded only in damaging one merchant ship. A few minutes later, Kummetz repeated his order to withdraw, and the battle was over.

Captain Sherbrooke was a lineal descendant of Sir John Jervis, the Earl of St. Vincent, who had similarly won a battle against overwhelming odds.* On his return to England, Sherbrooke, happy in the knowledge that he had done well, nearly as well as his famous ancestor, was awarded the Victoria Cross.

His sacrifice had paid off. The convoy reached Murmansk without a loss to the merchant ships.

But there were even more important consequences from this battle. The *Hipper* was repaired, but never went to sea again, and the *Lützow* was held back from an intended raid out in Atlantic waters.

When the news reached Hitler of the failure of the operation, he was furious. Despite the fact that it had been his own orders that had so hampered the big ships in their operations, he could not admit his fault. In a rage, he ordered all the big ships scrapped, the metal to be put to other war uses, and the crews to be transferred to the U-boat service. In vain Grand Admiral Raeder argued. The Führer would have his way. Raeder resigned his position as Commander in Chief of the German Navy in protest, and Hitler accepted his resignation, replacing him with Admiral Karl Dönitz, up to then head of the U-boat arm. Curiously enough Dönitz was able to get the scrapping order rescinded, but it was not until after six months of stalling.

Dönitz never had Raeder's grasp of the strategic uses of sea power, and from the time he took over as Commander in Chief, the efficiency of the German Navy went downhill. Only the U-boat arm continued to be effective, and the tide in that battle would turn the following May. In a very real sense, then, the battle in defense of convoy JW-51B was the final strategic defeat of the German surface navy.

---

* See page 217.

* * * * *

While the bitter fighting raged at sea, on land, and in the air, the restrictions of war at home were pressing ever tighter upon the American people. Manpower continued to be a knotty problem, not only for the armed services but also for the factories, the farms, and the offices. On December 5, Paul V. McNutt was appointed Chairman of the War Manpower Commission, with practically dictatorial powers over the allocation of men, including the Selective Service and employment of workers in war industries. He had the power to order that factories hire only through the U.S. Employment Service, which could establish quotas in men just as Nelson's OPM was establishing quotas in materials. He could similarly order management to give up workers in excess of their needs, although he could not order a worker to move to another community to take a job.

When McNutt moved into manpower management, Secretary of Agriculture Claude Wickard was given new powers to control the nation's food supply. Soon new foods were announced for rationing: coffee cut to a bare cup a day, canned fruits and vegetables to go "on points," butter sales halted for a time. Other restrictions were imposed. A temporary gasoline shortage caused all sales to be suspended in seventeen Eastern states for several days. Coming as these restrictions did at the Christmas season, they imposed real hardships on many families hoping for a last Christmas together before sons or husbands went overseas.

Clothing manufacture was restricted, with plainness the fashion of the day. Patch pockets, pleats, cuffs, and vests all vanished from the men's lines, while the women, too, had to be content with simplicity. A "Limitation Order on Feminine Apparel for Outer Wear and Certain Other Garments" forbade French cuffs, balloon, dolman, or leg-of-mutton sleeves, allover tucked, pleated, or shirred apparel, patch pockets on lined wool garments, inside pockets of wool cloth, bodices attached to wool skirts, and wool linings in woolen garments. The sweep and length of skirts were also limited, as they were in lounging robes. No hem could be more than two inches deep. The use of elastic for girdles and bras was almost entirely forbidden, so with many a groan, large numbers of women had to go back to the old whalebone or metal-stayed corset.

Silk stockings had been an early casualty of war, and the newly marketed nylons disappeared, as the "wonder fabric" was needed for parachutes. Rayon stockings were all that were available, and with their tendency to sag out of shape, milady was willing to go to almost any lengths to get a pair of nylons. On the black market, nylon stockings were bringing anywhere from twelve to twenty-five dollars a pair. The playboy or businessman on the make for the evening no longer said it with flowers; a pair of nylons discreetly laid on a table was usually enough to ensure a successful evening.

With full employment and with money in their pockets, American men and women turned to preparations for Christmas. The old order was changing, even to the death of the last lingering New Deal measure, with the abolition of the Work Projects Administration on December 4. Christmas shopping was decidedly limited and circumscribed by unwonted Government regulations. Even Santa Claus himself was not exempt. A War Labor Board order of December 4 stated: "Bona fide Santa Clauses shall be construed to be only such persons as wear a red robe, white whiskers, and other well recognized accoutrements befitting their station in life, and provided that they have a kindly and jovial disposition and use their high office of juvenile trust to spread the Christmas spirit." These paragons were officially declared exempt from the wage freeze.

The services made efforts to see to it that men still in the United States would have leave to get home for either the Christmas or the New Year's holiday. The result was such a transportation jam as had never before been experienced in the United States, but even at that, the men overseas had nothing but letters and Christmas parcels to remind them of families at home. Irving Berlin's sentimental song, "I'm Dreaming of a White Christmas," was sung from Tunisia to Guadalcanal, from Iceland to Espiritu Santo, from Britain to Australia.

Even before the Christmas season began, tragedy hit in Boston. On Saturday, November 28, Holy Cross had just beaten Boston College's football Eagles 55 to 12, and any people wound up in the nightclub Cocoanut Grove to celebrate or drown their sorrows. Soldiers, sailors, and civilians crowded the downstairs bar or took a turn on the dance floor. The floor show was about to start. No one noticed a bus boy standing on a bench trying to replace a light bulb some prankster had removed. The light was dim, so the bus boy lit a match to see better. Nearby was one of the artificial palm trees used for atmosphere in the club decoration. It was supposed to be fireproof, but it was not. Flames suddenly shot up. They spread along the draperies and up the stairs to the outside.

Panic ensued. Men and women pushed, and scrabbled to make their way out the revolving door, but thoughtless victims pushed on both sides at once, hopelessly jamming the door. Those in front had no chance to escape, for they were pushed ever harder against the unyielding door by those behind. The electric lights failed, and the only illumination was provided by the burning decorations and the human torches that men and women, their clothing and hair afire, had become.

An emergency exit was locked, but a few people managed to get out through the kitchen or service doors. When the firemen finally arrived and broke down the revolving door, they found the other side packed with the dead, six deep. Almost five hundred died in this disaster, including the cowboy movie star Buck Jones, who had been one of the heroes of the grim struggle for life.

Toward the end of the year, the Army moved its high command offices to a new building built for it across the Potomac from Washington. Called the Pentagon, the building was a world's wonder because of its odd shape, its bewildering maze of ramps, corridors, rings, and levels. Humorists set to work on the oddities of the building. Guides were supposed to get lost regularly. A high official, it was said, refused to leave his office because he knew he could never find it again. A Western Union messenger was reported to have entered to deliver a telegram; when he emerged three days later, he was a colonel in the Air Force. It was reputed that deep in the lower levels there was a kennel of Saint Bernard dogs complete with brandy casks to be used on rescue missions in the corridors of the building.

People continued to read and to go to the theaters and the movies. Most movie houses admitted servicemen at reduced rates, as did some theaters, concert halls, and sports arenas. Books produced under wartime restrictions had narrower margins, poorer paper, and weaker bindings. Some publishers and authors waived royalty payments for Armed Forces editions in paper, double-column format volumes issued without charge to the men overseas. These editions included everything from Westerns to mystery stories, novels, and serious nonfiction. Among the most popular were the reprints of Thorne Smith's *Topper* books and others of his madcap combination of sex and fantasy.

Professor Samuel Eliot Morison's biography of Columbus, *Admiral of the Ocean Sea,* was adjudged the best biography of the year. Morison himself was wearing Navy blue and was deeply involved in gathering material for the Navy's history of its operations in World War II. Morison had a small staff and the authority to go along on operations as he saw fit in order to get firsthand experience in the events he would later describe.

Most books continued to reflect the war, such as *How War Came* by Ernest K. Lindley and Forrest Davis, and William F. Kernan's *Defense Will Not Win the War.* Ernest Hemingway brought out a collection of short stories entitled *Men at War,* and in the preface, he advocated a somewhat startling suggestion. "Germany should be so effectively destroyed that we should not have to fight her again for a hundred years, or . . . forever. This can probably only be done by sterilization of all members of Nazi party organizations." Sterilization, he went on to say, "is little more painful than vaccination."

Pearl Buck's moving *Dragon Seed,* the story of a Chinese peasant family under Japanese invasion, quickly hit the bestseller lists. William Faulkner's *Go Down Moses* was less well received. Marjorie Kinnan Rawlings's *Cross Creek* was a sensitive picture of her part of the South. Humor lovers rejoiced in E. B. White's *One Man's Meat* and James Thurber's *My World—And Welcome to It.*

The theater had several hits on its hands by the end of the year. The highly successful *Star and Garter,* described as a $4.40 burlesque show, featured Bobby Clark and Gypsy Rose Lee. Maxwell Anderson produced *The Eve of St. Mark,* a story of an American farm boy who is sent to Bataan. *Rosalinda* was a partial success as a revival of the Johann Strauss, Jr., light opera *Die Fledermaus.* The most distinguished play of the year was Thorton Wilder's *The Skin of Our Teeth;* it was a fantasy dealing with man and his survival through catastrophe in all ages: the ice age, the flood, war (any war), and his own inventions.

The outstanding motion picture of the year, many critics believed, was Noel Coward's *In Which We Serve,* released in December. It was the story of a British destroyer from its building until its destruction by German air attack in the Mediterranean. Coward wrote both the script and the music and starred in the role of the ship's captain. Although criticized for its attitude of *noblesse oblige,* it was highly praised for its camera work, for the originality of the story telling, and for refreshing lack of the sentimentality that characterized most war films of the period.

On New Year's Eve the traditional crowds thronged Times Square in New York to sing the traditional "Auld Lang Syne," the war songs, and the popular hits. As the year passed into history, amid the gaiety of the celebration, tears were shed for those who were away from home and for those who would never return. Yet the worst was over. The struggle had not been won, but there was no chance that it could be lost.

EPILOGUE

Ring in the New

Expatiate free o'er all this scene of man;
A mighty maze! but not without a plan.
Pope, An Essay on Man

On January 7, 1943, President Roosevelt once again mounted the Speaker's dais in the House of Representatives to deliver the annual State of the Union Message to the Congress. In the galleries were representatives of most of the United Nations, including Lord Halifax of Great Britain, Maxim Litvinoff of the Soviet Union, and Dr. Wei Tao-ming of China.

As the strong, confident voice delivered the speech, it was interrupted with applause and cheers forty-five times in the forty-seven minutes it took to present the message.

A few insiders believed that Roosevelt would tear into the Republican party in revenge for Democratic losses at the polls in November. But the address completely avoided partisan politics; it was an address to the nation and the world. He reviewed the progress of the war in all theaters. "The Axis Powers [he said] knew that they must win the war in 1942—or eventually lose everything. I do not need to tell you that our enemies did not win this war in 1942." He reviewed

472

war production. "These facts and figures will give no aid and comfort to the enemy. On the contrary, I can imagine they will give him considerable discomfort. I suspect Hitler and Tojo will find it difficult to explain to the German and Japanese people just why it is that 'decadent, inefficient democracy' can produce such phenomenal quantities of weapons and munitions—and fighting men."

At least half the speech was devoted to his hopes for the postwar world, to man's longing for a lasting peace.

There are cynics and skeptics who say it cannot be done. The American people and all the freedom-loving peoples of this earth are now demanding that it must be done. And the will of these people shall prevail.

The philosophy of the Axis Powers is based on profound contempt for the human race. If, in the formation of our future policy, we were guided by the same cynical contempt, then we should be surrendering to the philosophy of our enemies, and our victory would turn to defeat.

The issue of this war is the basic issue between those who believe in mankind and those who do not—the ancient issue between those who put their faith in the people and those who put their faith in dictators and tyrants. There have always been those who did not believe in the people, who attempted to block their forward movement across history, to force them back to servility and suffering and silence.

The people have now gathered their strength. They are moving forward in their might and power—and no force, no combination of forces, no trickery, deceit or violence, can stop them now. They see before them the hope of the world—a decent, secure, peaceful life for all men everywhere.

Two days later Roosevelt and Hopkins and staff left the White House to take a train for Miami. The President was not simply getting away to bask in the Florida sunshine; he was embarked on a journey so secret that the regular porters, waiters, and cooks were taken off the train and replaced by trusted servants from Roosevelt's country retreat at Shangri-la. It is, however, impossible to keep the President's absence from Washington long a secret, and word quickly spread that Mr. Roosevelt had gone off somewhere. But no one knew where.

473

His destination was the city of Casablanca in French Morocco, only recently the scene of fighting, but now pacified and busy in its normal day-to-day life. Accompanied by his principal advisers and the Joint Chiefs of Staff, Mr. Roosevelt would meet Mr. Churchill and his entourage to plan Anglo-American strategy for the coming year.

Churchill and Roosevelt had planned the meeting for some weeks, and they had hoped to have Stalin present as well, but the Soviet leader had refused to leave the Kremlin and had seemed little interested in attending. His attitude seemed to be: You haven't done much in 1942—no second front. Until you keep your promise to Russia, there isn't much for us to talk about.

Roosevelt and his party flew from Miami to Belem, Brazil, then across the Atlantic to Bathurst in West Africa and so on to Casablanca. On a mound some four miles south of the city stands the Anfa Hotel. From its roof garden can be seen a splendid view of the African coast to the north and south and the rollers of the Atlantic ocean pounding up on the beach. In the hotel grounds are several villas. One of them was set aside for the Prime Minister and one for the President. In these luxurious and pleasant surroundings the work of the conference went forward.

Once again the American planners and the British disagreed on strategy. Under the leadership of General Alan Brooke, the British argued for exploiting the Mediterranean position, with the idea of driving Italy out of the war, bringing Turkey in on the Allied side, while building up for the invasion of France (Operation Roundup) in 1944.

General Marshall suspected the worst. He felt that the British scheme was to draw Allied forces so deeply into the Mediterranean that Roundup could never be staged. The British looked on Italy as a "bleeding ulcer" for Hitler, as Spain had been for Napoleon, but Marshall considered operations in the Mediterranean as a "vacuum into which the resources of the cross-Channel operation would be dissipated."

Admiral King urged that more attention be given to the Pacific. With the success of the Guadalcanal operations the American forces had some momentum, and this should be exploited lest the Japanese construct a series of impregnable fortifications. The idea of going on the offensive against Japan had a certain appeal to Marshall, since he realized that the cold logic of logistics would prevent a massive cross-Channel assault in 1943. He argued for going on the defensive in Europe during that year and putting everything available into the defeat of Japan.

Eventually the planners reached a compromise, and with good humor and accord presented their plans to the President and the Prime Minister. The most urgent task, as they saw it, was the defeat of the U-boat, because all other plans depended on getting troops and supplies across the oceans. The Allied forces in North Africa would try to clean up the Tunisian pocket as fast as possible, then in July they would invade Sicily to open the central Mediterranean as the first step in driving Italy out of the war. A headquarters would be established in London to plan for Roundup in 1944. Although the commander would not be selected for some time, a Chief of Staff, British Lieutenant General Sir Frederic E. Morgan, was selected with the title "Chief of Staff to the Supreme Allied Commander (Designate)." In the usual fashion, this title was quickly shortened to COSSAC.

The American ideas of daylight precision bombing were given the green light, a defeat for the British, who wanted control over all bombing and wanted to do it at night. To the United States was left the control of the war in the Pacific "with the resources available in the theater." Since these resources included most of the United States Navy, as well as other important forces, this provision was less than pleasing to the British, but it was the price they had to pay for operations in the Mediterranean. Another price the British paid for Sicily was to leave General Eisenhower in command. The British candidate was General Alexander, but because of Eisenhower's ability to get along with people of all nationalities and the high esteem that his British subordinates had for him, Ike remained.

While the Chiefs of Staff worked on the strategy of the war, Churchill and Roosevelt were more concerned with political matters. One burning issue was that of the French Government in North Africa. The death of Darlan had upset a working arrangement, and something needed to be done. Giraud was not particularly interested in political matters, and his desire was only to further French participation in the war against Germany. There remained de Gaulle.

De Gaulle was still furious because he had not been informed in advance of the North African landings. When he was invited to Casablanca he declined coldly. It took persuasion and threats on the part of Roosevelt and Churchill to bring him there at all, and throughout he remained unbending and aloof. He refused to make any commitments, and it was only several months later that he assumed direction of French interests in North Africa.

He did consent to make a brief appearance with Giraud for the press. American and British newsmen flown in for the press conference at the conclusion of the meetings were astounded to see the tall, haughty figure emerge and shake hands with Giraud. The expressions of the two men during that brief handclasp made one of the unintentionally comic photographs of the war. From their attitudes it seems as though each of them feared that the other's hand was coated with something foul.

At this same press conference, President Roosevelt made an offhand statement not for publication: "Peace [he said] can come to the world only by the total elimination of German and Japanese war power. . . . The elimination of German, Japanese, and Italian war power means the unconditional surrender of Germany, Italy, and Japan. . . . It does not mean the destruction of the population of Germany, Italy, or Japan, but it does mean the destruction of the philosophies in those countries which are based on conquest and the subjugation of other people."

Roosevelt always maintained that the phrase "unconditional surrender" popped into his head as he was speaking. Robert E. Sherwood, who was present, doubts this. He felt that the words were carefully chosen and stated at the moment to make the most dramatic impact, for they did not long remain secret. Much controversy arose over them. Critics argued that their use drove the Germans to desperation, thereby prolonging the war. No one can tell what might have been, but it is certain that Germany would never have surrendered on any conditions as long as Hitler lived. And he lived until just before the end. It seems highly unlikely that two words spoken at a press conference could have made much difference.

* * * * *

And so it was. The long year, with its triumphs and disasters, its victories and defeats, its joys and its sorrows, its

476

laughter and its tears, had finally come to an end, and a blueprint had been prepared for the next year. At the beginning of the year, the Axis was winning the war on every front. At the end, it was losing on every front. The key battles of the Coral Sea, Midway, Guadalcanal, El Alamein, North Africa, and Stalingrad had been fought and won. The Battle of the Atlantic was not yet won, but the weapons to win it were already at hand; in five months, the course of battle would change there as well. The battle of production, the battle of the home front, the battles of Whitehall and Pennsylvania Avenue were all being won.

Hard fighting and heavy sacrifices lay in the future. Many soldiers who celebrated the New Year of 1943 would not live to see another. Babies would be born never having known their fathers. Reputations would be made and lost, but the way was clear. Ahead lay victory for the Allies. Ahead lay disaster for Fascist Italy, Nazi Germany, and Bushidoistic Japan.

The year 1942 was the year that doomed the Axis.

Bibliography

The bibliography that follows is a highly selective list based on two criteria: authority and general interest. Some books written during the war cannot pretend to authority, but they have sufficient topical interest to be worth reading today. Some by participants have a natural bias, but their statements of feelings, ideas, reasons for decisions are valuable.

Extensive use has been made of magazine and newspaper files. *The New York Times, The Washington Post, The Detroit Free Press, Time, Life, Newsweek, U.S. News, The Saturday Evening Post,* and *The New Yorker* have been especially valuable.

AUPHAN, AMIRAL, et JACQUES MORDAL, *La Marine Française pendant la Seconde Guerre Mondiale.* Paris: Hachette, 1958.

BARNETT, CORRELLI, *The Desert Generals.* New York: The Viking Press, 1961.

BARUCH, BERNARD M., *The Public Years.* New York: Holt, Rinehart and Winston, 1960.

BRYANT, ARTHUR, *The Alanbrooke Diaries.* Vol. 1. *The Turn of the Tide.* New York: Doubleday & Co., 1957.

BUCHANAN, A. RUSSELL, *The United States and World War II.* 2 vols. New York: Harper & Row, 1964.

CAMPBELL, VICE ADMIRAL SIR IAN, AND CAPTAIN DONALD MACINTYRE, *The Kola Run.* London: Frederick Muller, 1958.

CARELL, PAUL, *The Foxes of the Desert.* New York: E.P. Dutton & Co., 1961.

Ciano's Diary, 1939-1943, MALCOLM MUGGERIDGE, ed. London: Heinemann, 1947.

CLARK, MARK, *Calculated Risk.* London: George C. Harris & Co., 1951.

DASCH, GEORGE J., *Eight Spies Against America.* New York: Robert M. McBride Co., 1959.

DAVIDSON, EUGENE, *The Trial of the Germans.* New York: The Macmillan Co., 1966.

DAVIS, KENNETH SYDNEY, *Experience of War: The*

United States in World War II. New York: Doubleday & Co., 1965.

EISENHOWER, DWIGHT D., *Crusade in Europe*. Garden City, N.Y.: Doubleday & Co., 1948.

FARAGO, LADISLAS, *Patton: Ordeal and Triumph*. New York: Dell Publishing Co., 1963.

FUCHIDA, MITSUO, and MASATAKE OKUMIYA, *Midway, the Battle That Doomed Japan: The Japanese Navy's Story*. Annapolis: U.S. Naval Institute, 1955.

GREENFIELD, KENT R., ed., *Command Decisions*. Washington, D.C: Office of the Chief of Military History, Department of the Army, 1960.

GRENFELL, CAPTAIN RUSSELL, RN, *Main Fleet to Singapore*. New York: The Macmillan Co., 1952.

GRIFFITH, SAMUEL B., *The Battle for Guadalcanal*. Philadelphia: J.B. Lippincott Co., 1963.

HALSEY, FLEET ADMIRAL WILLIAM F., USN, and LIEUTENANT COMMANDER J. BRYAN, III, USNR, *Admiral Halsey's Story*. New York: McGraw-Hill, 1947.

HARA, TAMEICHI, and F. SAITO, *Japanese Destroyer Captain*. New York: Ballantine Books, 1961.

HECKSTALL-SMITH, ANTHONY, *Tobruk: The Story of a Siege*. New York: W. W. Norton & Co., 1960.

HIGGINS, TRUMBULL, *Winston Churchill and the Second Front, 1940-1943*. New York: Oxford University Press, 1957.

HOWE, GEORGE F., *U.S. Army in World War II: Seizing the Initiative in the West*. Washington, D.C.: Office of the Chief of Military History, Department of the Army, 1957.

ISMAY, HASTINGS, *The Memoirs of General Lord Hastings Ismay*. New York: The Viking Press, 1960.

ITO, MASANORI, with ROGER PINEAU, *The End of the Japanese Imperial Navy*, trans. by Andrew Y. Kuroda and Roger Pineau. New York: W. W. Norton & Co., 1962.

JOHNSTON, STANLEY, *Queen of the Flat-Tops: The U.S.S. Lexington and the Coral Sea Battle*. New York: E. P. Dutton & Co., 1943.

KAMMERER, ALBERT, *Du Débarquement Américain au Meurtre de Darlan*. Paris: Flammarion, 1949.

———, *La Passion de la Flotte Française*. Paris: Librairie Arthème Fayard, 1951.

KARIG, WALTER, and WELBOURN KELLEY, *Battle*

Report: Pearl Harbor to Coral Sea. New York: Farrar and Rinehart, 1944.

KENNEY, WILLIAM, *The Crucial Years, 1940-1945*. New York: Macfadden Books, 1962.

KIMMEL, HUSBAND E., *Admiral Kimmel's Story*. Chicago: Henry Regnery Co., 1955.

KING, ERNEST J., and WALTER MUIR WHITEHILL, *Fleet Admiral King: A Naval Record*. New York: W. W. Norton & Co., 1952.

LANGER, WILLIAM L., and S. EVERETT GLEASON, *The Undeclared War 1940-1941*. New York: Harper & Bros., 1953.

LAWSON, DON, *The United States in World War II*. New York: Grosset & Dunlap, 1964.

LIDDELL HART, B. H., ed., *The Other Side of the Hill*. London: Cassell & Co., 1948.

MACARTHUR, DOUGLAS, *Reminiscences*. New York: McGraw-Hill, 1964.

MACINTYRE, DONALD, *U-Boat Killer*. New York: W. W. Norton & Co., 1956.

MANSTEIN, FIELD MARSHAL ERICH VON, *Lost Victories*. Chicago: Henry Regnery Co., 1958.

MERRILL, JAMES M., *Target Tokyo*. New York: Rand McNally, 1964.

MONTGOMERY, FIELD MARSHAL THE VISCOUNT, *Memoirs*. Cleveland and New York: World Publishing Co., 1958.

MORAN, LORD, *Churchill: Taken from the Diaries of Lord Moran*, Boston: Houghton Mifflin Co., 1966.

MORDAL, JACQUES, *Le Bataille de Casablanca*. Paris: Librairie Plon, 1952.

MORISON, SAMUEL ELIOT, *Coral Sea, Midway, and Submarine Actions, May 1942-August 1942*. Boston: Little, Brown & Co., 1951.

——, *Operations in North African Waters, October 1942-June 1943*. Boston: Little, Brown & Co., 1950.

——, *The Battle of the Atlantic, September 1939-May 1943*. Boston: Little, Brown & Co., 1954.

——, *The Rising Sun in the Pacific, 1931-April 1942*. Boston: Little, Brown & Co., 1948.

——, *The Struggle for Guadalcanal, August 1942-February 1943*. Boston: Little, Brown & Co., 1949.

MURPHY, ROBERT D., *Diplomat Among Warriors*. Garden City, N.Y.: Doubleday & Co., 1964.

NEWCOMB, RICHARD F., *Savo: The Incredible Naval Debacle off Guadalcanal*. New York: Holt, Rinehart and Winston, 1961.

PATTON, GEORGE S., *War as I Knew It: Battle Memoirs of General George S. Patton*. Boston: Houghton Mifflin Co., 1947.

PHILLIPS, C.E. LUCAS, *Alamein*. Boston: Little, Brown & Co., 1962.

——, *The Greatest Raid of All*. Boston: Little, Brown & Co., 1960.

POGUE, FORREST C., *George C. Marshall: Ordeal and Hope, 1939-1942*. New York: The Viking Press, 1966.

POTTER, E. B., and FLEET ADMIRAL C. W. NIMITZ, USN, eds., *Sea Power*. Englewood Cliffs: Prentice-Hall, 1960.

RACHLIS, EUGENE, *They Came to Kill*. New York: Random House, 1961.

REYNOLDS, QUENTIN, *Raid at Dieppe*. New York: Random House, 1943.

RIESENBERG, FELIX, JR., *Sea War: The Story of the U.S. Merchant Marine in World War II*. New York: Rinehart & Co., 1956.

ROBERTSON, TERENCE, *Channel Dash*. New York: E. P. Dutton & Co., 1958.

ROLLINS, ALFRED B., JR., ed., *Franklin D. Roosevelt and the Age of Action*. New York: Dell Publishing Co., 1960.

ROMMEL, ERWIN, *The Rommel Papers*, B. H. LIDDELL HART, ed. New York: Harcourt, Brace & Co., 1953.

ROOSEVELT, FRANKLIN D., *Nothing to Fear*, BENJAMIN D. ZEVIN, ed. New York: World Publishing Co., 1946.

ROSKILL, S. W., *The War at Sea*. 3 vols. in 4. London: H.M.S.O., 1954-1961.

SCHRAMM, PERCY E., ed., *Kriegstagebuch des Oberkommandos der Wehrmacht, 1940-1945*, Vol II, 1942. Frankfurt am Main, 1963.

SCHROTER, HEINZ, *Stalingrad,* trans. by Constantine Gibbon. New York: Ballantine Books, 1958.

SETH, RONALD, *Stalingrad: Point of Return*. New York: Coward-McCann, 1959.

SHERWOOD, ROBERT E., *Roosevelt and Hopkins*. 2 vols. New York: Harper & Bros., 1948.

SHIRER, WILLIAM L., *The Rise and Fall of the Third Reich*. New York: Simon and Schuster, 1960.

SLIM, FIELD MARSHAL THE VISCOUNT, *Defeat into Victory*. New York: David McKay Co., 1961.

SMITH, STAN, *The Battle of Savo*. New York: Macfadden, 1962.

———, *The Navy at Guadalcanal*. New York: Lancer Books, 1963.

STAFFORD, EDWARD P., *The Big E: Story of the U.S.S. Enterprise*. New York: Random House, 1962.

STAMPS, T. DODSON, and VINCENT J. ESPOSITO, *A Military History of World War II*. 4 vols. West Point, 1956.

THOMPSON, WALTER H., *Assignment: Churchill*. New York: Farrar, Straus & Cudahy, 1955.

TOLAND, JOHN, *But Not in Shame*. New York: Random House, 1961.

TREGASKIS, RICHARD, *Guadalcanal Diary*. New York: Random House, 1943.

VANDEGRIFT, A. A., and ROBERT B. ASPREY, *Once a Marine*. New York: W. W. Norton & Co., 1964.

VIAN, ADMIRAL OF THE FLEET SIR PHILIP, *Action This Day*. London: Frederick Muller, 1960.

WARLIMONT, WALTER, *Inside Hitler's Headquarters, 1939-1945*. New York: Praeger, 1964.

WERTH, ALEXANDER, *De Gaulle: A Political Biography*. New York: Simon and Schuster, 1965.

WILMOT, CHESTER, *The Struggle for Europe: World War II in Western Europe*. New York: Harper & Bros., 1952.

YOUNG, DESMOND, *Rommel: The Desert Fox*. New York: Harper & Brothers, 1951.

Index

484

487

492

493

500

212

502

503

507

508